基础培训

新东方AP考试指定辅导教

AP

微观经济学

Microeconomics

北京新东方学校AP教研中心·主编

于 宁·编著

群言出版社

QUNYAN PRESS

·北京·

图书在版编目(CIP)数据

AP微观经济学 / 于宁编著. —北京：群言出版社，
2010（2018.1重印）
ISBN 978-7-80256-206-6

Ⅰ. ①A… Ⅱ. ①于… Ⅲ. ①微观经济学—高等学校
—入学考试—自学参考资料 Ⅳ. ①F016

中国版本图书馆CIP数据核字（2010）第225090号

责任编辑：路淑双
封面设计：大愚设计

出版发行：群言出版社
地　　址：北京市东城区东厂胡同北巷1号（100006）
网　　址：www.qypublish.com（官网书城）
电子信箱：dywh@xdf.cn　qunyancbs@126.com
联系电话：010-62418641　65267783　65263836
经　　销：全国新华书店

印　　刷：廊坊十环印刷有限公司
版　　次：2011年5月第1版　2018年1月第9次印刷
开　　本：880mm×1230mm　1/16
印　　张：21.25
字　　数：421千字
书　　号：ISBN 978-7-80256-206-6
定　　价：60.00元

序 言

AP(Advanced Placement)课程在中国的成功登陆，无论是对中国高中教育的体系还是对中国高中教育的教学思路都是个不小的冲击。不同于国内高中"一刀切"(不论学习能力强弱，不论不同兴趣爱好，所有高中生都学习统一的标准课程)的教育体系，AP课程作为美国大学理事会(College Board)的明星产品，让学有余力的高中生能提前学习大学课程，不仅体现了分级教学的思想，更是满足了不同学习能力、不同学习兴趣的学生的学习需要。

据美国大学理事会的年度报告，申请顶尖名校的学生向大学招生办提供了平均4~5门AP成绩，而AP成绩在所有录取因素中以80.3%的影响力居第一位。因此，在SAT和TOEFL成绩的基础上，AP成绩成了步入名校竞争的新项目。随着中国学生留学大潮的涌来，加上AP课程在中国本土的开设，AP考试成为了时下最时髦的留学考试之一。

历史的实践告诉我们，无论是科学，还是技术，或小到一个考试，完全照搬西方肯定是行不通的。因此，AP在中国的教学、考试辅导等工作都已经悄然开展，不管是摸石头过河，还是模拟赶超，AP中国本土化势在必行。基于此，北京新东方学校成立了一支由博士学历教师组成的AP教研中心团队，大力开展了AP课程的教学教研活动。在近两年的研究过程当中，教材问题成为了当前最棘手的问题。在目前国内市面上，适合中国本土的AP教材几乎空白。为了帮助国内AP学习者更好地学习AP课程和准备AP考试，我们按照AP官方给出的考试大纲，编写了此套中英文结合的AP教材。AP考试不同于TOEFL等语言类考试，它是学科考试。学科知识无论用什么语言来描述都是同样的知识，因此本系列教材适当辅以中文解释，帮助考生更深入地理解。另一方面，为了让考生能够适合未来英文学习和英文考试的需要，本系列教材的定理展开、例题讲解等大部分内容都采用了英文描述。中英结合，易于中国考生对知识点的理解和把握。希望本套教材能给AP学习者助一臂之力。

最后，要感谢关心和支持本套书出版的大愚文化传播有限公司，北京新东方学校北美部的AP教研团队，是他们的努力才使得本书能够顺利地出版。限于水平，书中难免有不妥之处，望同行、读者不吝赐教。

范 猛

新东方国外考试推广管理中心主任

致　谢

　　一本好书的编著不是仅凭一人的力量就可以完成的，它的背后定有一支优秀的团队，本书亦如此。这本书的优秀团队由北京新东方 AP 微观和宏观经济学项目的老师们组成，他们都是我的好战友，而且无一例外地为本书的编写工作做出了极大的贡献。

　　首先，罗弥(北京大学中国经济研究中心)为本书模拟试题部分的编写和校对付出了巨大的心血，在此对她表示衷心的感谢；其次，张格（中国人民大学汉青经济与金融研究院)和张大印(中国人民大学汉青经济与金融研究院)为本书部分章节的编写和校对花费了很多时间和精力，对他们深表感谢；再次，感谢张强(中国人民大学财政金融学院)为本书部分章节的编写所做出的贡献。最后，感谢我教过的无数优秀而可爱的学生们，假如没有你们对本书的殷切期待和迫切需求，我恐怕没有如此大的动力在这么短的时间内促成本书的出版。

　　本书虽由我统稿和编校，但假如没有本书整个团队的努力和学生的殷切期盼，本书不会这么快就与大家见面。因此，再次向他们表示我诚挚的谢意。

于　宁

Contents

Introduction of AP Microeconomics Exam
AP 微观经济学考试简介

AP 是 Advanced Placement 的缩写，即大学预修课程。AP 课程及考试始于 1955 年。美国高中 AP 课程是由美国大学理事会（College Board）主办，在高中阶段开设的具有大学水平的课程，涵盖 22 个门类、37 个学科，已在美国 15000 多所高中普遍开设。它可以使高中学生提前接触大学课程，避免了高中和大学初级阶段课程的重复。目前，已有 40 多个国家的近 3600 所大学承认 AP 学分作为其入学参考标准，其中包括哈佛大学、耶鲁大学、牛津大学、剑桥大学等世界名牌大学。清华大学、北京大学、北京语言大学等也接受 AP 成绩。

美国每年约有 200 万高中毕业生，他们都要参加美国高考 SAT 和 AP 课程的考试。在美国，初等教育是免费的，但高等教育是收费的。美国高中生会在 11 年级时完成 SAT 的考试，在 12 年级（高中最后一年），则要完成两件大事。其一，根据 SAT 的考试成绩，申请大学和奖学金；其二，选修 AP 课程并准备考试。AP 考试的目的在于，利用高中最后一年免费教育的时间，提前完成一些美国大学的学分课程及考试。否则，在大学阶段完成相同的课程和学分，则需要支付高昂的学费。也就是说，AP 课程及考试可以帮助高中生减免大学学分、降低大学教育成本、缩短大学教育时间；其三，对中国学生而言，除可以获得美国大学学分，省时省钱外，还可以在国内提前解决在美国上大一时课程难适应的问题。

申请美国名牌大学时需要向学校招生办提供以下材料：申请论文（个人陈述）、年级排名（Rank）、在校总平均成绩（GPA）、入学考试（SAT）成绩、AP/A–LEVEL 成绩、推荐信、工作及实践经验等信息。通过对美国大学录取顾问委员会公布的影响大学录取因素的比较分析可以知道：AP 成绩以 80.3% 的影响力居第一，对大学录取过程起决定性作用，因为它向学校充分展示了学生的才智、专长及能力。因此，学习 AP 课程，参加 AP 考试不仅可以折抵大学学分，更可以让学生在名校录取的竞争中脱颖而出，占尽先机。

1989 年美国大学理事会（College Board）启动 AP 微观经济学考试，自此，参加 AP 微观经济学考试的学生数量增长迅速。到 2010 年，参加 AP 微观经济学考试的学生约达到 5 万。AP 微观经济学是 AP 考试中参考人数最多的考试之一。2010 年，AP 微观经济学考试的平均分为 3.02 分（满分 5 分）。多数大学接受 4 分或 5 分的成绩，另有少数大学接受 3 分的成绩。在 2010 年，约有 16.6% 的学生的分数为 5 分，约有 27.0% 的学生的分数为 4 分，约有 20.2% 的学生的分数为 3 分，共有约 63.8% 的学生的 AP 微观经济学成绩在 3 分以上。因此，对于考生来说，AP 微观经济学在众多 AP 考试科目中"性价比"较高，容易拿到不错的成绩，同时对于学商科和经济学的同学也很有帮助。

开设 AP 微观经济学课程的学校或者自学的学生，应该在高一、高二进行合理的时间安排，确定课程计划，以保证把学习微观经济学应具备的知识先行学习完毕。由于 AP 微观经济学是一门大学水平的课程，具有一定的挑战性，所以需要认真对待，多花时间和精力进行准备。

一、考试报名

AP 官方报名网址：http://www.collegeboard.com

香港考务局报名网址：https://www2.hkeaa.edu.hk

AP 微观经济学课程考试费用：约 87 美元

AP 微观经济学课程每年 3 月上旬报名截止，5 月初考试。

二、考试内容

AP 微观经济学的考试内容主要包括以下几部分：

主要内容	考试占比
Basic Economic Concepts（基本经济概念）	8%–14%
The Nature and Functions of Product Markets（产品市场的特征和公式）	55%–70%
Factor Markets（要素市场）	10%–18%
Market Failure and the Role of Government（市场失灵和政府角色）	12%–18%

具体见考试说明：AP Microeconomics Course Description (Effective Fall 2010)

下载地址：http://apcentral.collegeboard.com/apc/public/repository/ap–economics–course–description.pdf

三、考试概况

1. AP 微观经济学考试题型及时间安排

Multiple choice（选择题）	60 题/70 分钟
Free response（自由问答题）	3 题/50 分钟

2. AP 微观经济学成绩得分比例

AP 微观经济学得分比例（2010 年）

考试得分	Microeconomics	
	人数	百分比
5	8551	16.6
4	13925	27.0
3	10421	20.2
2	7651	14.8
1	11053	21.4
学生总数	51601	
3 分及以上	32897	63.8
平均分	3.02	
标准差	1.39	

3. 考试成绩评定

AP 考试的成绩评定实行 5 分制。

5 分——具有非常好的资格；

4 分——具有好的资格；

3 分——具有资格；

2 分——可能有资格；

1 分——不予推荐。

一般而言，3 分及以上的成绩为大多数大学所接受，即可以在进入大学后折抵大学学分。少数顶尖大学要求 4 分或 5 分才能折抵大学学分，而哈佛大学要求 5 分才能折抵大学学分。

四、主要备考资料

1. 考试说明 AP Microeconomics Course Description (Effective Fall 2010)。考试说明为考生必读资料，不仅列有考试大纲，并且还有真题及评分示范。在备考时和考前都要重点研究考试说明。

2. AP 官网上的所有 free-response 都是可以免费下载的。

3. 曼昆编著的《经济学原理(微观经济学部分)》，第 5 版。

4. 本书：内容翔实，题目和真题接近，具有极高的参考价值。

五、备考时间安排

时间	周数	安排
12.1 – 12.5	1	了解 AP 微观经济学。下载考试说明以及考试报名的说明，学习一些基本的微观经济学术语及其英文表述
12.6 – 12.31	3	将教材从头到尾看一遍，要求基本看懂、看通(建议参加辅导班，疏理一遍考试内容的框架)
1.1 – 2.28	8	再次研读教材，将所有例题和练习题至少做两遍
3.1 – 4.15	6	研究真题，做模拟题(建议至少做两遍)，按照考试要求的时间进行练习，总结知识点及解题方法
4.16 – 4.30	2	回顾知识点，继续做真题(建议至少做两遍)，查漏补缺
5.1 – 考试	1	考前调节心态，重点温习，准备考试用品

主要内容和概念讲解

  经济(economy)这个词可以说是现代社会中日常应用最广泛的一个词了，考察其来源，"经济"一词源于希腊语，意思是指管理家庭事务的人(one who manages a household)。初看，似乎觉得这个解释有点奇特，但如果把家庭看作是一个小型的社会，就会发现经济的这种本源定义是合理的。以下我们分三个层面进行解释。

  对于个人(individual)或家庭(household)来说，肯定会面临着许多决策。哪些家庭成员去做家务？做哪些家务？谁去做晚饭？谁去打扫房间？谁有权掌控遥控器选择自己喜欢看的电视节目？每个家庭都会考虑家庭成员的能力、努力程度和意愿，将这些稀缺资源合理配置给各个成员。

  与此类似的是，厂商(firms)也面临着大量的决策。究竟哪些人去工作？生产什么东西或提供什么服务？生产多少？在生产过程中需要投入的资源有哪些？这些生产出来的产品和劳务到底以什么样的价格销售出去才合算？比如，社会需要一部分人去从事第一产业农业，一部分人去制造鞋子、衣服等，从事第二产业工业，还有一部分人去经营餐馆、旅店、理发店等第三产业服务业。生产多少粮食合适，制造多少衣服足够消费，在生产过程中需要投入多少人力、物力，粮食、衣服、饭菜价格多少，才能让买卖双方都皆大欢喜，社会稳定。

  同理，一个国家也存在着做经济决策、制定财政货币政策以解决资源最优化配置的问题。早在 2000 多年前，老子在《道德经》里就说过"治大国若烹小鲜"，其中就包含着深刻的经济决策、经济管理的哲理。

  选择之所以关系重大，是由于稀缺性(scarcity)的存在。在经济学中，稀缺性担当着重要的角色。稀缺性就是指社会资源的有限性(the limited nature of society's resource)。我们只有一个地球，它所能提供的资源显然不能满足我们所有的欲望。人类的主观需求是无止境的，但客观上满足这些需求的手段或者说生产这些物品的资源总是不足的。中国有句俗话："人心不足蛇吞象。"相对于人类无限的欲望，任何资源都是有限的。我们可能会认为，像比尔·盖茨这样的世界首富，似乎可以获得他想要的任何东西。我们可能会认为在他的字典里没有"稀缺"这个词。然而如果把时间当做一种资源来考虑的话，情形就会不同，盖茨也必须做好工作安排，确保时间花在刀刃上。在时间面前，盖茨和普通人是一样的。

  由于稀缺性的普遍存在，我们就要利用好、管理好这些资源。在现代社会中，大多数资源都不是由一个中央计划者来配置的，而是通过个人、企业、政府和其他组织等共同配置的。对这一复杂问题的研究促使经济学诞生和发展。简单地说，经济学就是研究社会如何管理自己的稀缺资源的科学（Economics is the study of how society manages its scare resources.）。具体一点，就是研究社会中的个人、厂商和政府等组织如何进行选择，以及这些选择如何决定社会资源的使用方式。

经济学首先研究日常生活中人们是如何做出决策的（how people make decisions）：工作多少，购买多少，储蓄多少，以及如何把储蓄用于投资。在个人决策的基础上，经济学还研究人们是如何相互交易的（how people interact with each other），产品和劳务的价格是如何在买卖者达成共识的。在这些微观局部分析的基础上，经济学还分析影响整个经济的力量和趋势（analyze the forces and trends that affect the economy as a whole），包括国内生产总值的大小、人均收入的增长、失业率、消费物价指数等。

经济学作为一门成熟的学科，跟其他学科类似，都有一些基础的原理或理论。曼昆在所著的经典经济学教材《经济学原理》中，总结出了十大经济学原理（ten principles of economics）。这些经济学原理为绝大多数经济学家所认同，在现实中应用最为广泛，经济学大厦也正是建立在这些基本原理的基础之上的。接下来我们将会看到，即使是最复杂的经济分析，也是由这些基本经济原理所构建的。

谈起经济，无论是说北京经济还是中国经济乃至世界经济，指的无非是在生活中相互交易、相互交往、相互影响的一群人。经济学首先反映了组成这种经济活动的个人行为，因此研究经济的十大原理首先从研究个人如何做出决策开始，主要包括四个原理：1. 人们面临权衡取舍；2. 某种东西的成本是为了得到它而放弃的东西；3. 理性人考虑边际量；4. 人们会对激励做出反应。

人是社会动物，在漫长而又短暂的一生中，我们的决策不仅仅影响我们自身，也会直接或间接地影响到其他相关的人。关于人们相互交易的经济学原理有三个：5. 贸易能使每个人的状况更好；6. 市场通常是组织经济活动的一种好方法；7. 政府有的时候可以改善市场结果。

从个人决策开始到人们间的相互交易，这些行为最终组成了"经济"。整体不同于个体和局部，有着自身特殊的规律。最后三个原理就涉及经济的整体运行：8. 一国的生活水平取决于它生产产品与劳务的能力；9. 当政府发行了过多的货币时，物价上升；10. 社会面临通货膨胀与失业之间的短期权衡取舍。

总之，从个人、厂商和国家三个层面来说，个人追求效用（utility）最大化，厂商追求利润（profit）最大化，国家追求福利（welfare）最大化。

下面我们针对这十大经济学原理一一进行介绍。

原理一：人们面临权衡取舍（**People face tradeoffs.**）。中国人说"鱼和熊掌不可兼得"，西方也有"天下没有免费的午餐（no free lunch）"这一谚语。为了得到我们喜爱的东西，通常不得不放弃另一件我们所钟爱的东西，最终的决策要求我们在两者之间进行权衡取舍。

以学生为例，时间是他最宝贵的资源。他可以把时间全部用在学习英语上，也可以把时间全部用在学习数学上，或者既学英语又学数学，或者出去兼职，当然也可以睡大觉。哈佛图书馆馆训"此刻睡觉，你将做梦，此刻学习，你将圆梦"，幽默地揭示出了时间分配利用的意义和价值。休闲和工作是一个人一生中大部分时间都要面临的选择。对于家庭来说，如何进行消费支出始终是个重大问题。食物和衣着消费支出是一个普通家庭日常所要面临的经常性选择。在家庭投资中，一家之主既可以决定购买房产，也可以决定购买黄金，或者干脆投资股市,博弈一番。在国家层面,同样也面临着各种不同的权衡取舍。国防建设和经济发展,被通俗地比喻为"大炮和黄油"(guns vs. butter),环境污染和经济增长之间也存在着某种此消彼长的矛盾。

在社会中有一种权衡取舍最为政治学家、社会学家和普通百姓所关注,那就是效率(efficiency)与平等(equity)之间的权衡,效率是指社会从其稀缺资源中所能得到的最多东西,平等则是指将这些所得公平地分配给社会成员。换一种容易理解的说法,效率就是经济蛋糕(pie)的大小,效率越高蛋糕就做得越大,而平等则是指如何分割这些蛋糕。在现实生活中,两个目标往往不一致。应该说,平等与效率是人类面临的永恒命题。在此只举一例:政府一方面利用诸如失业保险、贫困补助等各项福利制度来帮助底层弱势群体,提高基层劳动者的收入,另一方面利用各种企业所得税和个人所得税加大对政府从富人向穷人的转移支付比重,增加政府收入。这种为了维持社会和谐、减小贫富差距、有助社会平等的政策,却忽视了对辛勤工作者的激励。工作减少,生产的产品和劳务也就减少了,最终会牺牲社会效率。

原理二:某种东西的成本是为了得到它而放弃的东西(**The cost of something is what you give up to get it.**)。正如原理一所说,人们经常面临着权衡取舍,所以在做决策时都会不自觉地考虑各种方案的成本和收益。相对来说,收益一般很容易看清,但是成本有时会让人雾里看花看不清楚。假设现在市场上的电影票价是50元,别人问你看一场电影的成本是什么,你也许会不假思索地答道"50元"。但如果你仔细思考取舍的概念,就会发现答案似乎不是那么简单。首先,50元可以买到其他相等价格的东西。另外,你的时间是稀缺资源(scarce resource),在计算时也应考虑在内。这些钱和时间代表你为了看电影而放弃的机会,这些就是经济学中的机会成本。机会成本(opportunity cost)是指为了得到某种东西而必须放弃的东西。比如,你上大学的成本只是学费和食宿费吗?如果你选择直接去工作,4年的收入是20万,那么这就是你上大学的机会成本,在做决策时这个成本也必须考虑在内。在美国职业篮球联盟(NBA)里,不少高中生直接参加选秀,放弃大学深造,提前成为职业球员,收获巨额年薪。科比、詹姆斯、加内特等球星就是这样的典型例子,他们读大学的机会成本会比普通人高很多。

考虑一个简单的金融案例,假如你投资某支股票,花了1万元,但是经过一年的摸爬滚打,结果还算不错,没有亏损,小赚了1000元。此时,你可能会简单地认为自己的收益率是10%。但如果假设同期的固定储蓄利率是5%,那么你的实际收益率就要打折扣。因为用机会成本来进行分析,你的实际成本(real cost)是10500元,而不是1万元。

另外再考虑一个例子:高中毕业打算申请美国学校的同学需要参加美国高考(SAT),我们分析一下SAT考试中阅读部分的机会成本问题。如果做题速度加快,就会影响正确率,而减慢做题速度又可能做不完。所以,做题速度快的机会成本就是正确率下降,而做题速度慢、正确率高的机会成本是做不完题目。

原理三:理性人考虑边际量(**Rational people think at the margin.**)。"边际"这个词来源于数学,用数学的专业解释就是因变量随着自变量的变化而变化的程度,即自变量变化一个单位,因变量会因此而改变的量。在现实生活中,许多决策涉及对现有行动计划进行微小的增量调整（small, incremental adjustments to an existing plan of action），经济学家把这些调整称为边际变动(marginal changes)。

在许多情况下，人们可以通过考虑边际量来做出最优决策(optimal decision)。我们来看一个很有价值的例子，假设一架有 250 个座位的飞机在国内飞行一次，航空公司的成本是 15 万元。在这种情况下，每个座位的平均成本是 15 万元除以 250，即 600 元。大家可能会得出结论：航空公司的票价决不应该低于 600 元。但航空公司可以通过考虑边际量而增加利润。如果一架飞机即将起飞时仍有 5 个空位，而在登机口等待退票的乘客愿意支付 400 元买一张票。航空公司应该卖票给他吗？当然应该。如果飞机有空位，多增加一位乘客的成本是微乎其微的。虽然一位乘客的平均成本是 600 元，但边际成本(marginal cost)仅是这位额外乘客将消费的一包花生米和一罐汽水的成本而已，甚至可能连免费餐饮都没有。只要等退票的乘客愿意支付的钱大于边际成本，那么卖给他机票就完全有利可图。类似于这样的现实商业例子有很多，比如，每到季末，各个商家都会打折低价清货，道理就在于把货物卖出去回收部分现金总比把货物放在库里既占用空间又占用资金要强。

人们在做决策时，会理性地比较边际成本和边际收益，边际成本是做某件事时的额外成本，边际收益相对于边际成本而言，是指做某件事的额外收益(additional revenue)。具体地说，边际成本(收益)(marginal cost /revenue)就是多增加一个单位产品的生产或消费所带来的成本(收益)。当边际收益大于边际成本时，人们才会继续生产和消费。比如，一个刚刚本科毕业且有机会到英国继续读应用硕士(1 年制)的大学生，就可以应用边际成本和边际收益来进行分析以做出决策。

原理四：人们会对激励做出反应(**People respond to incentives.**)。由于人们通过比较成本(cost)和收益(benefit)做出决策，所以当成本或收益变动时，人们的行为也会改变。也就是说，人们会对激励做出反应。例如，当包子的价格上升时，人们就决定多吃蒸饺少吃包子，因为购买包子的成本提高了。同时，早餐店主也会愿意雇佣更多工人并多生产包子，因为出售包子的收益高了。深入一点，联想原理三：理性人考虑边际量，那么我们就能得出，成本和收益的边际变动激励人们做出反应（Marginal changes in costs or benefits motivate people to respond.）。

事实上，激励可以被视为经济学的核心。如果没有激励，为什么人们每天早上要去上班?谁会冒险开发新产品?谁会在平时减少消费而增加储蓄?谁会努力工作?如果没有激励，谁会这么做呢？由于公共政策可以改变个人行动的成本和收益，所以决策者可以利用这些政策改变人们的行为。但是，当决策者未能考虑到政策对激励产生的影响时，最终会产生意想不到、南辕北辙的结果。因此，当我们分析任何一项公共政策时，不仅应该考虑直接影响，而且还要考虑到激励发生作用的间接影响。

在曼昆的《经济学原理》一书中，举了一个关于"安全带和汽车安全"(seat belts and car safety)的公共政策，说明激励可能产生意想不到的结果。为了保护汽车上的驾驶员和乘客的安全，法律规定所有的汽车都要有安全带。由于更多的人系安全带，在重大车祸发生时，驾驶员存活的概率提高了。从这种意义上说，安全带拯救了一些人的生命。安全带对安全的这种直接影响正是实施该法律的动机。

但是在这种情况下，相关的激励机制是驾驶员开车时的速度和谨慎程度。缓慢而谨慎地开车是有代价的,因为这要耗费驾驶员的时间和精力。当决定谨慎开车的程度时,理性人要比较谨慎开车的边际收益和边际成本。当边际收益大于边际成本时,他们就会更慢、更谨慎地开车。这就可以解释为什么人们在道路结冰时会比道路洁净时更缓慢而谨慎地开车。

现在来考虑安全带法律如何改变了一个理性驾驶员的"成本—收益"(cost-benefit)计算。由于安全带降低了伤亡的概率,减小了驾驶员的车祸代价,因此,安全带法律减少了缓慢而谨慎开车的收益。人们对安全带的反应和对道路状况改善的反应一样,即更快更放肆地开车。这样,安全带法律最终的结果是更多的车祸次数。

这个法律如何影响开车死亡的人数呢?系安全带的驾驶员在任何一次车祸中存活的可能性都更大了,但他们很可能发现车祸的次数也更多了。最终的综合效应是不确定的。此外,安全开车程度的下降对行人(以及没有系安全带的驾驶员)显然有不利的影响。他们会由于这一法律而面临危险,因为他们很可能发现自己遇上了车祸而又没有安全带的保护。因此关于安全带的法律倾向于增加行人死亡的人数。

这种关于激励与安全带的讨论初看起来,似乎是毫无根据的猜测。但是经济学家的实证研究表明,实际上汽车安全法有许多此类意想不到的影响。数据显示,这些法律减少了每次车祸的死亡人数而增加了车祸的次数。结果是驾驶员死亡人数变动很小,而行人死亡人数增加了。这样的结果,绝不是制定此类法律的初始目的。

原理五:贸易能使每个人的状况更好(Trade can make everyone better off.)。 如果交易双方、多方以及两国之间存在资源或生产力差异,那么就存在使各方都获得好处的贸易机会。在小孩之间,经常会看到互相交换玩具、卡片的情景,这就是一个很好的例子。同样的道理对于国与国之间的关系也是适用的。美国农业发达,有着大量的过剩农产品,但缺乏石油。而科威特有着丰富的石油资源,食物却不足。显然,两国之间进行贸易对双方都有利。

试想一下,如果把你的家庭与其他所有家庭隔绝开来,那么你的家庭就必须自力更生(self-sufficiency),自己种粮食,自己做衣服,盖自己住的房子,生活付出的成本会很高,生活质量就会大大降低,甚至无法生活。显然,你的家庭在与其他家庭交易的活动中互通有无,受益匪浅。无论是在耕种、做衣服或盖房子方面,通过与其他人交易,人们可以以较低的价格(成本)买到各种各样的产品与劳务(By trading with others, people can buy a greater variety of goods and services at lower cost.),同时贸易也使每个人可以专门从事自己最擅长的活动(Trade allows people to specialize in what they do best.),形成专业化分工:农民种粮食,裁缝做衣服,建筑工人盖房子。

从这些简单的例子可以看出,贸易是一个双赢(win-win)的过程,双方都会获益。在现代社会中,每一个人都既是生产者,又是消费者,通过贸易,既为别人提供产品和劳务,又能享受到别人为我们提供各种丰富产品和劳务的好处。

原理六:市场通常是组织经济活动的一种好方法(Markets are usually a good way to organize economic activity.)。 经济学中的市场(market)是指任何可以进行交换的场合,包括有形和无形的市场,买者和卖者不必出现同一地点,商品交换也不必在同一时间发生。传统的集市、社区里的菜市场、拥挤的零售市场和批发市场里到处可见讨价还价的情景,这是我们最熟悉的市场。但在现代社会,百货商场和大型购物中心已很少见到讨价还价,超市更是明码标价。随着信息技术和网络的发展，在如淘宝网上进行的无形交易在市场中所占的比重会越来越大。

在以市场为核心的经济活动中，所有参与人必然面临生产什么、为谁生产、如何生产这三个基本问题(what, for whom, how to produce)。实际上，这就是经济学所要研究的三个基本问题。在市场经济(market economy)中，企业决定雇用谁和生产什么(decide who to hire and what to produce)；家庭决定为哪家企业工作，以及用自己的收入购买什么（who to work for and what to buy）。

回顾人类历史，组织经济活动的方式或者说是资源配置方式主要有两种。一种是计划经济（central planning），就如同当年的苏联，中央政府决定生产什么产品与提供何种劳务，生产多少，以及谁来生产和消费这些产品与劳务。他们认为，只有政府组织经济活动，才能更好地促进整个社会的经济福利。另一种，就是市场经济(market economy)。随着以苏联为首的东欧社会主义阵营的解体，加之中国等国的市场化改革，现在世界上绝大多数国家都实行市场经济。在一个市场经济中，中央计划者的决策被千百万家企业和家庭的决策所取代。市场经济就是指众多企业和家庭在产品和劳务市场上相互交易，通过它们的分散决策来配置资源的经济（an economy that allocates resources through the decentralized decisions of many firms and households as they interact in markets for goods and services）。在企业和家庭的相互交易中，价格和个人利益引导着它们的决策。

关于市场经济，最为经典的理论是亚当·斯密于1776年在《国富论》(*An Inquiry into the Nature and Causes of the Wealth of Nations*)里提出的"看不见的手"(invisible hand)。亚当·斯密观察到，关心自己利益的企业和个人在决定买卖时，会盯着价格(look at prices)。价格不仅反映了一种物品的社会价值，也反映了生产该物品的社会成本(social costs)。因此，市场参与者就会不知不觉地考虑其行为的社会成本(unknowingly take into account the social costs of their actions)。最终结果却使得价格引导众多决策者实现了社会总体福利最大化。亚当·斯密揭示出，看似杂乱无章的市场交易行为背后，各个企业和个人，仿佛被一只"看不见的手"——价格所指引，导致了合意(desirable)的市场结果。

关于"看不见的手"指引经济活动有一个重要的推论：当政府阻止价格根据供求自发地调整时，它就限制了"看不见的手"协调组成经济的千百万家庭和企业的能力。单纯的计划经济的彻底失败即源于此。

原理七：政府有的时候可以改善市场结果 （Governments can sometimes improve market outcomes.）。

正如原理六所揭示的，市场通常是组织经济活动的一种好方法。但是这个规律也有例外，"看不见的手"有时由于各种原因，并不能有效地配置资源(allocate resources)。经济学家用市场失灵(market failure)这个词来指代市场本身不能有效配置资源的情况(a situation in which a market left on its own fails to allocate resources efficiently)。对于市场失灵，政府有必要也有动力对经济进行干预。原理七是对原理六的补充。一般说来，政府干预经济基于两大原因：促进效率和促进平等(to promote efficiency and to promote equity)。

市场为什么会失灵？一个可能原因是外部性。外部性(externality)是一个人的行为对旁观者福利的影响(the impact of one person's or firm's actions on the well-being of a bystander)。

污染就是一个典型的例子。如果一家水泥厂不承担它排放烟尘的全部成本，比如引起附近空气质量下降和增加附近居民患病的风险，它就会大量排放烟尘。在这种情况下，政府就可以通过征收排污税或发放排污许可证的方式进行环境保护来增加经济福利。当然，污染是一个负外部性（negative externality）的例子，它减少旁观者的福利。如果增加旁观者的福利，就会产生正外部性（positive externality）。发明创造就是正外部性的典型例子。一项有用的发明研究出来，除了发明者本身外，其他很多人也会享受到它的好处。

市场失灵的另一个可能原因是市场势力（market power）。市场势力是指一个人（或一小群人）不适当地影响市场价格的能力。例如，假设某一地区的每户家庭都需要电，但当地只有一家发电厂，并且外地的电网难以接入。这家发电厂的所有者对电的销售就有市场势力——在这种情况下，它是一个垄断者。这家发电厂的所有者并不受残酷竞争的限制，可以借势加价，而在正常情况下，"看不见的手"正是凭借竞争来制约个人的私利。

当然，针对市场失灵，我们说政府有时可以改善市场结果，但并不意味着总能如此。公共政策并不是由天使制定的，而是通过极不完善的政治程序制定的。有时政策只是为了利于政治上有权势的人，有时政策由动机良好但信息掌握不充分的领导人制定。因此，相对于市场失灵，有时会出现政府失灵。

原理八：一国的生活水平取决于它生产产品与劳务的能力（A country's standard of living depends on its ability to produce goods and services.）。

当今世界各国生活水平（living standards）的差异惊人。2009 年，美国人均收入为 4.7 万美元，同年中国的人均收入为 3590 美元，而非洲地区肯尼亚的人均收入仅为 770 美元。而这种平均收入的巨大差别也反映在生活质量的各种衡量指标上。高收入国家的公民比低收入国家的公民拥有更多房产、更多汽车，享受更好的营养、更好的医疗保健，以及拥有更长的预期寿命（life expectancy）。

纵向来看，随着时间的推移，一国生活水平的变化也很大。就中国而言，改革开放 30 多年来 GDP 年均增长 10%，按照这一速率，人均收入每七年就会翻一番，这一速度在人类历史上恐怕都是绝无仅有的。而美国 GDP 以接近 2% 的速度增长，虽然与中国相比两个数字相差较大，但是由于美国经济生活水平远高于我国，绝对经济增长量庞大，那么 2% 的增长率也是相当惊人的。

用什么来解释各国和不同时期生活水平的巨大差别呢？答案之简单出乎人的意料。几乎所有生活水平的变动都可以归因于各国生产率的差别——也就是一个工人一小时内所生产的产品与劳务量的差别（the amount of goods and services produced from each hour of a worker's time）。一国的生产增长率决定了平均收入增长率，较高的生产率会带来更高的生活水平。在那些每单位时间内工人能生产大量产品与劳务的国家，大多数人享有较高的生活水平；而在那些工人生产率低下的国家，大多数人必须忍受贫困的生活。

当然影响生活水平的因素有很多，比如自然条件、经济制度、市场竞争等，只是相对于这些，生产率的作用要大得多，生产率是生活水平最直接的影响因素。通俗的理解就是财大气粗，有钱好办事。生产率本身也是一个复杂的问题，人力资本、良好的教育、先进的设备、一流的生产技术水平都有助于提高生产率。

原理九：当政府发行了过多的货币时，物价上升（**Prices rise when the government prints too much money.**）。

按照老百姓的通俗说法，就是钱多了，东西不值钱了。用普通大众都知道的专业术语来说就是"通货膨胀"。21世纪最有名的通货膨胀就是津巴布韦的货币贬值，达百分之十亿，被称为"真实的笑话"。不过这比起1922年的德国，还要逊色不少。1921年1月，德国一份日报的价格为0.3马克。在不到两年的时间里，即1922年11月，一份同样的报纸价格为7000万马克。且其他所有商品的价格都以类似的程度上升。这一事件是历史上最为惊人的通货膨胀案例。

在经济学里，通货膨胀一般是指经济中物价总水平的上升（an increase in the overall level of prices in the economy）。虽然在现代社会，如前述的恶性通货膨胀非常少见，但通货膨胀却始终是政府必须面对的一个重大经济问题和政治问题。在上世纪90年代初期，中国通货膨胀率达到两位数，1994年达到最高，为24.1%。2006年至2008年中国资本流动性过剩，投资过热，股市、房市繁荣，通货膨胀率达到5%左右。由于通货膨胀会给社会带来各种损失，给债权人、纳税人、现金持有者造成伤害，所以世界各国都在对通货膨胀进行全方位的分析，并把保持低通货膨胀率作为经济政策的一个目标。

是什么引起了通货膨胀？在大多数严重或持续的通货膨胀中，罪魁祸首总是相同的——货币量的增长（the growth in the quantity of money）。当一个政府发行了大量货币时，货币的价值就下降了（the value of the money falls）。对历史的实证研究表明，各国通货膨胀率居高不下之时，都伴随着货币量的迅速增长。而通货膨胀率较低的时候，货币量一般都增长缓慢。

原理十：社会面临通货膨胀与失业之间的短期权衡取舍（**Society faces a short-run tradeoff between inflation and unemployment.**）。

如果通货膨胀是由于原理九所揭示的过度发行货币这一简单原因引起的，那么为什么政府有时却在解决通货膨胀问题上面临很大困难呢？原因之一在于人们通常认为降低通货膨胀会引起失业的暂时增加。通货膨胀与失业之间的这种此消彼长的关系图被称为菲利普斯曲线（Phillips curve），是因为发现这一统计规律的是新西兰经济学家菲利普斯。

虽然菲利普斯曲线在经济学中仍然是一个有争议的理论，但大多数经济学家现在接受了这样一种思想：通货膨胀与失业之间存在短期权衡取舍关系（the tradeoff between inflation and unemployment）。根据普遍的解释，这种权衡取舍关系的产生是由于价格调整缓慢所造成的。例如，假定政府减少了经济中的货币量，在长期中，这项政策变动的唯一后果是物价总水平将下降。但并不是所有的价格都将立即做出同步调整，而是极为缓慢地进行变动。这就是说，价格在短期中是具有粘性（sticky）的。

由于价格是具有粘性的，各种政府政策都具有不同于长期效应的短期效应。例如，当政府减少货币量时，它就减少了人们支出的数量。较低的支出与居高不下的价格结合在一起就减少了企业销售的产品与劳务量。销售量减少又导致企业解雇员工。因此，在价格的变动做出完全调整之前，货币量减少就暂时增加了失业。

通货膨胀与失业之间的权衡取舍关系只是暂时的，但可以持续数年之久。因此，菲利普斯曲线对理解经济中的许多发展是至关重要的，特别是决策者在运用各种政策工具时就可以利用这种关系。短期内决策者可以通过改变政府支出量、税收量和发行的货币量来影响通货膨胀与失业。由于货币与财政政策工具（monetary and fiscal policy instruments）具有如此大而复杂的潜在力量，所以，决策者应该如何运用这些工具来控制经济，一直是一个有争议的问题。另外，上世纪 70 年代美国经济出现的滞涨（stagflation）使得菲利普斯曲线的可信度受到了质疑，也促使人们对菲利普斯曲线做了相应的理论调整，以便能够解释滞涨现象。

原理十之所以存在与原理九所揭示的货币因素有一定关系。原理十所揭示的经济问题也从反面印证原理六和原理七这两项互补原理的正确性，原理十所强调的短期权衡取舍也可以看作是原理一的具体例子。政府在解决这个问题时，就要考虑到原理二，即在追求经济增长还是追求社会和谐、维持低失业率之间做出具体的成本收益分析，否则就会走向原理七所揭示的反面——政府失灵。

至此，我们对经济学到底研究什么有了一个初步的了解。在以后的学习中，我们将进一步深入分析个人、厂商与国家之间的经济关系，将会看到经济学这门学科是建立在可以应用于许多不同情况的少数几个基本原理和思想之上的。同时，后续的研究也将加深我们对这些基本原理的深入理解。

重要名词解释

1. **Scarcity**：the limited nature of society's resource
2. **Economics**：the study of how society manages its scare resources
3. **Efficiency**：the property of society getting the maximum benefits from its scarce resources
4. **Equity**：the property of distributing economic prosperity uniformly among the members of society
5. **Opportunity cost**：whatever must be given up in order to obtain some item
6. **Marginal change**：small, incremental adjustments to a plan of action
7. **Market economy**：an economy that allocates resources through the decentralized decisions of many firms and households as they interact in markets for goods and services
8. **Market failure**：a situation in which a market left on its own fails to allocate resources efficiently
9. **Externality**：the impact of one person's actions on the well-being of a bystander
10. **Market power**：the ability of a single economic actor（or small group of actors）to have a substantial influence on market prices
11. **Productivity**：the quantity of goods and services produced from each unit of labor input
12. **Inflation**：an increase in the overall level of prices in the economy
13. **Phillips curve**：a curve that shows the short-run tradeoff between inflation and unemployment

模拟试题

1. The basic economic problem of all countries is the existence of
   （A）Tax increases and budget deficits.
   （B）Limited resources and unlimited wants.
   （C）Unemployment and inflation.
   （D）Government and private industry.
   （E）Unions and monopoly firm.

   Key：B

   Analysis：It examines the basic understanding of economics. Economics is the study of how society manages its scare resources. The scarcity means limited resources relative to human desire.

2. Which of the following is the best example of a negative externality?
   （A）An increase in the price of oil due to the imposition of environmental regulations
   （B）An increase in the price of oil due to action taken by the Organization of Petroleum Exporting Countries（OPEC）
   （C）A decline in oil stock prices as a result of bad management
   （D）Oil leakages from drilling platforms in the Gulf of Mexico
   （E）Restrictions on the importation of foreign-made cars

   Key：D

   Analysis：The question examines the concept of negative externality, which means the negative impact of one person's or firm's actions on the well-being of a bystander. The oil leakages from drilling platforms in the Gulf of Mexico contaminate the sea, and cause environmental pollution.

3. The study of economics is primarily concerned with which of the following?
   （A）The testing of hypotheses under controlled conditions
   （B）The allocation of scarce resources, given unlimited wants
   （C）The fair and equal treatment of all households
   （D）The provision of conclusive answers to public policy issues
   （E）The development of the dynamics of group behavior

   Key：B

   Analysis：The question examines the glossary of economics. Economics is the study of how society manages its scare resources. That means the allocation of scarce resources, given unlimited wants. Therefore, optimal use of resources is desirable.

4. An opportunity cost is entailed in which of the following situations?
   ［I］A student decides to attend college full-time.
   ［II］A family uses its $20,000 savings to purchase an automobile.
   ［III］A farmer decides to grow more wheat and less corn.
   （A）I only

(B) II only

(C) III only

(D) I and III only

(E) I, II, and III

Key： E

Analysis： The opportunity cost of an item is what you give up to obtain that item. It always exists as long as people make a choice.

5. As nations specialize in production and trade in international markets, they can expect which of the following domestic improvements?

[I] Allocation of domestic resources

[II] Standard of living

[III] Self-sufficiency

(A) I only

(B) II only

(C) III only

(D) I and II only

(E) I, II and III

Key： D

Analysis： According to the 5th principle, trade can make everyone better off. By international trade, a nation can export the goods in excess and import for shortage. So trade can improve the standard of living. The domestic economy can no longer maintain self-sufficiency if it involves in trade.

6. The word "economy" comes from the Greek word "oikonomos", which means

(A) "Environment."

(B) "Production."

(C) "One who manages a household."

(D) "One who makes decisions."

(E) "One who trade in the market."

Key： C

Analysis： It examines the original definition of economics. As a Chinese old saying goes, "Governing a large country is just like cooking a delicate dish". Managing the household and the country share a lot in common, too.

7. Resources are

(A) Scarce for households but plentiful for economies.

(B) Plentiful for households but scarce for economies.

(C) Scarce for households and scarce for economies.

(D) Plentiful for households and plentiful for economies.

(E) Plentiful for both if human can avoid the waste.

Key： C

Analysis: Scarcity is the limited nature of society's resources. Therefore we cannot produce all the goods and services that people desire.

8. The adage, "There is no such thing as a free lunch," means

　(A) Even people on welfare have to pay for food.

　(B) The cost of living is always increasing.

　(C) People face tradeoffs.

　(D) All costs are included in the price of a product.

　(E) Goods are scarce.

Key: C

Analysis: Due to scarcity of resources, people have to face tradeoffs, and to get something you must give up something else.

9. Which of the following is correct concerning opportunity cost?

　(A) Except to the extent that you pay more for them, opportunity costs should not include the cost of things you would have purchased anyway.

　(B) To compute opportunity costs, you should subtract benefits from costs.

　(C) Opportunity costs and the idea of tradeoffs are not closely related.

　(D) Rational people should compare various options without considering opportunity costs.

　(E) None of them.

Key: A

Analysis: What you give up to obtain an item is called opportunity cost. To compute opportunity costs, you should add benefits to costs. Rational people face tradeoffs, and they should compare various options, considering opportunity costs.

10. A rational decision maker takes an action only if the

　(A) Marginal benefit is less than the marginal cost.

　(B) Marginal benefit is greater than the marginal cost.

　(C) Average benefit is greater than the average cost.

　(D) Marginal benefit is greater than both the average cost and the marginal cost.

　(E) Marginal benefit is greater than the average cost.

Key: B

Analysis: People make decisions by comparing costs and benefits at the margin. Only if marginal benefit is greater than marginal cost, it is desirable. Rational people think at the margin, not the average.

11. People are likely to respond to a policy change

　(A) Only if they think the policy is a good one.

　(B) Only if the policy changes the costs of their behavior.

　(C) Only if the policy changes the benefits of their behavior.

　(D) If the policy changes either the costs or benefits of their behavior.

　(E) Only if they think the policy is a bad one

Key: D

Analysis: Marginal changes in costs or benefits motivate people to respond. Because people make decisions by comparing costs and benefits, their behavior may change when the costs or benefits change.

12. Which is the most accurate statement about trade?

   (A) Trade can make every nation better off.

   (B) Trade makes some nations better off and others worse off.

   (C) Trading for a good can make a nation better off only if the nation cannot produce that good itself.

   (D) Trade helps rich nations and hurts poor nations.

   (E) Trade sometimes may make every nation worse off.

   Key: A

   Analysis: By trading with others, people can buy a greater variety of goods and services at a lower cost. According to the 5th principle, trade can make everyone better off.

13. Which of the following statements best characterizes a basic difference between market economies and centrally-planned economies?

   (A) Society relies more upon prices to allocate resources when the economy is centrally-planned than when it is market-based.

   (B) The self-interest of households is reflected more fully in the outcome of a centrally-planned economy than in the outcome of a market economy.

   (C) Government plays a larger role in the economic affairs of a market economy than in the economic affairs of a centrally-planned economy.

   (D) None of the above are correct.

   (E) A, B and C are all true.

   Key: D

   Analysis: In a market economy, the decisions of a central planner are replaced by the decisions of millions of firms and households. Market economy is an economy that allocates resources through the decentralized decisions of many firms and households as they interact in markets for goods and services.

14. What is the most important factor that explains differences in living standards across countries?

   (A) The quantity of money

   (B) The level of unemployment

   (C) Productivity

   (D) Equality

   (E) Natural resources

   Key: C

   Analysis: Productivity is the amount of goods and services produced from each hour of a worker's time. Almost all variation in living standards is attributable to differences in countries' productivity. The higher productivity is, the higher standard of living shall be.

15. The short-run tradeoff between inflation and unemployment implies that, in the short run,

（A）A decrease in the growth rate of the quantity of money will be accompanied by an increase in the unemployment rate.

（B）An increase in the growth rate of the quantity of money will be accompanied by an increase in the unemployment rate.

（C）Policymakers are able to reduce the inflation rate and, at the same time, reduce the unemployment rate.

（D）Policymakers can influence the inflation rate, but not the unemployment rate.

（E）Policymakers can't influence both of them.

Key：A

Analysis：The Phillips curve illustrates the tradeoff between inflation and unemployment: higher inflation, lower unemployment. This is the short-run tradeoff.

Chapter 3

Thinking like an Economist
像经济学家一样思考

主要内容和概念讲解

我们从小学习至今，会发现每门课都会有自己的专业名词和特殊的思维方式。语文谈论语法、中心思想、修辞方法。数学谈论方程、函数、几何、公理。经济学也一样，有自己的专业名词。比如，供给（supply）、需求（demand）、弹性（elasticity）、消费者剩余（consumer surplus）、无谓损失（deadweight loss）、机会成本（opportunity cost）等。它们看起来有点神秘，但其实只是对日常经济现象和问题的提炼，是一种学术化的定义。它们的最大好处是为我们提供了一种全新的思考角度和方式。一个学过经济学的人在看待日常经济现象时，会不自觉地运用这些名词去分析现象背后的经济学本质，相比那些没有学过经济学的人来说，他们的看法一般要更为深入和透彻。这些专业术语的具体含义我们会在后面一一解释。但是，必须要指出的是，这些只是最基本的方法论，学完它们只是让你有一个感性的认识，而要成为经济学者或者经济学家还差得远呢。

在现代社会中，经济学家一般会扮演两种角色。一种是类似自然科学家那样的研究者（researcher），另一种则是政府的政策顾问（policy adviser）。显然，类似于自然科学家的研究者角色是基础和关键，但不可否认政府的政策顾问角色也很重要，因为经济学是一门"经世致用"之学，与实际生活紧密相连，其目的是把经济思想应用到实际经济管理中去。

作为科学家，经济学家们提出理论、收集资料，分析这些资料以努力证明或否定他们的理论。这与物理学家、化学家或者生物学家的研究方法一样。经济学家设法用科学家的客观态度来解决问题。但是，很显然，经济学家与物理学家、生物学家等有一个最大的区别，那就是经济学家无法进行实验，而物理学家和生物学家可以利用各种仪器进行研究。因此，经济学始终受到很多人的质疑。

我们先把这个争论放在一边，换一种思路，考虑一下科学的本质是什么？科学的本质是科学方法（scientific method），即冷静地建立并检验有关世界如何运行的各种理论。从这种意义上说，经济学和物理学以及其他自然科学一样，科学既包括研究地心引力也包括研究一国经济。爱因斯坦就曾指出："全部科学不过是日常所思的提炼罢了（The whole of science is nothing more than the refinement of everyday thinking.）。"下面我们就来谈谈经济学家运用科学逻辑来考察经济如何运行的一些方法，他们是如何观察（observation）、提炼理论（theory），然后再进一步观察检验（more observation）的。

我们都知道，在物理学中，牛顿观察到苹果落地现象后通过深入思考发现了万有引力定律。这一定律不仅适用于苹果，而且适用于我们所观察到的宇宙中的绝大多数物体。在实际应用中，万有引力定律能够解释绝大多数自然现象。因此，这个理论就是一条很好的理论。但是，随着天文现象观察的深入，有些天文现象用牛顿的万有引力定律并不能解释。这就促使科学家们进行进一步的理论思考，以弥补万有引力定律的不足。爱因斯坦发现的相对论，就很好地做到了这一点。同样，在经济学中也存在这种观察和理论的互动关系。以十大经济学原理中的原理九为例，在一个价格迅速上升的国家中，经济学家通过观察得出了通货膨胀理论：当政府发行了过多的货币时，物价上升。为了检验这个理论，经济学家可以收集并分析许多不同国家和货币的资料。如果货币量的增长完全与价格上升的速度无关，那么这个理论就难以成立。相反，如果在国际统计资料中货币增长与通货膨胀密切相关，那么这个理论成立的可能性很大。事实上，正如我们介绍的，它是正确的。

　　虽然经济学家像其他科学家一样运用理论和观察，但他们面临着更大的挑战。经济学中，实验通常是很困难的。研究重力理论的物理学家可以在实验室里多次重复比伽利略的试验更精确的自由落体实验。但是，在经济学中实验就困难更多。可以想象，总不能为了让经济学家得到有用的数据而人为改变一国货币的供给。经济学家和天文学家、生物学家一样，通常不得不将突发的事件作为研究的对象。为了弥补实验的不足，经济学家只能寄希望于历史提供的"自然实验"。例如，1929 年的美国经济大萧条（Great Depression），大量银行破产，经济陷入衰退，广大民众生活困难。政府制定经济政策时，当局想尽办法以应对危机。但对经济学家来说，这却提供了很好的研究经济危机、财政和货币政策等重大问题的难得机会。凯恩斯发表了《就业、利息与货币通论》，宏观经济学就此诞生。后续的很多学者，至今仍在研究大萧条。弗里德曼等人通过分析大量的历史数据，认为大萧条在很大程度上源于货币供给不足的政策失误。因此，经济学与历史紧密相关，历史一方面为我们提供了很好的素材和数据，另一方面也可以使我们以史为鉴，阐释和评价现行的经济理论。

　　同自然科学研究一样，经济学研究的第一步也是做出假设（assumptions）。比如在高楼上令铁球做自由落体运动，其落地所需时间就可以通过简单的公式计算得出。我们自然而然地假设空气对铁球的摩擦可以忽略不计。虽然依照理论，空气会使铁球下降速度减慢。但是我们通过假设铁球在真空中下落会使问题简单化，而且对答案没有实质影响。

　　类似地，经济学的这些假设也会大大简化（simplify）问题，而又能得出非常有用的结论。利用假设，经济学家解释这个世界就变得更为容易。例如，研究国际贸易（international trade），就可以假设世界只由两个国家组成，每个国家只生产两种商品。当然，现实远比这复杂，全世界有 200 多个国家，每个国家都生产无数种不同类型的商品。但我们通过假设可以方便思考。一旦我们理解了只有两个国家和两种商品这种假设世界中的国际贸易，我们就可以很好地理解现实复杂世界中的国际贸易。

　　那么做出什么样的假设才有助于解决问题呢？假设从楼上抛下来的不是铁球，而是气球，那么由于空气摩擦对气球的影响力要比对铁球大得多，使用原来的计算方法就会导致结果偏差很大。显然，没有摩擦的假设在新的情况下不再适用，此时就要用到新的假设。同样，经济学家也会采用不同的假设来回答不同的问题。在分析企业生产行为时，你就会发现在短期和长期中，企业所面临的情况是不一样的。在短期中，如果某种因素导致商品需求旺盛，价格上升，但企业很难调整生产规模，最多只能把现有规模发挥到极致，而在长期中，企业则可以通过扩建厂房、增加生产线等扩大生产规模。同时，由于有盈利机会，会有新的厂商加入到商品的生产中。所以在研究问题时，需要做出不同的假设，这导致了短期市场供给曲线和长期市场供给曲线的不同。选择不同的假设正是科学思考的艺术，这没有固定的规律可循，但一切假设都需要有创造性。

在假设的基础上，需要建立经济模型（economic model）来进行深入分析。我们常见的模型有很多，比如玩具、火箭、飞机等实物模型，水箱中的潜艇和风洞中的物理模型，还有地图、电路图和分子结构图等符号模型。模型是为了达到一定的目的，对客观事物的一部分进行简缩、抽象、提炼出来的原型的替代物，集中反映了原型中人们所需要了解的那一部分的特征。我们从小到大所做的数学应用题就是数学模型的应用。

经济学也用模型来了解世界，通常包括图表（figure）和方程式（equation）。正如生物老师用塑料人体模型来讲授人体主要构造一样，经济模型也会忽略很多细节，以便我们能够发现什么才是真正重要的。人体模型并不包括所有的肌肉和血管，经济模型也不反映经济的每一个特征。

所有的模型都是基于假设构建而成的，假设至关重要，如果假设条件不同，模型就会相应地做出改动。这些模型简化了现实（simplify reality），有助于增进我们对现实的理解。

下面我们来看经济学中最基础的模型之一：循环流向图（The circular-flow diagram）。什么是循环流向图？我们知道在市场中，主要的参与者是家庭（households）和企业（firms）、当然也包括政府等其他组织。但是在这个模型及很多模型中，我们都假设市场是由家庭和企业构成的。在它们组成的经济社会中，存在着各种经济活动：购买、出售、工作、雇佣、制造等等。在这些活动中，你会发现有种东西在市场间流通，那就是货币，以前被称为通货（currency）。循环流向图就是说明货币如何通过市场在家庭与企业之间流动的直观经济模型。它通过这种简单的方法，很直观地揭示出经济中家庭和企业之间的交易往来（a visual model of the economy that shows how dollars flow through markets among households and firms, a simple way to visually show the economic transactions that occur between households and firms in the economy.）。

The Circular-Flow Diagram

在市场中，企业用劳动力、土地和资本（建筑物和机器）这些投入品来生产产品与提供劳务，这些投入品被称为生产要素（factors of production）。家庭拥有、出售生产要素并消费企业生产的所有产品与劳务（goods and services）。家庭和企业在两类市场上相互交易。在产品与劳务市场上，企业是卖者，而家庭是买者，购买企业生产的产品与劳务。在生产要素市场上，家庭是卖者，企业是买者，购买家庭所提供的用于生产产品与劳务的投入品。

　　循环流向图的内圈代表家庭与企业之间产品与劳务的流向。家庭在生产要素市场上把劳动力、土地和资本出售给企业使用，然后企业用这些要素生产产品与劳务，这些产品与劳务又在产品与劳务市场上出售给家庭。因此，生产要素从家庭流向企业，而产品与劳务由企业流向家庭。

　　循环流向图的外圈代表相应的货币流向。家庭支出货币以购买企业的产品与劳务。企业用销售的部分收益对生产要素进行支付，刨除企业工人的工资和办公场所的租金，所剩下的部分是企业所有者的利润。企业所有者本人也是家庭成员。因此，对产品与劳务的支出从家庭流向企业，而收入以工资、租金和利润的形式从企业流向家庭。

　　这个循环流向图是一个简单的经济模型，删去了很多细节。一个更为复杂、更为现实的循环流向模型还应该包括政府和国际贸易。但这些细节对于我们理解经济是如何组织的并不重要。恰恰因为该图的简单性，能帮助我们很好地理解经济活动的内在联系，但其背后所蕴含的深刻意义是值得仔细琢磨的。

　　我们接下来要介绍的第二个模型是生产可能性边界（the production possibilities frontier），这一模型是用数学图表的形式来建立的。它指的是一个图形，表明在既定的可供利用的生产要素和技术条件下，经济所能生产的各种产量的组合（a graph showing the various combinations of output that the economy can possibly produce given the available factors of production and technology）。下面我们来详细分析这个模型，你会发现这个模型体现了最基本的经济思想。

The Production Possibilities Frontier

　　假定在一个经济体中，只生产两种商品：电脑和汽车。所有的生产要素都全部用来生产这两种商品。在生产要素和生产技术为既定时，该经济体所能生产的最大产量是一系列不同的组合，比如 2000 台电脑、700 辆汽车或者 2200 台电脑和 600 辆汽车，如图中的 A、C 点所示。极端情况下，如果全部资源都用于汽车行业，该经济体可以生产 1000 辆汽车而生产电脑为 0；如果全部资源都用于电脑行业，该经济体可以生产 3000 台电脑而生产汽车为 0。正如图中的 F、E 两个端点所示。我们把这些最大产量的组合连在一起，就是一条生产可能性边界线。在这条边界线之外的 D 点，是一个不可能实现的情况，因为资源是稀缺的（scarce），现有资源不足以支持那种生产水平。而 B 点则表示资源没有得到充分利用。由此，我们得出结论，经济体可以在生产可能性边界线上或它之内的任何一点上进行生产，但不能在该边界以外任何一点上进行生产。

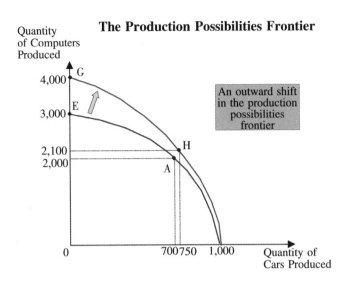

生产可能性边界也不是一成不变的。当某种或者全部商品的生产率、资源数量发生改变时，生产可能性边界就会随之变化。比如，电脑行业的技术进步提高了工人的劳动率，每个工人每周生产的电脑数量会增加。如果全部资源用来生产电脑，电脑可以多生产出 1000 台，即从 E 点移动到 G 点。在汽车产量为既定时，现在整个经济体可以生产更多电脑，结果就会导致生产可能性边界线向外移动。由于产出增长，社会生产可以从 A 点移动到 H 点，即大家可以享有更多电脑和更多汽车。

生产可能性边界曲线不仅大大简化了复杂的经济问题，而且有助于我们深刻理解经济学的思想。现在我们可以借助于生产可能性边界曲线来阐述一些基本概念。第一个概念是稀缺性。正因为资源是稀缺的，所以不可能无限制地生产，最终的产出是受到约束的，不可能超越生产可能性边界曲线之外，如 D 点。第二个概念是效率（efficiency）。如果经济体可以充分利用它所得到的全部稀缺资源投入生产，那么最终的结果就是有效率的。生产可能性边界线上的各点就代表有效率的生产水平。而在边界线内的 B 点，则说明还有资源没有被充分利用。如果消除了无效率的根源，则会促使产出从 B 点移动到 A 点或 C 点，生产出的电脑和汽车都会大大增加。我们可以看到，在边界线上的每一点，如果不减少一种商品的生产，就不能增加另一种商品的生产。由此引出了之前我们介绍过的权衡取舍的概念。例如当社会生产从 A 点移动到 C 点时，社会生产了更多的电脑，但却要以减少生产汽车为代价。是多生产电脑还是多生产汽车？这就要在二者之间有个取舍。权衡取舍（tradeoff）本质上就与机会成本（opportunity cost）的概念相联系。经济学十大原理告诉我们，机会成本是为了得到某种东西所放弃的东西，即所得必有所失。生产可能性边界曲线直观地告诉我们，从另一种商品的角度可以衡量这种商品的机会成本。当社会把一些生产要素从汽车行业配置到电脑行业，即从 A 点移动到 C 点时，它为了得到额外的 200 台电脑而必须放弃 100 辆汽车。换句话说，在 A 点时，200 台电脑的机会成本是 100 辆汽车。最后一个概念是经济增长（economic growth）。我们看到生产可能性边界曲线向外扩张，就是表明社会能够生产出更多的产品供大家消费，从而改善了大家的生活质量，此时就是经济增长。其原因无外乎生产要素的增加和生产技术的改良，平常说的管理改善其实也是一种技术的改良。

需要提醒大家的是，我们所画的生产可能性边界曲线是向外凸出的（convex），这包含着深刻的经济学哲理。在经济学里，我们称之为"边际转换率递增"（increasing marginal rate of transformation）。现在抛开学术定义，以图为例，先看一下它的具体含义。从图形与 X 轴的交点开始，当社会用它的大部分资源生产汽车而非电脑时，生产可能性边界是非常陡峭的。因为在最适合生产电脑的熟练工人和优良机器都用于生产汽车时，只要稍做变动，哪怕是最差的工人和最落后的设备退出转而生产电脑，每放弃一辆汽车所引起的电脑数量的增加也相当可观。与此相比，在图形与 Y 轴交点附近，当社会把其大部分资源用于生产电脑而非汽车时，生产可能性边界非常平坦。在这种情况下，最适合生产电脑的资源已经用于电脑行业，每放弃一辆汽车所引起的电脑数量的增加是微乎其微的。在逐渐增加汽车生产的过程中，即由 E 点到 F 点，以电脑衡量的汽车的机会成本是逐渐递增的。这种边际转换率递增的原因在于生产要素的边际报酬递减（diminishing marginal return）和所使用的要素的比例的差异等。这点在后续的学习中会做进一步的讲解。

在介绍完这两个最基础的经济模型之后，我们来对经济学进行划分。生物学研究涉及分子、细胞、动植物到生物圈等不同层面，物理学涉及原子、分子等粒子层面以及星系和宇宙等极其宏大的层面。同以上学科目一样，经济学至少也分为两种不同的层面。由循环流向图可知，一方面，我们可以研究个别家庭与企业如何做出决策，或者研究某种产品与劳务市场上家庭与企业之间的相互交易。另一方面，我们还可以研究整体经济的运行，这里所说的整体经济就是所有市场上参与交易的所有决策者活动的总和。

对应这种部分与整体、局部与全局的关系，经济学一般可以划分为微观经济学和宏观经济学（Microeconomics and Macroeconomics）。微观经济学研究家庭和企业是如何做出决策以及它们在市场上是如何相互交易的，它关注经济中的个体行为（Microeconomics focuses on the individual parts of the economy. It is the study of how households and firms make decisions and how they interact in markets.）。宏观经济学研究整体经济现象，这些现象包括通货膨胀、失业和经济增长等，它把经济看作是一个整体（Macroeconomics looks at the economy as a whole. It is the study of economy-wide phenomena, including inflation, unemployment, and economic growth.）。

举例如下，一个微观经济学家可以研究煤价、电价上调对居民生活的影响，也可以研究国外农产品的大量进口对国内农业的影响，或者提高高等教育入学率对职工收入水平的影响。而一个宏观经济学家则可以研究人民币汇率（RMB exchange rate）的波动对我国国民收入和经济稳定的影响，也可以研究减少通货膨胀（inflation）的具体措施，或者失业率（rate of unemployment）对经济增长（economic growth）的影响。

微观经济学和宏观经济学显然是密切相关的（closely intertwined）。千百万人的分散决策最终导致了整体经济的变动。因此，不考虑相关的微观经济决策而要理解宏观经济的发展是不可能的。宏观经济学在研究政府削减个人所得税对整个市场中产品与劳务生产的影响时，就必须要考虑所得税减少究竟是如何影响普通家庭购买产品与劳务支出的决定的。

尽管微观经济学与宏观经济学之间存在着固有的联系，但它们还是有着很多本质上的不同。宏观经济学并非微观经济学的简单加总，宏观经济学有着自己独特的研究问题和解决方法。在微观经济学中适用的规律并不适用于宏观经济学，简单加总会导致合成谬误：1+1≠2。

在划分完经济学的分类之后，我们再来谈一谈研究经济学的经济学家。在现代社会，人们总是对很多经济问题感到迷惑，例如，为什么黄金价格一直见长，它与一般大宗商品有什么关系？并希望知道藏在经济现象背后的原因，此时人们往往求助于经济学家。有时候，人们也寄希望于经济学家提出改善经济状况的政策建议。例如，如何控制诸如农产品这样的大宗商品的价格涨幅，从而减少人们的基本生活开支？当经济学家试图去解释世界时，他们是科学家。而当经济学家想要改善世界时，他们是政策顾问或者决策者。

由于科学家和决策者这两种身份和研究目的不同，经济学家所使用的表达方式（statements）也会有所差别。举例来说，现在有两种不同的表述，一种是最低工资法引起了失业，另一种是政府应该提高最低工资。这两种说法有什么不同？显然这两种说法所要达到的目的是不同的。第一种说法像出自科学家之口，做出了一种关于世界是什么样（what the world is）的表述。而第二种说法像是某位决策者说的，做出了想如何改变世界、世界应该是什么样（what the world should be）的表述。

一般说来，关于世界的表述就可分为类似以上例子的两种类型。第一类是实证表述（positive statements）。实证表述是描述性的（descriptive），是关于世界是什么样的表述。第二类是规范表述（normative statements）。规范表述是价值判断性的（prescriptive），是关于世界应该是什么样的表述。

实证表述与规范表述是紧密联系在一起的。我们对世界究竟是什么样的实证认识决定了我们倾向于哪种带有特定价值判断的规范观点。如果说最低工资的确会引起失业，那么我们很有可能就会否决政府应该上调最低工资的结论。当然，规范结论并不仅仅依靠实证分析。很多结论既需要实证分析，又需要价值判断。

实证表述和规范表述的主要区别是如何判断它们的正确性。理论上说，可以通过检验证据而确认或否定实证表述，即实证表述能被证实和证伪（confirm and falsify）。经济学家可以通过分析某一时期内最低工资变动和失业变动的数据来评价第一种表述。然而，评价规范表述则涉及价值观和事实。仅仅靠研究数据并不能提供多少帮助。究竟什么样的政策是好政策，这绝不是一个简单的科学问题，它涉及人们对伦理、宗教、政治、哲学的各种看法。

下面有四个常见的表述，它们究竟是实证表述还是规范表述？1. 最低工资的上调会引起非熟练工人的失业。2. 较高的联邦预算赤字会引起利率增加。3. 相对于上调最低工资而导致就业的少量减少，其增加收入的效果更重要。4. 政府应该对烟草企业征税用来治疗因吸烟患病的穷人。四个表述中，前两个只是陈述事实，是实证表述。而后面两个带有价值判断，是规范表述。注意，实证表述并不一定是正确的。

在学习经济学时，要始终牢记实证表述与规范表述的区别。经济学中很大一部分内容仅仅是试图解释世界是什么样的，但经济学的目标往往是改变世界。当你听到经济学家做出规范表述时，你就知道，他们已经跨过了界线（cross the line），从科学家变成了决策者。

作为政策顾问的经济学家参与政策的制定过程。以美国华盛顿政府为例，它雇用许多经济学家来提供政策建议。这些经济学家主要在三个部门中为政府服务，即立法部门、行政部门、司法部门（legislative, executive, judicial）。另外，美国总统还有一个经济顾问委员会（consultative committee），直接为总统提供经济咨询和建议。

但是，只要你留意一下这些经济学家的言论，你就会发现它们很少一致。大文豪萧伯纳就曾嘲讽："如果把所有的经济学家首尾相连地排成一队，他们也得不出一个结论（If all economists were laid end to end, they would not reach a conclusion.）。"罗纳德·里根总统曾经开玩笑地说：对于经济学家来说，100个问题会有3000个答案。

　　为什么经济学家往往会给决策者提出相互矛盾的建议呢? 为什么他们经常看法相左? 有两个基本原因: 一是经济学家可能对世界是什么样的不同实证理论的正确性看法不一致。二是经济学家可能有不同的价值观, 因此对政策应该实现的目标就有不同的规范观点。

　　关于第一个原因, 我们在自然科学中也经常遇到。光的波粒二象性、爱因斯坦的相对论都说明人们对世界认识的加深。但随着研究的深入, 科学家对真理的认知有分歧, 这一点也不奇怪。经济学家通常也会由于同样的原因而有分歧。经济学是一门年轻的学科, 还有许多问题需要探讨。经济学家们有时意见不一致, 这是因为他们对不同理论的正确性或不同数据的分析结论看法不同而造成的, 本质是由于经济学家的世界观和价值观不同。例如, 经济学家对于政府是应该根据家庭收入还是消费(支出)来征税的看法就不一致。支持把现行所得税改为消费税的人认为, 这种变动会鼓励家庭更多地储蓄, 因为用于储蓄的收入并不征税, 而高储蓄又会引起生产率和生活水平更快地增长。支持现行所得税的人认为, 家庭储蓄并不会对税法的改变做出多大反应。这两派经济学家对税制具有不同的规范观点, 是因为他们关于储蓄对税收激励反应程度的实证观点不同。

　　关于第二个原因, 我们来看一个简单的例子。假设政府征税, 对于年收入为 20 万美元的中产阶层征税 2 万美元, 占收入的 10%; 对于年收入为 5 万美元的底层征税 1 万美元, 占收入的 20%。这种税收政策公平吗? 如果不公平的话, 谁支付的太多了, 而谁支付的太少了? 低收入是因为身体残疾的原因还是由从事的职业所决定的? 哪个理由更重要? 中产阶层的较高收入是由于遗产所得还是勤奋工作所致? 哪个理由更重要? 所有这些问题都将引起很大争议。如果现在有两个经济学家提出了一致的建议, 那我们倒要严重怀疑了。这个简单的例子说明了为什么经济学有时对公共政策的看法不同。正如我们在之前关于规范分析和实证分析的讨论中所了解的, 不能只根据科学来判断政策。经济学家有时提出了不一致的建议是因为他们有不同的价值观和世界观。

　　的确, 由于科学判断的差别和价值观的不同, 经济学家之间的分歧是不可避免的。但也不应该夸大这种分歧。在许多情况下, 经济学家们的确有一致的看法。例如, 租金上限减少了可供住房的数量, 也降低了住房的质量, 关税(tariff)和进口配额(import quota)通常会降低一般经济福利(economic welfare)等等。

　　到现在为止, 我们已经学习了一些最基本的经济学观点与方法。在以后的学习中, 我们将会不断加深对这些基础理论的认识。在经济学的学习中, 我们需要广泛涉猎, 利用各种知识和技能。伟大的宏观经济学创始人约翰·梅纳德·凯恩斯的一些忠告对我们的学习很有价值:

　　经济学研究似乎并不需要任何极高的特殊天赋。与更高深的哲学或纯科学相比, 经济学不是……一门极其容易的学科吗? 一门容易的学科, 但这学科中很少有人能出类拔萃! 对于这个悖论的解释也许在于杰出的经济学家应该具有各种天赋。在某种程度上他应该是数学家、历史学家、政治家和哲学家。他必须了解符号并用文字表达出来。他必须根据一般性来深入思考特殊性, 并在抽象与具体问题之间游刃有余。他必须根据过去、为着未来而研究现在。他必须考虑到人性或社会制度等各种影响因素。他必须同时保持果断而客观的情绪; 并且像艺术家一样冷漠而不流俗, 但有时又要像政治家一样脚踏实地。

　　(The study of economics does not seem to require any specialized gifts of an unusually high order. Is it not...a very easy subject compared with the higher branches of philosophy or pure science? An easy subject, at which very few excel! The paradox finds its explanation, perhaps, in that the master-economist must possess a rare combination of gifts. He must be mathematician, historian, statesman, philosopher—in some degree. He must understand symbols and speak in words. He must contemplate the particular in terms of the general, and touch abstract and concrete in the same flight of thought. He must study the present in the light of the past for the purposes of the future. No part of man's nature or his institutions must lie entirely outside his regard. He must be purposeful and disinterested in a simultaneous mood; as aloof and incorruptible as an artist, yet sometimes as near the earth as a politician.)

这是一个很高的标准。但通过大量实践，至少我们将会越来越习惯于像经济学家一样，从经济学的视角、利用经济学的方法来深入思考社会问题。

重要名词解释

1. **Circular-flow diagram:** It is a visual model of the economy that shows how dollars flow through markets among households and firms, a simple way to visually show the economic transactions that occur between households and firms in the economy.

2. **Production possibilities frontier:** It is a graph showing the various combinations of output that the economy can possibly produce given the available factors of production and technology.

3. **Microeconomics:** the study of how households and firms make decisions and how they interact in markets

4. **Macroeconomics:** the study of economy-wide phenomena, including inflation, unemployment, and economic growth

5. **Positive statements:** claims that attempt to describe the world as it is

6. **Normative statements:** claims that attempt to prescribe how the world should be

主要计算

1.

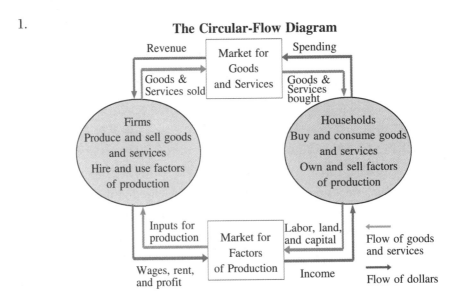

The Circular-Flow Diagram

2.

The Production Possibilities Frontier

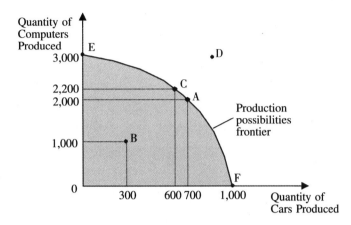

3.

The Production Possibilities Frontier

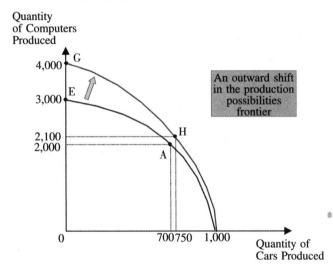

模拟试题

Questions 1-2 refer to the following graph of a country's production possibilities curve.

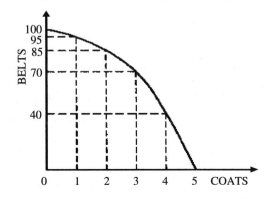

1. If two coats are currently being produced, the opportunity cost of producing the third coat is

   (A) 85 belts

   (B) 75 belts

   (C) 40 belts

   (D) 15 belts

   (E) 10 belts

   Key: D

   Analysis: It examines the definition of opportunity cost, which is whatever must be given up in order to obtain some items. From the graph, if we produce 1 coat more, we must give up 10 (85−70) belts.

2. The best combination of belts and coats for this economy to produce is

   (A) 95 belts and 1 coat

   (B) 85 belts and 2 coats

   (C) 70 belts and 3 coats

   (D) 40 belts and 4 coats

   (E) Indeterminate with the available information

   Key: E

   Analysis: From the definition of opportunity cost, A−D are all efficient productions. However, we lack sufficient information to determine the demand of the society and people's preference.

3. The table below represents points on an economy's current production possibilities curve.

Good X	Good Y
1,000	0
990	100
980	200
970	300

   The opportunity cost of increasing the production of good Y from 0 to 200 is

   (A) 1,000 units of X

   (B) 980 units of X

   (C) 200 units of X

   (D) 20 units of X

   (E) 5 units of X

   Key: D

   Analysis: According to the definition of opportunity cost, if the amount of good Y produced increases from 0 to 200, then the amount of good X must be cut down from 1,000 to 980, so the corresponding opportunity cost is 20.

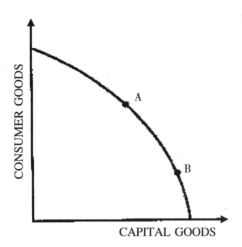

4. The diagram above shows an economy's current production possibilities curve for capital goods and consumer goods. If the society chooses point B over point A, it is choosing

（A）More future consumption in exchange for less current consumption

（B）More current capital goods in exchange for less future consumption

（C）More future and current consumption

（D）Less future consumption in exchange for more current consumption

（E）Less current capital goods in exchange for greater future consumption

Key：A

Analysis：Capital goods refer to the buildings and machines that are used to produce goods or provide the services. They are the factors of production, not for the current consumption but for the future consumption.

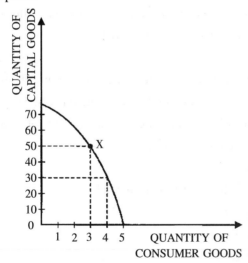

5. According to the graph above, if a country is currently producing at point X, the opportunity cost of producing another consumer good is

（A）20 capital goods

（B）More than 20 capital goods

（C）Fewer than 20 capital goods

(D) 20 consumer goods

(E) Fewer than 20 consumer goods

Key: A

Analysis: At point X, the country produces 3 consumer goods and 50 capital goods. If it produce 1 more consumer good (to 4 consumer goods), then the capital goods must decrease from 50 to 30, so the corresponding opportunity cost is 20 capital goods.

6. Economists, like mathematicians, physicists, and biologists,

    (A) Make use of the scientific method.

    (B) Try to address their subject with a scientist's objectivity.

    (C) Devise theories, collect data, and then analyze these data in an attempt to verify or refute their theories.

    (D) All of the above are correct.

    (E) Just devise theories.

    Key: D

    Analysis: This question examines the role of economist as a scientist.

7. Which of the following statements about economic models is correct?

    (A) Economic models are built to mirror reality exactly.

    (B) Economic models are useful, but they should not be used for the purpose of improving public policies.

    (C) Because economic models omit many details, they allow us to see what is truly important.

    (D) Economic models seldom incorporate equations or diagrams.

    (E) Economic models are simplifications of reality, and in this respect economic models are very different from other scientific models.

    Key: C

    Analysis: It examines the understanding of economic models. Economic models are built to simplify reality in the same way as other scientific models. They are most often composed of diagrams and equations. They can be used for improving public policies.

8. Economists build economic models by

    (A) Generating data.

    (B) Conducting controlled experiments in a lab.

    (C) Making assumptions.

    (D) Reviewing statistical forecasts.

    (E) Equations or diagrams.

    Key: C

    Analysis: Economists build economic models by making assumptions just as the other scientists.

9. A circular-flow diagram is a model that

    (A) Helps to explain how participants in the economy interact with one another.

(B) Helps to explain how the economy is organized.

(C) Incorporates all aspects of the real economy.

(D) Both (A) and (B) are correct.

(E) Help to explain how the money circulates.

Key: D

Analysis: A circular-flow diagram is a simple way to visually show the economic transactions that occur between households and firms in an economy. It simplifies the real economy.

10. Factors of production are

(A) The mathematical calculations firms make in determining their optimal production levels.

(B) Social and political conditions that affect production.

(C) The physical relationships between economic inputs and outputs.

(D) Inputs of the production process.

(E) All of the above are correct.

Key: D

Analysis: The factors of production are the inputs of the production process, such as land, labor and capital.

11. In economics, capital refers to

(A) The finances necessary for firms to produce their products.

(B) Buildings and machines used in the production process.

(C) The money households use to purchase firms' output.

(D) Stocks and bonds.

(E) Money.

Key: B

Analysis: It examines the definition of capital. Capital is used for production, not for current consumption. The money, stocks and bonds can be used to purchase the buildings and machines. They contribute to the accumulation of capital.

12. In the markets for goods and services in the circular-flow diagram,

(A) Households and firms are both buyers.

(B) Households and firms are both sellers.

(C) Households are buyers and firms are sellers.

(D) Households are sellers and firms are buyers.

(E) All of the above are wrong.

Key: C

Analysis: It examines the understanding of the circular-flow diagram. The diagram includes two market: the market for goods and services, and the market for factors of production. In the market for goods and services, households are buyers and firms are sellers.

13. In the circular-flow diagram, which of the following items does not flow from households to

firms?

(A) Revenue

(B) Land, labor, and capital

(C) Factors of production

(D) Profit

(E) A, B and C.

Key: D

Analysis: It examines the understanding and application of economic models: circular-flow diagram. In the market for goods and services, the households give the revenue (income) to firms, and in the market for factors of production, the households supply the factors of production: land, labor, and capital.

14. The production possibilities frontier is a graph that shows the various combinations of output that an economy can possibly produce given the available factors of production and

(A) Society's preferences.

(B) The available production technology.

(C) A fair distribution of the output.

(D) The available demand for the output.

(E) Natural resources and the national wealth.

Key: B

Analysis: The production possibilities frontier is a graph showing the various combinations of output that an economy can possibly produce given the available factors of production and technology.

15. When constructing a production possibilities frontier, which of the following assumptions is not made?

(A) The economy produces only two goods or two types of goods.

(B) Firms produce goods using factors of production.

(C) The technology available to firms is given.

(D) The quantities of the factors of production that are available are increasing over the relevant time period.

(E) The firm makes the best of the factors of production.

Key: D

Analysis: It examines the definition of the production possibilities frontier. The concept does not include the assumption of increasing factors of production.

16. If an economy is producing efficiently, then

(A) There is no way to produce more of one good without producing less of another good.

(B) It is possible to produce more of both goods without increasing the quantities of inputs that are being used.

(C) It is possible to produce more of one good without producing less of another good.

(D) It is not possible to produce more of any good at any cost.

（E）It is uncertain.

Key：A

Analysis：An outcome is said to be efficient if the economy is getting all it can from the scarce resources available. In that case, it shall have to face the tradeoff. In order to obtain some item, you must give up something else.

17. A production possibilities frontier shifts outward when

（A）The economy experiences economic growth.

（B）The desires of the economy's citizens change.

（C）At least one of the basic principles of economics is violated.

（D）Opportunity costs are lessened.

（E）B and C

Key：A

Analysis：The production possibilities frontier shows the tradeoff between the productions of different goods at a given time, but the tradeoff can change over time due to technological advances for example. Then the production possibilities frontier will shift outward. That results in economic growth.

18. Which of the following areas of study typifies microeconomics as opposed to macroeconomics?

（A）The impact of minimum-wage laws on employment in the fast food industry.

（B）The effect of changes in household saving rates on the growth rate of national income.

（C）The impact of faster money growth on the rate of inflation.

（D）A comparison of alternative tax policies and their respective impacts on the rate of the nation's economic growth.

（E）The effect of an increasing inflation rate on national living standards.

Key：A

Analysis：Microeconomics focuses on the individual parts of the economy. It is the study of how households and firms make decisions and how they interact in markets. Macroeconomics looks at the economy as a whole. It is the study of economy-wide phenomena, including inflation, unemployment, and economic growth. B, C, D and E are the topic of Macroeconomics.

19. Which of the following areas of study typifies macroeconomics as opposed to microeconomics?

（A）The effects of rent control on the availability of housing in New York City.

（B）The economic impact of tornadoes on cities and towns in Oklahoma.

（C）How tariffs on shoes affects the shoe industry.

（D）The effect on the economy of changes in the nation's unemployment rate.

（E）The impact of minimum-wage laws on employment in the fast food industry.

Key：D

Analysis：A, B, C and E study how households and firms make decisions and how they interact in markets. They focus on the individual parts of the economy.

20. Which of the following statements best captures the relationship between microeconomics and macroeconomics?

    (A) For the most part, microeconomists are unconcerned with macroeconomics, and macroeconomists are unconcerned with microeconomics.

    (B) Microeconomists study markets for small products, whereas macroeconomists study markets for large products.

    (C) Microeconomics and macroeconomics are distinct from one another, yet they are closely related.

    (D) Microeconomics is oriented toward policy studies, whereas macroeconomics is oriented toward theoretical studies.

    (E) None of all.

    Key: C

    Analysis: The two subfields are different in terms of focus of study. Microeconomics is the basic foundation. Despite the inherent link between microeconomics and macroeconomics, the two fields are distinct. Microeconomics and macroeconomics address different questions; they sometimes take quite different approaches as well.

21. One way to characterize the difference between positive statements and normative statements is as follows:

    (A) Positive statements tend to reflect optimism about the economy and its future, whereas normative statements tend to reflect pessimism about the economy and its future.

    (B) Positive statements offer descriptions of the way things are, whereas normative statements offer opinions on how things ought to be.

    (C) Positive statements involve advice on policy matters, whereas normative statements are supported by scientific theory and observation.

    (D) Economists outside of government tend to make normative statements, whereas government-employed economists tend to make positive statements.

    (E) Positive statements are affirmative, which justify existing economic policy. Normative statements are pessimistic, putting the worst possible interpretation on things.

    Key: B

    Analysis: Positive statements are descriptive. They make a claim about how the world is. Normative statements are prescriptive. They make a claim about how the world ought to be. They have nothing to do with right or false, optimistic or pessimistic.

22. You know an economist has crossed the line from policy adviser to scientist when he or she

    (A) Claims that the problem at hand is widely misunderstood by non-economists.

    (B) Makes positive statements.

    (C) Talks about values.

    (D) Makes a claim about how the world should be.

    (E) Makes normative statements.

Key: B

Analysis: The scientist makes the positive statements, but does not discuss values.

23. "Prices rise when the quantity of money rises rapidly" is an example of a

(A) Negative economic statement.

(B) Positive economic statement.

(C) Normative economic statement.

(D) Statement that contradicts one of the basic principles of economics.

(E) Definitely economic law.

Key: B

Analysis: It examines the definition of a positive statement. Such a statement makes a claim about what the world is.

24. Sometimes economists disagree because their scientific judgments differ. Which of the following instances best reflects this source of disagreement?

(A) One economist believes income tax cuts are unfair to those with low incomes; another economist believes income tax cuts are not unfair to those with low incomes.

(B) One economist believes unemployment causes more human suffering than does inflation; another economist believes inflation causes more human suffering than does unemployment.

(C) One economist believes the policies of the Democratic Party offer the best hope for America's future; another economist believes the policies of the Republican Party offer the best hope for America's future.

(D) One economist believes increases in the minimum wage increase unemployment; another economist believes increases in the minimum wage do not increase unemployment.

(E) All of them.

Key: D

Analysis: Why economists disagree? For two reasons: 1. They may disagree about the validity of alternative positive theories about how the world works. 2. They may have different values and, therefore, different normative views about what policy should try to accomplish. A, B and C are for the second reason.

25. Sometimes economists disagree because their values differ. Which of the following instances best reflects this source of disagreement?

(A) One economist believes the North American Free Trade Agreement (NAFTA) has led to a loss of American jobs; another economist disputes this claim.

(B) One economist believes that when income taxes are cut, people will increase their spending; another economist believes that when income taxes are cut, people will increase their saving.

(C) One economist advises against increases in sales taxes because she thinks such increases are unfair to low-income people; another economist disputes the idea that increases in sales taxes are unfair to low-income people.

(D) One economist believes that, prior to the Civil War, slavery contributed to economic growth in the South; another economist believes that slavery held back the South's economic growth.

(E) If the government were to set a maximum legal price on gasoline, then there would be a shortage of gasoline.

Key: C

Analysis: A, B, D and E are positive statements without carrying any value. C involves the attitude towards low-income people.

26. Which of the following statements is correct about the extent of disagreement among economists?

(A) There is a great deal of agreement among economists on virtually every economic issue.

(B) There is a great deal of agreement among economists on many important economic issues.

(C) All disagreements among economists are attributable to differences in their values.

(D) All disagreements among economists are attributable to the fact that different economists have different degrees of faith in the validity of alternative economic theories.

(E) All disagreements among economists are attributed to their academic level.

Key: B

Analysis: A, B, D and E give too absolute conclusions. But, in fact, there is indeed a great deal of agreement among economists on many important economic issues.

Economic Interdependence and the Gains from Trade 经济的相互依存性与贸易的好处

主要内容和概念讲解

如果从太空中俯瞰地球你就会发现，地球上发达的现代经济非常像一个巨大的蚂蚁王国。如果把人比做蚂蚁的话，那么每只蚂蚁都有着明确的分工。有的在收割作物，有的在制作食物，有的在分配食物，有的在工厂工作，有的在办公室办公，有的在家打扫房屋。人们忙忙碌碌的原因是什么呢?天下熙熙皆为利来，天下攘攘皆为利往。人们都有着共同的利益追求，但这里的"利"并不能简单地用钱来衡量，而应该解释为"生活的舒适和方便"。那么怎样才能做到让人们都能够生活得更好呢?

我们首先想一下我们的日常生活。从早晨起床开始，也许你穿的衣服是中国生产的，但是是由国外某品牌设计的。你穿的运动鞋，比如耐克、阿迪达斯分别是由美国、德国设计的，但是是在东南亚生产的。你早晨或许喝的是咖啡，那可能是巴西等南美国家生产的，也或许是豆浆，其原料大豆很有可能是从美国、阿根廷进口的。你乘坐的公交车或者汽车，其零部件是由很多不同国家生产组装的。你看的电视、电影节目也是由不同地区、不同国家制作的。你用的苹果、诺基亚、三星、黑莓等手机，你所用的苹果电脑等等都是外国设计的，虽然部分零部件是中国的富士康等企业制造的。

而为你提供产品和劳务的这些人你并不认识。他们为你提供这些，并不是发善心，当然也没有人或者政府命令他们这样做。他们之所以这样做是出自相互交易的目的，他们从交易中得到了想要的回报。在前面我们已经介绍了十大经济学原理，其中的原理五:Trade can make everyone better off 揭示的就是这个道理。下面我们就来看看交易怎样使每个人都得到好处，人们又为何选择相互依存(interdependence)。

首先我们对现代复杂的经济社会进行简化，这正是我们之前了解的经济学研究中经常用到的方法。设想一个经济体中只有两种商品——土豆和牛肉，只有两个人——农民和牧牛人。农民种植土豆，牧牛人生产牛肉。

显然，这时候交易能给他们带来很大的好处。如果这两人的胃口是正常的，农民不大可能坚持吃一两个月的土豆，牧牛人也不大可能坚持一两个月吃牛肉，无论是土豆做成土豆泥、炸土豆、烤土豆，还是牛肉做成烤牛肉、水煮牛肉、熏牛肉、牛肉干等，两人最终肯定都会吃腻的。

但如果双方进行交易，两人马上都能享用到汉堡包和炸薯条，或者营养丰富的土豆炖牛肉。贸易的好处非常明显。

再延伸下去，如果双方都能生产对方的产品，但是生产的成本相当高，比如农民去养牛是费力不讨好的事，那么此时贸易的好处也非常明显。

再进一步思考以下这种情况：如果牧牛人生产牛肉和土豆都比农民擅长，是个全能人才，此时贸易的好处就不那么明显，那么牧牛人和农民是自给自足还是继续相互交易呢？

针对这种情况，我们需要详细深入地分析。为了方便分析，我们假设如表所示。

农民生产 1 磅牛肉需要 20 小时，生产 1 磅土豆需要 10 小时。牧牛人的效率就高得多，生产 1 磅牛肉需要 1 小时，且生产土豆也比农民高效，8 小时就能生产 1 磅土豆。

假定一周双方都工作 40 小时，则农民一周能生产 2 磅牛肉、4 磅土豆，牧牛人一周能生产 40 磅牛肉、5 磅土豆。另一种计算方法是，生产 1 磅牛肉，农民需要 20 小时，牧牛人需要 1 小时，而生产 1 磅土豆，农民需要 10 小时，牧牛人需要 8 小时。此时，牧牛人占有绝对优势。

	Hours Needed to Make 1 lb. of:		Amount Produced in 40 Hours（1 week）	
	Beef	**Potatoes**	**Beef**	**Potatoes**
Farmer	20 hours/lb	10 hours/lb	2 lbs	4 lbs
Rancher	1 hour/lb	8 hours/lb	40 lbs	5 lbs

根据这个结果，我们可以分别画出生产可能性边界（production possibilities frontiers）曲线，它们分别代表农民、牧牛人所能生产的各种商品的产量组合。

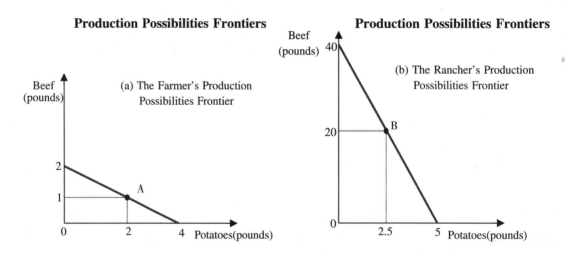

在第一幅图里，农民面临着生产牛肉和土豆的权衡取舍（tradeoff）。不同于之前介绍的向外凸出（bowed outward）的生产可能性边界曲线，由于农民生产牛肉和土豆的技术决定了他能以不变的比率在两种商品之间转换，从而使得生产可能性边界曲线是一条直线。

图中 A 点表示，当农民每周用一半时间生产牛肉、一半时间生产土豆时，会得到 1 磅牛肉、2 磅土豆。

同样再看第二幅图，该图表示牧牛人的生产可能性边界曲线。如果一周时间全部用来生产牛肉，能生产 40 磅；如果时间全部用来生产土豆，能生产 5 磅。B 点表示牧牛人每周用一半时间生产牛肉、一半时间生产土豆，则会产出 20 磅牛肉和 2.5 磅土豆。

如果自给自足，双方互不交易，这样每个消费者所消费的就是他所生产的，生产可能性边界就是消费可能性边界。我们将会看到，没有贸易，整体经济收益是低下的，自力更生（self-dependence）往往并不能丰衣足食（be well-fed and well-clothed）。

如果农民和牧牛人都专门（specialize）生产自己所擅长的商品，然后相互贸易，结果将会如何？农民应该专心生产土豆，牧牛人应该专心生产牛肉吗？我们的结论是肯定的，但是具体原因是什么呢？

	What They Produce and Consume
Farmer	1 lb beef（A）
	2 lbs potatoes
Rancher	20 lbs beef（B）
	2.5 lbs potatoes

来看这张原始表格，假定农民和牧牛人的初始生产和消费偏好分别是 A 点和 B 点，就是农民生产和消费 1 磅牛肉、2 磅土豆，牧牛人生产和消费 20 磅牛肉、2.5 磅土豆。这时农民和牧牛人荤素搭配得还不错，土豆和牛肉都有的吃。

此时，如果牧牛人向农民提议说："哥们，我用 3 磅牛肉来交换你的 1 磅土豆，如何？你就专门生产土豆。我呢，多生产点牛肉，一周由 20 小时改为 24 小时生产牛肉，相应地缩短土豆的生产时间，改为 16 小时生产土豆。"农民想："土豆我都吃腻了，有的是，就想多吃点牛肉，还有这样的好事？好，不管你葫芦里卖什么药，我先换了再说！"如果是各位读者，你们会答应吗？傻子才不干！除非他有牛肉恐惧症或者是素食主义者。

这样交换后，农民的 4 磅土豆减去交换出去的 1 磅，总共还有 3 磅土豆，又获得了牧牛人给的 3 磅牛肉；牧牛人获得农民给的 1 磅土豆后，原来的 2 磅加上 1 磅总共为 3 磅土豆，原来的 24 磅牛肉减去 3 磅牛肉，为 21 磅牛肉。这样农民可以消费 3 磅土豆和 3 磅牛肉，而牧牛人可以消费 3 磅土豆和 21 磅牛肉。结果如下表所示：

The Outcome with Trade

	What They Produce	What They Trade	What They Consume
Farmer	0 lb beef	Gets 3 lbs beef	3 lbs beef（A*）
	4 lbs potatoes	for 1 lb potatoes	3 lbs potatoes
Rancher	24 lbs beef	Gives 3 lbs beef	21 lbs beef（B*）
	2 lbs potatoes	for 1 lb potatoes	3 lbs potatoes

我们来看下面这张图。A 点是没有交易之前的农民的消费组合，而 A* 是交易后的新的消费组合，农民能享用到 3 磅土豆和 3 磅牛肉，显然农民能享受到更好的福利（welfare）。

Trade Expands the Set of Consumption Possibilities

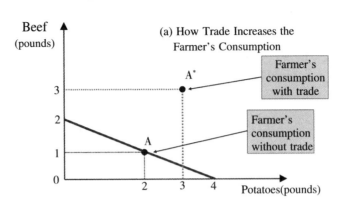

再看下面这张图。B 点是没有交易之前牧牛人的消费组合，B* 是交易后的新的消费组合，即 3 磅土豆和 21 磅牛肉。同样，牧牛人也获得了好处。

Trade Expands the Set of Consumption Possibilities

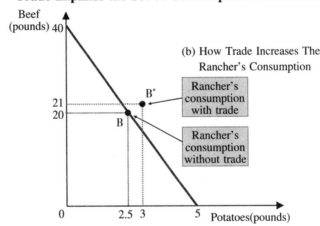

总结前面的表格我们会发现，通过交易，相对于之前各自的自给自足，农民现在多获得 2 磅牛肉、1 磅土豆，而牧牛人则多获得 1 磅牛肉、0.5 磅土豆。

通过前面的例子我们会发现，不同生产者的生产成本存在差异，这种差异会决定究竟谁生产什么东西。这里我们不禁要问，究竟谁生产土豆的成本更低，是农民还是牧牛人？

为了回答这个问题，我们必须弄清楚两种衡量生产成本方式的区别。第一种是常见的方法，即生产一单位产品所需要的时间。例如农民生产 1 磅土豆需要 10 小时，这属于绝对成本，即会计成本核算方法。如果没有学经济学，很多分析可能就此为止了。但是我们已经学习过机会成本的经济学理念，在这里就可以派上用场了。机会成本（opportunity cost）是指为了得到某种东西而要牺牲的东西。比如，农民为了多得到牛肉，就必须牺牲土豆，放弃生产土豆的时间去生产牛肉。

针对第一种常见方法，如果某个生产者拥有较高的生产率（productivity），也就是从更小的投入生产同样的产品（注意这里的投入是以会计成本核算的），我们就可以称这个生产者拥有绝对优势（absolute advantage）。绝对优势指的就是用比另一个生产者更少的投入生产某种商品的能力。

　　针对第二种衡量生产成本的方法，也就是机会成本，经济学里有比较优势(comparative advantage)的概念。如果谁的机会成本低，即为了得到某种东西而放弃的东西更少，则谁就具有比较优势。比较优势指的就是一个生产者以低于另一个生产者的机会成本生产一种商品的能力。

　　下面我们运用机会成本来分析农民和牧牛人的案例。农民生产1磅牛肉的时间是20小时，而20小时能够生产2磅土豆，所以生产1磅牛肉就要放弃2磅土豆，也就是生产1磅牛肉的机会成本是2磅土豆。相反，农民生产1磅土豆的机会成本是1/2磅牛肉。

　　再来看牧牛人，牧牛人生产1磅牛肉只需1小时，而牧牛人1小时只能够生产1/8磅土豆，所以其生产1磅牛肉的机会成本是1/8磅土豆。相反，牧牛人生产1磅土豆的机会成本是8磅牛肉。

　　从表中不难看出，对于同一个生产者来说，其生产的两种商品的机会成本互为倒数(inverse)。

	Opportunity Cost of:	
	1 lb Beef	**1 lb Potatoes**
Farmer	2 lb potatoes	1/2 lb beef
Rancher	1/8 lb potatoes	8 lb beef

　　接下来，我们来看看，谁拥有绝对优势？是农民还是牧牛人？

　　显然，牧牛人生产1磅土豆、1磅牛肉所需的时间都少于农民，拥有绝对优势。

　　那么，谁拥有比较优势？是农民还是牧牛人？

　　从上表可以看出，牧牛人生产牛肉的机会成本为1/8磅土豆，远比农民生产牛肉的机会成本(2磅土豆)要低，所以牧牛人在生产牛肉上拥有比较优势。同样，农民生产土豆的机会成本为1/2磅牛肉，而牧牛人生产土豆的机会成本为8磅牛肉，比农民要高得多，因此农民在生产土豆上拥有比较优势。

　　机会成本的差异和比较优势的存在促使贸易双方都能够获益。如果每个人都能专门生产自己占比较优势的商品，经济的总产量就会增加。经济蛋糕、总规模的增大会使每个人的状况都得到改善。

　　为什么能够获得这样的好处？这是因为每个人都能集中精力从事于他有较低机会成本的生产活动。考虑一下铅笔的生产。我们需要砍伐适当材质的树木，然后把它们运到木材厂，切成能进一步加工成装笔芯的木条。而铅笔中的石墨、顶端的橡皮头，以及把橡皮头和铅笔连在一起的金属片都需要由受过专门训练的人来生产。铅笔是一种很常用的文具，但如果要全部亲自生产却要耗费大量的钱财和时间。如果由铅笔厂各个岗位的熟练工人来做，则能在短时间内以较低的成本生产出大量铅笔来。美国福特汽车公司当初之所以迅速增长，就是因为其著名的福特制——福特制保证高效的流水线作业，工人分工绝对明确，因此最终的产量也是十分惊人的。

　　因此我们可以得出结论：贸易能够使每个人获益，是因为它使人们可以专门从事具有比较优势的活动。基本理由有三：首先，专业化节约了工人从一种生产任务向另一种生产任务转换的时间。其次，通过重复做同一种工作，会使工人更加熟练。第三，专业化为发明创造提供了肥沃的土壤，也使得业务愈加熟练。

最早对专业化分工及贸易行为进行深入分析的是伟大的经济学家亚当·斯密（Adam Smith）。他被认为是经济学的鼻祖。亚当·斯密在 1776 年出版了著名的《国富论》一书，这本书的英文名字是：*An Inquiry into the Nature and Causes of the Wealth of Nations*，所以也可以译为《国民财富的本质和原因研究》。在这本书里，亚当·斯密运用生活中的例子生动地对贸易和经济的相互依存性进行了详细分析。至今，很多经济学家仍然追随这一理论。

在亚当·斯密的书里，亚当·斯密以裁缝、鞋匠和农民为例。裁缝绝不会制作自己穿的鞋子，鞋匠也不会制作自己穿的衣服，农民既不会制作鞋子也不会制作衣服，要雇用不同的工匠来做。如果购买一件东西的价钱比亲自生产的花费小，那么永远不要亲自生产。大家都认同为了自身的利益，应当把全部精力集中用到比他人有利的地方。然后，出售自己所生产的部分产品，以购买自己所需要的其他任何商品。

大卫·李嘉图（David Ricardo）在其 1817 年的经典著作《政治经济学与赋税原理》（*Principles of Political Economy and Taxation*）中，提出了我们现在所熟知的比较优势原理。李嘉图对自由贸易的辩护也是基于这一原理之上，他反对限制粮食进口的谷物法，相信贸易能够使每个人受益。

接下来我们来分析一个实际案例。虽然近年来泰格·伍兹深陷性丑闻和离婚纠纷，但是这对他的收入并没有太大的影响。伍兹的收入主要来源于广告商的赞助，而非参赛的奖金。下面我们来设想一下，伍兹会为自己家的草坪割草吗？

这并不排除伍兹哪天心血来潮，或者为了作秀会偶尔修剪一下草坪。这里我们假设伍兹修剪草坪要 2 小时，而佣人阿甘体质差了不少，修剪草坪就没那么快，需要 4 小时。假设伍兹如果去做他的本职工作打球，2 小时能赚 1 万美元。阿甘如果出去打零工，则 4 小时只能赚 20 美元的较低工资。

	Mow Lawn	**Work**
Tiger Woods	2 hours	$10,000
Forrest Gump	4 hours	$20

此时，显然伍兹在修剪草坪上具有明显的绝对优势，但是从机会成本的角度来分析，其机会成本是 1 万美元，而阿甘的机会成本是 20 美元。阿甘在修剪草坪上具有明显的比较优势。所以泰格·伍兹还是专心打高尔夫球，修剪草坪的事还是让阿甘来做比较合理。

把比较优势的理论推而广之，我们来分析国家间的贸易行为。国家间的贸易往来主要分为两种，即进口和出口。进口品是指那些在国外生产而在国内销售的产品，出口品是指那些在国内生产而在国外销售的产品。

	Food（per month）	**Cars（per month）**
America	2 tons	1
Japan	1 ton	1

假设美国和日本都生产两种商品，分别是食物和汽车。若全部资源用于生产食物，美国每月能生产 2 吨粮食，日本则只能生产 1 吨粮食；若全部资源用于生产汽车，由于美国和日本在科技水平和投入上差不多，每月都能生产 1 辆汽车，如上表所示。

先来看汽车：美国生产 1 辆汽车的机会成本是 2 吨食物，而日本生产 1 辆汽车的机会成本是 1 吨食物，其机会成本较低，具有比较优势。因此日本应该专心生产汽车，美国则应专心生产食物。

最后我们来总结一下本章的内容：我们应该充分认识到我们是生活在一个相互依存的世界中的，每个人都享用着全世界所生产的产品和劳务。大家互相依存，通过交易，获得了丰富多彩的商品。谁投入更低，谁就拥有绝对优势；谁的机会成本更低，谁就拥有比较优势。

贸易可以使各国的福利水平增加，因为各国的比较优势不同。贸易之所以使每个人的状况变得更好，是因为它使得人们可以专门从事自己占比较优势的活动。比较优势不仅适用于个人，也适用于国家。经济学家通常运用比较优势原理来支持自由贸易。

如今国际政治斗争往往以贸易问题作为落脚点。美国一直对中国的大量出口产品怀有很大敌意，会定期制造紧张局势。但是，回到贸易的本质上来，从相互依存和贸易的重要性来看，贸易是一个双赢的过程。美国消费了大量物美价廉、由中国制造的产品，却得了便宜还不卖乖。当今国际，中国离不开世界，世界更离不开中国。当然，中国不能永远依靠廉价的劳动力和资源，而应该转走高科技和创新路线，实现从制造大国向创新大国的转变。

比较优势从另一个层面向我们揭示了合作的重要性，不是每个人都具有绝对优势，但每个人都拥有比较优势，可以互相合作共同完成某项任务。上帝赋予了每个人独一无二的价值，因此，我们要认识到自己的比较优势，实现我们存在的价值。

重要名词解释

1. **Absolute advantage**：the comparison among producers of a good according to their productivity
2. **Opportunity cost**：whatever must be given up to obtain some items
3. **Comparative advantage**：the comparison among producers of a good according to their opportunity cost
4. **Imports**：goods produced abroad and sold domestically
5. **Exports**：goods produced domestically and sold abroad

主要图表

1.

Production Possibilities Frontiers

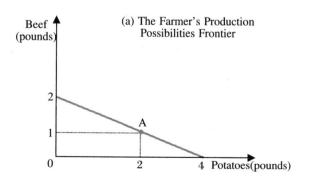

(a) The Farmer's Production Possibilities Frontier

2.

Trade Expands the Set of Consumption Possibilities

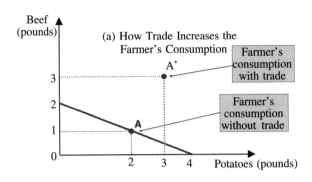

主要计算

Juanita and Shantala run a business that programs and tests cellular phones. Assume that Juanita and Shantala can switch between programming and testing cellular phones at a constant rate. The following table applies.

	Minutes Needed to		Number of Cellular Phones Programmed or Tested in a 40-Hour Week	
	Program 1 Cellular Phone	Test 1 Cellular Phone	Cellular Phones Programmed	Cellular Phones Tested
Juanita	?	2	160	1,200
Shantala	10	4	240	600

1. According to the table, the number of minutes needed by Juanita to program a cellular phone is

   a. 4.

   b. 5.

   c. 7.5.

   d. 15.

   Key：d

   Analysis： 40×60/160=15

2. According to the table, which of the following points would be on Juanita's production possibilities frontier, based on a 40-hour week?

   a. (120 cellular phones programmed, 295 cellular phones tested)

   b. (130 cellular phones programmed, 225 cellular phones tested)

   c. (140 cellular phones programmed, 155 cellular phones tested)

   d. Both (a) and (b) would be on Juanita's production possibilities frontier.

Key: b

Analysis: 130×15+225×2=2400

3. According to the table, which of the following points would be on Shantala's production possibilities frontier, based on a 40-hour week?

   a. (120 cellular phones programmed, 250 cellular phones tested)

   b. (180 cellular phones programmed, 150 cellular phones tested)

   c. (240 cellular phones programmed, 600 cellular phones tested)

   d. More than one of the above would be on Shantala's production possibilities frontier.

   Key: b

   Analysis: 180×10+150×4=2400

4. According to the table, Juanita has an absolute advantage in

   a. Programming cellular phones and a comparative advantage in programming cellular phones.

   b. Programming cellular phones and a comparative advantage in testing cellular phones.

   c. Testing cellular phones and a comparative advantage in programming cellular phones.

   d. Testing cellular phones and a comparative advantage in testing cellular phones.

   Key: d

   Analysis: It examines the definition of absolute advantage and comparative advantage. The absolute advantage and the comparative advantage of Juanita happen to be the same.

5. According to the table, Shantala has an absolute advantage in

   a. Programming cellular phones and a comparative advantage in programming cellular phones.

   b. Programming cellular phones and a comparative advantage in testing cellular phones.

   c. Testing cellular phones and a comparative advantage in programming cellular phones.

   d. Testing cellular phones and a comparative advantage in testing cellular phones.

   Key: a

   Analysis: It examines the definition of absolute advantage and comparative advantage. Here is the opposite case of the question above.

Uzbekistan's Production Possibilities Frontier

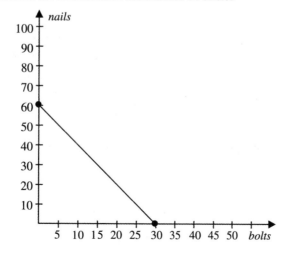

45

Azerbaijan's Production Possibilities Frontier

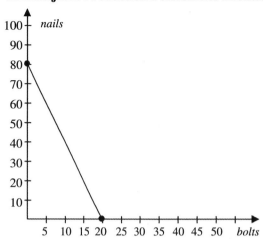

6. According to the figures above, if Uzbekistan and Azerbaijan each divides its time equally between making bolts and making nails, then the total production is

   a. 15 bolts and 40 nails.

   b. 25 bolts and 70 nails.

   c. 30 bolts and 80 nails.

   d. 50 bolts and 140 nails.

   Key: b

   Analysis: In this case, Uzbekistan's production combination is 15 bolts and 30 nails. Azerbaijan's production combination is 10 bolts and 40 nails. So the total production is 25 bolts and 70 nails.

7. According to the figures above, if the production possibilities frontiers shown are each for two days of production, then which of the following combinations of bolts and nails could Uzbekistan and Azerbaijan together make in a given 2-day production period?

   a. 12 bolts and 120 nails

   b. 24 bolts and 96 nails

   c. 38 bolts and 50 nails

   d. 44 bolts and 24 nails

   Key: d

   Analysis: Suppose a is correct, then we assume Azerbaijan specializes in producing 80 nails, then 120-80=40, and Uzbekistan must produce 40 nails. But according to the production possibilities frontiers of Uzbekistan（$2x+y=60$）, Uzbekistan can produce 10 bolts at the best and can't produce 12 bolts. So a is false. Similarly, we can check b, c and d. Only d is possible.

8. According to the figures above, if the production possibilities frontiers shown are each for two days of production, then which of the following combinations of bolts and nails could

Uzbekistan and Azerbaijan together not make in a given 2-day production period?

a. 9 bolts and 122 nails

b. 21 bolts and 98 nails

c. 36 bolts and 56 nails

d. 46 bolts and 18 nails

Key: d

Analysis: Use the same logic as the above question. The Azerbaijan's production possibilities frontiers is 4x+y=80, so a, b and c are all possible.

9. According to the figures above, Azerbaijan's opportunity cost of one nail is

a. 1/4 bolt and Uzbekistan's opportunity cost of one nail is 1/2 bolt.

b. 1/4 bolt and Uzbekistan's opportunity cost of one nail is 2 bolts.

c. 4 bolts and Uzbekistan's opportunity cost of one nail is 1/2 bolt.

d. 4 bolts and Uzbekistan's opportunity cost of one nail is 2 bolts.

Key: a

Analysis: It examines the definition of opportunity cost. It means whatever must be given up in order to obtain some item. 20/80=1/4, 30/60=1/2.

10. According to the figures above, suppose Uzbekistan decides to increase its production of bolts by 10, what is the opportunity cost of this decision?

a. 1/2 nail

b. 2 nails

c. 5 nails

d. 20 nails

Key: d

Analysis: $10 \times (60/30) = 20$

11. According to the figures above, suppose Azerbaijan is willing to trade 3 nails with Uzbekistan for every bolt that Uzbekistan makes and sends to Azerbaijan, which of the following combinations of bolts and nails could Azerbaijan then consume, assuming Uzbekistan specializes in making bolts and Azerbaijan specializes in making nails?

a. 8 bolts and 56 nails

b. 14 bolts and 44 nails

c. 18 bolts and 32 nails

d. 20 bolts and 26 nails

Key: a

Analysis: $8 \times 3 + 56 = 80$

12. According to the figures above, Uzbekistan has an absolute advantage in the production of

a. Bolts and a comparative advantage in the production of bolts.

b. Bolts and a comparative advantage in the production of nails.

c. Nails and a comparative advantage in the production of bolts.

d. Nails and a comparative advantage in the production of nails.

Key: a

Analysis: As for the production of bolts, Uzbekistan's 30>Azerbaijan's 20, and the opportunity cost of Uzbekistan's bolts is 2<4, which is the opportunity cost of Azerbaijan's bolts. So Uzbekistan also has a comparative advantage in the production of bolts.

13. According to the figures above, Azerbaijan has an absolute advantage in the production of

    a. Bolts and a comparative advantage in the production of bolts.

    b. Bolts and a comparative advantage in the production of nails.

    c. Nails and a comparative advantage in the production of bolts.

    d. Nails and a comparative advantage in the production of nails.

    Key: d

    Analysis: Similarly as the above question.

14. According to the figures above, if Uzbekistan and Azerbaijan switch from each country dividing its time equally between the production of bolts and nails to each country spending all of its time producing the good in which it has a comparative advantage, then the total production will increase by

    a. 5 bolts and 10 nails.

    b. 15 bolts and 40 nails.

    c. 20 bolts and 50 nails.

    d. 30 bolts and 80 nails.

    Key: a

    Analysis: At the beginning, the total production is 25 bolts and 70 nails. Then we have 30 bolts and 80 nails. So the total production will increase by 5 bolts and 10 nails.

15. According to the figures above, if Uzbekistan and Azerbaijan each spends all its time producing the good in which it has a comparative advantage and trade takes place at a price of 12 bolts for 36 nails, then

    a. Neither Uzbekistan nor Azerbaijan will gain from this trade.

    b. Uzbekistan will gain from this trade, but Azerbaijan will not.

    c. Azerbaijan will gain from this trade, but Uzbekistan will not.

    d. Both Uzbekistan and Azerbaijan will gain from this trade.

    Key: d

    Analysis: Trade can make everyone better off.

16. According to the figures above, without trade, Uzbekistan produced and consumed 12 bolts and 36 nails and Azerbaijan produced and consumed 14 bolts and 24 nails. Then, each country agreed to specialize in the production of the good in which it has a comparative advantage and trade 16 bolts for 38 nails. As a result, Uzbekistan gained

    a. 2 bolts and 2 nails and Azerbaijan gained 2 bolts and 18 nails.

    b. 4 bolts and 2 nails and Azerbaijan gained 2 bolts and 14 nails.

    c. 14 bolts and 38 nails and Azerbaijan gained 16 bolts and 42 nails.

    d. 16 bolts and 38 nails and Azerbaijan gained 16 bolts and 38 nails.

    Key: a

Analysis: (nail, bolts), (36, 12) and (24, 14)→(0, 30) and (80, 0)→(38, 14) and (42, 16), so for Uzbekistan 38−36=2, 14−12=2, and for Azerbaijan, 42−24=18, 16−14=2.

模拟试题

1. When can two countries gain from trading two goods?

   a. When the first country can only produce the first good and the second country can only produce the second good.

   b. When the first country can produce both goods, but can only produce the second good at great cost, and the second country can produce both goods, but can only produce the first good at great cost.

   c. When the first country is better at producing both goods and the second country is worse at producing both goods.

   d. Two countries could gain from trading two goods under all of the above conditions.

   e. It depends on the specific condition.

   Key: d

   Analysis: Trade can make everyone better off.

2. Regan grows flowers and makes ceramic vases. Jayson also grows flowers and makes ceramic vases, but Regan is better at producing both goods. In this case, trade could

   a. Benefit both Jayson and Regan.

   b. Benefit Jayson, but not Regan.

   c. Benefit Regan, but not Jayson.

   d. Benefit neither Jayson nor Regan.

   e. None of the above.

   Key: a

   Analysis: Jayson does not have the absolute advantage, but has the comparative advantage. He can specialize in one job in which he has the comparative advantage. This way everyone could be better off.

3. Ben bakes bread and Shawna knits sweaters. Ben and Shawna both like to eat bread and wear sweaters. In which of the following cases is it impossible for both Ben and Shawna to benefit from trade?

   a. Ben cannot knit sweaters and Shawna cannot bake bread.

   b. Ben is better than Shawna at baking bread and Shawna is better than Ben at knitting sweaters.

   c. Ben is better than Shawna at baking bread and at knitting sweaters.

   d. Both Ben and Shawna can benefit from trade in all of the above cases.

   e. b and c

   Key: d

Analysis: Gains are from specialization and trade.

4. Shannon bakes cookies and Justin grows vegetables. In which of the following cases is it impossible for both Shannon and Justin to benefit from trade?

   a. Shannon does not like vegetables and Justin does not like cookies.

   b. Shannon is better than Justin at baking cookies and Justin is better than Shannon at growing vegetables.

   c. Justin is better than Shannon at baking cookies and at growing vegetables.

   d. Both Shannon and Justin can benefit from trade in all of the above cases.

   e. Shannon is better than Justin at growing vegetables and Justin is better than Shannon at baking cookies.

   Key: a

   Analysis: Gains are from specialization and trade. But trade fails when people do not like and need the goods.

5. An economy's production possibilities frontier is also its consumption possibilities frontier

   a. Under all circumstances.

   b. Under no circumstances.

   c. When the economy is self-sufficient.

   d. When the rate of tradeoff between the two goods being produced is constant.

   e. When the rate of tradeoff between the two goods being produced is diminishing.

   Key: c

   Analysis: It examines the understanding and application of economic models: production possibilities frontier.

6. A production possibilities frontier is bowed outward when

   a. The more resources the economy uses to produce one good, the fewer resources it has available to produce the other good.

   b. An economy is self-sufficient instead of interdependent and engaged in trade.

   c. The rate of tradeoff between the two goods being produced is constant.

   d. The rate of tradeoff between the two goods being produced depends on how much of each good is being produced.

   e. None of all

   Key: d

   Analysis: If the rate of tradeoff between the two goods being produced is constant, the production possibilities frontier is a linear line. In general, the marginal rate of transformation is increasing.

7. A production possibilities frontier is a linear line when

   a. The more resources the economy uses to produce one good, the fewer resources it has available to produce the other good.

   b. An economy is interdependent and engaged in trade instead of self-sufficient.

   c. The rate of tradeoff between the two goods being produced is constant.

d. The rate of tradeoff between the two goods being produced depends on how much of each good is being produced.

e. The marginal rate of transformation are increasing.

Key: c

Analysis: Only if the rate of tradeoff between the two goods being produced is constant, the production possibilities frontier is a linear line.

8. The following table contains some production possibilities for an economy for a given month.

Sweaters	Gloves
4	300
6	?
8	100

If the production possibilities frontier is a straight line, then "?" must be

a. 100.

b. 150.

c. 200.

d. 250.

e. 180.

Key: c

Analysis: $300-(300-100)/(8-4)\times(6-4)=200$

9. The following table contains some production possibilities for an economy for a given year.

Cars	Newspapers
10	400
12	360
14	?

If the production possibilities frontier is bowed outward, then "?" could be

a. 340.

b. 330.

c. 320.

d. 310.

e. 350.

Key: d

Analysis: If the production possibilities frontier is a linear line, the answer is 320. But this one is bowed outward, so it must be less than 320.

10. A farmer has the ability to grow either corn or cotton or the combination of the two. Given no other information, it follows that the farmer's opportunity cost of a bushel of corn multiplied by his opportunity cost of a bushel of cotton

a. Is equal to 0.

b. Is between 0 and 1.

c. Is equal to 1.

d. Is greater than 1.

e. Is equal to 1/2.

Key: c

Analysis: It examines the understanding of the opportunity cost. The opportunity cost of each other is reciprocal.

11. Suppose a gardener produces both green beans and corn in her garden. If she must give up 14 bushels of corn to get 5 bushels of green beans, then her opportunity cost of 1 bushel of green beans is

   a. 0.36 bushel of corn.

   b. 2.8 bushels of corn.

   c. 14 bushels of corn.

   d. 70 bushels of corn.

   e. 25.2 bushels of corn.

   Key: b

   Analysis: 14/5=2.8

12. Comparative advantage is related most closely to which of the following?

   a. Output per hour

   b. Opportunity cost

   c. Efficiency

   d. Bargaining strength in international trade

   e. Productivity

   Key: b

   Analysis: The producer who has the smaller opportunity cost of producing a good is said to have a comparative advantage in producing that good.

13. Specialization and trade are closely linked to

   a. Absolute advantage.

   b. Comparative advantage.

   c. Gains to some traders that exactly offset losses to other traders.

   d. Shrinkage of the economic pie.

   e. Productivity.

   Key: b

   Analysis: Differences in opportunity cost and comparative advantage create the gains from trade.

14. Suppose that a worker in Agland can produce either 10 units of organic grain or 2 units of incense per year, and a worker in Zenland can produce either 5 units of organic grain or 15 units of incense per year. There are 20 workers in Agland and 10 workers in Zenland. Currently the two countries do not trade. Agland produces and consumes 100 units of grain

and 20 units of incense per year. Zenland produces and consumes 50 units of grain and no incense per year. If each country made the decision to specialize in producing the good in which it has a comparative advantage, then the combined yearly output of the two countries would increase by

a. 30 units of grain and 100 units of incense.

b. 30 units of grain and 150 units of incense.

c. 50 units of grain and 90 units of incense.

d. 50 units of grain and 130 units of incense.

e. 50 units of grain and 150 units of incense.

Key: d

Analysis: At the beginning, (grain, incense) is (100, 20) and (50, 0). Then they specialize, and (gain, incense) is (200, 0) and (0, 150).

15. Suppose that a worker in Boatland can produce either 5 units of wheat or 25 units of fish per year, and a worker in Farmland can produce either 25 units of wheat or 5 units of fish per year. There are 10 workers in each country. Political pressure from the fish lobby in Farmland and from the wheat lobby in Boatland has prevented trade between the two countries on the grounds that cheap imports would kill the fish industry in Farmland and the wheat industry in Boatland. As a result, Boatland produces and consumes 25 units of wheat and 125 units of fish per year while Farmland produces and consumes 125 units of wheat and 25 units of fish per year. If the political pressures were overcome and trade was to occur, each country would completely specialize in the product in which it has a comparative advantage. If trade were to occur, the combined output of the two countries would increase by

a. 25 units of wheat and 25 units of fish.

b. 50 units of wheat and 50 units of fish.

c. 75 units of wheat and 75 units of fish.

d. 100 units of wheat and 100 units of fish.

e. 75 units of wheat and 100 units of fish.

Key: d

Analysis: (25, 125)+(125, 25)→(0, 250)+(250, 0). Boatland specializes in fish, and Farmland specializes in wheat.

Supply, Demand and Equilibrium
供给、需求与均衡

Chapter 5

主要内容和概念讲解

　　供给（supply）与需求（demand）是经济学里经常用到的两个词。在市场经济中，供给与需求也是驱动市场正常运转的力量（force）。我们已经学过，面对稀缺性进行决策是经济学所要解决的基本问题。我们在进行商品和劳务交易时，它们的价格就是我们所要付出的代价。价格实际上是对稀缺程度的度量。但究竟由谁来决定价格呢？答案就是——供给与需求。供给与需求决定价格，价格传递着供求双方的关键信息，继而配置经济中的稀缺资源（allocate the economy's scarce resources），也决定了每种商品和劳务的产量以及价格。

　　在现代经济中，我们到处能感受到供给与需求的存在。天气因素影响农商品的价格，战争和远洋运输影响石油价格，这些都明显与供求关系有关。还有一些较为复杂的问题，比如提高最低工资对工人有利还是有弊，身陷困境的航空企业如何制定价格，如何解决诸如北京等大城市中交通拥堵的问题等等，都可以归结为供给与需求的问题。如果想知道某件事或者某项政策如何影响经济，那么就需要考虑它如何影响供给与需求。实际上，很多问题都可以用供给和需求的理论来解释，虽然有些不合乎情理，比如恋爱、婚姻、家庭等，但仍有助于我们认清事物的本质。

　　供给与需求在市场上的相互作用，指的是人们在市场上相互交易的行为。市场可分为两个对立的群体：买者（buyer）和卖者（seller）。市场就是由某种商品或劳务的买者与卖者所组成的一个群体（a group of buyers and sellers of a particular good or service）。买者作为一个群体决定了这种商品或劳务的需求（Buyers determine demand.），而卖者作为另一个群体决定了供给（Sellers determine supply.）。

　　在研究买者和卖者的行为之前，我们先看看它们所处的市场是什么，以及有哪些不同的市场类型（market type）。

　　在日常生活中我们会看到很多不同的市场，如服装市场、大型超市、家电卖场、专卖店，当然还有家门口的菜市场等等。那么经济学是如何划分这些市场，从而发掘出市场背后的规律的呢？需要注意的是经济学家不是根据商品的类型来划分市场的，他们透过现象抓本质，依据厂商数量、商品差异、进入或退出的难易程度以及市场信息的充分程度来进行划分。

　　先来看一下我们身边最为直观和熟悉的市场。例如农商品市场，无论是批发还是零售，都组织得井井有条。在这些市场中，买者和卖者在特定的时间和地点相聚，双方自由讨价还价，市场中还有交易中介帮助确定价格和销售。古代和现在农村里的赶集活动就是这一市场的集中体现。当然有的市场组织得也并不是很严密，例如我们身边的蛋糕市场。蛋糕的买者并不会在某一时段相聚在一起。蛋糕的众多卖者也分布在不同的地方，他们提供略有差别的商品。这种市场上也没有权威的交易中介制定统一价格，而是由各个蛋糕店主自己制定价格。各个买家也是自主决定在哪家蛋糕店购买多少蛋糕。尽管这个市场没有人组织，但蛋糕的买者群体和卖者群体也形成了一个市场。每个买蛋糕的人都知道市场上总有一些正在出售的蛋糕可供选择。而每个蛋糕店主也都意识到，他的商品与其他卖者提供的商品是相似的。蛋糕的价格和销量并不是由任何一个买者或卖者决定的。确切地说，蛋糕的价格和销量是由所有买者和卖者在市场上的相互交易所决定的。

蛋糕市场和经济中的大多数市场一样充满了竞争。竞争市场（competitive market）是指这样的市场，在这个市场里有许多买者与卖者，以至于每一个人对市场价格的影响都微乎其微（in which there are many buyers and many sellers so that each has a negligible impact on the market price）。每一个蛋糕卖者对价格的控制都是有限的，因为其他卖者也提供类似的商品。如果要价高的话，买者会转去其他蛋糕店购买。卖者也没有理由收取低于现行市场价格的价钱，因为利薄难以承受低价，即使低价可以多吸引买者，也难以抵消低价所带来的损失。何况低价有时会让买者认为蛋糕质量有问题。另外，由于价格具有粘性，如果降了价以后再涨价会影响不好，难度也大。同样，没有一个蛋糕买者能影响蛋糕的价格，因为每个买者的购买量都很少，而且由于蛋糕有保质期，团购蛋糕基本不可能。

竞争市场根据竞争程度可进一步划分，首先可分为完全竞争市场（perfectly competitive market）和其他类市场。在一个完全竞争市场里，商品是一样的（Products are the same.），买者与卖者人数众多，以至于没有任何一个买者或卖者可以影响市场价格（numerous buyers and sellers so that each has no influence over price），也就是说，每个人都是"价格接受者"（Buyers and sellers are price takers.）。在本章的学习中，我们假定市场就是一个完全竞争市场。现实中，有些市场非常符合以上条件，接近于完全竞争市场。例如，在水稻市场上有成千上万出售水稻的农民和千百万个购买水稻和水稻商品的消费者。由于没有一个买者或卖者能影响水稻价格，所以，每个人都把价格作为既定的因素。

但是也有许多商品与劳务市场并不是完全竞争的。一些市场只有一个卖者，而且由这个卖者决定价格。这个卖者被称为垄断者（monopolist），这个市场被称为完全垄断市场（monopoly market），例如各地的有线电视公司、燃气公司、自来水厂和电力公司等。当地的居民基本上只能从一家有线电视公司、一家燃气公司、一家自来水厂或一家电力公司购买劳务。在中国，铁路向来有"铁老大"的称号，就是绝对的垄断。

有一些市场只有少数几个卖者，而且这些卖者之间并不经常主动进行带有攻击性的竞争。这样的几个卖者被称为寡头（oligopolist），这样的市场被称为寡头垄断市场（oligopoly market），例如运动鞋市场中，耐克、阿迪达斯、彪马等几个少数厂商就是全球市场的寡头。大家如果留意网球市场，就会发现全球市场基本上被四家公司——威尔逊、宾州、邓禄普和斯伯丁（Wilson, Penn, Dunlop, and Spalding）所瓜分。而且你会发现，这些公司尽量避免激烈竞争，基本不打价格战，至少表面上看起来很和气。当然，它们背后都在拼命加大研发和营销力度。有的寡头，比如航空公司有时会互相串通，以维持较高的机票价格。在中国，电信市场就是个典型的寡头市场。

最后还有一种常见的市场类型：在这个市场上有许多卖者，它们提供的商品略有差异，并且每个卖者都可以为自己的商品定价。这种市场在经济学里被称为垄断竞争市场（monopolistically competitive market），例如知名的品牌服装市场。市场上的服装有很多不同的品牌，这些衣服的差异并不大，新的款式很快就被他人模仿，而且服装公司可以为自己的商品制定价格。

应该说，在当今世界，我们能看到各种各样的市场类型，但是基本上都可归入以上四种。只是这四种市场类型的划分并不是很严格，现实生活中有很多市场同时具有两种不同市场类型的特点。比如，运动服装市场就既有垄断竞争市场的特点，又有寡头垄断市场的特点。我们之前介绍过经济学研究要采用假设，因此我们对现实中的市场进行抽象简化，从最基本的完全竞争市场开始研究。虽然完全竞争市场最容易分析，但是由于大多数市场或多或少都有不同程度的竞争，因此我们在研究完全竞争市场下供给与需求所得到的许多基本结论也适用于更复杂的市场。

在对市场类型有了简单的了解之后，现在我们再回到供给和需求这个市场背后的推手上来。从常理出发，我们先来看需求。肯尼迪说过："不要问你们的国家能为你们做些什么，而要问你们能为国家做些什么（Ask not what your country can do for you, ask what you can do for your country.）。"小时候我们经常听老师说："我为人人，人人为我"、"给予比索取更幸福"。但是现实生活中，人类基于自私的本性，总是需求在前。正如我们之前所学过的，稀缺性本质上就表现为相对于人类无限的欲望，一切资源都是有限的。其实，供给和需求就是我们所要面临的权衡取舍。是现在满足需求进行消费呢，还是进行生产再投资，提高将来的供给呢？现实生活中，这可是个非常复杂的问题。

那么，什么是需求（demand）呢？ 一种商品的需求量是指在某一特定的时间内，在各种可能的价格下，消费者愿意而且能够购买的该商品的数量（the amount of a good that buyers are willing and able to purchase）。

那么是什么决定了个人的需求量呢？经济学总结出五个主要因素：价格、收入、相关商品的价格、偏好和预期（price, income, prices of related goods, taste and expectation）。下面我们分别介绍一下这几个因素。

在选购商品时，价格因素往往是我们首先考虑的。试想你在买包子的时候，每个包子涨0.5元，你就很可能会少买；但如果便宜0.5元，你就会多买。由于需求量随着价格上升而减少，随着价格下降而增加，因此说需求量与价格负相关。价格与需求量之间的这种关系对经济中大部分商品来说都是正确的，而且，实际上这种关系很普遍，所以经济学家称之为需求定律（law of demand）。当其他条件不变时，一种商品的价格上升，该商品的需求量将会减少，这就是需求定律（Other things equal, the quantity demanded of a good falls when the price of the good rises.）。

收入可能是我们一生都在考虑的问题。相信很多人都曾有过囊中羞涩的经历，而且收入会制约我们的消费需求。试想你现在只有10元钱，这是你一天的零花钱，你还会早餐吃包子就把它全花完吗？即使你很能吃，你也会省着花。穷人恨不得一分钱当两分用，每天节衣缩食；富人呢，一般花起钱来大手大脚，甚至铺张浪费，所以奢侈品从来都是属于富人的。中国有句话叫做"由俭入奢易，由奢入俭难"，社会上也流行一句口头禅——"男人有钱就变坏"，这里面都暗含了收入因素对个人的影响。在经济学里，如果其他条件不变，当收入减少时，一种商品的需求随之减少，这种商品就称为正常品（normal goods）。现实生活中的大多数商品都是正常品，但并不是所有的商品都是正常品。如果当收入减少时，一种商品的需求却随之增加，这种商品就被称为低档品，也叫劣等品（inferior goods）。街头的小餐馆和公共汽车就属于这类商品。当收入降低时，你一般不大会去环境幽雅的中高档餐厅或者乘坐出租车。

　　相关商品的价格也是我们在购物时经常考虑的一个因素。假定包子的价格上升,包子是正常品,需求定律表明你将会少买包子。同时,你也许就会多买蒸饺。因为包子和蒸饺都是面食,里面的馅也差不多,只是包子丰满,而蒸饺脸上多了褶子而已,但是它们能够满足我们相似的食欲。当一种商品价格上升(减少)会增加(减少)另一种商品的需求时,这两种商品被称之为替代品(substitutes)。生活中有很多成对的替代品,比如可口可乐和百事可乐、可乐和果汁、汉堡和面包、米线和面条等。联想之前学到的垄断,如果一个垄断厂商把一种商品的所有替代品都控制了,就将完全控制消费者,消费者要么接受,要么就只好不再消费此类商品。现在我们假设豆浆的价格上升,此时你将会少买豆浆。因为人们吃早餐时习惯边喝豆浆边吃包子,所以你也会少买包子,至少在一段时间内是这样的。有着类似关系的商品还有电脑和软件、汽油与汽车、花生米和饮料等。当一种商品的价格上升(下降)会减少(增加)另一种商品的需求时,我们称它们为互补品(complements)。商家可以利用互补品的这种性质进行促销,比如在电影院,花生米、爆米花可以很便宜,而饮料的价格可以适当调高,这样影院的总体收益反而会有所增加。

　　偏好(taste),专业的说法也叫嗜好(preference),它对需求的影响也很明显。如果你喜欢吃包子,那就会多买,而如果你看到包子就没胃口,那你就会少买或不买。由于萝卜青菜,各有所爱,经济学家一般不会深究偏好这一因素,而且它也很难解释,因为偏好多与心理、文化、历史因素有关。

　　最后是预期因素(expectation)。"预期"这个词在经济学里是个很重要的概念。宏观经济学里就有一个理性预期学派。这里举例来说,如果你预期下个月会得到一笔不小的收入,可能就不会省着花钱,而是现在多消费。另外,假使你预期下个月包子会由于面粉价格的上涨而上调价格,你就会在这个月多吃包子,甚至会多买面粉。预期这个概念在股市、房地产市场里表现得淋漓精致,在那里人们的预期变化很频繁。

　　在这五个因素中,我们尤其要关注价格因素。当然,购买商品的消费者数量(number of buyers)也会影响需求量。前面介绍的需求定律,揭示了商品的需求量与价格负相关。在其他条件不变时,商品的需求量会随着价格的上升而逐渐减少。为了直观地反映这种关系,我们采用需求表来表示。需求表就是表示一种商品的价格与其需求量之间关系的表格。

　　如图所示,当冰激凌蛋卷免费的时候,一个人最多会需要12个。当价格提升为0.5美元时,一个人最多需要10个,数量减少两个。当价格继续上涨至1美元时,需求量降为8个。直至价格升为3美元时,如此贵的价格使得消费者只能与冰激凌蛋卷说再见了。这样的表格就像列车时刻表,因此经济学家通常称之为需求表(demand schedule)。

冰激凌蛋卷的价格(美元)	冰激凌蛋卷的需求量(个)
0.00	12
0.50	10
1.00	8
1.50	6
2.00	4
2.50	2
3.00	0

根据这张表我们可以画出需求曲线。以需求量作为横坐标，以价格作为纵坐标（经济学中的惯例做法），把各个点连在一起形成一条曲线，这就是需求曲线，它反映了一种商品的价格和需求量之间的关系，反映在图形上，是一条向下倾斜（downward-sloping）的曲线。

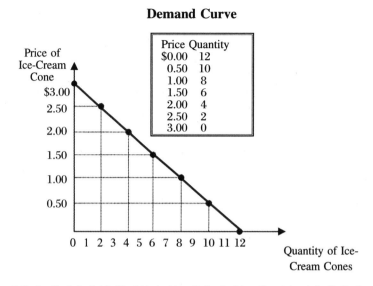

Demand Curve

Price	Quantity
$0.00	12
0.50	10
1.00	8
1.50	6
2.00	4
2.50	2
3.00	0

在这里，要注意到需求曲线背后的条件。我们之所以能画出需求曲线来，是因为假设其他条件不变。上图的需求曲线表明，只有当冰激凌蛋卷的价格变动时，冰激凌蛋卷的需求量才会改变，而影响需求量的其他因素，如收入、相关商品的价格、偏好、预期等都保持不变。经济学家用 ceteris paribus（字面意思是"其他条件相同"）这个术语表示，除了正在研究的变量之外，所有相关变量都保持不变。需求曲线之所以向下倾斜，就是因为在其他条件不变时，较低的价格意味着更多的需求量（Lower prices mean a greater quantity demanded.）。

显然"其他条件不变"这种假设不太符合现实情况。在现实世界中，很多事情是同时变动的。正如我们之前对经济模型所做的假设一样，假设有助于我们看清事情的本质和事物间的联系。假设没有问题，关键是我们在运用供给与需求工具来分析事件或政策时，需要记住什么是不变的条件，什么是变化的条件。

到现在为止我们一直在讨论这条曲线。但这条曲线代表谁的需求情况呢？你的？我的？还是其他人的？决定个人需求的基本因素似乎就是个人偏好了。但是，实际上我们要研究的是市场需求曲线。市场是由无数的人构成的，所以市场需求曲线自然是个人需求曲线的加总。

X：商品的数量 Y：商品的价格

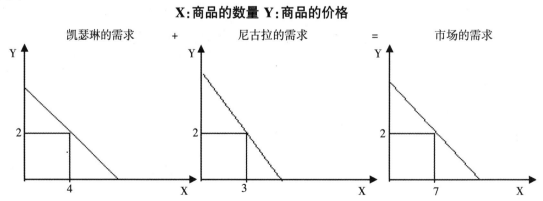

如果市场只由两个人组成，在价格是 2 元的时候，凯瑟琳和尼古拉的需求分别是 4 个单位和 3 个单位商品。市场需求（market demand）就是所有人对某种商品或劳务需求的总和（refers to the sum of all individual demands for a particular good or service），把个人需求曲线横轴上表示的个人需求量相加即得，也即此时市场需求是 7 个单位商品。把个人需求曲线水平（horizontally）相加就得出了市场需求曲线（market demand curve）。我们所要关注、分析的是市场到底是如何运作的，所以主要用到的是市场需求曲线。

市场需求曲线与个人需求曲线一样，是假设除价格可以变化外，其他影响需求量的因素都是固定的。当这些除价格以外影响需求的因素发生变化时，比如收入、相关商品的价格、偏好和期望等发生改变时，需求曲线就会移动，要么向左，要么向右。

现在，假定中国医学协会突然宣布经常吃包子的人更健康也更长寿。那么，这条新闻对包子铺会有什么影响？我们很容易想到，在某一既定价格时，消费者会愿意购买更多的包子。也就是市场需求曲线会向右移动。反之，任何一种减少购买意愿的事件发生，就会使得市场需求曲线向左移动。比如，最近新闻报道说早餐行业里很多包子都是用劣质的面粉做的，或者馅料含有致癌物质，这些都会使得人们减少或者不购买包子。

不同于表现为需求曲线向左或向右移动的需求变动，需求量的变动是特指商品价格变动所导致的需求沿着曲线本身的移动（movement along the demand curve）。如图所示，当价格上升时，商品的需求量就会减少，即从 A 点移动到 B 点。

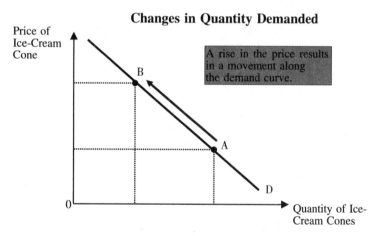

简言之，需求曲线表示在其他所有决定需求的因素不变时一种商品的价格变化，该商品的需求量会发生什么变化。而当其他决定因素中的一种发生变化时，需求曲线就会平移（shift），如下表所示。注意，影响市场需求曲线的还有市场中买者的数量（number of buyers）。

Change in Quantity Demanded versus Change in Demand

Variables that Affect Quantity Demanded	A Change in This Variable...
Price	Represents a movement along the demand curve
Income	Shifts the demand curve
Prices of related goods	Shifts the demand curve
Taste	Shifts the demand curve
Expectation	Shifts the demand curve
Number of buyers	Shifts the demand curve

接下来考虑一个实际案例。吸烟有害健康，这已是世界各国的共识。因此，公共政策制定者考虑运用政策来减少吸烟民众的数量，现在有两种方法，一种是使香烟或其他烟草商品的需求曲线移动。公益广告、香烟盒上有害健康的警告以及禁止在电视上做香烟广告等，都旨在在任何一种既定价格水平时减少香烟的需求量。如果确实能够减少香烟的需求量，那么这些政策就使香烟的需求曲线向左移动。第二种方法是提高香烟的价格。例如，如果政府对香烟制造商征税，烟草公司就会以提高价格的方式把税收负担转嫁给消费者。较高的价格会促使吸烟者减少吸烟量。在这种情况下，吸烟量的减少就不再表现为需求曲线的移动。相反，它表现为沿着同一条需求曲线移动到价格更高而数量较少的一点上。

但是，这两种方法有可能使得吸烟者转而吸食大麻——如果大麻是香烟的替代品的话。那么就会产生新的问题。但如果大麻与香烟是互补品的话，情况就要好得多。因此，政策制定者还得调查市场中吸食香烟和大麻的实际情况，这样才能使政策发挥最大效果。

现在我们来考察卖者(seller)的行为。任何一种商品或劳务的供给量(quantity supplied)都是卖者愿意而且能够出售的数量。需求有需求定律，供给也有供给定律(law of supply)。供给定律指的是：在其他条件不变时，一种商品的价格上升，该商品的供给量就会增加。假设包子的市场价格上涨，那么老板肯定愿意多生产包子，因为包子卖出去的话会有更多收入，从而获得更高的利润。而且会有更多的、以前不卖包子的小餐馆转而卖包子。

但是除了价格(price)外，还有哪些因素会影响供给量? 同需求相似，它们分别是投入品的价格、生产技术、预期和生产厂商的数量(input price, technology, expectation, and number of producers)。以包子行业为例，面粉、蔬菜、猪肉等投入品的价格上涨，工人工资的增加都会使得生产成本更高，在价格一时难以提高的情况下，老板会决定减少生产；反之，老板则会增加生产。类似地，在生产技术提高的情况下，比如工人更加熟练、绞肉机等更加先进的情况下，老板也会增加生产。而如果预期到包子在下个月会涨价，那么很多老板在这个月会减少生产。

对于总的市场供给来说，如果厂商数量多，自然供给就多。但是，对于单个厂商来说，这个因素就不存在。因为我们分析的假设条件是完全竞争市场。实际生活中，开包子铺确实需要考虑市场中已有包子铺的数量。

我们来看冰激凌蛋卷市场中的某个卖家的供给表(supply schedule)。供给表是表示一种商品的价格与其供给量之间关系的表格。当价格是 0 时，卖家显然不愿意生产。当价格涨为 0.5 美元时，卖家还是觉得赔本，不会生产。当价格涨为 1 美元时，卖家有了点利润，开始生产 1 个。根据供给定律，随着价格的上涨，供给量会增加。等价格达到 3 美元时，卖家愿意生产 5 个。

把这种关系反应在图形上，就是供给曲线(supply curve)。供给曲线是表示一种商品的价格与其供给量之间关系的图形，它是向上倾斜的(upward-sloping)曲线。如图所示，以供给量作为横坐标，以价格作为纵坐标，标出各个点，然后连在一起就是供给曲线。

Supply Curve

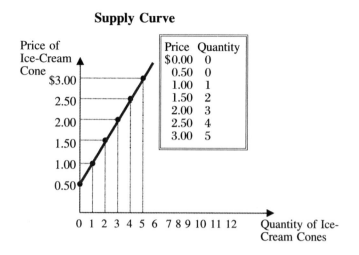

与市场需求是所有买者需求的总和一样，市场供给（market supply）也是所有卖者供给的总和（the sum of all individual supplies for all sellers of a particular good or service）。因此，我们在水平方向上加总个人供给曲线就能得到市场供给曲线。如图所示，如果市场中只有 2 个卖者，在价格是 2 美元时，一个卖家愿意供给 3 个单位商品，另一个卖家愿意供给 4 个单位商品，则市场总供给就是 7 个单位商品。

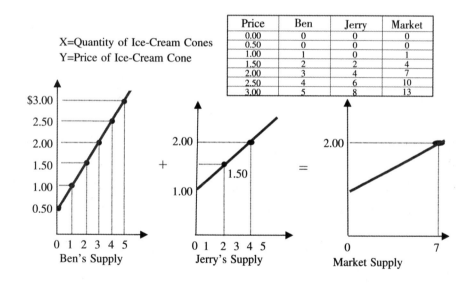

在供给分析中，同样要区分两个概念。一个是供给量的变动（change in quantity supplied），一个是供给的变动（change in supply）。如下图所示，供给量的变动是指沿着供给曲线的移动（movements along the supply curve），它的起因是商品市场价格的变化。供给的变动则表现为供给曲线的左右移动，它的起因是除价格以外其他影响供给量的因素的变动。

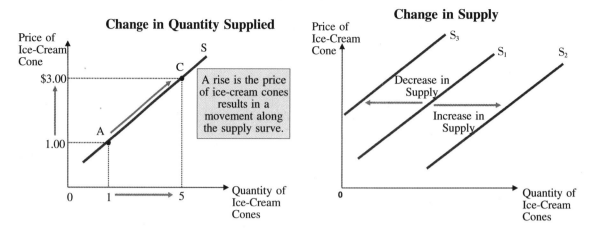

简言之，供给曲线表示在所有其他决定供给的因素不变时，一种商品的价格变化，该商品的供给量会发生什么变化。当其他决定因素中的一种发生变化时，供给曲线移动，如下表所示。注意影响市场供给曲线的还有市场中买家的数量。

Variables that Affect Quantity Suppiled	A Change in This Variable...
Price	Represents a movement along the supply curve
Input price	Shifts the supply curve
Technology	Shifts the supply curve
Expectation	Shifts the supply curve
Number of sellers	Shifts the supply curve

到此为止，我们已经分别分析了供给和需求。现在我们可以把它们结合起来，说明它们是如何决定市场上一种商品的销量和价格的。

在经济学里我们使用均衡(equilibrium)这个专业名词来表示供给和需求平衡的状态(a situation in which supply and demand have been brought into balance)。均衡价格(equilibrium price)就是指使得供给与需求平衡的价格(the price that balances supply and demand)。当价格调整到使供给与需求平衡时，此时的供给量和需求量就是均衡数量（equilibrium quantity）。反映在图表中，供给曲线与需求曲线相交时的纵坐标就是均衡价格，而横坐标就是均衡数量，此时供给量和需求量相等。均衡价格也叫做市场出清价格(market-clearing price)，因为在此价格下，生产出来的商品正好满足消费，市场中没有剩余的商品，且市场上的每一个人都得到了满足，买者买到了他想买的所有商品，而卖者也卖出了他想卖的所有商品。

为了更深入地了解市场出清，我们来看两种情况：过度供给和过度需求，经济学里分别称之为超额供给(excess supply)和超额需求(excess demand)。

超额供给如下图所示。

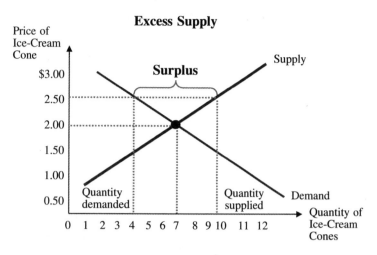

当价格高于均衡价格（2 美元）时，例如为 2.5 美元，此时由供给曲线可得，生产商愿意提供 10 个冰激凌蛋卷。而由需求曲线可得，消费者只需要 4 个冰激凌蛋卷。此时，市场中就会有 6 个商品积压，冰激凌蛋卷生产商怎么也卖不出去剩余商品。超额供给就是指这种供给量大于需求量的状态（a situation in which quantity supplied is greater than quantity demanded）。

这种情况下该怎么办呢? 供过于求时，供给一方就会降低价格以卖出商品。价格会趋向均衡价格移动，直到降到市场均衡价格为止。此时，厂商生产出来的全部商品才能都卖出去。

而超额需求（Excess Demand）如下图所示。

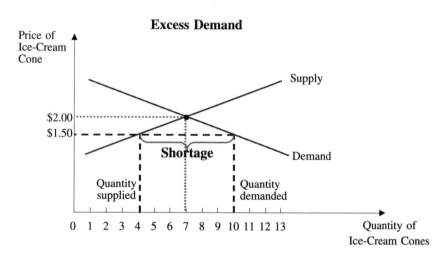

假设价格低于均衡价格，为 1.50 美元，此时由供给曲线可得，生产商只愿意提供 4 个冰激凌蛋卷。而由需求曲线可得，消费者需要 10 个冰激凌蛋卷。此时，市场中就会有 6 个商品的短缺，太多的买家抢购太少的商品，消费者怎么也买不到足够的商品。超额需求就是指这种需求量大于供给量时的状态（a situation in which quantity demanded is greater than quantity supplied）。

此时又该怎么办呢? 供不应求时，供给方就会觉得有可乘之机，会提高价格，价格也会趋向均衡价格移动，直到升到市场均衡价格为止。此时，厂商生产出来的全部商品都会卖出去，愿意以这一价格购买商品的买家都会买到想要的商品。市场也会把那些不愿意以更高价格购买商品的潜在买家清出市场。

因此，总体来看，许多买者与卖者的行为自发地把市场价格推向均衡价格。一旦市场达到其均衡价格，所有买者和卖者都会得到满足，也就不存在价格上升或下降的压力。在不同市场上达到均衡价格的速度是不同的，这取决于价格调整的快慢。但是，在大多数自由市场上，由于价格最终要变动到均衡价格，所以，过剩与短缺都只是暂时的。实际上，这种现象普遍存在，所以被称为供求定律（law of supply and demand）：即任何一种商品价格的调整都会使该商品的供给与需求达到均衡状态（the claim that the price of any good adjusts to bring the supply and demand for that good into balance）。

到现在为止，我们已经分析了供给与需求如何共同导致市场均衡，市场均衡又如何决定商品价格，以及买者所购买和卖者所生产的商品数量。显然，在图形中，供给和需求曲线的位置决定了均衡价格和数量。但当某些事件使这两条曲线中的一条或两条都移动时，市场上的均衡就改变了。关于这种变动的分析，经济学中称之为比较静态分析法，因为它涉及原均衡与新均衡的比较。

在分析某一事件影响市场导致均衡变动时，通常按照三个步骤进行。第一，确定该事件是使供给曲线移动，还是需求曲线移动，还是使两种曲线都移动（decide whether the event shifts the supply or demand curve （or both））。第二，确定曲线是向右移动还是向左移动（decide whether the curve(s) shift(s) to the left or to the right.）。第三，用供求图来分析这种移动如何影响均衡价格和数量（examine how the shift affects equilibrium price and quantity）。

下面我们就用供求图来简单阐述一下这三个步骤。

一、需求变动(a change in demand)。

假设某一年夏季天气特别热，那么这种情况是如何影响冰激凌蛋卷市场的呢？为了分析这个问题，我们分三个步骤进行。

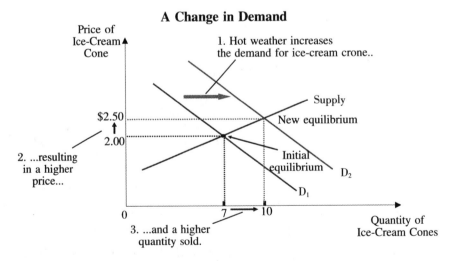

1. 天气热通过改变人们对冰激凌蛋卷的偏好而影响需求曲线。这就是说，天气改变了人们在任何一种既定价格时想购买的冰激凌蛋卷的数量。供给曲线则不变，因为天气并不直接影响销售冰激凌蛋卷的企业。

2.由于天气热使人们想吃更多的冰激凌蛋卷，需求增加了，所以，需求曲线向右移动。这种移动表明，在每种价格时，冰激凌蛋卷的需求量都增加了。

3.由图可知，天气热提高了冰激凌蛋卷的价格，增加了冰激凌蛋卷的销售量。

需要注意的是，当天气炎热使冰激凌蛋卷价格上升时，尽管供给曲线不变，但企业供给的冰激凌蛋卷数量增加了。在这种情况下，价格沿着供给曲线移动，供给量增加，但供给未变，因为供给量是指卖者希望出售的数量，而供给是指供给曲线的位置。要注意这与日常用语的区别。同样，需求曲线平移称为需求变动，而沿着一条固定需求曲线的移动称为需求量的变动。

二、供给和需求同时变动（a change in both supply and demand）。

假设天气炎热和地震同时发生。我们知道天气炎热会影响需求曲线，而地震破坏了当地的冰激凌工厂，使得生产被迫缩减，从而影响供给曲线。现在这两个事件共同影响市场。

我们仍遵循三个步骤进行。

1.我们可以确定，两条曲线都会移动。天气炎热影响需求曲线，因为它改变了买者在任何一种既定价格时想要购买的冰激凌蛋卷的数量。同时，地震改变了供给曲线，因为它改变了卖者在任何一种既定价格时想要出售的冰激凌蛋卷的数量。

2.需求增加，需求曲线向右移动，而供给减少，供给曲线向左移动。

3.由图可知，这会导致两种可能的结果，取决于需求和供给移动的相对幅度。在这两种情况下，均衡价格都会上升，而均衡数量则不同。一种是需求有大幅度增加，而供给减少很小，均衡数量会增加。与此相反，另一种是供给大幅度减少，而需求增加很少，均衡数量会减少。当然，还有一种临界情况，即需求和供给变动幅度相同，则均衡数量不变。因此，这些事件肯定会提高冰激凌蛋卷的价格，但它们对冰激凌蛋卷销售量的影响是不确定的。如下面两幅图所示。

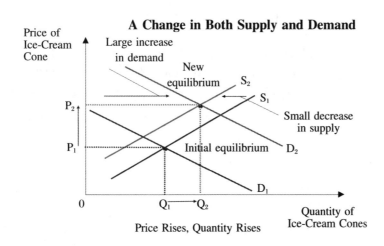

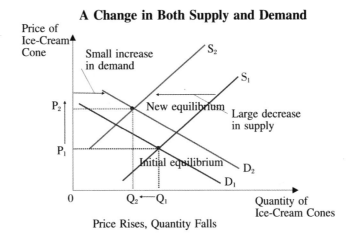

A Change in Both Supply and Demand

Price Rises, Quantity Falls

由于供求两条曲线都有不变、增加和减少三种情况，因此最终的组合结果会有9种。我们把它们进行一个简单的总结，如下表所示。我们会看到，在两条曲线都移动时，均衡数量或均衡价格是不确定的。在图形上我们会看到，这与曲线的斜率和曲线的移动量有关。

What Happens to Price and Quantity When Supply or Demand Shifts?

	No Change In Supply	An Increase In Supply	A Decrease In Supply
No Change In Demand	P same Q same	P down Q up	P up Q down
An Increase In Demand	P up Q up	P ambiguous Q up	P up Q ambiguous
A Decrease In Demand	P down Q down	P down Q ambiguous	P ambiguous Q down

到此为止，我们对供给和需求有了一个初步的认识。供给和需求共同决定了经济中各种不同商品和劳务的价格。价格反过来就成了指导资源配置的信号。究竟谁可以得到这些资源？答案就是那些愿意并有能力支付价格的人。比如，考虑一下北京历史悠久的四合院的配置。由于这些四合院非常有限，并不是每一个人都能享受到四合院的优雅生活。谁能得到这种资源呢？答案是愿意并且有能力支付这种四合院价格的人。因此，四合院的价格要一直进行调整，直至四合院的需求与供给达到均衡。因此，在市场经济中，价格是配置稀缺资源的机制。

同样，价格决定了每种商品由谁来生产和生产多少。我们可以考虑一下建筑工人的情况。由于人们需要住房，因而保证一些人从事建筑业是至关重要的。但什么因素决定谁是农民，谁是建筑工人呢？在一个自由的社会中，并没有做出这种决策并确保住房供给充足的政府机构，而即使有，实际中也很难操作。相反，把农民配置到建筑业中是由于千百万农民的个人工作决策所导致的。这种分散的决策制度运行良好，就是因为这些决策依赖于价格。农作物价格和建筑工资(劳动的价格)的调整，确保了有足够的人选择走出农村去当建筑工人。

　　价格使分散决策能够避免混乱，价格可以用来协调千百万有着不同能力与需求的人的具体行动，价格可以保证整个经济所需要做到的在实际生活中也最终得到实现。如果市场经济被"看不见的手"所引导，正如亚当·斯密所揭示的那样，价格系统就是"看不见的手"所持的指挥棒，可以用来指挥整个经济的运作。

　　最后，我们要谨记，供给和需求是非常普遍的经济现象。因此，供求模型是一种十分有用的分析工具，在以后的学习中，我们会经常用到这个模型。通过简单地了解市场是如何运作的，有助于我们更好地理解十大经济学原理之一：市场通常是组织经济活动的一种好方法。在任何一种经济制度中，为了确保效率，资源都要配置到更具竞争性的行业中。市场经济正是利用供给与需求的力量来实现这个目标的。

重要名词解释

1. **Market**：a group of buyers and sellers of a particular good or service
2. **Competitive market**：a market in which there are many buyers and many sellers so that each has a negligible impact on the market price
3. **Quantity demanded**：the amount of a good that buyers are willing and able to purchase
4. **Law of demand**：the claim that, other things equal, the quantity demanded of a good falls when the price of the good rises
5. **Normal good**：a good for which, other things equal, an increase in income leads to an increase in demand
6. **Inferior good**：a good for which, other things equal, an increase in income leads to a decrease in demand
7. **Substitutes**：two goods for which an increase in the price of one leads to an increase in the demand for the other
8. **Complements**：two goods for which an increase in the price of one leads to a decrease in the demand for the other
9. **Demand schedule**：a table that shows the relationship between the price of the good and the quantity demanded
10. **Demand curve**：a graph of the relationship between the price of a good and the quantity demanded
11. **Ceteris paribus**：a Latin phrase that means all variables other than the ones being studied are assumed to be constant
12. **Quantity supplied**：the amount of a good that sellers are willing and able to sell
13. **Law of supply**：the claim that, other things equal, the quantity supplied of a good rises when the price of the good rises
14. **Supply schedule**：a table that shows the relationship between the price of the good and the quantity supplied
15. **Supply curve**：a graph of the relationship between the price of a good and the quantity

supplied

16. **Equilibrium**：a situation in which supply and demand have been brought into balance

17. **Equilibrium price**：the price that balances supply and demand. On a graph, it is the price at which the supply and demand curves intersect.

18. **Equilibrium quantity**：the quantity supplied and the quantity demanded when the price has adjusted to balance supply and demand

19. **Surplus**：a situation in which quantity supplied is greater than quantity demanded

20. **Shortage**：a situation in which quantity demanded is greater than quantity supplied

21. **Law of supply and demand**：the claim that the price of any good adjusts to bring the supply and demand for that good into balance

主要图表

1.

Equilibrium of Supply and Demand

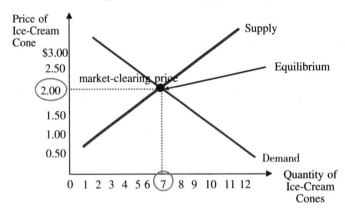

2.

A Change in Demand

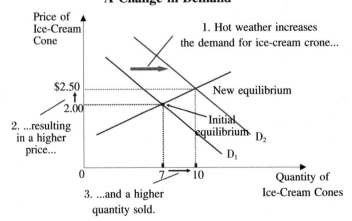

3.

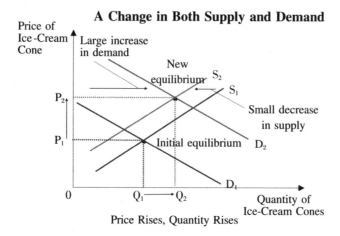

A Change in Both Supply and Demand

Price Rises, Quantity Rises

4.

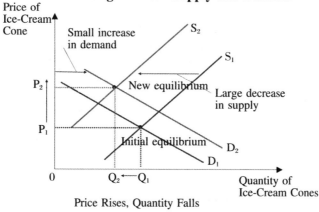

A Change in Both Supply and Demand

Price Rises, Quantity Falls

模拟试题

1. The short-run aggregate supply curve is likely to shift to the left when there is an increase in
   （A）The cost of productive resources.
   （B）Productivity.
   （C）The money supply.
   （D）The federal budget deficit.
   （E）Imports.
   Key：E
   Analysis：It examines the understanding of the supply curve and imports. Imports refer to the goods produced abroad and sold domestically, so imports reduce the quantity supplied, which makes the supply curve shift to the left.

2. Assume that for consumers, pears and apples are substitutes. It is announced that pesticides used on most apples may be dangerous to consumers' health. As a result of this

announcement, which of the following market changes is most likely to occur in the short run in the pear market?

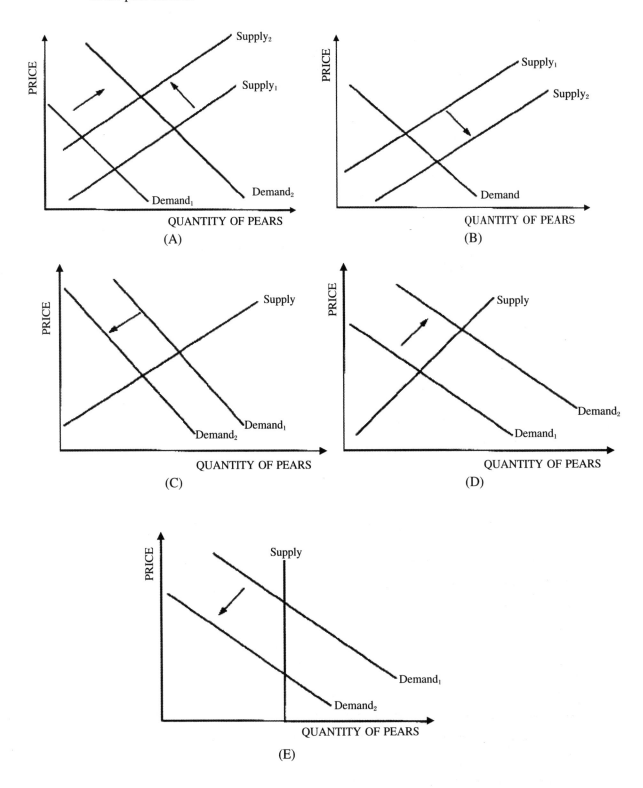

Key: D

Analysis: Pears and apples are substitutes. Now people may not choose apples or choose fewer. So people choose more pears. This will cause the demand curve of the pears shift to the right. But its supply curve remain unchanged.

3. Assume that popcorn and movie attendance are complements and that Salty Concession grows corn suitable for popping. Mr. Concession will most likely sell a greater quantity of popping corn at a higher price if which of the following occurs?

   (A) The wages of farm workers and movie theater employees increase.

   (B) A technological improvement results in less expensive and more efficient harvesting of corn.

   (C) The introduction of new fat-free potato chips provides new competition in the snack-food market.

   (D) The release of three summer movies sets records for movie attendance.

   (E) New government regulations force movie theaters to hire more security guards at each theater.

Key: D

Analysis: Complements refer to two goods for which an increase in the price of one leads to a decrease in the demand for the other. High attendance means people will consume more popcorn. Demand for popcorn will increase. So the supplier can sell more at a high price.

4. In a perfectly competitive market, which of the following shifts in the supply and demand curves will definitely cause both the equilibrium price and quantity to decrease?

	Supply Curve	Demand Curve
(A)	Shifts to the left	Shifts to the left
(B)	Shifts to the left	No shift
(C)	Shifts to the right	Shifts to the right
(D)	No shift	Shifts to the right
(E)	No shift	Shifts to the left

Key: E

Analysis: It examines the equilibrium of supply and demand. Just recall and draw a graph.

5. If bologna is an inferior good, which of the following must be true?

   (A) The demand curve for bologna is vertical.

   (B) The demand curve for bologna is horizontal.

   (C) An increase in the price of bologna will decrease the supply of bologna.

   (D) An increase in consumer income will decrease the demand for bologna.

   (E) A decrease in consumer income will decrease the supply of bologna.

Key: D

Analysis: Inferior good is a good for which, other things equal, an increase in income leads to a decrease in demand.

6. Which of the following events will cause the demand curve for hamburgers to shift to the right?

   (A) An increase in the price of pizza, a substitute for hamburgers.

   (B) An increase in the price of French fries, a complement to hamburgers.

   (C) An increase in the price of hamburgers.

   (D) A decrease in the price of hamburgers.

   (E) A decrease in the cost of producing hamburgers.

   Key: A

   Analysis: B will cause the demand curve to shift to the left. C and D will cause a movement along the demand curve. E will influence the supply curve.

7. Which of the following best describes a perfectly competitive market?

   (A) Many small firms is producing differentiated products and facing significant barriers to entry.

   (B) Many small firms producing a homogeneous product and facing significant barriers to entry.

   (C) Many small firms producing a homogeneous product and facing no significant barrier to entry.

   (D) A single large firm producing a unique product and facing significant barriers to entry.

   (E) A few large firms producing a differentiated product and facing no significant barriers to entry.

   Key: C

   Analysis: This question examines the understanding of perfectly competitive market. In such a market, products are the same, there are numerous buyers and sellers so that each has no influence on price, and buyers and sellers are price takers.

8. Assume that a competitive industry producing a normal good is in long-run equilibrium. If average consumer income decreases, which of the following changes will occur?

	Short-Run Price	Short-Run Industry Output	Movement of Firms
(A)	Increase	Increase	Enter
(B)	Increase	Decrease	Exit
(C)	Decrease	Increase	Exit
(D)	Decrease	Decrease	Enter
(E)	Decrease	Decrease	Exit

   Key: E

   Analysis: This will cause the demand curve to shift to the left. And the supply curve keeps fixed. So at the new equilibrium, the price and the output both will decrease. Due to no excess profit, no firms will enter.

9. If a normal good is produced in a competitive market, which of the following combinations of events could cause the price of the good to increase and the quantity to decrease?

   (A) An increase in the average income of consumers and an increase in the number of producing firms.

(B) An increase in the average income of consumers and an increase in the price of a variable input.

(C) An increase in the price of a substitute good and an increase in the number of producing firms.

(D) A decrease in the number of consumers and a decrease in the price of a variable input.

(E) A decrease in the average income of consumers and an increase in the number of producing firms.

Key: B

Analysis: Try to eliminate the wrong choices one by one.

10. If the price for a product produced in a competitive market increases, which of the following is most likely to occur in the labor market for workers who produce that product?

(A) The demand for labor and the number of workers hired both increase.

(B) The supply of labor and the number of workers hired both increase.

(C) The demand for labor and the number of workers hired both decrease.

(D) The supply of labor and the number of workers hired both decrease.

(E) There is a movement along the demand curve for labor, and firms hire more workers.

Key: A

Analysis: For price increasing, the firm must want to produce more, so the demand for labor and the number of workers hired both increase. There is a shift in the demand curve for labor.

11. Which of the following situation best illustrates the law of demand?

(A) As the incomes of United States citizens have decreased over the past year, the demand for housing has also decreased.

(B) Recent decreases in the price of imported wine have led to an increase in the consumption of domestic wine.

(C) In the past several months, as the price of compact disc players has decreased, the quantity of compact disc players sold has increased.

(D) The increase in the price of quality health foods has increased the revenues of firms producing these goods.

(E) As the demand for computers has increased, the number of workers in the computer industry has increased.

Key: C

Analysis: The law of demand is the claim that, other things equal, the quantity demanded of a good falls when the price of the good rises.

12. The graph below shows the supply and demand curves for gasoline. Which of the following will occur if the government establishes a price ceiling of $1.20 per gallon?

(A) A shortage of 900 million gallons.

(B) A shortage of 200 million gallons.

(C) A shortage of 100 million gallons.

(D) A surplus of 100 million gallons.

(E) Neither a surplus nor a shortage.

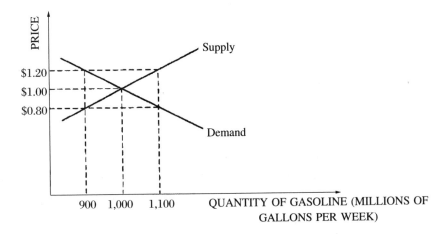

Key: E

Analysis: The price ceiling of $1.2 per million gallons is not binding.

13. Which of the following will decrease the demand for beef?

(A) An increase in the price of pork, if pork and beef are substitute goods.

(B) An increase in the price of potatoes, if potatoes and beef are complementary goods.

(C) A decrease in the cost of transporting beef to consumers.

(D) An increase in the income levels of most consumers, if beef is a normal good.

(E) Research showing beef is better for your health than chicken.

Key: B

Analysis: A, D and E will cause an increase. C deals with the supply curve.

14. Suppose that a large number of unskilled workers enter a nation's labor market. If the labor market is competitive, the number of unskilled workers hired and the wage rate will most likely change in which of the following ways?

Number of Unskilled Workers Hired	Wage Rate
(A) Increase	Increase
(B) Increase	Decrease
(C) Increase	Not change
(D) Decrease	Increase
(E) Decrease	Decrease

Key: B

Analysis: It examines the equilibrium of supply and demand. Just recall and draw a graph. There will be a shift in the supply of unskilled workers.

15. Mr. Carpenter devotes his working time to producing tables and chairs. An increase in the demand for chairs will result in

(A) An increase in the amount of time he devotes to producing tables.

(B) An increase in his opportunity cost of producing tables.

(C) A decrease in the price of tables.

(D) A decrease in the price of chairs.

(E) A decrease in his total revenue.

Key: B

Analysis: It examines the law of demand and the opportunity cost.

16. Assume that consumers consider potatoes to be an inferior good, but consider rice to be a normal good. An increase in consumers' incomes will most likely affect the equilibrium price and quantity of potatoes and rice in which of the following ways?

	Potato		Rice	
	Price	Quantity	Price	Quantity
(A)	Decrease	Decrease	Increase	Increase
(B)	Decrease	Increase	Increase	Decrease
(C)	Decrease	Decrease	Decrease	Decrease
(D)	Increase	Increase	Decrease	Decrease
(E)	Increase	Decrease	Increase	Decrease

Key: A

Analysis: According to the definition of the inferior good and the normal good, the consumers will buy less potatoes and more rice. Then use the law of demand to analyze.

17. Assume that a consumer spends all her income on the purchase of two goods. If the consumer's income doubles and the prices of the two goods also double, the quantity of the two goods purchased will

(A) Also double.

(B) More than double.

(C) Increase, but it will be less than double.

(D) Not change.

(E) Depend on the slope of the demand curve.

Key: D

Analysis: P×Q=Income

18. Which of the following tends to increase the gap in earnings between skilled and unskilled workers over time?

(A) An increase in the demand for unskilled workers relative to skilled workers.

(B) An increase in the supply of skilled workers relative to unskilled workers.

(C) A decrease in the demand for unskilled workers relative to skilled workers.

(D) A decrease in both the demand for and the supply of skilled workers.

(E) An increase in both the demand for and the supply of unskilled workers.

Key: C

Analysis: It examines the law of demand. C can decrease the demand for unskilled workers and increase the demand for skilled workers.

19. Which of the following would cause the equilibrium price of good X to increase?

   (A) Producers of good X and a new technology that reduces the cost of producing X.

   (B) The price of an essential input in the production of good X increases.

   (C) Goods X and Y are complements, and the government imposes a tax on good Y.

   (D) Good X is a normal good, and the government increases income taxes by 3%.

   (E) Good X is an inferior good, and the government decreases income taxes by 10%.

   Key: B

   Analysis: For A, the supply curve shifts to right, so the price shall decrease. For C, it decreases the demand, the demand curve shifts to left, so the price will be lower. For E, it will increase the consumers' income, so they reduce their demand for X.

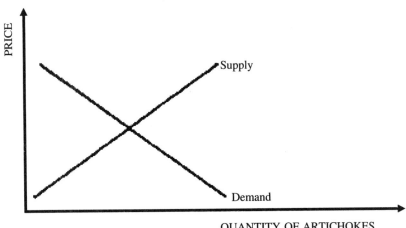

QUANTITY OF ARTICHOKES

20. The graph above shows the supply and demand curve for artichokes. The surgeon general announces that eating an artichoke a day dramatically reduces one's likelihood of developing cancer. Simultaneously an infestation of the artichoke weevil severely damages the crop. Which of the following will definitely occur as a result?

   (A) The supply of artichokes will increase.

   (B) The price of artichokes will increase.

   (C) The demand for artichokes will decrease.

   (D) The quantity of artichokes grown will decrease.

   (E) The profits of farmers who specialize in growing artichokes will decrease.

   Key: B

   Analysis: This examines the understanding of the equilibrium of supply and demand. The demand curve shifts to right. The supply curve shifts to left. So the price will increase while the equilibrium of quantity is uncertain.

21. If the demand for good Y increases as the price of good X decreases, it can be concluded that

   (A) X and Y are substitute goods.

   (B) X and Y are complementary goods.

   (C) X is an inferior good and Y is a superior good.

   (D) X is a superior good and Y is an inferior good.

（E）Both X and Y are inferior goods

Key： B

Analysis： The complements are two goods for which an increase in the price of one leads to a decrease in the demand for the other.

22. If a perfectly competitive firm increases its price above the market equilibrium price, which of the following will be true for this firm?

（A）Its total revenue will increase.

（B）Its profit will increase.

（C）Its sales will decrease but profit will not be affected.

（D）Its demand curve will become downward sloping.

（E）It will not be able to sell any output.

Key： E

Analysis： Quantity supplied is greater than quantity demanded, which leads to surplus.

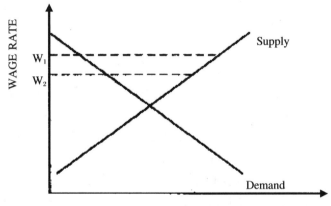

NUMBER OF TEENAGE WORKERS

23. The graph above illustrates the labor market for teenage workers. The current minimum wage for all workers is W_1. If the Congress introduces a subminimum wages W_2 that applies only to teenagers, what is the most likely effect on teenage employment?

（A）Teenage employment will increase because firms will want to hire more teenagers at W_2 than at W_1.

（B）Teenage employment will increase because more teenagers will want to work at W_2 than at W_1.

（C）Teenage employment will decrease because fewer teenagers will want to work at W_2 than at W_1.

（D）Teenage employment will decrease because firms will want to hire fewer teenagers at W_2 than at W_1.

（E）Teenage employment will not change because the market-clearing wage is lower than W_1 and W_2.

Key： A

Analysis： Demand will increase and the supply will decrease. The gap of unemployment will reduce.

Chapter 6 Elasticity and Its Application
弹性及其应用

主要内容和概念讲解

如果明天全国的超市都将大米价格或者面粉价格下调 5%, 这些商品的需求量将不会有很大变化。但是如果粮油或者牛奶价格下调相同的幅度, 需求量相对而言就会大幅增加。为什么有时价格变动的影响比较小, 有时影响比较大呢? 从前一章所学的供求分析图中, 我们可以得知这主要是因为供给与需求曲线的形状, 陡峭(steeper)的反应大, 平滑(flatter)的反应小。那么如何衡量曲线的形状呢? 由数学常识可以猜测这与斜率(slope)有很大关系。实际上, 我们应用弹性(elasticity)来进行分析发现, 它与斜率的确关系密切。

首先, 我们给出弹性的定义。弹性广义上是指一个变量对另一个变量变动的反应程度(a measure of the responsiveness of an variable to the other variable)。在这里, 我们考虑供给与需求框架下的弹性。它指的是需求量或供给量对其决定因素中某一种的反应程度的度量(a measure of the responsiveness of quantity demanded or quantity supplied to one of its determinants)。我们之前的分析大多是定性的(qualitative), 现在我们可以应用弹性进行更加精确的定量分析(quantitative analysis)。在需求方面, 有需求价格弹性、需求收入弹性、需求交叉价格弹性 (price elasticity of demand, income elasticity of demand, cross-price elasticity of demand)。在供给方面, 主要就是供给价格弹性。在下面的学习中, 我们主要就这几类弹性进行介绍。

首先来看需求价格弹性。需求定律(the law of demand)表明, 一种商品价格的下降会使需求量增加。需求价格弹性就是衡量需求量对价格变动的反应敏感程度(a measure of how much the quantity demanded of a good responds to a change in the price of that good), 用需求量变动的百分比除以价格变动的百分比来计算(computed as the percentage change in quantity demanded divided by the percentage change in price)。

如果一种商品的需求量对价格变动的反应大(substantially), 那么可以说这种商品的需求是富有弹性的(elastic)。如果一种商品的需求量对价格变动的反应小(slightly), 则可以说这种商品的需求是缺乏弹性的(inelastic)。这是一种定性的划分, 在下面我们介绍弹性的具体计算时, 我们会给出定量的标准。

那么是什么因素决定了一种商品的需求是富有弹性的还是缺乏弹性的呢(determinants of price elasticity of demand)? 其实, 任何一种商品的需求都取决于消费者的偏好(preference), 所以需求的价格弹性取决于许多种构成个人欲望的经济、社会和心理因素。根据经验, 我们可以给出一些决定需求价格弹性的因素。

首先, 必需品(necessity)和奢侈品(luxury)之间的弹性差异很大。必需品倾向于需求缺乏弹性, 而奢侈品倾向于需求富有弹性。当衣服的价格上升时, 尽管人们可能会适当减少购买次数和购买数量，但不会大幅度减少需求量。与此相比，当豪华游艇的价格上升时，游艇需求量会大幅度减少。原因就在于大多数人把衣服看作必需品，而把游艇看作奢侈品。当然，一种商品是必需品还是奢侈品并不取决于商品本身固有的性质，而取决于买者的偏好。对于一个热衷于航行而不太关注自己穿着的节俭富翁来说，游艇可能是需求缺乏弹性的必需品，而衣服则是需求富有弹性的奢侈品。

其次，相近替代品的可获得性（availability of close substitutes）也会影响商品的需求弹性。例如，大豆油和花生油就很容易相互替代。如果消费者从这种商品转向其他商品较为容易，那么这种商品的需求弹性就大。假设大豆油的价格不变，花生油价格略有上升，就会引起花生油的销量大幅度减少。而由于鸡蛋是一种没有相近替代品的食物，鸡蛋的需求弹性肯定小于花生油。

再次，市场的定义（definition of the market）。这一点似乎不是很直观。但通过举例说明大家就很容易理解。比如食物是一个很广泛的范畴，它的需求相当缺乏弹性是因为没有替代品。但是，苹果就是一个很狭义的范畴，它的需求就较富有弹性，因为人们容易用其他水果来代替苹果。红富士苹果就是一个更狭义的范畴，它的需求就更富有弹性，人们完全可以转而购买国光等其他类苹果。

最后一个影响因素是时间范围（time horizon）。因为当时间比较长时，寻找替代品和进行其他调整总是比较容易。因而，需求弹性在可以进行所有调整的长期，一般大于某些调整不能进行的短期。以汽油为例，当汽油价格较大幅上升时，在最初的几个月中汽油的需求量只会略有减少，人们一时还没法调整。但是，随着时间推移，人们会购买更省油的汽车，改乘公共交通工具，或搬家到离工作近的地方。在一两年内，汽油的需求量会较大幅度减少。

总结一下，如果某一商品是奢侈品，相近的替代品数量越多，市场的定义越狭窄，时间段越长，则需求更富有弹性（Demand tends to be more elastic.）。

现在我们就来具体说明需求价格弹性是如何计算（compute）的。根据定义，它等于需求量变动的百分比除以价格变动的百分比（the percentage change in the quantity demanded divided by the percentage change in price）。来看一个简单的实例。假定冰激凌蛋卷的价格从 2 美元上升到 2.2 美元使得你购买的冰激凌蛋卷数量从每月 10 个减少为 8 个。我们计算出价格变动百分比：

价格变动百分比=（2.20−2.00）÷2.00×100%=10%

同样，我们计算出需求量变动百分比：

需求量变动百分比=（10−8）÷10×100%=20%

在这种情况下，你的需求价格弹性是：20%/10%=2，反映了需求量变动的比例是价格变动比例的两倍，需求量对价格的变动还是比较敏感的。

$$\frac{\dfrac{(10-8)}{10}\times100\%}{\dfrac{(2.20-2.00)}{2.00}\times100\%}=\frac{20\%}{10\%}=2$$

由于一种商品的需求量与其价格负相关，所以，数量变动的百分比与价格变动的百分比总是相反的符号。在这个例子中，价格上升，价格变动的百分比是正的 10%，而需求量减少，需求量变动的百分比是负的20%。因此，需求价格弹性实际上为负数，但一般做法是取绝对值，变负为正。需求价格弹性越大，意味着需求量对价格越敏感。

如果你想计算一条需求曲线上两点之间的需求价格弹性，你很快就会注意到计算结果有差异。从A点到B点的弹性似乎不同于从B点到A点的弹性。例如，考虑上例的数字：

A点：价格=2美元，数量=10

B点：价格=2.2美元，数量=8

从A点到B点，我们刚才计算出的需求价格弹性是2。从B点到A点：

价格变动百分比=(2.20-2.00)÷2.20×100%=9.1%

同样，我们计算出需求量变动百分比：

需求量变动百分比=(10-8)÷8×100%=25%

在这种情况下，你的需求价格弹性是：25%/9.1%=2.75，反映了需求量变动的比例是价格变动比例的2.75倍，需求量对价格的变动显得更加敏感。

同样的数字，计算的结果却不一样。为了避免这种方向性偏差，我们采用更好的中点法（midpoint formula）来计算弹性。不管变动的方向如何，它都能给出一个确切的结果。中点法不再采用变动量除以原先水平的标准方法来计算变动的百分比。例如，上例中，2美元和2.2美元的中点是2.1美元，根据中点法，无论是从2美元到2.2美元还是从2.2美元到2美元，上升和下降的比例都约是9.5%。同理，数量的中点是9，变动的比例是2/9×100%≈22%。最后的需求价格弹性为2.33。

Midpoint formula

$$\frac{\dfrac{(10-8)}{(10+8)}\times100\%}{2} \Bigg/ \frac{\dfrac{(2.20-2.00)}{(2.20+2.00)}\times100\%}{2}=2.33$$

在规定了弹性的具体计算方法后，经济学家根据需求曲线弹性的大小对需求曲线进行了分类。当弹性小于1，即需求量变动的比例小于价格变动的比例时，需求是缺乏弹性的（inelastic demand）。当弹性大于1，即需求量变动的比例大于价格变动的比例时，需求是富有弹性的（elastic demand）。下图中的需求就是富有弹性的。

Computing the Price Elasticity of Demand

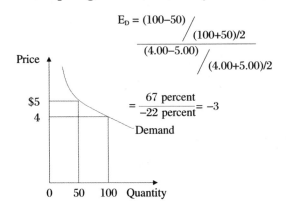

　　如果弹性正好是1，即需求量与价格同比例变动，需求就是单位弹性(unit elastic)。还有两种极端的情况：一种是无论价格如何变动，需求量总是不变。此时弹性数值为0，我们称之为完全无弹性（perfectly inelastic）；另一种是价格极小变动就会引起需求量极大变动，此时弹性趋近为无穷大，称之为完全有弹性(perfectly elastic)。

　　由于需求的价格弹性测量的是需求量对价格的反应程度，因此它与需求曲线的斜率紧密相关。通过给定点的需求曲线越平坦(flatter)则需求价格弹性越大，越陡峭(steeper)则需求价格弹性越小。其实，通过简单的数学推导，可以得知：

弹性=1/斜率×(P/Q)

显然弹性与斜率成反比关系。

　　下面我们把这五种需求价格弹性通过图形形象地展示出来。

Perfectly lnelastic Demand
— Elasticity equals 0

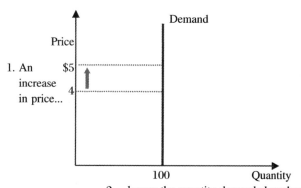

2. ...leaves the quantity demanded unchanged.

　　这是完全无弹性的需求价格弹性图。它垂直于横轴。如图所示，当价格由4美元升为5美元时，需求数量都是100，需求数量没有任何变化，弹性为0。

Inelastic Demand
— Elasticity is less than 1

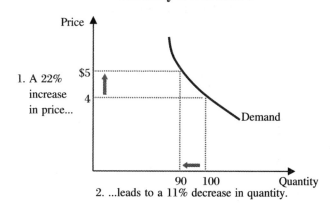

2. ...leads to a 11% decrease in quantity.

　　这是需求缺乏弹性图，如图所示，价格变化幅度大，而需求数量变化幅度较小，因此弹性小于1。

Unit Elastic Demand
— Elasticity equals 1

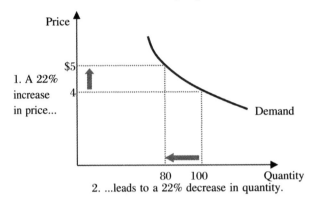

这是单位弹性图，价格变化和需求数量变化幅度一样，需求价格弹性为1。

Elastic Demand
— Elasticity is greater than 1

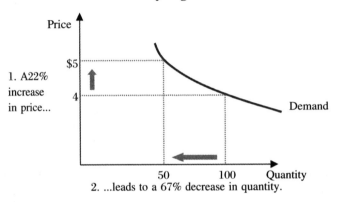

这是富有弹性图，如图所示，价格变化幅度小，而需求数量变化幅度较大，因此弹性大于1。

Perfectly Elastic Demand
— Elasticity equals infinity

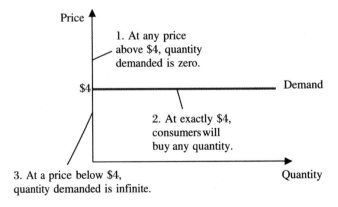

这是完全富有弹性图,价格只要高于 4 美元,需求数量就是 0。当价格低于 4 美元时,需求数量是无限大。当价格正好是 4 美元时,消费者将会买任意数量的商品。需求价格弹性趋于无穷大。

注意:以上弹性计算法,都是采用中点法计算的,考试和练习中也应该采用中点法计算。

当研究市场上供给或需求的变动时,我们经常想研究的一个变量是总收益(total revenue),即某种商品在交易中由买者支付、由卖者得到的货币总量,用该商品的价格乘以销售量来计算。在任何一个市场上,总收益都是 P×Q,即一种商品的价格乘以该商品的销售量。我们可以像下图那样用图形来表示总收益。需求曲线下面阴影方框的高是 P,宽是 Q。这个方框的 P×Q 就等于这个市场的总收益。在图中,P=4 美元,Q=100,总收益是 4 美元×100=400 美元。

Elasticity and Total Revenue

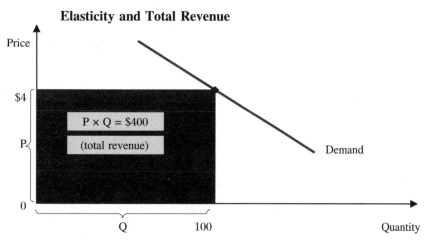

总收益如何沿着需求曲线的变动而变动呢? 答案取决于需求的价格弹性。价格和需求量成反比关系,此消彼长,所以总收益就取决于二者中哪个变动比较大。如果需求是缺乏弹性的,如下图所示,那么,价格上升引起总收益增加。在图中,价格从 1 美元上升到 3 美元使需求量从 100 减少到 80,因此,总收益从 100 美元增加到 240 美元。价格上升引起 P×Q 增加,是因为 Q 减少的比例小于 P 上升的比例。

Elasticity and Total Revenue: Inelastic Demand

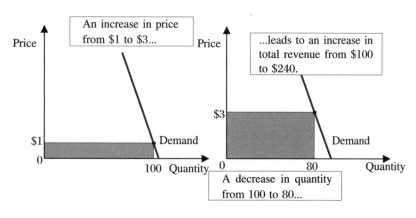

如果需求富有弹性，则得出相反的结果：价格上升引起总收益减少。例如，在下图中，当价格从 4 美元上升到 5 美元时，需求量从 50 减少为 20，因此，总收益从 200 美元减少为 100 美元。由于需求富有弹性，当需求量大幅减少时，价格上升所带来的总收益增量将不足以弥补需求量降低的损失。也就是说，价格上升而 P×Q 减少是因为 Q 减少的比例大于 P 上升的比例。

Elasticity and Total Revenue: Elastic Demand

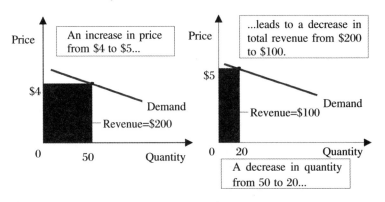

通过以上两个图例，我们可以得出一般规律：当需求价格弹性小于 1 时，即需求价格较无弹性时，价格上升使总收益增加，价格下降使总收益减少。当需求价格弹性大于 1 时，即需求价格富有弹性时，价格上升使总收益减少，价格下降使总收益增加。在需求弹性等于 1 的特殊情况下，价格的变动不影响总收益。利用此规律，商家就可以考虑是采用降价还是提价措施来提高收益，而关键就在于认清商品的需求价格弹性是否大于 1。

此时，我们就会想知道，在既定的需求曲线上，到底什么时候需求价格弹性大于 1，什么时候小于 1，什么时候等于 1？我们以简单的线性需求曲线为例来进行具体分析。请看以下图表（注：表中计算均采用中点法）：

Price	Quantity	Total Revenue （Price × Quantity）	Percent Change in Price	Percent Change in Quantity	Elasticity	Description
$0	14	$0	200%	15%	0.1	Inelastic
1	12	12	67%	18%	0.3	Inelastic
2	10	20	40%	22%	0.6	Inelastic
3	8	24	29%	29%	1	Unit elastic
4	6	24	22%	40%	1.8	Elastic
5	4	20	18%	67%	3.7	Elastic
6	2	12	15%	200%	13	Elastic
7	0	0				

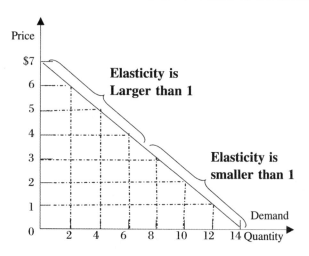

　　我们会发现，在需求曲线中点，需求价格弹性为 1。在需求曲线中点以上，价格弹性大于 1，在需求曲线中点以下，价格弹性小于 1。之前，我们得知弹性=1/斜率×(P/Q)，由于线性需求曲线的斜率是固定的，因此，曲线上各个点的弹性主要取决于 P 和 Q 的比值。随着价格的递增，即线性需求曲线向左上方移动，P/Q 逐渐增加，因此弹性增加，直至趋于无穷大。反之，随着需求的递增，线性需求曲线向右下方移动，P/Q 逐渐减小，因此弹性递减，直至趋于 0。而在中点，斜率恰好等于中点的(P/Q)值，所以弹性等于 1。

　　决定需求的因素除了价格外，还有收入、相关商品价格等因素。因此，经济学家还要考虑需求收入弹性(income elasticity of demand)和需求交叉价格弹性(cross-price elasticity)。

　　首先来看需求收入弹性。经济学家用需求收入弹性来衡量消费者收入变动时需求量如何变动(measures how much the quantity demanded of a good responds to a change in consumers' income)。它是衡量一种商品需求量对消费者收入变动的反应程度，用需求量变动百分比除以收入变动百分比来计算(computed as the percentage change in the quantity demanded divided by the percentage change in income)，即：

　　需求收入弹性=需求量变动百分比/收入变动百分比

　　正如我们在第五章中所讨论的，大多数商品是正常品(normal goods)，收入提高会增加需求量。由于需求量与收入同方向变动，因此正常品的收入弹性为正数。少数商品是低档品(inferior goods)，收入提高会减少需求量，例如搭乘公共汽车或去小餐馆就餐。由于需求量与收入反方向变动，所以低档品的收入弹性为负数。

　　即使在正常品中，收入弹性的大小差别也很大。像食物、汽油、衣服、公共设施和医疗服务这类必需品(necessity)往往收入弹性小，因为消费者无论收入多低也要选择购买一些此类商品。而像越野车和皮衣这类的奢侈品(luxury)往往收入弹性大，因为消费者明白，如果他们收入极低，他们可以根本不购买这类商品。经济学里，一般认为收入弹性小于 1 的为必需品，大于 1 的为奢侈品。

　　再来看需求交叉价格弹性。它衡量的是一种商品的需求量对另一种商品价格变动的反应程度(a measure of how much the quantity demanded of one good responds to a change in the price of another good)，是用第一种商品的需求量变动百分比除以第二种商品的价格变动百分比(computed as the percentage change in quantity demanded of the first good divided by the percentage change in the price of the second good)，即：

需求交叉价格弹性=商品1需求量变动百分比/商品2价格变动百分比

联想前一章我们所介绍的替代品(substitutes)和互补品(complements)，你就会发现，替代品的需求交叉价格弹性是大于零的，为正值，而互补品则是小于零的，为负值。具体数值的大小反映了两种商品之间的替代性或互补性的强弱。

到现在为止，我们已经将需求的相关弹性都做了简单的介绍。接下来我们来介绍供给弹性。你会发现，理解了各种需求弹性之后，再来学习供给弹性就会驾轻就熟。

供给定律表明，当其他因素不变时，一种商品价格上升，卖者会增加供给量。除了价格，决定供给量的还有其他一些因素。比如，当投入品价格下降，或者技术取得进步时，该商品的卖者就会增加供给量。同需求中的弹性分析一样，为了从定性表述转向定量表述，我们又要用到弹性的概念。

供给价格弹性衡量的是供给量对价格变动的反应程度，是用供给量变动百分比除以价格变动百分比来计算。如果供给量对价格变动的反应很大，就可以说这种商品的供给是富有弹性的(elastic)。如果供给量对价格变动的反应很小，就可以说这种商品的供给是缺乏弹性的(inelastic)。

那么决定供给价格弹性的因素有哪些呢？一是伸缩性(flexibility)，二是时间长短(time period)。伸缩性是指卖者改变它们生产的商品产量的灵活性和适应性。例如，海滩土地供给缺乏弹性是因为几乎不可能生产出这种土地。与此相比，诸如书、汽车和电视这类制成品的供给富有弹性，是因为生产这些商品的企业可以对价格上升做出反应而让工厂更长时间地运行。在这里，价格的激励作用非常明显。

在大多数市场上，供给价格弹性最关键的决定因素是时间的长短。供给在长期中的弹性通常都大于短期。在短期中，企业不能轻易地改变工厂的规模来增加或减少一种商品的生产。因此，在短期中供给量对价格不太敏感。与此相比，在长期中，企业可以建立新工厂或关闭旧工厂。此外，新企业也可以进入一个市场，旧企业也可以退出。因此，在长期中供给量可以对价格做出相当大的反应，供给价格弹性也会变大。

下面我们举例说明供给价格弹性是如何计算的。假设每加仑牛奶的价格从2.85美元上升到3.15美元，牧场主每月生产的牛奶量从9000加仑增加到1.1万加仑。我们计算出价格变动百分比如下：

价格变动百分比=(3.15-2.85)/3.00×100%=10%

同样，我们计算出供给量变动百分比如下：

供给量变动百分比=(11000-9000)/10000×100%=20%

在这种情况下，供给价格弹性是：20%/10%=2

可见，牛奶的供给是富有弹性的。

由于供给价格弹性衡量的是供给量对价格的反应程度，所以它直接反映在供给曲线的形状上。同需求价格弹性的划分一样，我们可以把供给价格弹性划分为五种。对于供给富有弹性的商品来说，具体有三种：一种是完全有弹性的供给(perfectly elastic)，弹性等于无穷大；一种是相对富有弹性的供给(relatively elastic)，弹性大于1；一种是单位弹性(unit elastic)，弹性等于1。对于供给缺乏弹性的商品来说，具体有两种：一种是相对缺乏弹性(relatively inelastic)，弹性小于1；一种是供给完全无弹性(perfectly inelastic)，弹性为0。具体请看下面的图形。

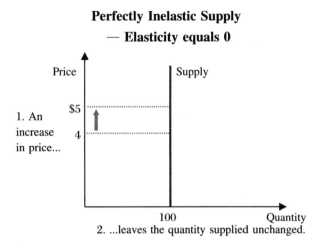

Perfectly Inelastic Supply
— **Elasticity equals 0**

Price

Supply

$5

1. An increase in price...

4

100   Quantity

2. ...leaves the quantity supplied unchanged.

这是完全无弹性的供给曲线图,供给曲线垂直于横轴。当价格上涨时,供给量并不会发生改变,供给价格弹性为 0。

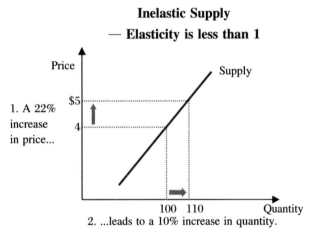

Inelastic Supply
— **Elasticity is less than 1**

Price

Supply

$5

1. A 22% increase in price...

4

100   110   Quantity

2. ...leads to a 10% increase in quantity.

这是缺乏弹性的供给曲线图,显得比较陡峭。供给增加的幅度小于价格上涨的幅度,供给价格弹性小于 1。

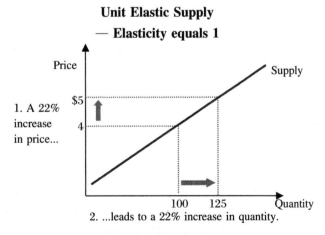

Unit Elastic Supply
— **Elasticity equals 1**

Price

Supply

$5

1. A 22% increase in price...

4

100   125   Quantity

2. ...leads to a 22% increase in quantity.

这是单位弹性的供给曲线图。供给增加的幅度与价格上涨的幅度相等,供给价格弹性等于 1。

Elastic Supply
— Elasticity is greater than 1

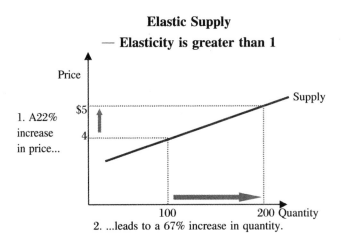

这是富有弹性的供给曲线图，曲线显得比较平缓。供给增加的幅度大于价格上涨的幅度，供给价格弹性大于1。就实际情况而言，这种商品涨价后利润空间也比较大。

Perfectly Elastic Supply
— Elasticity equals infinity

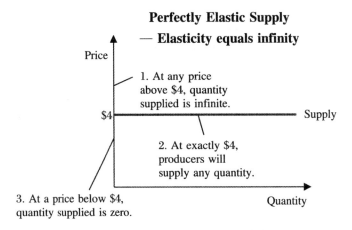

这是完全有弹性的供给曲线图，曲线是平行于横轴的，从中可以看出价格极小的变动就会引起供给量很大的变动。如图所示，当价格大于4美元时，供给量是无限的。当价格低于4美元时，供给量为0。当价格等于4美元时，生产商愿意生产任何数量的商品。在完全竞争市场中，众多卖家所面临的情况差不多都是这样的，4美元就是它们的成本底线，稍有涨价，大家就会觉得有利润可赚，就都会增加生产。

由以上分析可知，随着弹性增加，供给曲线越来越平坦，这表明供给量对价格变动的反应越来越大。

下图反映出一个典型（typical）行业的情形，在这个行业中企业的生产能力是有限的。在供给量水平低时，供给弹性高，这表明企业对价格变动能做出相当大的反应。价格少量增加，企业也会扩大生产。在这一范围内，企业存在未被利用的生产能力，例如全天或部分时间处于闲置状态的厂房和设备。价格少量增加使得企业利用这种闲置的生产能力是有利可图的。

随着供给量增加，企业开始达到其生产能力的极限。一旦生产能力完全得到利用，再增加生产就需要建立新工厂。要使企业能承受这种额外支出，价格就必须大幅度上升，因此，供给变得缺乏弹性。沿着曲线向右移动，供给弹性逐渐走低，直至趋于0。在短时间内，即使价格再高，企业一时也难以生产。

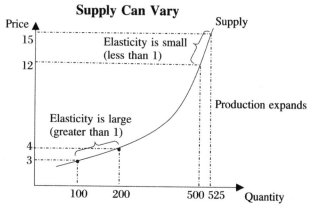

How the Price Elasticity of Supply Can Vary

在介绍完需求和供给弹性之后，我们要综合运用供给、需求和弹性（supply, demand, and elasticity）这三个因素来考虑实际问题。

我们来考虑三个典型的实际问题。农业技术进步的好消息是农民的坏消息吗？为什么OPEC即石油输出国组织不能保持石油的高价格呢？禁毒（drug interdiction）是增加还是减少了与毒品相关的犯罪呢？乍一看，这些问题似乎没有什么共同之处。但这三个问题都与市场相关，而且，所有市场都要服从于供给与需求的支配。在这里我们将用供给、需求和弹性这些工具来回答这些看似复杂的问题。

为此我们需用到在上一章中学到的三个步骤。第一，我们确定该事件是使供给曲线还是需求曲线移动。第二，我们考虑曲线向哪个方向移动。第三，我们用供求图说明市场均衡如何变动。下面，我们就用这个方法来分析这三个案例。

现在来看第一个案例。假如研究所里的农业科学家培育出比现有品种更高产的小麦新杂交品种时，种小麦的农民会发生什么变化，小麦市场又会发生什么变动呢？

显然新杂交品种的培育会影响供给曲线。由于杂交品种提高了每英亩土地上所能生产的小麦量，所以，现在农民愿意在任何一种既定的价格水平时供给更多小麦。换句话说，供给曲线向右移动。需求曲线仍然不变，因为消费者在任何一个既定价格水平时购买小麦商品的愿望并不受新杂交品种引进的影响。以下图为例，当供给曲线从 S_1 移动到 S_2 时，小麦销售量从 100 增加到 110，而小麦的价格从 3 美元下降为 2 美元。

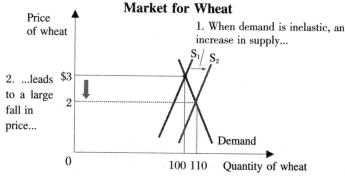

An Increase in Supply in the Market for Wheat

1. When demand is inelastic, an increase in supply...

2. ...leads to a large fall in price...

3. ...and a proportionately smaller increase in quantity sold. As a result, revenue falls from $300 to $220.

但是，新品种的培育使农民的状况变好了吗？要简单明了地回答这个问题，就要考虑农民得到的总收益发生的变动。农民的总收益是 P×Q，即小麦价格乘以销售量。新品种的培育以两种相矛盾的方式影响农民。杂交品种使农民生产了更多小麦（Q 增加），但现在每吨小麦售价下降了（P 下降）。

当农业技术进步使小麦供给从 S₁ 移到到 S₂ 时，小麦价格下降。由于小麦需求缺乏弹性（此处运用中点法计算弹性是 0.24，远小于 1），销售量从 100 增加到 110 的比例小于价格从 3 美元下降为 2 美元的比例。结果农民的总收益从 300 美元（3 美元×100）减少为 220 美元（2 美元×110）。

总收益增加还是减少取决于需求弹性。在现实生活中，像小麦这种基本食品的需求一般是缺乏弹性的，因为这些东西较为便宜，而且，很少有好的替代品。当需求曲线缺乏弹性，如上图所示时，价格下降引起总收益减少。在这个图中你可以看到：小麦价格大幅度下降，而小麦销售量增加很少，总收益从 300 美元减少为 220 美元。因此，新杂交品种的培育减少了农民从销售农作物中所得到的总收益。

如果这种新杂交品种的培育使农民的状况变坏了，那么他们为什么还要采用这种新品种呢？要回答这个问题我们首先要理解竞争市场是如何运行的。由于每个农民都是小麦市场上微不足道的分子，因此对他们而言，小麦价格是既定的。对任何一个既定的价格来说，使用新品种以便生产并销售更多小麦会更好一些。但当所有农民都这样做时，小麦的供给增加了，价格下降了，因而，农民的状况变坏了。

尽管这个例子乍看起来只是假设，但实际上它有助于解释过去一个世纪以来世界经济的巨大变化。一百多年前，世界上大部分人口居住在农村。受制于科学技术的落后，农业生产方法的传播方式是相当原始的，以至于大多数人不得不当农民，以生产足够的食物。但随着时间的推移，农业技术进步增加了每个农民所能生产的食物量。这种食物供给增加与食物需求缺乏弹性相结合就引起农民收益减少，鼓励人们离开农业。这些都可以从统计数据中反映出来。农村人口的减少与农业生产率的巨大进步是一致的，农业产量非但没有因为从业人员的大幅减少而减少，反而大幅地增加，供给量极大丰富。

这种对农商品市场的分析也有助于解释那些看似自相矛盾的公共政策：某些农业计划努力帮助农民减少某些作物的生产。为什么用这些计划来减少某些作物的生产呢？它们的目的主要是为了减少农商品的供给，从而提高价格。由于需求缺乏弹性，如果农民向市场供给的作物减少了，他们作为一个整体便会得到更多的总收益。没有一个农民愿意从自己的立场出发选择毁坏农作物，因为每个农民都把市场价格看作既定价格。但是，如果所有的农民都一起来这样做，他们每个人的状况就会变得好些。

当我们分析农业技术或农业政策的影响时，需要注意，对农民有利的不一定对整个社会也有利。这里面存在着复杂的关系。农业技术进步可能对农民是坏事，但对能以低价买到食物的消费者而言肯定是好事。同样，旨在减少农商品供给的政策可以增加农民的收入，但这样做的代价却是提高了食物对于消费者的成本。

下面来看第二个关于石油的案例。石油是当今世界最重要的商品，有着"黑金"之称。石油市场关乎全球经济的发展。由于石油的自然属性特殊，世界石油市场有着一定的天然垄断性。OPEC（石油输出国组织）就是典型的石油垄断机构。在 70 年代，OPEC（石油输出国组织）的成员决定提高世界石油价格，以增加它们的收入。这些国家通过同时减少它们提供的石油产量而实现了这个目标。从 1973 年到 1974 年，石油价格（根据总体通货膨胀进行了调整)上升了50%以上。然而,几年之后OPEC又一次故伎重演。1979年石油价格上升了14%,随后1980年上升了34%,1981年上升了34%;但OPEC发现要维持高价格是很困难的。从1982年到1985年,石油价格每年下降10%左右。不满与混乱很快蔓延到OPEC各国。1986年OPEC成员国之间的合作完全破裂了,石油价格猛跌了45%。1990年石油价格(根据总体通货膨胀进行了调整)又回到1970年开始时的水平,而且在上世纪90年代的大部分年份中一直保持在这种低水平上。

在分析这个案例时,我们需要注意短期和长期市场的区别。供给与需求在短期与长期中的状况是不同的。

在短期中,石油的供给和需求都是较为缺乏弹性的。供给缺乏弹性是因为已知的石油储藏量和石油开采能力不能迅速改变。需求缺乏弹性是因为购买习惯不会立即对价格变动做出反应。例如,许多老式耗油车的驾驶员只能支付高价格的油钱。因此,正如下图所示,短期供给和需求曲线都是陡峭的。当石油供给从 S_1 移动到 S_2 时,价格从 P_1 到 P_2 的上升幅度是大的。

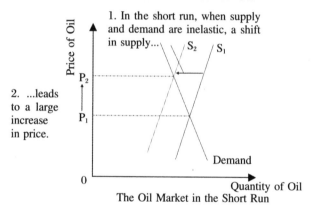

A Reduction in Supply in the World Market for Oil

The Oil Market in the Short Run

长期的情况则大不相同。在长期中,欧佩克以外的石油生产者对高价格的反应是增加石油勘探并提高开采能力。消费者的反应是更加节俭,例如用新型节油车代替老式耗油汽车。因此,正如下图所示,长期供给和需求曲线都更加富有弹性。在长期中,由供给曲线的移动而引起的价格变动比短期小得多。

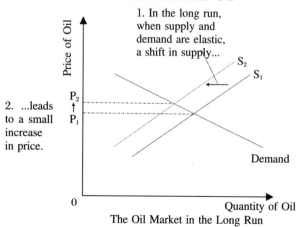

A Reduction in Supply in the World Market for Oil

The Oil Market in the Long Run

这种分析表明,为什么 OPEC 只在短期内成功地保持了石油的高价格。当 OPEC 各国一致同意减少它们的石油生产时,供给曲线向左移动。尽管每个 OPEC 成员国销售的石油少了,但短期内价格上升幅度很大,因此 OPEC 的总体收入增加了。与此相比,在长期内,当供给和需求较为富有弹性时,用供给曲线水平移动来体现的供给减少只引起价格的小幅度上升。因此,这证明了 OPEC 共同减少供给在长期中无利可图。

现在 OPEC 仍然存在。你也会偶尔听到有关 OPEC 国家官员召开会议的新闻。但是,OPEC 国家之间的合作现在越来越少,部分原因就是该组织过去在保持高油价上的失败。当然 OPEC 组织还是一个寡头垄断组织(oligopoly),这在后面章节还会讲到,由于其组织形式的特殊性各国之间是既合作又竞争的关系。

最后,我们来看禁毒的案例。我们的社会面临的一个长期问题是非法毒品的使用,比如海洛因、可卡因和大麻等。这些非法毒品的使用有很多不利影响。一是毒品依赖会毁掉吸毒者及其家庭的生活。二是吸毒上瘾的人往往会实施抢劫或其他暴力犯罪,以得到吸毒所需要的钱。为了限制非法毒品的使用,各国政府每年都投入大量人力物力来减少毒品的流入。现在我们用供给和需求工具来分析这些禁毒政策。

假设政府增加打击毒品走私的工作人员的数量。非法毒品市场会发生什么变动呢?与通常的做法一样,我们分三个步骤回答这个问题。第一,是供给曲线移动还是需求曲线移动。第二,移动的方向。第三,这种移动如何影响均衡价格和数量。

虽然禁毒的目的是减少毒品的使用,但它的直接影响对象是毒品的卖者而不是买者。当政府禁止某些毒品进入国内并逮捕更多的走私者时,这就增加了出售毒品的成本,从而减少了在任何一种既定价格时的毒品供给量。但毒品需求方——买者在任何一种既定价格时想购买的数量却并不会改变。正如下图所示,禁毒使供给曲线从 S_1 向左移动到 S_2,而需求曲线不变。毒品的均衡价格从 P_1 上升为 P_2,均衡数量从 Q_1 减少为 Q_2。均衡数量减少表明禁毒减少了毒品的使用。

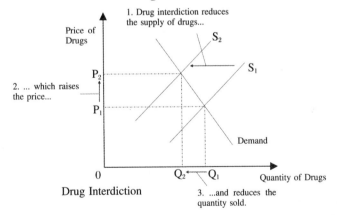

Does Drug Interdiction Increase or Decrease Drug-Related Crime?

但是,与毒品相关的犯罪情况如何呢?为了回答这个问题,需要考虑吸毒者为购买毒品所支付的总量。由于受毒品价格上升的影响而根除不良习惯的瘾君子很少,他们的选择会是再高的价格也要购买,所以,很可能的情况是,毒品的需求缺乏弹性,正如图中所示。如果需求是缺乏弹性的,那么,价格上升就会使毒品市场总收益增加。也就是说,由于禁毒导致价格提高的比例大于毒品使用量减少的比例,结果便是增加了吸毒者为毒品支付的总货币量，当然也增加了贩毒者的收入。那些已经以行窃来维持吸毒的瘾君子为了得到更多钱会变本加厉地进行犯罪。因此在一定程度上，禁毒会增加与毒品相关的犯罪。

由于禁毒的这种不利影响，一些分析家提出了另一些解决毒品问题的方法。决策者不是要减少毒品供给，而应该通过禁毒教育的劝说努力减少需求。禁毒教育的效应如下图所示。需求曲线向左由 D_1 移动到 D_2。结果，均衡数量从 Q_1 减少到 Q_2，而均衡价格从 P_1 下降到 P_2，总收益即价格乘以数量也减少了。因此，与打击毒贩相对比，禁毒教育更能减少吸毒和与毒品相关的犯罪。

**Does Drug Interdiction Increase
Or decrease Drug-Related Crime?**

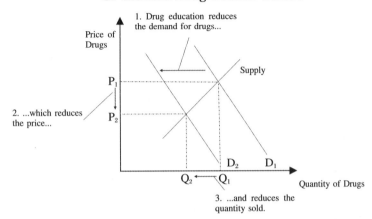

在这种情况下，禁毒支持者会争辩说，禁毒政策在长期与短期内的效应是不同的，因为需求弹性可能取决于时间的长短。在短期内，毒品需求也许是缺乏弹性的，因为高价格对已有的瘾君子吸毒没有实质性影响。但在长期内需求也许是较富有弹性的，因为高价格限制了年轻人中尝试吸毒的人数，而且随着时间的推移，这也有助于减少瘾君子的数量。在这种情况下，禁毒在短期内增加了与毒品相关的犯罪，而在长期内会减少这种犯罪。

通过以上三个案例的分析，我们已经对供给和需求有了进一步的认识，体会到供给和需求及其弹性的妙用。西方有种说法，一只鹦鹉只要学会说"供给与需求"就可以成为一个经济学家。通过这两章的学习你可能会体会到，这种说法还是有一定的道理的。有了供给与需求这对分析工具，你就可以分析许多重大事件以及影响经济的重大政策。

重要名词解释

1. **Elasticity**：a measure of the responsiveness of quantity demanded or quantity supplied to one of its determinants

2. **Price elasticity of demand**：a measure of how much the quantity demanded of a good responds to a change in the price of that good, computed as the percentage change in quantity demanded divided by the percentage change in price

3. **Total revenue**：the amount paid by buyers and received by sellers of a good, computed as the price of the good times the quantity sold

4. **Income elasticity of demand**: a measure of how much the quantity demanded of a good responds to a change in consumers' income, computed as the percentage change in quantity demanded divided by the percentage change in income

5. **Cross-price elasticity of demand**: a measure of how much the quantity demanded of one good responds to a change in the price of another good, computed as the percentage change in quantity demanded of the first good divided by the percentage change in the price of the second good

6. **Price elasticity of supply**: a measure of how much the quantity supplied of a good responds to a change in the price of that good, computed as the percentage change in quantity supplied divided by the percentage change in price

主要图表

1.

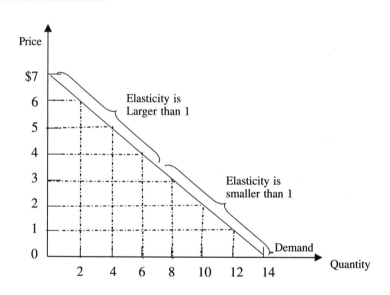

2.

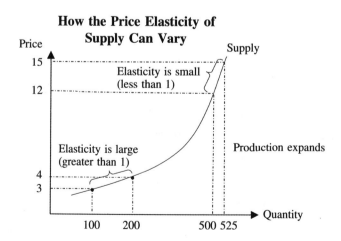

3.

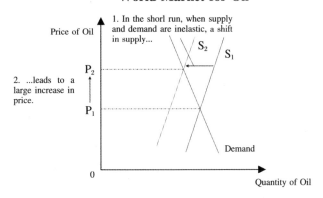

**A Reduction in Supply in the
World Market for Oil**

1. In the shorl run, when supply
and demand are inelastic, a shift
in supply...

Price of Oil

S_2 S_1

P_2

2. ...leads to a
large increase in
price.

P_1

Demand

0   Quantity of Oil

主要计算

1. 需求价格弹性

假定冰激凌蛋卷的价格从 2 美元上升到 2.2 美元,使得你购买的冰激凌蛋卷数量从每月 10 个减少为 8 个。计算需求价格弹性。

解答:价格变动百分比=(2.20−2.00)÷2.00×100=10%

需求量变动百分比=(10−8)÷10×100=20%

需求价格弹性=需求量变动百分比÷价格变动百分比=20%÷10%=2

2. 中点法计算需求价格弹性

假定某种商品的价格由 5 元降为 4 元时,需求量由 50 增加到 100,运用中值法计算需求价格弹性。

解答:价格的中值=(4.00+5.00)/2=4.50

需求量的中值=(100+50)/2=75

价格变动百分比=(4.00−5.00)÷4.50×100%=−22%

需求量变动百分比=(100−50)÷75×100%=67%

需求价格弹性=需求量变动百分比÷价格变动百分比=67%÷(−22%)=−3

3. 中点法计算供给价格弹性

假设每加仑牛奶的价格从 2.85 美元上升到 3.15 美元,牧场主每月生产的牛奶量从 9000 加仑增加到 1.1 万加仑。求牛奶的供给价格弹性。

解答:价格变动百分比=(3.15−2.85)/3.00×100=10%

供给量变动百分比=(11000−9000)/10000×100%=20%

在这种情况下,供给价格弹性=供给量变动百分比/价格变动百分比=20%/10%=2

模拟试题

1. Which of the following will most likely occur in an economy if more money is demanded than is supplied?

   (A) The amount of investment spending will increase.

   (B) Interest rate will decrease.

   (C) Interest rate will increase.

   (D) The demand curve for money will shift to the left.

   (E) The demand curve for money will shift to the right.

   Key: D

   Analysis: It examines the understanding of supply and demand of money. Money is a special good. The supply of money is fixed and the increase of money demand causes the demand curve of money to shift to the right. The graph of the demand and supply of money is as follows.

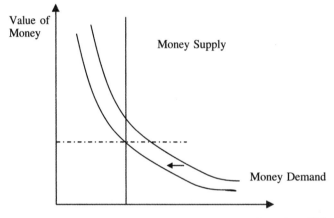

2. An increase in the money supply is most likely to have which of the following short-run effects on real interest rates and real output?

   (A) Decrease Decrease

   (B) Decrease Increase

   (C) Increase Decrease

   (D) Increase No change

   (E) No change Increase

   Key: A

   Analysis: Excessive money leads to devaluation. So real interest rates decrease and real output also decreases.

3. If a normal good is produced in a competitive market, which of the following combinations of events could cause the price of the good to increase and the quantity to decrease?

   (A) An increase in the average income of consumers and an increase in the number of producing firms

   (B) An increase in the average income of consumers and an increase in the price of a variable input

(C) An increase in the price of a substitute good and an increase in the number of producing firms

(D) A decrease in the number of consumers and a decrease in the price of a variable input

(E) A decrease in the average income of consumers and an increase in the number of producing firms

Key: B

Analysis: It examines the understanding of competitive market and normal good. In a competitive market, P=MR=MC, AR=P≥AC, for the short term. Normal good refers to a good for which, other things equal, an increase in income leads to an increase in demand.

4. Which of the following must be true if the revenues of wheat farmers increase when the price of wheat increases?

(A) The supply of wheat is price elastic.

(B) The supply of wheat is income elastic.

(C) The supply of wheat is income inelastic.

(D) The demand for wheat is price elastic.

(E) The demand for wheat price inelastic.

Key: E

Analysis: When a demand curve is inelastic(with a price elasticity less than 1), a price increase raises total revenue, and a price decrease reduces total revenue.

5. The demand curve for a normal good slopes down for which of the following reasons?

[I] An increase in the price of the good induces consumers to purchase substitute products.

[II] An increase in the price of the good reduces consumers' purchasing power.

[III] An increase in the price of the good increases consumers' utility from consuming that good.

(A) I only

(B) II only

(C) III only

(D) I and II only

(E) I and III only

Key: D

Analysis: Substitutes refer to two goods for which an increase in the price of one leads to an increase in the demand for the other. The consumers face the budget constraint.

6. A factor of production will NOT earn economic profit when its supply is

(A) Elastic

(B) Inelastic

(C) Unit elastic

(D) Perfectly elastic

(E) Perfectly inelastic

Key: D

Analysis: It examines the understanding of all kinds of the price elastic of supply. For the case of perfectly elastic supply, the price is fixed.

7. In the short run, a decrease in production costs of a product will shift

 (A) Both the demand curve and the supply curve to the right

 (B) The demand curve to the left and the supply curve to the right

 (C) Only the supply curve to the right

 (D) Only the supply curve to the left

 (E) Only the demand curve to the left

 Key: C

 Analysis: A decrease in production costs of a product influences the supply only, not the demand. The supplier is now willing to produce more at any given price. So the supply curve shifts to the right.

8. Which of the following is true in the elastic range of a firm's demand curve?

 (A) The firm should expand output to increase economic profits.

 (B) An increase in price will also lead to an increase in total cost.

 (C) A decrease in price will likely lead to an increase in total revenue.

 (D) Marginal revenue is negative.

 (E) The firm is maximizing total revenue.

 Key: C

 Analysis: Other choices have nothing to do with the elasticity. Only C is possible when the elasticity of demand curve is more than 1.

9. To alleviate a financial crisis, a university increases student fees. This action will increase university revenues if the price elasticity of demand for university education is

 (A) Inelastic

 (B) Unit elastic

 (C) Elastic

 (D) Equal to the price elasticity of supply

 (E) Equal to 1

 Key: A

 Analysis: When a demand curve is inelastic （a price elasticity less than 1）, a price increase raises total revenue, and a price decrease reduces total revenue.

10. Assume that both the supply of and the demand for a good are relatively price elastic. The imposition of a per-unit excise tax on the sale of the good would cause the equilibrium and the quantity to change in which of the following ways?

	Price	Quantity
(A)	Increase	Increase
(B)	Increase	No change
(C)	Increase	Decrease
(D)	Decrease	No change
(E)	Decrease	Decrease

Key：C

Analysis：See the graph.

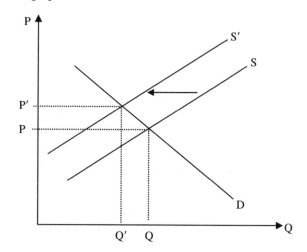

11. The price of an airline ticket is typically lower if a traveler buys the ticket several weeks before the flight's departure date rather than on the day of departure. This pricing strategy is based on the assumption that

（A）Travelers are not aware of how airline prices change across time.

（B）Travelers do not have alternative modes of transportation.

（C）Travelers will pay any price to travel as the departure date approaches.

（D）The marginal cost of the last few seats on an airplane higher than that for the first few seats.

（E）Travelers' demand becomes less elastic as the departure date approaches.

Key：E

Analysis：We can eliminate the wrong choices one by one.

12. Leather and beef are jointly produced such that an increase in the production of one results in an equal increase in the production of the other. An increase in the demand for leather will most likely cause

（A）A decrease in the price of leather

（B）A decrease in the price of beef

（C）A decrease in the equilibrium quantity of beef sold

（D）An increase in the demand for beef in the short-run

（E）An increase in the supply of leather

Key：B

Analysis：An increase in the demand for leather will lead to more production of leather. Because they are jointly produced, the supply of beef will increase. The supply exceeds the demand in short-term, thus the price of beef will decrease.

13. Generally, a firm is more willing and able to increase quantity supplied in response to a price change when

(A) The relevant time period is short rather than long.

(B) The relevant time period is long rather than short.

(C) Supply is inelastic.

(D) The firm is experiencing capacity problems.

(E) The demand curve which it faces is inelastic.

Key: B

Analysis: The determinants of elasticity of supply are flexibility and time period.

14. If two supply curves pass through the same point and one is steep and the other is flat, which of the following statements is correct?

(A) The flatter supply curve represents a supply that is inelastic relative to the supply represented by the steeper supply curve.

(B) The steeper supply curve represents a supply that is inelastic relative to the supply represented by the flatter supply curve.

(C) Given two prices with which to calculate the price elasticity of supply, the elasticity is the same for both curves.

(D) A decrease in demand will increase total revenue if the steeper supply curve is relevant, while a decrease in demand will decrease total revenue if the flatter supply cure is relevant.

(E) None of the above is true.

Key: B

Analysis: The flatter the supply curve that passes through a given point is, the greater the price elasticity of supply shall be. The steeper the supply curve that passes through a given point is; the smaller the price elasticity of supply shall be. So the steeper supply curve represents a supply that is inelastic relative to the supply represented by the flatter supply curve. D depends on the demand curve, not the supply curve.

15. Assume that bread and butter are complementary goods. The government begins to subsidize the production of wheat, which is an input in the production of bread.

(a) For each of the following markets, draw correctly labeled supply and demand graphs and show the effect of the subsidy on the equilibrium price and quantity in the short run.

(i) The wheat market

(ii) The bread market

(iii) The butter market

(b) If the demand for bread is price elastic, how will total revenues for the bread producers change as a result of the government subsidy?

Key: 5 points (4 + 1)

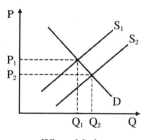

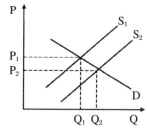

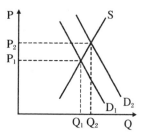

Wheat Market   Bread Market   Bread Market

(a) 4 points:

One point is earned for drawing correctly labeled supply and demand graphs for all three markets.

One point is earned for showing a rightward shift of the supply curve in the wheat market with price decreasing and quantity increasing.

One point is earned for showing a rightward shift of the supply curve in the bread market with price decreasing and quantity increasing.

One point is earned for showing a rightward shift of the demand curve in the butter market with price increasing and quantity increasing.

(b) 1 point:

One point is earned for concluding that the total revenue will increase.

16. Steve is a utility-maximizing consumer who spends all of his income on peanuts and apples, both of which are normal goods.

(a) Assume that the last unit of peanuts consumed increased Steve's total utility from 40 utils to 48 utils and that the last unit of apples consumed increased his total utility from 52 utils to 56 utils.

(i) If the price of a unit of peanuts is $1 and Steve is maximizing utility, calculate the price of a unit of apples.

(ii) If the price of a unit of peanuts increases and the price of a unit of apple remains unchanged from the price you determined in part (a) (i), how will Steve's purchase of peanuts change?

(b) Assume that the cross-price elasticity of demand between peanuts and apples is positive. A widespread disease has destroyed the apple crop. What will happen to the equilibrium price and quantity of peanuts in the short run? Explain.

(c) Assume that the price of bananas increases.

(i) Will the substitution effect increase, decrease, or have no effect on the quantity of apple demanded?

(ii) What happens to Steve's real income?

Key: 6 points (2 + 2 + 2)

(a) 2 points:

One point is earned for calculating the price of a unit of apples, $4/8 = $0.50.

One point is earned for stating that Steve will purchase fewer peanuts.

(b) 2 points:

One point is earned for stating that the equilibrium price and the quantity of peanuts will both increase.

One point is earned for explaining that peanuts and apples are substitutes, and since the price of apples increased, it would cause the demand for peanuts to increase.

(c) 2 points:

One point is earned for stating that the substitution effect causes the quantity of apples demanded to decrease.

One point is earned for stating that Steve's real income will decrease.

17. Utility and price elasticity of demand are important concepts in explaining consumer behavior.

(a) Define marginal utility.

(b) The table below shows the quantities, prices, and marginal utilities of two goods, fudge and coffee, which Nancy purchases.

	Fudge	**Coffee**
Quantity of purchase	10 pounds	7 pounds
Price per pound	$2	$4
Marginal utility of last pound	12	20

Nancy spends all her money and buys only these two goods. In order to maximize her utility, should Nancy purchase more fudge and less coffee, purchase more coffee and less fudge, or maintain her current consumption? Explain.

(c) Assume that consumers always buy 20 units of good R each month regardless of its price.

(i) What is the numerical value of the price elasticity of demand for good R?

(ii) If the government implements a per-unit tax of $2 on good R, how much of the tax will the seller pay?

Key: 5 points $(1 + 2 + 2)$

(a) 1 point:

One point is earned for defining marginal utility as the extra satisfaction received from consuming an additional unit of a good or service.

(b) 2 points:

One point is earned for concluding that Nancy should purchase more fudge and less coffee.

One point is earned for explaining that the per dollar MU for fudge is greater than the per dollar MU for coffee.

(c) 2 points:

One point is earned for stating that the price elasticity of demand for good R is zero.

One point is earned for stating that none of the tax will be paid by the seller of good R, or that buyers pay all of the tax.

Chapter 7

Supply, Demand and Government Policies
供给、需求和政府政策

主要内容和概念讲解

在前面的学习中，我们已经初步了解到，在一个自由的、没有管制的（free, unregulated）市场系统中，市场自身的供求力量决定均衡价格和均衡数量（Market forces establish equilibrium prices and exchange quantities.）。各种事件通过影响供给和需求来改变均衡价格和数量，使得市场处于有效率的状态。但是，市场有效并不代表大家都满意（Not everyone is satisfied.）。效率与公平的矛盾始终存在。此时，经济学家就要站出来解决这个问题了。他们不再局限于科学家的身份只提出并检验解释我们周围世界的理论，而是试图成为决策者，运用经济学理论去改造世界，使世界变得更好。

我们先从探讨直接控制价格的政策开始。价格管制政策不仅在原来的计划经济中很常见，就连在像美国这种最发达的市场经济国家，也是最为常见的一种政策。例如，租金控制法规定了房东可以向房客收取的最高租金。最低工资法规定了企业可以向工人支付的最低工资。当决策者认为一种商品或劳务的市场价格对买者或卖者不公平时，通常就会实施价格管制（usually enacted when policymakers believe the market price is unfair to buyers or sellers），包括规定价格上限（price ceiling）和价格下限（price floor）。但正如我们将看到的，这些政策本身也会引起一些不公平（unfair）。

何谓价格上限？何谓价格下限？我们举个例子来看。兰州拉面是全国闻名的小吃。在兰州市，如果没有政府管制，由于市场上有众多买家和卖家自由竞争，拉面的价格调整最终会使得市场供求平衡。在均衡价格时，众多买者想买的拉面数量正好等于卖者想卖的拉面数量。具体来说，假设均衡价格是每碗4元。

但是，并不是每个人对这个自由市场达到的结果都感到满意。比如说，兰州市消费者协会或者工会会提出异议，认为4元价格太高，很多低收入的普通民众不可能每天都吃得起。同时，拉面行业协会也会抱怨，4元的价格太低了，生产拉面的厂家很难得到利润。实际生活中，会有很多相关利益集团游说政府，以便通过一项直接控制市场价格的法律规定改变市场结果。

由于任何一种商品的买者总希望价格越低越好，而卖者总希望价格越高越好，所以双方的利益是冲突的。如果拉面消费者在游说中成功了，政府就会制定法律规定拉面的最高价格。如果拉面生产商游说成功，政府就会制定法律规定拉面的最低价格。价格上限就是指可以出售一种商品的法定最高价格（a legally established maximum price at which a good can be sold），比如租金控制。价格下限指的是可以出售一种商品的法定最低价格（a legally established minimum price at which a good can be sold），比如最低工资。

下面我们就通过冰激凌蛋卷市场来依次考虑这两种政策的影响。当政府受冰激凌蛋卷消费者抱怨的鼓动对冰激凌蛋卷市场实行价格上限时,根据价格的高低,可能有两种结果,即有限制作用的(binding)和无限制作用的(unbinding)。

A Price Ceiling That Is Not Binding...

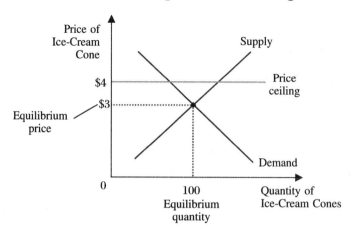

上图中,政府规定每个冰激凌蛋卷的价格上限为4美元。在这种情况下,由于使供求平衡的价格(3美元)低于上限,价格上限没有限制作用。市场力量自然而然地使经济向均衡变动,而且,价格上限没有影响。当然,政府一般不太可能做这样的无用功。下一种结果,会更有可能,也更有意义。

A Price Ceiling That Is Binding...

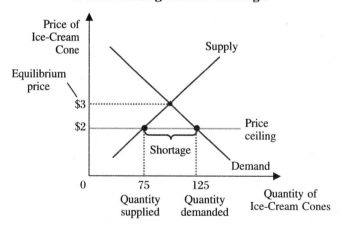

在这种情况下,政府规定每个冰激凌蛋卷的价格上限2美元。由于均衡价格(3美元)在价格上限之上,所以,价格上限对市场有一种限制性作用。供求力量趋向于使价格向均衡变动,但当市场价格达到上限时,就不能再上升了。因此,市场价格等于价格上限。在这种价格时,冰激凌蛋卷的需求量(图中为125个)超过了供给量(75个),存在冰激凌蛋卷短缺。因此,一些在现行价格时想买冰激凌蛋卷的人会买不到。

当冰激凌蛋卷短缺的形成是由于这种价格上限时,一些配给冰激凌蛋卷的机制就会出现。这种机制可能是排长队(long lines):那些愿意提前来并排队等候的人得到一个冰激凌蛋卷,而另一些不愿意等候的人得不到。另一种方法是,卖者可以根据它们自己的偏好来配给冰激凌蛋卷,如只卖给朋友、亲戚或同一种族或民族的成员。要注意的是,尽管价格上限是出于帮助冰激凌蛋卷买者的愿望而制定的，但并不是所有买者都能从这种政策中受益。一些买者尽管不得不排队等候但以较低的价格得到冰激凌蛋卷，而另一些买者根本买不到任何冰激凌蛋卷。

冰激凌蛋卷市场的例子反映了一条一般规律：当政府对竞争市场规定限制性价格上限时，就会产生商品的短缺，而且，卖者必然要在大量潜在买者中配给稀缺商品。这种价格上限之下产生的配给机制(allocative mechanism)很少是合意的。排长队是无效率的，因为这样浪费了买者的时间。因为商品并没有配给给对它评价最高的买者，根据卖者偏好配给的机制既无效率又可能是不公平的。与此相比，在自由竞争市场中，商品配给通过价格来实现，这种配给机制既有效率又客观。当冰激凌蛋卷市场达到均衡时，任何一个想支付市场价格的人都可以买到冰激凌蛋卷。

总的说来，有限制作用的价格上限会使得需求量大于供给量，造成商品短缺，例如1970年的石油危机(oil crisis)。短缺现象的存在，就会迫使卖家必须采用非价格性的配给手段，例如排队和人为地有区别性地对待消费者。

我们采用汽油的案例来进行简单分析。1973年石油输出国组织OPEC提高了世界石油市场的原油价格。由于原油是用于生产汽油的主要投入品，较高的石油价格减少了汽油的供给。加油站前排起的长队成了司空见惯的现象，而且，驾车人常常不得不为了买几加仑汽油而等待几个小时。

是什么引起了加油排队呢？大多数人将此归咎为OPEC。的确，如果OPEC不提高原油价格，汽油的短缺就不会出现。但经济学家把它归咎为政府对石油公司采取的汽油价格管制。

The Price Ceiling on Gasoline Is Not Binding...

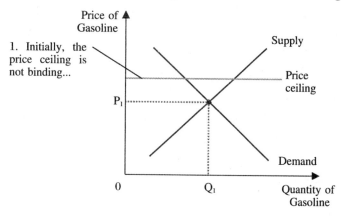

我们用供求图来分析所出现的情况。正如上图所示，在OPEC提高原油价格之前，汽油的均衡价格为P_1，低于最高限价。因此，价格管制没有影响。但是，当原油价格上升时，情况发生了改变。原油价格上升增加了生产汽油的成本，也就减少了汽油的供给。

The Price Ceiling on Gasoline Is Binding...

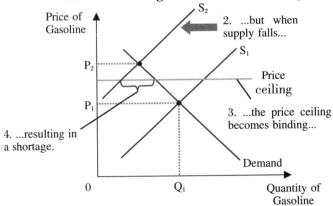

正如上图所示，供给曲线从 S_1 向左移动到 S_2。在一个没有管制的市场上，供给的这种移动将使汽油的均衡价格从 P_1 上升为 P_2，而且不会引起短缺。相反，价格上限使价格不能上升到均衡水平。在存在价格上限时，生产者愿意出售的量小于消费者愿意购买的量。因此，供给移动引起了存在管制价格时的严重短缺。

最后，对汽油价格管制的法律被撤销了。而这项法律的制定者也终于明白他们要为美国人排队等候买汽油而浪费的大量时间承担部分责任。现在，当原油价格变动时，汽油的价格也得以调整以使供求均衡。

在分析了汽油案例之后，我们再来看租金管制(rent control)这一典型的价格上限案例。在许多城市，地方政府都规定了房东能向房客收取的租金上限（Rent controls are ceilings placed on the rents that landlords may charge their tenants.）。这项政策的目的是帮助穷人能够租得起住房(help the poor by making housing more affordable)。但是，经济学家却经常抨击租金管制，认为这是一种帮助穷人提高生活水平的极无效率的方法。一个经济学家称租金管制是"除了轰炸之外毁灭一个城市的最好方法"(the best way to destroy a city, other than bombing)。

租金管制的不利影响对一般人并不明显，因为这些影响要在许多年后才能显现出来。短期中，房东出租的公寓数量是固定的，而且，他们不能随着市场状况的变动而迅速调整这一数量。此外，短期中，在一个城市寻找住房的人的数量对租金也并不会非常敏感，因为人们调整自己的住房安排要花时间。因此，住房的短期供给与需求都是较为缺乏弹性的(inelastic)。下图表示的就是租金管制对住房市场的短期影响。与任何一种价格上限一样，租金管制引起短缺。但由于短期中供给与需求缺乏弹性，因此由租金管制引起的短缺并不严重，其中的主要影响是降低了租金。

Rent Control in the Short Run...
(supply and demand are inelastic)

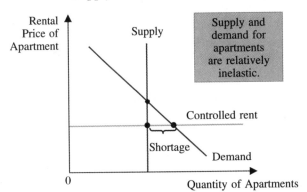

长期的情况却完全不同,因为随着时间的推移,租赁住房的买者与卖者对市场状况反应较大。在供给一方,房东对低租金的反应是不建新公寓,也不维修现有的公寓。在需求一方,低租金鼓励人们去找自己的公寓(而不是与父母或室友同住),而且也会引起更多的人迁移到城市的情况。因此,长期中供给与需求都是较为富有弹性的(elastic)。

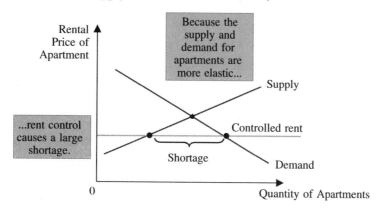

Rent Control in the Long Run...
(supply and demand are elastic)

上图说明了租金管制对长期住房市场的影响。当租金管制把租金压低到均衡水平以下时,公寓的供给量大幅度减少,而公寓的需求量大幅度增加,其结果是出租住房大量短缺(shortage)。

在那些存在租金管制的城市里,房东采用各种机制来配给住房。有些房东选择让租房者长期等待。也有一些房东喜欢没有孩子的房客。还有一些房东根据种族采取不同待遇。有时公寓分配给了那些愿意暗中向大楼管理者付钱的人。实际上,这些贿赂使公寓总价格(包括贿赂(bribe))接近均衡价格。为了充分了解租金管制的影响,我们可以回想一下在最开始介绍的经济学十大原理之一:人们会对激励做出反应。在自由市场中,房东会努力使自己的公寓保持洁净而安全,因为令人满意的公寓可以获得更高的价格。与此相比,当租金管制引起短缺和排队等待时,就没有什么激励(motivation)能使房东对房客关心的问题做出反应。在现有住房供不应求的状况下,房东还有动力花钱来维修并改善住房状况吗? 显然不会。最后的结果是,房客虽然付出了低租金,但他们也得到了低质量的住房。

决策者对租金管制的这种影响的反应通常是实行额外的管制。例如,认定住房方面的种族歧视为非法,并制定法律规定房东提供适于居住的居房的最低条件。但是,这些法律实施起来很困难而且费用巨大。与此相比,当取消租金管制并由市场竞争力调节住房市场时,这些法律就没有必要存在了。在一个自由市场上,住房价格的调节会消除供给短缺。

分析完价格上限后,再来看看价格下限(price floor),分析一下它又是如何影响市场结果的。我们再回到冰激凌蛋卷市场。现在设想政府被冰激凌蛋卷制造商组织的借口说服了。在这种情况下,政府将制定价格下限。价格下限和价格上限一样,都是政府要使价格保持在与均衡水平不同的水平上。价格上限是确定价格法定的最高限,而价格下限则是确定价格法定的最低限(a legally established minimum price at which a good can be sold)。

当政府实行价格下限时,也可能会有两种结果(outcomes)。如果价格下限低于均衡价格,则不具有约束作用。如果价格下限高于均衡价格,就有约束作用,即使商品过剩。

如果当冰激凌蛋卷的均衡价格是3美元时，政府确定的价格下限是2美元，我们可以从下图中得出以下结果：在这种情况下，由于均衡价格高于价格下限，价格下限没有限制性。市场力量自然而然地使经济向均衡变动，价格下限没有任何影响。

A Price Floor That Is Not Binding...

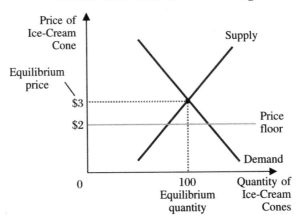

当政府把价格下限定为每个冰激凌蛋卷4美元时，如下图所示。在这种情况下，由于均衡价格3美元低于价格下限，价格下限对市场有限制性约束。供求力量使价格向均衡价格变动，但当市场价格达到下限时，就不能再下降了。市场价格等于价格下限。在这种价格时，冰激凌蛋卷的供给量（120个）超过了需求量（80个）。一些想以现行价格出售冰激凌蛋卷的人卖不出去。因此，限制性的价格下限引起商品过剩。

A Price Floor That Is Binding

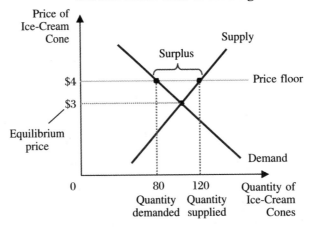

由这个简单的例子可以看出，价格下限阻止了供给和需求向均衡价格和均衡数量移动（A price floor prevents supply and demand from moving toward the equilibrium price and quantity.）。当价格向下移动触碰到价格下限时，就不能再进一步下降了，市场价格就等于价格下限（When the market price hits the floor, it can fall no further, and the market price equals the floor price.）。

总之，有限制性的价格下限，会使得供给量大于需求量，造成过剩，即一些卖者不能按市场价格出售商品。过剩现象的存在,就会导致具有歧视标准(discrimination criteria)的非价格配给机制取代自由市场中的价格配给机制。那些也许由于种族或家族之故而受买者青睐的卖者能比那些不受青睐的卖者更好地出售自己的商品。现实生活中价格下限的典型例子有最低工资(the minimum wage)和农业价格支持(agricultural price supports)。

最低工资是价格下限最重要的例子。最低工资法规定了任何一个雇主可以支付的最低劳动力价格 (Minimum wage laws dictate the lowest price possible for labor that any employer may pay.)。

为了分析最低工资的影响,我们必须考虑劳动力市场(labor market)。下图表示劳动力市场,它和所有市场一样服从于供求的力量。工人决定劳动供给,而企业决定需求。在没有政策干预时,工资调整使劳动力的供求平衡。

The Minimum Wage

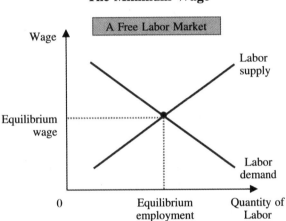

下图表示的是有最低工资的劳动力市场。如果最低工资高于均衡水平,如图中所示,劳动供给量大于需求量,结果会造成失业。因此,最低工资增加了有工作工人的收入,但减少了那些找不到工作的工人的收入。

The Minimum Wage

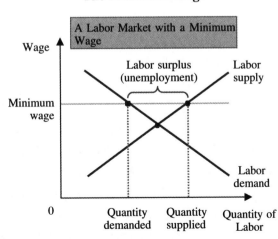

　　为了充分了解最低工资,我们需要注意,经济不只包括一种单一的劳动力市场(a single labor market),而是包括由许多不同类型工人构成的劳动力市场。最低工资的影响取决于工人的技能与经验(skill and experience of the worker)。技术水平高且经验丰富的工人不受影响,因为他们的均衡工资大大高于最低工资。对于这些工人,最低工资没有限制性。

　　最低工资对青少年(teenager)劳动力市场的影响最大。青少年的均衡工资往往较低,因为青少年属于技术水平最低而且也是经验最少的劳动力成员。此外,青少年往往愿意接受较低的工资以换取在职培训。实际上,有些青年人愿意以"实习"(internship)之名来工作而不要任何报酬。但是,由于实习不支付工资,所以,最低工资不适用于实习。总之结果是,最低工资对青少年的限制比对其他劳动力成员都大。

　　除了改变劳动力的需求量之外,最低工资还改变了劳动力的供给量。由于最低工资增加了青少年可以赚到的工资,它也就增加了选择寻找工作的青少年的人数。国外一些研究发现,较高的最低工资会影响那些已经就业的青少年。当最低工资提高以后,一些正在上学的青少年会选择退学去参加工作。这些新退学的青少年代替了那些之前已退学就业的青少年,对就业市场产生冲击,使他们现在成为失业者。

　　最低工资是西方政治争论中常见的话题。最低工资的支持者认为这项政策是增加贫穷工人的收入、改善(better off)他们生活的一种方法。他们指出,那些赚取最低工资的工人只能勉强度日,这一点是毫无争议的。例如,从 2009 年开始,美国联邦政府将最低工资标准定为每小时 7.25 美元,一年中每周工作 40 小时、领取最低工资的两个成年人每年的总收入只有 30160 美元,不及中产家庭年收入的一半。许多最低工资的支持者也承认,它有一些不利影响包括失业,但他们认为,这些影响并不大,而且,考虑到所有情况之后,最关键的是较高的最低工资可以使穷人的状况变好。

　　最低工资法的反对者认为,这并不是解决贫穷问题的最好办法。从劳动力的需求角度来说,它并不直接影响那些工资高于最低工资的年轻人,最低工资在实际生活中的执行也不是很彻底。假如最低工资上升 10%,就会使青少年的就业减少 1%–3%,这个数字已经相当大,即较高的最低工资会引起失业。从劳动力的供给角度来说,最低工资法会促使更多的年轻人选择寻找工作,鼓励青少年退学(drop out),从而使得原有的一些不熟练的工人无法得到他们所需的在职培训(on-the-job training)。

　　此外,最低工资法的反对者还指出,最低工资法是一种目标欠妥的政策(poorly targeted policy)。在领取最低工资的人中,只有不到 1/3 的家庭生活在贫困线以下。许多最低工资的领取者是中产阶级家庭的青少年,他们是为了赚取零花钱而从事业余工作。

　　现在,我们回忆一下之前介绍的十大经济学原理之一:市场通常是组织经济活动的一种好方法。这个原理解释了为什么经济学家几乎总是反对价格上限和价格下限。在经济学家看来,价格并不是某些偶然过程的结果。他们认为,价格是隐藏在供给和需求曲线背后的千百万个企业和消费者共同决策的结果。价格有平衡供求从而协调经济活动的关键作用。决策者通过规定价格的方法来确定价格的做法模糊了正常指引社会资源配置的信号(obscure the signals that normally guide the allocation of society's resources)。

　　经济学十大原理的另一个原则是政府有时可以改善市场结果。实际上,决策者进行价格控制是因为他们认为市场结果是不公平的(view the market's outcome as unfair)。价格管制的目标往往是帮助穷人。例如，租金管制法是想要使每个人都住得起房子，而最低工资法的目的是帮助人们摆脱贫困。

但价格管制往往会伤害它想要帮助的人（hurt those they are trying to help）。租金管制可以保持低租金，但它无法鼓励房东维修住房，并使找房变得困难。最低工资法会增加一些工人的收入但也会使其他工人成为失业者。这些政策总会顾此失彼，此时政府就需要进行权衡取舍（tradeoff）。

政府也可以用除了价格管制以外（other than controlling prices）的方法来帮助那些需要帮助的人。例如，政府可以通过给贫困家庭部分租金补贴来使他们租得起房子。与租金管制不同，这种租金补贴并不会减少住房供给量，也就不会引起住房短缺。同样，工资补贴提高了贫穷工人的生活水平又不会刺激企业减少雇员数量。工资补贴的方法之一就是减免劳动收入税收。

虽然这些替代性政策（alternative policies）往往比价格管制好，但也不完美（imperfect）。租金和工资补贴要花费政府资金，这就要求更高的税收收入。正如我们在下一部分所要说明的，税收也有自己的成本。

富兰克林说过，税收是现代经济中最普遍的现象。所有政府，无论是中国还是美国，无论是从中央政府（国税）还是到地方政府（地税），都利用税收为公共支出筹资（raise revenue for public projects）。税收是一种非常重要的政策工具，在许多方面影响着我们的生活，所以，税收研究是经济学研究中的另一个重要课题。在这一部分我们将从税收如何影响经济开始研究。

为了拟定我们分析的场合，设想某一地方政府决定举办年度冰激凌蛋卷节，到时会有游行、烟火以及本镇官员做演讲。为了给这项活动筹集经费，该政府决定对每个冰激凌蛋卷的销售征收 0.5 美元的税。当这项计划公布时，有两个游说集团立即采取行动。全国冰激凌蛋卷制造商组织声称，它的成员在竞争市场上正在为生存而挣扎，并认为冰激凌蛋卷买者应该支付税收。全国冰激凌蛋卷消费者协会则声称，冰激凌蛋卷消费者入不敷出，并认为冰激凌蛋卷卖者应该支付税收。市长为了达成一致，提出买者支付一半税收，卖者支付一半税收。

为了分析这些建议，我们需要问一个简单而敏感的问题：当政府对一种商品征税时，究竟谁来承担税收负担？是买者？还是卖者？或者，如果买者与卖者分摊税收负担，是什么因素决定如何分配？政府能像这位市长的建议那样简单地来用立法来分配税收负担吗？还是要由经济中更基本的力量来决定税收负担分配？经济学家用税收归宿这个术语来解释关于税收负担分配的问题。税收归宿，简单地说就是研究由谁来承担税收负担（the study of who bears the burden of a tax）。正如我们将看到的，我们运用供求工具分析税收归宿，会得到一些令人惊讶的结论。

当然，在分析之前，我们都知道，税收肯定会导致市场均衡的改变（Taxes result in a change in market equilibrium.）。直觉和经验告诉我们，无论税收由谁来承担，买者都会支付更多，卖者获得更少（Buyers pay more and sellers receive less, regardless of whom the tax is levied on.）。下面我们用实际案例来进行分析。

我们首先考虑对一种商品的买者征税。例如，假设当地政府通过一项法律，要求冰激凌蛋卷的买者为他们购买的每个冰激凌蛋卷向政府支付 0.5 美元的税。这项法律会如何影响冰激凌蛋卷的买者和卖者呢？为了回答这个问题，我们可以遵循分析供给与需求时常用的三个步骤：(1)确定该法律影响供给曲线还是需求曲线；(2)确定曲线移动的方向；(3)分析这种移动如何影响均衡。

这项税收最初会影响冰激凌蛋卷的需求。供给曲线并不受影响，因为在任何一种既定的价格时，卖者向市场提供冰激凌蛋卷的激励是相同的。与此相比，买者只要购买冰激凌蛋卷就不得不向政府交税(并付款给卖者)。因此，税收使冰激凌蛋卷的需求曲线移动。

移动的方向很明显。由于对买者征税使冰激凌蛋卷的吸引力变小了，在每种价格时买者需要的冰激凌蛋卷量也少了。因此，需求曲线向左下移动。

在这种情况下，我们可以更准确地了解需求曲线移动多少，由于向买者征收 0.5 美元的税。所以，对买者的有效价格现在比市场价格高 0.5 美元。例如，如果每个冰激凌蛋卷的市场价格正好是 2 美元，对买者的有效价格就应该是 2.5 美元。由于买者看的是包括税收的总成本，所以，他们购买的冰激凌蛋卷的市场价格其实比实际价格高出 0.5 美元——尽管他们自己可能并没有意识到这一点。换句话说，为了诱使买者需要任何一种既定的数量，市场价格现在必须降低 0.5 美元，以弥补税收的影响。因此，如下图所示，税收使需求曲线向下从 D_1 移动到 D_2，其移动幅度正好是税收量（0.5 美元）。

Impact of a 50¢ Tax Levied on Buyers...

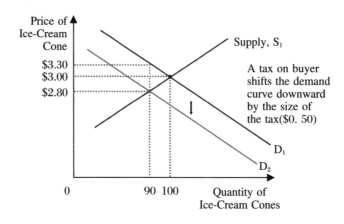

为了说明税收的影响，我们来比较原来的均衡与新均衡。在图中可以看到，冰激凌蛋卷的均衡价格从 3 美元下降到 2.8 美元，而均衡数量从 100 个减少为 90 个。由于在新均衡时，卖者卖得少了，买者也买得少了，所以对冰激凌蛋卷征税缩小了冰激凌蛋卷市场的规模。现在我们回到税收归宿问题：谁支付了税收？虽然买者向政府支付了全部税收，但买者与卖者分摊了负担。当引进了税收时，市场价格从 3 美元下降为 2.8 美元，卖者卖出一个冰激凌蛋卷比没有税收时少收入 0.2 美元。因此，税收使卖者的状况变坏了。买者付给卖者较低的价格(2.8 美元)，包括税收在内的有效价格从征税前的 3 美元上升为有税收时的 3.3 美元(2.8 美元+0.5 美元=3.3 美元)。因此，税收也使买者的状况变坏了。

Impact of a 50 c Tax Levied on Buyers...

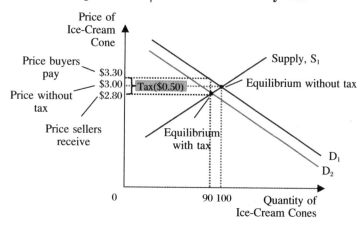

总之，以上分析得出了两个一般性结论：1.税收抑制了市场活动。当对一种商品征税时，该商品在新的均衡时销售量减少了（Taxes discourage market activity. When a good is taxed, the quantity of the good sold is smaller in the new equilibrium.）。2.买者与卖者分摊税收负担。在新的均衡时，买者为该商品支付得多了，而卖者得到的少了（Buyers and sellers share the burden of taxes. In the new equilibrium, buyers pay more for the good, and sellers receive less.）。

在分析完买者之后，现在考虑向一种商品的卖者征税。假设地方政府通过法律要求冰激凌蛋卷的卖者每卖一个冰激凌蛋卷向政府支付 0.5 美元。这项法律会有什么影响呢？

在这种情况下，税收最初会影响冰激凌蛋卷的供给。由于政府并不向买者征税，在任何一种既定价格时，冰激凌蛋卷的需求量是相同的，所以，需求曲线不变。与此相比，对卖者征税增加了销售冰激凌蛋卷的成本，这就使得卖者在每一价格水平时供给的数量减少，供给曲线向左上移动。

我们可以精确地知道移动的幅度。在任何一种冰激凌蛋卷的市场价格时，卖者的有效价格即它们在纳税之后得到的价格要降低 0.5 美元。例如，如果一个冰激凌蛋卷的市场价格正好是 2 美元，卖者得到的有效价格将是 1.5 美元。无论市场价格是多少，卖者仿佛是在比市场价格低 0.5 美元的价格来供给冰激凌蛋卷。换个说法，为了使卖者供给任何一种既定的数量，现在的市场价格必须比之前高 0.5 美元，以弥补税收的影响。因此，如下图所示，供给曲线向上从 S_1 移动到 S_2，移动幅度正好是税收量 0.5 美元。

Impact of a 50¢ Tax on Sellers...

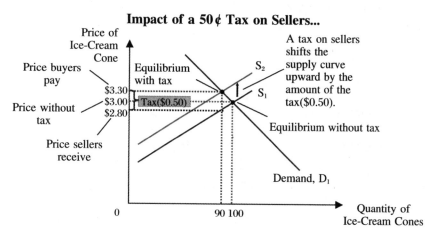

当市场从旧均衡向新均衡移动时，冰激凌蛋卷的均衡价格从 3 美元上升到 3.3 美元，而均衡数量从 100 个减少为 90 个。税收又减少了冰激凌蛋卷市场的规模。而且，买者与卖者又一次分摊税收负担。由于市场价格上升，买者为每个冰激凌蛋卷比纳税前多支付了 0.3 美元。卖者得到的价格高于没有税收时，但有效价格（纳税之后）从 3 美元下降到 2.8 美元。

比较前两幅图可以得出一个令人惊讶的结论：对买者征税和对卖者征税的效果是相同的（Taxes on buyers and taxes on sellers are equivalent.）。在这两种情况下，税收在买者支付的价格和卖者得到的价格之间都打入了一个楔子（places a wedge）。无论税收是向买者征收还是向卖者征收，买者价格与卖者价格之间的楔子是相同的（The wedge between the buyers' price and the sellers' price is the same, regardless of whether the tax is levied on buyers or sellers.）。在这两种情况下，这个楔子都使供给和需求曲线的相对位置移动（shifts the relative position）。在新均衡时，买者和卖者分摊税收负担（share the burden of the tax）。对买者征税和对卖者征税的唯一差别就是谁把钱交给政府（who sends the money to the government）。

如果我们设想政府在每家冰激凌蛋卷店的柜台上放一只碗来收取 0.5 美元的冰激凌蛋卷税时，也许就很容易理解这种征税方式的一致性了。当政府向买者征税时，就相当于要求买者每买一个冰激凌蛋卷就往碗里放 0.5 美元。当政府向卖者征税时，要求卖者每卖出一个冰激凌蛋卷往碗里放 0.5 美元。无论 0.5 美元是直接从买者的口袋放入碗内，还是间接从买者的口袋放入碗内都无关紧要。一旦市场达到新均衡，无论向谁征税，都是由买者与卖者分摊负担。

下面我们再来看与每个家庭都相关的工资税（the payroll tax）。对于城市里每个有正式工作的人来说，每月在收到工资单时会发现，实际领到的钱是从自己赚到的钱中扣除了税收之后的剩余部分。国家利用这些税收收入来支付社会保障与维持政府运转。工资税指的是政府对企业支付给工人的工资征税。那么，你认为谁应该承受工资税的负担——是企业还是工人？当政府通过这项立法时，它试图规定税收负担的分摊。根据这项法律，企业支付一半税收，工人支付一半税收。这就是说，一半税收从企业收益中扣除，而另一半税收从工人工资中扣除。而你的工资单上的扣除量就是工人应支付的部分。

但是，对税收归宿的分析表明，法律制定者并不能这样轻而易举地分摊税收负担。为了说明这一点，我们可以把工资税看作对商品征收的税来分析，在这里商品是劳动力，而价格是工资。工资税的关键特征是，它是放在企业支付的工资和工人得到的工资之间的一个楔子，如下图所示。当征收工资税时，工人得到的工资减少了，而企业支付的工资增加了。最后，工人和企业像立法所要求的那样分摊了税收负担。但税收负担在工人和企业之间的这种分摊与立法的分摊无关：图中税收负担的分摊并不一定是一半对一半，而且，如果法律规定向工人征收全部税收或向企业征收全部税收，也会出现同样的结果。

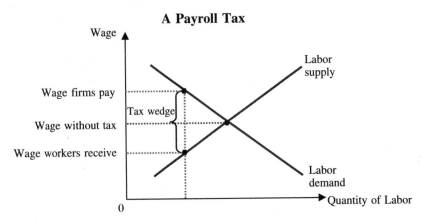

A Payroll Tax

这个例子说明，公共政策争论中往往忽略了税收归宿最基本的结论。法律制定者可以决定税收是来自买者的口袋还是来自卖者的口袋，但它们不能用立法规定税收的真正负担。确切地说，税收归宿取决于供给和需求的力量。

当对一种商品征税时，该商品的买者与卖者分摊税收负担。但税收负担如何确切地分摊呢（How exactly is the tax burden divided?）？只有在极少数情况下是平均分摊的。那么怎样比较（compare）对卖者征税和对买者征税的效应？这个问题的答案取决于需求弹性和供给弹性（depend on the elasticity of demand and the elasticity of supply）。

为了说明税收负担如何分摊，考虑以下两幅图中两个市场的税收影响。在这两种情况下，该图表示了最初的需求曲线、最初的供给曲线和插入买者支付的量与卖者得到的量之间的楔子。两幅图中都没有画出新的供给、需求曲线。哪一条曲线移动取决于税收是向买者征收还是向卖者征收。正如我们已经说明的，这与税收归宿无关。这两幅图的差别是供给和需求的相对弹性。

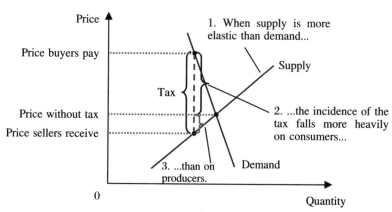

Elastic Supply, Inelastic Demand...

上图表示的是供给相对富有弹性而需求较为缺乏弹性的市场上的税收。也就是说，卖者对某种商品的价格非常敏感，而买者非常不敏感。当对这样的市场征税时，卖者得到的价格并没有下降多少，因此卖者只承担了一小部分负担；与此相比，买者支付的价格大幅度上升，表示买者承担了大部分税收负担。

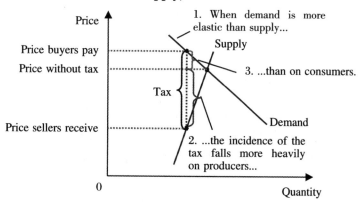

Inelastic Supply, Elastic Demand...

上图表示的是供给较为缺乏弹性而需求相对富有弹性的市场上的税收。在这种情况下，卖者对价格不敏感，而买者却非常敏感。该图表示，当征收税收时，买者支付的价格上升幅度并不大，而卖者得到的价格大幅度下降。因此，卖者承担了大部分税收负担。

上面的两幅图说明了一个关于税收负担分摊的一般结论：税收负担更多地落在缺乏弹性的市场一方身上（The burden of a tax falls more heavily on the side of the market that is less elastic.）。为什么是这样呢？弹性实际上衡量的是当条件变得不利时，买者或卖者离开市场的意愿（measures the willingness of buyers or sellers to leave the market when conditions become unfavorable）。需求弹性小意味着买者对消费这种商品没有适当的替代品（alternatives）。供给弹性小意味着卖者对生产这种商品没有适当的替代品。当对这种商品征税时，市场中拥有较少替代选择的一方不能轻而易举地离开市场，从而必须承担更多的税收负担（The side of the market with fewer good alternatives cannot easily leave the market and must, therefore, bear more of the burden of the tax.）。那么，在工资税中，谁承担更多的税收负担呢？一般说来，劳动力供给缺乏弹性，而劳动力需求则更有弹性，因此更多地由工人承担税收负担。

我们再来看一个很典型的案例。在 1990 年，美国国会针对游艇、私人飞机、皮衣、珠宝和豪华轿车这类商品通过了一项新的奢侈品税，其目的就是向那些承担税收负担最少的人增加税收。由于只有富人能买得起这类奢侈品，所以，对奢侈品征税看似是向富人征税的一种合理方式。

但是，当透过供给与需求来分析问题时，会发现结果与国会所期望的完全不同。比如，考虑游艇市场。游艇的需求是极其富有弹性的。百万富翁不买游艇是很容易的；他们可以用钱去买更大的房子，去欧洲度假，或者留给继承人大笔遗产。与此相比，游艇的供给至少在短期中是较为缺乏弹性的。游艇工厂不能轻而易举地转向其他用途，而且，建造游艇的工人也不愿意由于市场状况的改变而改换职业。

在这种情况下，通过分析我们可以明确做出以下预测：由于富有弹性的需求与缺乏弹性的供给，税收负担主要落在供给者身上。也就是说，对游艇征税的主要负担落在建造游艇的企业和工人身上，因为最后的结果是它们的商品价格下降了，但工人并不会变富裕。因此，奢侈品税收的负担落在中产阶级身上的比落在富人身上的多。

在这种税收付诸实施之后，关于奢侈品税归宿的错误假设很快就显现了出来。奢侈品供给者使国会议员认识到了它们所面临的经济困境。最终美国国会在 1993 年废除了大部分奢侈品税。

重要名词解释

1. **Price ceiling**：a legal maximum on the price at which a good can be sold
2. **Price floor**：a legal minimum on the price at which a good can be sold
3. **Tax incidence**：the study of who bears the burden of taxation

主要图表

1.

A Price Ceiling That Is Binding...

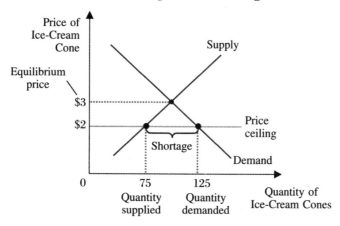

2.

The Price Ceiling on Gasoline Is Binding...

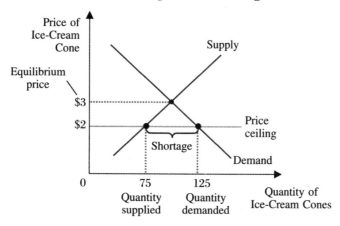

3.

A Price Floor That Is Binding...

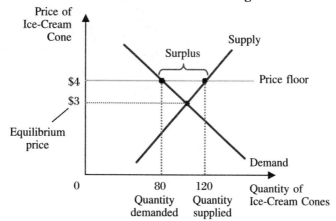

4.

A Payroll Tax

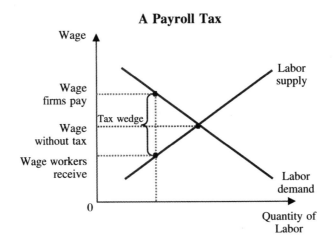

5.

Elastic Supply, Inelastic Demand...

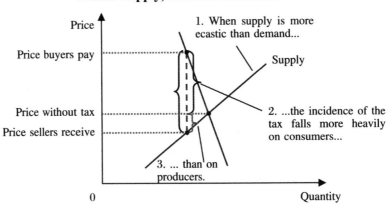

6.

Inelastic Supply, Elastic Demand...

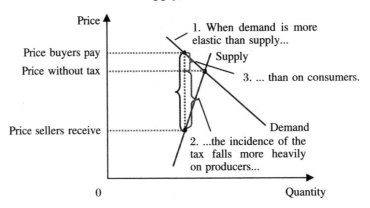

模拟试题

1. Rent-control laws dictate

    a. The exact rent that landlords must charge tenants.

    b. A maximum rent that landlords may charge tenants.

    c. A minimum rent that landlords may charge tenants.

    d. A minimum rent and a maximum rent that landlords may charge tenants.

    e. The fixed rent that landlords charge tenants.

    Key：b

    Analysis：It examines the definition of rent control.

2. Minimum-wage laws dictate

    a. The exact wage that firms must pay workers.

    b. A maximum wage that firms may pay workers.

    c. A minimum wage that firms may pay workers.

    d. A minimum wage and a maximum wage that firms may pay workers.

    e. A minimum wage that firms may pay for teenager workers.

    Key：c

    Analysis：It examines the definition of minimum wage.

3. Price controls are usually enacted

    a. As a means of raising revenue for public purposes.

    b. When policymakers believe that the market price of a good or service is unfair to buyers or sellers.

    c. When policymakers detect inefficiencies in a market.

    d. When inflation is really serious.

    e. All of the above are correct.

    Key：b

    Analysis：Price controls are usually enacted when policymakers believe that the market price is unfair to buyers or sellers.

4. A price ceiling is

    a. Often imposed on markets in which "cutthroat competition" would prevail without a price ceiling.

    b. A legal maximum on the price at which a good can be sold.

    c. Often imposed when sellers of a good are successful in their attempts to convince the government that the market outcome is unfair without a price ceiling.

    d. A source of efficiency in a market.

    e. All of the above are correct.

    Key：b

    Analysis：It examines the definition of price ceiling.

5. Which of the following is the most likely explanation for the imposition of a price ceiling on

the market for milk?

a. Policymakers have studied the effects of the price ceiling carefully, and they recognize that the price ceiling is advantageous for society as a whole.

b. Buyers of milk, recognizing that the price ceiling is good for them, have pressured policymakers into imposing the price ceiling.

c. Sellers of milk, recognizing that the price ceiling is good for them, have pressured policymakers into imposing the price ceiling.

d. Buyers and sellers of milk have agreed that the price ceiling is good for both of them and have therefore pressured policymakers into imposing the price ceiling.

e. All of the above are wrong.

Key: b

Analysis: It depends on the circumstances that who succeed in persuading the government. If the side of demand wins, it will impose the price ceiling. By contrast, if the side of supply wins, it will impose the price floor.

6. Which of the following observations would be consistent with the imposition of a binding price ceiling on a market?

a. A smaller quantity of the good is bought and sold after the price ceiling becomes effective.

b. A smaller quantity of the good is demanded after the price ceiling becomes effective.

c. A larger quantity of the good is supplied after the price ceiling becomes effective.

d. The consumer will enjoy more benefit.

e. All of the above are correct.

Key: a

Analysis: If there is a binding price ceiling, the quantity of bought and sold will decrease, but the demand will not change, leading to the shortage.

7. Suppose the equilibrium price of a physical examination （"physical"） by a doctor is $200, and the government imposes a price ceiling of $150 per physical. As a result of the price ceiling,

a. The demand curve for physicals shifts to the right.

b. The supply curve for physicals shifts to the left.

c. The quantity demanded of physicals increases and the quantity supplied of physicals decreases.

d. The number of physicals performed stays the same.

e. None of them.

Key: c

Analysis: Because $150 is below the equilibrium price($200), more people want to buy and less doctors want to supply. So the shortages appear.

8. As rationing mechanisms, prices

a. And long lines are efficient.

b. Are efficient, but long lines are inefficient.

c. Are inefficient, but long lines are efficient.

d. And long lines are inefficient.

e. It's hard to say.

Key: b

Analysis: In general, the prices are always and the only efficient way to allocate the resources.

9. Long lines

a. And discrimination according to seller bias are both inefficient rationing mechanisms because they both waste buyers' time.

b. And discrimination according to seller bias are both inefficient rationing mechanisms because the good does not necessarily go to the buyer who values it most highly.

c. Are an inefficient rationing mechanism because they waste buyers' time, and discrimination according to seller bias is an inefficient rationing mechanism because the good does not necessarily go to the buyer who values it most highly.

d. Are an inefficient rationing mechanism because the good does not necessarily go to the buyer who values it most highly, and discrimination according to seller bias is an inefficient rationing mechanism because it wastes buyers' time.

e. None of all.

Key: c

Analysis: Long lines waste buyers' time, and discrimination causes the good not necessarily going to the buyer who values it most highly.

10. Economists generally believe that rent control is

a. An efficient and fair way to help the poor.

b. Inefficient, but the best available means of solving a serious social problem.

c. A highly inefficient way to help the poor raise their standard of living.

d. An efficient way to allocate housing, but not a good way to help the poor.

e. An efficient but not fair way to help the real poor.

Key: c

Analysis: Particularly, one economist called rent control "the best way to destroy a city, other than bombing."

11. Which of the following is the most likely explanation for the imposition of a price floor on the market for corn?

a. Policymakers have studied the effects of the price floor carefully, and they recognize that the price floor is advantageous for society as a whole.

b. Buyers and sellers of corn have agreed that the price floor is good for both of them and have therefore pressured policymakers into imposing the price floor.

c. Buyers of corn, recognizing that the price floor is good for them, have pressured policymakers into imposing the price floor.

d. Sellers of corn, recognizing that the price floor is good for them, have pressured policymakers into imposing the price floor.

e. All of the above are wrong.

Key: d

Analysis: Sellers always want the price floor and the buyers always want the price ceiling.

12. A surplus results when

    a. A nonbinding price floor is imposed on a market.

    b. A nonbinding price floor is removed from a market.

    c. A binding price floor is imposed on a market.

    d. A binding price floor is removed from a market.

    e. All of the above are right.

Key: c

Analysis: A binding price floor causes a surplus because quantity supplied is larger than quantity demanded. When there is no binding price floor or the price floor is not binding, the market will keep the original equilibrium.

13. When a binding price floor is imposed on a market to benefit sellers,

    a. Every seller in the market benefits.

    b. Every buyer in the market benefits, too.

    c. Every seller who wants to sell the good will be able to do so, but only if they appeal to the personal biases of the buyers.

    d. Some sellers will not be able to sell any amount of the good.

    e. Some buyers will benefits.

Key: d

Analysis: The price floor is binding if set above the equilibrium price, leading to a surplus.

14. Which of the following is correct?

    a. Workers determine the supply of labor, and firms determine the demand for labor.

    b. Workers determine the demand for labor, and firms determine the supply of labor.

    c. The labor market is a single market for all different types of workers.

    d. The price of the product produced by labor adjusts to balance the supply of labor and the demand for labor.

    e. The price of the product produced by labor determines the demand for labor.

Key: a

Analysis: In the labor market, the wage is the price, workers supply the labor and firms demand the labor.

15. A minimum wage that is set above a market's equilibrium wage will result in

    a. An excess demand for labor, that is, unemployment.

    b. An excess demand for labor, that is, a shortage of workers.

    c. An excess supply of labor, that is, unemployment.

    d. An excess supply of labor, that is, a shortage of workers.

    e. A new equilibrium.

Key: c

Analysis: The wage is higher, so the supply exceeds the demand, leading to unemployment.

16. The term "tax incidence" refers to

    a. Whether buyers or sellers of a good are required to send tax payments to the government.

    b. Whether the demand curve or the supply curve shifts when the tax is imposed.

    c. The distribution of the tax burden between buyers and sellers.

    d. Widespread view that taxes will always be a fact of life.

    e. None of all.

    Key: c

    Analysis: Tax incidence is the study of who bears the burden of a tax.

17. When a tax is placed on the sellers of a product,

    a. Buyers pay more and sellers receive more than they did before the tax.

    b. Buyers pay more and sellers receive less than they did before the tax.

    c. Buyers pay less and sellers receive more than they did before the tax.

    d. Buyers pay less and sellers receive less than they did before the tax.

    e. None of the above.

    Key: b

    Analysis: The taxes place a wedge between the price that buyers pay and the price that sellers receive. In the new equilibrium, buyers pay more for the good, and sellers receive less.

18. If the government levies a $500 tax per car on sellers of cars, then the price received by sellers of cars would

    a. Decrease by less than $500.

    b. Decrease by exactly $500.

    c. Decrease by more than $500.

    d. Increase by an indeterminate amount.

    e. Increase less than $500.

    Key: a

    Analysis: This tax burden will be partly transformed to the buyers, so it must decrease by less than $500.

19. Buyers of a good bear the larger share of the tax burden when a tax is placed on the product for which

    a. The supply is more elastic than the demand.

    b. The demand is more elastic than the supply.

    c. The tax is placed on the sellers of the product.

    d. The tax is placed on the buyers of the product.

    e. a and c are right.

    Key: a

    Analysis: The burden of a tax falls more heavily on the side of the market that is less elastic.

20. Which of the following statements is true?

a. A tax levied on buyers will never be partially paid by sellers.

b. Who actually pays more for a tax depends on the price elasticities of supply and demand.

c. Government can decide who actually pays a tax.

d. A tax levied on sellers always will be passed on completely to buyers.

e. A tax burden falls more heavily on the side of the market that is less inelastic.

Key: b

Analysis: Buyers and sellers share the burden of the tax. And the burden of a tax falls more heavily on the side of the market that is less elastic. Government cannot decide who actually pays a tax.

Consumers, Producers and the Efficiency of Markets
消费者、生产者与市场的有效性

主要内容和概念讲解

在开始这一章之前，让我们先回顾一下之前学习过的市场均衡（market equilibrium）概念，我们知道，市场自身的供求力量决定了均衡价格与均衡数量。但是，这个均衡的价格与数量是否使得买者与卖者的福利达到最大化了呢（Do the equilibrium price and quantity maximize the total welfare of buyers and sellers?）？要回答这个问题，我们就要讨论福利经济学（welfare economics）。如果说市场均衡反映了市场是如何分配稀缺资源（scarce resources）的，那么福利经济学就是评判这种市场配置（market allocation）是否是令人满意的分支学科。

福利经济学是一门研究资源配置如何影响经济生活（economic well-being）的学科。消费者与生产者期望通过参与市场活动达到利益最大化，也就是说，市场使得这两方的福利达到最大化，同时达到市场均衡。下面我们来介绍一组福利经济学中的重要概念——消费者剩余与生产者剩余。消费者剩余（consumer surplus）度量的是消费者也就是买方的经济福利；相对地，生产者剩余（producer surplus）度量生产者即卖方的经济福利。接下来我们来看看具体如何计算。

要计算消费者剩余，首先我们必须知道消费者的意愿支出（willingness to pay）是多少，也就是消费者愿意且能够（willing and able）为这个商品付出的最大价格，它体现了买方对产品或劳务的价值估计。而消费者剩余就是消费者的意愿支出与实际购买支出之差。下面我们通过一个具体的例子来分析。假设有四个可能的消费者，他们的意愿支出如下表所示：

Buyer	Wilingness to Pay
Jack	$100
Peter	80
Bob	70
Mike	50

根据这张表，我们就能列出需求计划表（demand schedule）并画出需求曲线（demand curve）。比如当商品的价格高于100美元时，没有一个人愿意购买此商品，也就是需求量为0，当价格高于80小于100美元时，只有 Jack 一人愿意购买，因此需求量为1，以此类推，可得到需求计划表，如下图：

Price	Buyer	Quantity Demanded
More than $ 100	None	0
$ 80 to $ 100	Jack	1

Price	Buyer	Quantity Demanded
$ 70 to $ 80	Jack, Peter	2
$ 50 to $ 70	Jack, Peter, Bob	3
$ 50 or less	Jack, Peter, Bob, Mike	4

由此，可以画出如下的需求曲线：

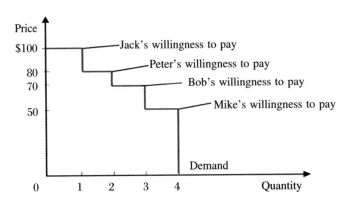

如果市场上商品的售价 Price=80 美元，那么 Jack 的消费者剩余就应该是 100-80=20（美元），如下图(a)所示；如果 Price=70 美元，那么购买者变成 Jack 和 Peter，他们各自的消费者剩余分别为 30 美元和 10 美元，因此总消费者剩余为 40 美元，如下图(b)所示。

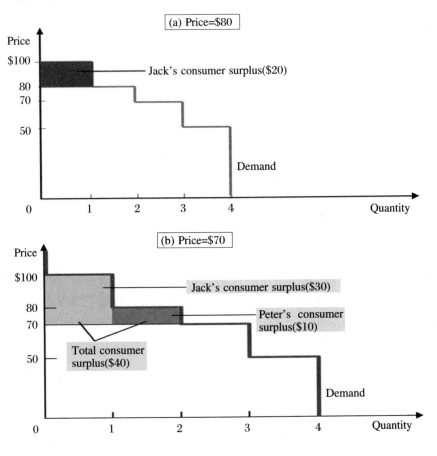

由以上两幅图我们可以看到,在消费者需求曲线之下而位于价格线之上的区域面积就是市场中的消费者剩余。我们已经知道了消费者剩余的计算方法,接下来我们来看一看价格是如何影响消费者的福利也就是消费者剩余的。

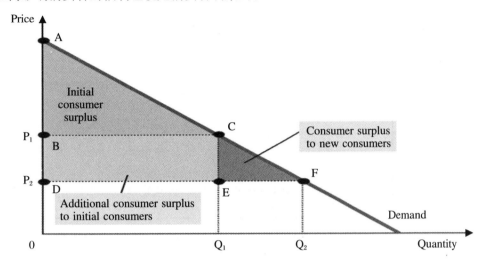

如上图,向右下方倾斜的直线代表需求曲线。如果市场价格定在 P_1 时,市场上的消费者剩余为三角形 ABC 的面积。当市场价格下降至 P_2 时,消费者剩余增大为三角形 ADF 的面积,这代表消费者福利的增加,其中既包括原来的消费者因为商品价格下降而获得的额外利益(长方形 BCED),也包括由于价格下降市场上新增加的消费群体的利润(三角形 CEF)。

学习完何为消费者剩余后,就更容易理解什么是生产者剩余了。生产者剩余(producer surplus)度量生产者在参与市场活动中获得的利润,它是生产者卖出商品所得减去生产该商品的成本(seller's cost)。同样,我们假设市场上只有四个生产者,生产成本分别如下表所示:(假设只有当市场价格高于生产成本时才会出售)

Seller	Cost
Marina	$ 900
Nancy	800
Crystal	600
Nicole	500

用同样的方法,可以画出供给曲线,并用供给曲线得出生产者剩余。

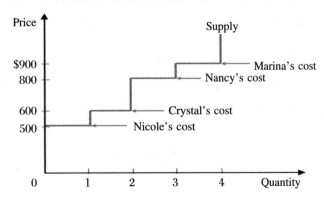

当市场价格 Price=600 美元时，市场上只有 Nicole 一个供给者，因此生产者剩余为 600−500=100（美元），如图（a）所示。而当市场 Price=800 美元时，市场上有两个供应商。他们的生产者剩余如下图（b）所示。

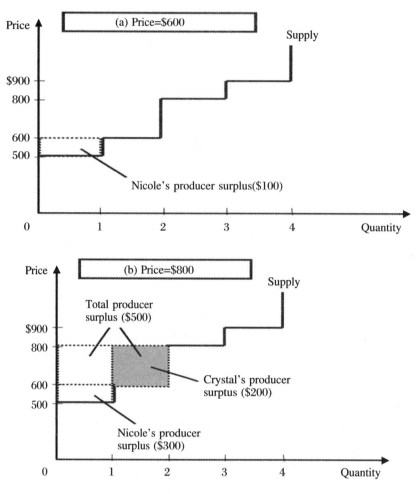

由此可见，生产者剩余是供给曲线之上而位于市场价格线之下的区域面积。市场价格对生产者剩余的影响也可以通过下图得出：

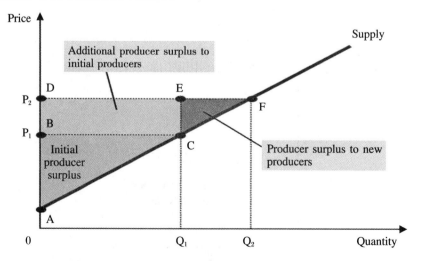

如上图,向右上方倾斜的直线代表供给曲线。如果市场价格定在 P_1 时,市场上的生产者剩余为三角形 ABC 的面积。当市场价格上升至 P_2 时,生产者剩余增大为三角形 ADF 的面积,价格上升代表生产者福利的增加,其中既包括原来的生产者因为商品价格上升而获得的额外利益(长方形 BCED),也包括由于价格上升市场上新增加的供给群体利润(三角形 CEF)。

在充分了解了消费者剩余和生产者剩余过后,我们就可进入本章的核心问题——市场效率(market efficiency)。在一个自由市场(free market)中资源配置是不是各个行为体都满意的呢?我们运用本章上面所描述的消费者剩余和生产者剩余两个概念来探讨这个问题。

Consumer Surplus = Value to Buyers – Amount Paid by Buyers

Producer Surplus = Amount Received by Sellers – Cost to Sellers

因此:

Total Surplus = Consumer Surplus + Producer Surplus

= Value to Buyers – Cost to Sellers

那么我们就可以这样定义市场效率:它是使得社会所有成员的总剩余最大化时的资源配置。同时,在考虑市场效率时,作为一个经济计划者,我们需要把平等也就是生活资源在买卖双方之间的公平分配考虑进去。下图可以很好地说明市场效率。

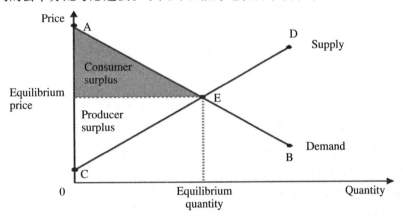

我们知道,自由市场有几个隐含意义。首先,商品会最先分配给那些出价最高的消费者;其次,成本最低的生产者最先卖出商品。由此,我们可以探讨自由市场决定的商品数量是否使消费者和生产者剩余最大化。我们不妨看下面这样一幅图:

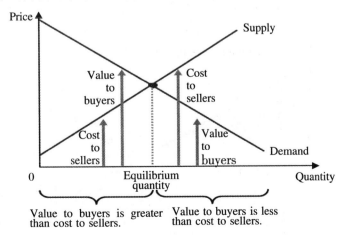

可以看到，当市场上商品数量少于均衡数量时，买者的意愿支出大于卖者的成本，由总剩余的公式可知，此时多卖出一单位商品，社会总剩余会增加。因此市场上的商品数量增加。相反，当市场上商品数量多于均衡数量时，买者的意愿支出小于卖者的成本，由总剩余的公式可知，此时多卖出一单位商品，社会总剩余会减少。因此为了使社会福利最大化，市场中的商品会减少，直至达到均衡数量。由此我们就能得出这样一个结论：自由市场上决定的均衡数量达到了社会福利的最大化水平。因此，作为经济计划者的我们，可以放心把产量交由市场自行决定。

而当市场达不到完全竞争，即不是自由市场时，市场势力（market power）就会开始起作用。当市场势力开始起作用时，市场便开始失灵，因为它使得市场价格和交易数量偏离均衡价格和均衡数量。这里我们引入一个新的概念——外部性（externality）。外部性是指由于市场活动而给除买者与卖者之外的第三方造成的成本。比如，你在地铁上吃了个韭菜馅的大包子，空气中弥漫的韭菜味就对你身边的人造成了强烈的负效用，损害了他的社会福利，这就是负外部性。我们在考虑社会福利时必须把外部性考虑进去，否则此时市场自身做出的决策就是失效的，也就是说此时达到的均衡也是失效的。我们会在之后的章节中进一步讲解外部性的有关内容。

重要名词解释

1. **Welfare Economics**：the study of how the allocation of resources affects economic well-being
2. **Consumer Surplus**：economic welfare from the buyer's side
3. **Producer Surplus**：economic welfare from the seller's side
4. **Market Efficiency**：the property of a resource allocation of maximizing the total surplus received by all members of society
5. **Externalities**：created when a market outcome affects individuals other than buyers and sellers in that market

主要图表

1.

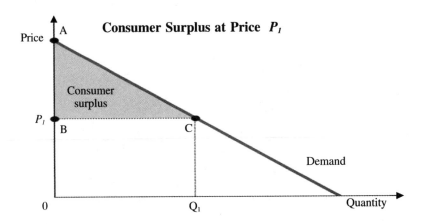

2.

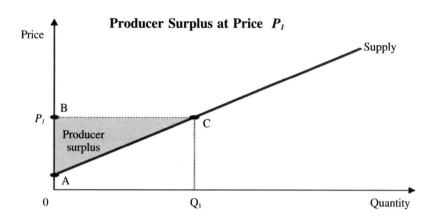

3.

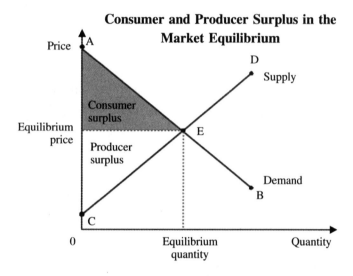

1. Welfare economics is the study of how

    A. The allocation of resources affects economic well-being.

    B. A price ceiling compares to a price floor.

    C. The government helps poor people.

    D. A consumer's optimal choice affects his/her demand curve.

    E. How technology is best put to use in the production of goods and services.

    Key: A

    Analysis: It examines the definition of welfare economics.

2. Which of the Ten Principles of Economics does welfare economics explain more fully?

    A. The cost of something is what you give up to get it.

    B. Rational people think at the margin.

    C. Markets are usually a good way to organize economic activity.

    D. People respond to incentives.

E. People face tradeoffs.

Key: C

Analysis: Definition.

3. Welfare economics explains which of the following in the market for DVDs?

   A. The government sets the price of DVDs; firms respond to the price by producing a specific level of output.

   B. The government sets the quantity of DVDs; firms respond to the quantity by charging a specific price.

   C. The market equilibrium price for DVDs maximizes the total welfare to DVD buyers and sellers.

   D. The market equilibrium price for DVDs maximizes consumer welfare but minimizes producer welfare.

   E. None of them.

   Key: C

   Analysis: The total welfare maximization will be realized at the market equilibrium price.

4. The maximum price that a buyer will pay for a good is called the

   A. Cost.

   B. Willingness to pay.

   C. Equity.

   D. Efficiency.

   E. Deadweight loss.

   Key: B

   Analysis: The definition of willingness to pay.

5. A consumer's willingness to pay directly measures

   A. The extents to which advertising and other external forces have influenced the consumer's preferences.

   B. The cost of a good to the buyer.

   C. How much a buyer values a good.

   D. Consumer surplus.

   E. The price they afford.

   Key: C

   Analysis: Willingness to pay directly measures the buyer's value for a good.

6. A demand curve reflects each of the following except the

   A. Willingness to pay of all buyers in the market.

   B. Value each buyer in the market places on the good.

   C. Highest price buyers are willing to pay for each quantity.

   D. Ability of buyers to obtain the quantity they desire.

   E. C and D

Key: D

Analysis: A demand curve does not reflect the ability of buyers to obtain the quantity they desire.

7. Consumer surplus

   A. Is the amount of a good that a consumer can buy at a price below equilibrium price.

   B. Is the amount a consumer is willing to pay minus the amount the consumer actually pays.

   C. Is the number of consumers who are excluded from a market because of scarcity.

   D. Measures how much a seller values a good.

   E. Is the value of a good to a consumer.

   Key: B

   Analysis: It examines the definition of consumer surplus.

8. On a graph, the area below a demand curve and above the price measures

   A. Producer surplus.

   B. Consumer surplus.

   C. Deadweight loss.

   D. Willingness to pay.

   E. The return of the consumer.

   Key: B

   Analysis: It examines the typical graph of surplus.

9. Consumer surplus in a market can be represented by the

   A. Area below the demand curve and above the price.

   B. Distance from the demand curve to the horizontal axis.

   C. Distance from the demand curve to the vertical axis.

   D. Area below the demand curve and above the horizontal axis.

   E. None of them.

   Key: A

   Analysis: Consumer surplus is the amount a consumer is willing to pay minus the amount the consumer actually pays. So it can be represented by the area below the demand curve and above the price.

10. In a market, the marginal buyer is the buyer

    A. Whose willingness to pay is higher than that of all other buyers and potential buyers.

    B. Whose willingness to pay is lower than that of all other buyers and potential buyers.

    C. Who is willing to buy exactly one unit of the good.

    D. Who would be the first to leave the market if the price were any higher.

    E. Who is willing to pay more than the price.

    Key: D

    Analysis: The marginal buyer is the buyer whose willingness to pay equals the price. If the price is a bit higher, he would leave the market.

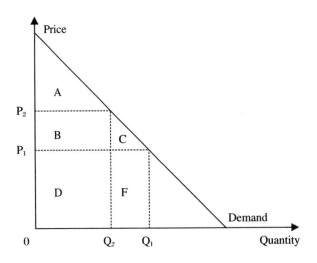

11. Refer to the figure above. When the price is P_1, consumer surplus is

   A. A.

   B. A+B.

   C. A+B+C.

   D. A+B+D.

   E. A+B+C+D+F.

   Key: C

   Analysis: Consumer surplus in a market can be represented by the area below the demand curve and above the price.

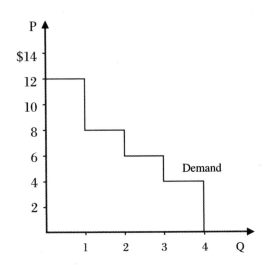

12. Refer to the figure above. If the price of the good is $6, then consumer surplus is

   A. $4.

   B. $6.

   C. $8.

   D. $10.

   E. $12.

Key: C

Analysis:（12–6）+（8–6）=8

13. Cost is a measure of the

    A. Seller's willingness to sell.

    B. Seller's producer surplus.

    C. Producer shortage.

    D. Seller's willingness to buy.

    E. Seller's opportunity cost.

    Key: A

    Analysis: The definition of the willingness to sell.

14. Producer surplus is

    A. Measured by using the demand curve for a good.

    B. Always a negative number for sellers in a competitive market.

    C. The amount a seller is paid minus the cost of production.

    D. The opportunity cost of production minus the cost of producing goods that go unsold.

    E. The costs to sellers of participating in a market.

    Key: C

    Analysis: The definition of the producer surplus.

15. Karen sharpens knives in her spare time for extra income. Buyers of her service are willing to pay $2.50 per knife for as many knives as Karen is willing to sharpen. On a particular day, she is willing to sharpen the first knife for $1.75, the second knife for $2.25, the third knife for $2.75, and the fourth knife for $3.25. Assume Karen is rational in deciding how many knives to sharpen. Her producer surplus is

    A. $0.25.

    B. $0.50.

    C. $1.00.

    D. $1.75.

    E. $2.00.

    Key: C

    Analysis: Karen will sharpen 2 knives. If she continues to sharpen, the price 2.50 < her willingness（2.75）, so she will stop sharpening. Then 2.50×2–（1.75+2.25）=1.

16. At Nick's Bakery, the cost to make homemade chocolate cake is $3 per cake. As a result of selling three cakes, Nick experiences a producer surplus in the amount of $19.50. Nick must be selling his cakes for

    A. $6.50 each.

    B. $7.50 each.

    C. $9.50 each.

    D. $10.50 each.

    E. $12.50 each.

Key: C

Analysis: 19.5/3+3=9.5

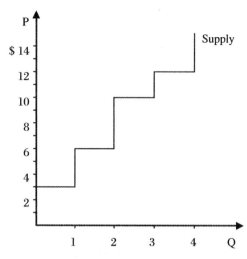

17. Refer to the figure above. If the price of the good is $8.50, then producer surplus is

    A. $2.50.

    B. $6.50.

    C. $8.00.

    D. $11.00.

    E. $13.00.

Key: C

Analysis: $(8.5-3)+(8.5-6)=8$

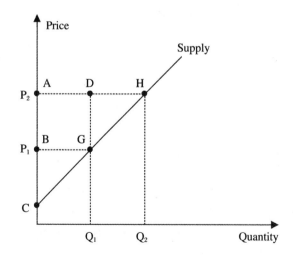

18. Refer to the figure above. When the price rises from P_1 to P_2, which area represents the increase in producer surplus to existing producers?

    A. BCG

    B. ACH

    C. DGH

D. ABGD

E. ABGH

Key：D

Analysis：DGH is the producer surplus to new producers.

19. Total surplus is equal to

    A. Value to buyers – Profit to sellers.

    B. Value to buyers – Cost to sellers.

    C. Consumer surplus × producer surplus.

    D. （Consumer surplus + Producer surplus）× Equilibrium quantity.

    E. Value to buyers + Profit to sellers.

    Key：B

    Analysis：It also equals consumer surplus + producer surplus.

20. The decisions of buyers and sellers that affect people who are not participants in the market create

    A. Market power.

    B. Externalities.

    C. Profiteering.

    D. Market equilibrium.

    E. Market failure

    Key：B

    Analysis：It examines the definition of externalities.

Application: the Cost of Taxation
应用：税收成本

主要内容和概念讲解

上一章我们讨论了有关福利经济学的基本内容，也了解了福利经济学是研究资源配置对经济生活的影响的。买方与卖方通过参与市场活动获得利益，而在自由市场下达到的均衡正好可以使得它们的社会总福利水平最大化。但是，这只是考虑了消费者与生产者的状况，如果政府加入，情况会变成什么样呢？我们知道不论是买方还是卖方，都要向政府交纳税收。那么，我们就从税收入手，看一看税收是如何影响市场参与者的经济生活的。

首先，我们知道，无论商品的税收是由买者交纳还是由卖者支出，无疑都会导致这样一种负面效应：要么消费者需要支付更多的钱用于购买商品，要么生产者的销售利润降低。也就是说，由于税收的存在，消费者支付的价格不再等于生产者的所得，其中有一部分要作为税收上交政府。我们不妨看一下下面这幅图：

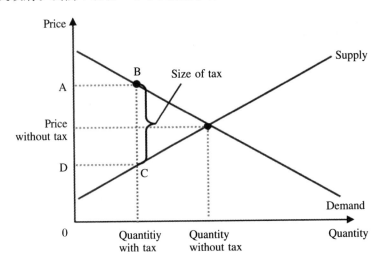

可以看出，当不存在税收时，市场达到均衡数量与均衡价格，但是当税收存在时，买价等于卖价与税收之和。由于卖价降低，生产者的销售量会沿着供给曲线向下移动，直到买价与卖价之差足以弥补税收才停止变动。此时，从图中可以很明显地看出来，税收存在状态下达到的商品销售量明显低于自由市场中的均衡数量，也就是说，此时市场中的商品规模减小了。如果假设 T 为单位商品的税额（size of tax），Q 为销售商品的数量，则政府税收（government's tax revenue）即为 T×Q，在上图中我们就可以表示为长方形 ABCD 的面积。而对于税收，我们可以认为这是政府福利，也包括在社会总剩余中。

那么，结合上一章学到的消费者剩余和生产者剩余的知识，就可以分析税收是如何影响社会福利的。我们先来看下面这幅图：

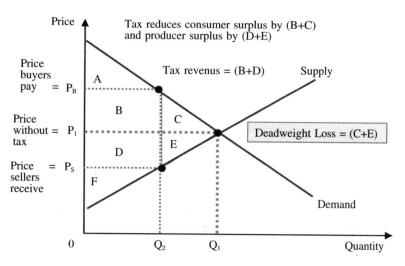

如上图，我们知道，当不存在税收时，自由市场达到均衡价格 P_1 和均衡数量 Q_1，社会总剩余(social total surplus)为(A+B+C+D+E+F)面积之和，其中消费者剩余为(A+B+C)，生产者剩余为(D+E+F)。而在政府征税后，消费者支出价格为 P_B，于是消费者剩余变为 A(需求曲线与支出价格之间的面积)，而生产者实际收入价格则为 P_S，生产者剩余变为 F(供给曲线与生产者实际收入价格之间的面积)。因此我们可以知道，由于税收的存在，消费者剩余减少了(B+C)，而生产者剩余减少了(D+E)。这减少的福利中有(B+D)变为政府税收，是政府福利，而(C+E)就成了税收造成的无谓损失(deadweight loss)，也就是由于市场扭曲而造成的社会总剩余减少。我们可以用下表来总结我们上述的分析：

	Without Tax	**With Tax**	**Change**
Consumer Surplus	A+B+C	A	−(B+C)
Producer Surplus	D+E+F	F	−(D+E)
Tax Revenue	None	B+D	+(B+D)
Total Surplus	A+B+C+D+E+F	A+B+D+F	−(C+E)

这时，我们就可以得出税收对社会福利造成的影响。从整体上说，税收会导致社会总福利的无谓损失(deadweight loss)。而这其中的福利变化，包括消费者剩余和生产者剩余的减少、政府福利由于税收的增加，以及最终的无谓损失。

接下来，我们来讨论一下有关无谓损失(deadweight loss)的有关问题。首先，无谓损失到底是如何形成的呢？从上述分析中我们不难发现，无谓损失是由于税收的存在而使得买价与卖价之间存在差额，从而使得买方与卖方无法从交易中实现它们的全部利润。而在交易中损失的利润造成了社会福利的无谓损失。那又是什么决定了税收导致无谓损失的大小呢？由上述图形描述，我们知道无谓损失的大小就是小三角形的面积，那么是什么决定了小三角形的面积呢？那就是价格变动一个单位时，消费者的需求数量与生产者的供给数量的变化状况。而这很容易使我们联想到之前学过的一个概念——价格弹性(price elasticity)。也就是说，无谓损失的大小取决于需求曲线与供给曲线的价格弹性。我们不妨用下图来具体分析一下。

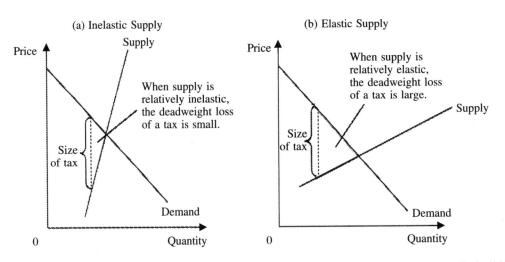

如图(a)和(b)所示,我们分别给出了供给曲线弹性变化的两种情况。当供给曲线弹性小时,供给曲线的斜率大,也就是说,在固定单位税额(size of tax)的情况下,它与需求曲线形成的小三角形面积明显小于供给弹性大的情况。这就表明,供给曲线弹性越大,税收所造成的无谓损失越大。

同理可分析需求曲线变化的两种情况,如图(c)和(d)。当需求曲线弹性小时,需求曲线的斜率大,也就是说,在固定单位税额的情况下,它与供给曲线形成的小三角形面积,明显小于需求弹性大的情况。这就表明,需求曲线弹性越大,收税所造成的无谓损失越大。

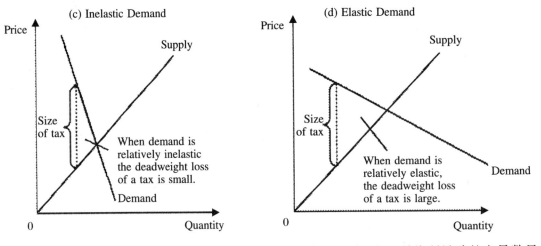

因此,可以得出一个结论,当需求与供给的弹性越大时,由于税收所导致的交易数量减少的越多,社会总福利水平损失越大,即由此造成的社会无谓损失也就越大。对于这个结论一些经济学家也有很多自己的看法,比如一些经济学家认为对劳动力征税(labor taxes)会更大程度扭曲经济,造成更大的社会无谓损失,因为他们认为劳动力的供给曲线富有弹性。又例如,那些可以自行决定工作时间的自由作家、以及那些可以自行决定退休时间的老年人,甚至那些从事不法事业的人员,他们都有更多自由的选择,因此对于外界刺激,比如工资价格变动时,他们会做出更大反应。

最后我们来研究一下,当税额变动时对无谓损失和税收的影响。下面三幅图很好地说明了税额由大到小时无谓损失和税收大小的变化。

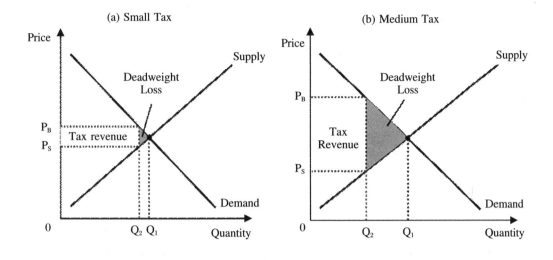

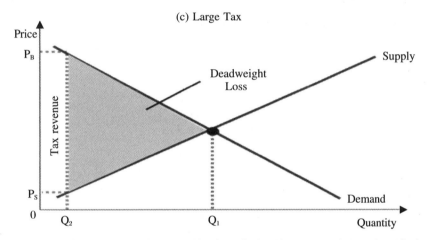

可以看到，随着单位税额的增加，无谓损失一直在增加，而且增速也在不断变大，也就是说增长得越来越快。而对于税收收入，当单位税额很小时，税收收入也很少，随着单位税额的增大，税收收入不断增加，但当增加到一定程度时，随着税额的增加，税收收入反而会开始减小，因为此时高税额开始缩小市场份额，也就是说单位税额的增加无法弥补由于交易数量减少所带来的损失。可以用下面两幅图来表示：

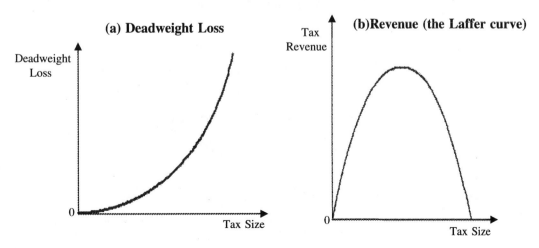

上图(b)用于描述单位税额与政府税收收入之间的关系，这里有一个专门名词叫做拉斐曲线(Laffer curve)。而拉斐(Laffer)和里根(Reagan)共同提出了卖方经济(supply-side economics)的概念，他们认为适当减少税额，可以吸引更多人加入生产，从而提高增加税收收入的潜能。

重要名词解释

1. **Tax revenue**：the size of the tax × the quantity of the good sold
2. **Deadweight loss**：the fall in total surplus; the fall in the sum of consumer surplus, producer surplus and tax revenue
3. **The Laffer curve**：a curve depicts the relationship between tax rates and tax revenue
4. **Supply-side economics**：the views of Reagan and Laffer who proposed that a tax cut would induce more people to work and thereby have the potential to increase tax revenues

主要图表

1.

The Effects of a Tax

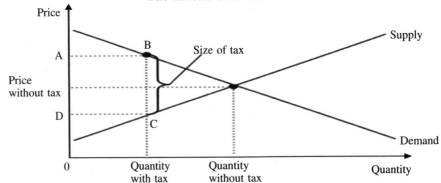

2.

How a Tax Affects Welfare

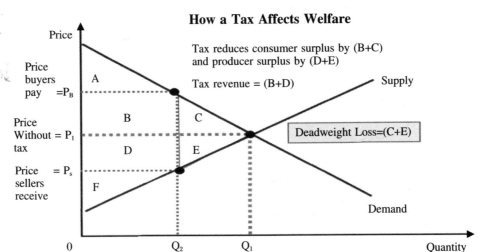

3.

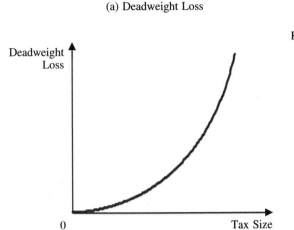

(a) Deadweight Loss

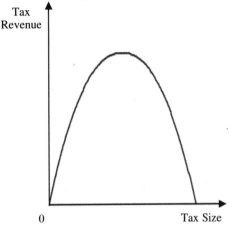

(b) Revenue (the Laffer curve)

模拟试题

1. To fully understand how taxes affect economic well-being, we must
    A. Assume that economic well-being is not affected if all tax revenue is spent on goods and services for the people who are being taxed.
    B. Compare the taxes raised in the United States with those raised in other countries, especially France.
    C. Compare the reduced welfare of buyers and sellers to the amount of revenue the government rises.
    D. Take into account the fact that almost all taxes reduce the welfare of buyers, increase the welfare of sellers, and raise revenue for the government.
    E. Compare the profits earned by firms to the losses incurred by consumers.
    Key：C
    Analysis：It examines the understanding of the taxes and economic welfare.
2. When a tax is levied on a good, the buyers and sellers of the good share the burden,
    A. Provided the tax is levied on the sellers.
    B. Provided the tax is levied on the buyers.
    C. Provided a portion of the tax is levied on the buyers, with the remaining portion levied on the sellers.
    D. Regardless of how the tax is levied.
    E. All of the above ore wrong.
    Key：D
    Analysis：It does not matter whether a tax on a good is levied on buyers or sellers of the good. When taxed a good, the price paid by buyers rises, and the price received by sellers falls.
3. When a tax is placed on a product, the price paid by buyers
    A. Rises, and the price received by sellers rises.

B. Rises, and the price received by sellers falls.

C. Falls, and the price received by sellers rises.

D. Falls, and the price received by sellers falls.

E. Rises, and the price received by sellers remains the same.

Key: B

Analysis: It examines the understanding of the effects of a tax.

4. A tax affects

   A. Buyers only.

   B. Sellers only.

   C. Buyers and sellers only.

   D. Buyers, sellers, and the government.

   E. The government.

   Key: D

   Analysis: A tax affects three group: buyers, sellers, and the government.

5. The government's benefit from a tax can be measured by

   A. Consumer surplus.

   B. Producer surplus.

   C. Tax revenue.

   D. Total surplus.

   E. All of the above are correct.

   Key: C

   Analysis: Tax revenue is the government's benefit.

6. What happens to the total surplus in a market when the government imposes a tax?

   A. Total surplus increases by the amount of the tax.

   B. Total surplus increases but by less than the amount of the tax.

   C. Total surplus decreases.

   D. Total surplus is unaffected by the tax.

   E. Total surplus decreases to zero.

   Key: C

   Analysis: The losses to buyers and sellers exceed the revenue raised by the government. This fall in total surplus is called the deadweight loss.

7. When a good is taxed,

   A. Both buyers and sellers of the good are made worse off.

   B. Only buyers are made worse off, because they ultimately bear the burden of the tax.

   C. Only sellers are made worse off, because they ultimately bear the burden of the tax.

   D. Neither buyers nor sellers are made worse off, since tax revenue is used to provide goods and services that would otherwise not be provided in a market economy.

   E. At last, the tax revenue is used to provide public goods and services, so it will be better off.

   Key: A

   Analysis: The consumer surplus and the producer surplus both decrease. The losses to buyers and sellers exceed the revenue raised by the government.

8. Deadweight loss is the

    A. Decline in total surplus resulted from a tax.

    B. Decline in government revenue when taxes are reduced in a market.

    C. Decline in consumer surplus when a tax is placed on buyers.

    D. Loss of profits to business firms when a tax is imposed.

    E. Decline in producer surplus when a tax is placed on sellers.

    Key: A

    Analysis: The fall in total surplus is called the deadweight loss.

9. For good B, the supply curve is the typical upward-sloping straight line, and the demand curve is the typical downward-sloping straight line. When good B is taxed, the area on the relevant supply-and-demand graph that represents

    A. Government's tax revenue is a rectangle.

    B. The deadweight loss of the tax is a triangle.

    C. The loss of consumer surplus caused by the tax is neither a rectangle nor a triangle.

    D. The loss of producer surplus caused by the tax is neither a rectangle nor a triangle.

    E. All of the above are correct.

    Key: E

    Analysis: It examines the understanding of the typical graph of deadweight loss.

10. In the market for widgets, the supply curve is the typical upward-sloping straight line, and the demand curve is the typical downward-sloping straight line. The equilibrium quantity in the market for widgets is $200 per month when there is no tax. Then a tax of $5 per widget is imposed. As a result, the government is able to raise $750 per month in tax revenue. We can conclude that the equilibrium quantity of widgets has fallen by

    A. 25 per month.

    B. 50 per month.

    C. 75 per month.

    D. 100 per month.

    E. 125 per month.

    Key: B

    Analysis: 200−750/5=50

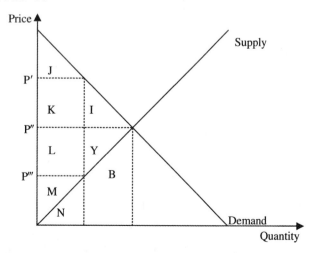

11. Refer to the figure above. Suppose the government imposes a tax of P′—P‴. The area measured by I+Y represents the

A. Deadweight loss due to the tax.

B. Loss in consumer surplus due to the tax.

C. Loss in producer surplus due to the tax.

D. Total surplus before the tax.

E. Tax revenue.

Key: A

Analysis: It examines the understanding of the graph of deadweight loss.

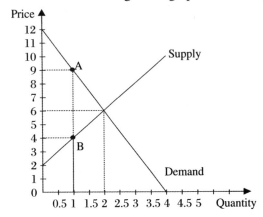

12. Refer to the figure above. The loss of producer surplus for those sellers of the good who continue to sell it after the tax is imposed is

A. $0.

B. $1.

C. $2.

D. $3.

E. $4.

Key: C

Analysis: Notice that "who continue to sell it after the tax is imposed" is different from "the sellers dropping out of the market". 2×1=2.

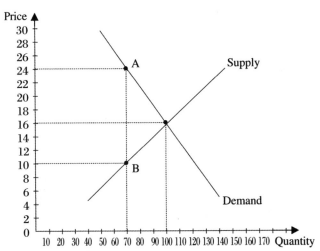

13. Refer to the figure above. The tax results in a loss of producer surplus that amounts to

   A. $90.

   B. $180.

   C. $420.

   D. $510.

   E. $210.

   Key: D

   Analysis: （100+70）×（16−10）/2=510

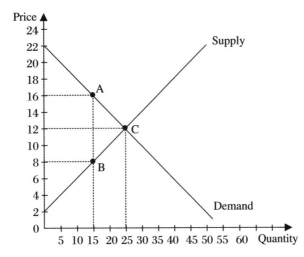

14. Refer to the figure above. The deadweight loss associated with this tax amounts to

   A. $60 and this figure represents the amount by which tax revenue to the government exceeds the combined loss of producer and consumer surpluses.

   B. $60 and this figure represents the surplus that is lost because the tax discourages mutually advantageous trades between buyers and sellers.

   C. $40 and this figure represents the amount by which tax revenue to the government exceeds the combined loss of producer and consumer surpluses.

   D. $40 and this figure represent the surplus that is lost because the tax discourages mutually advantageous trades between buyers and sellers.

   E. All of the above are wrong.

   Key: D

   Analysis: The triangle ABC represents the deadweight loss. （16−8）× （25−15）/2=40.

15. The price elasticities of supply and demand affect

   A. Both the size of the deadweight loss from a tax and the tax incidence.

   B. The size of the deadweight loss from a tax but not the tax incidence.

   C. The tax incidence but not the size of the deadweight loss from a tax.

   D. Neither the size of the deadweight loss from a tax nor the tax incidence.

   E. Either the size of the deadweight loss from a tax or the tax incidence.

   Key: A

Analysis: It examines the understanding of deadweight loss and tax incidence.

16. Buyers of a product will bear the larger part of the tax burden, and sellers will bear a smaller part of the tax burden, when the

    A. Tax is placed on the sellers of the product.

    B. Tax is placed on the buyers of the product.

    C. Supply of the product is more elastic than the demand for the product.

    D. Demand for the product is more elastic than the supply of the product.

    E. Supply of the product is elastic, and the demand for the product is inelastic.

    Key: C

    Analysis: The elasticities of supply and demand measure how much sellers and buyers respond to the changes in the price and, therefore, determine how much the tax distorts the market outcome. Hence, the greater the elasticities of supply and demand are, the greater the deadweight loss of a tax shall be.

17. The deadweight loss from a $1 tax will be smallest in a market with

    A. Inelastic supply and elastic demand.

    B. Inelastic supply and inelastic demand.

    C. Elastic supply and elastic demand.

    D. Elastic supply and inelastic demand.

    E. Unit elastic supply and unit elastic demand.

    Key: B

    Analysis: The greater the elasticities of supply and demand are, the greater the deadweight loss of a tax shall be.

18. Other things equal, the deadweight loss of a tax

    A. Decreases as the size of the tax increases.

    B. Increases as the size of the tax increases, but the increase in the deadweight loss is less rapid than the increase in the size of the tax.

    C. Increases as the size of the tax increases, and the increase in the deadweight loss is more rapid than the increase in the size of the tax.

    D. Increases as the price elasticity of demand and/or supply increase, but the deadweight loss does not change as the size of the tax increases.

    E. All of the above are wrong.

    Key: C

    Analysis: As the size of a tax rises, the deadweight loss grows larger and larger. Indeed, the deadweight loss of a tax rises even more rapidly than the size of the tax.

19. Labor taxes may distort labor markets greatly if

    A. Labor supply is highly inelastic.

    B. Many workers choose to work 40 hours per week regardless of their earnings.

    C. The number of hours many part-time workers want to work is very sensitive to the wage rate.

D. "Underground" workers do not respond to changes in the wages of legal jobs because they prefer not to pay taxes.

E. Elderly can't choose when to retire.

Key: C

Analysis: We can eliminate the wrong choices one by one.

20. Suppose the tax on liquor is increased so that the tax goes from being a "medium" tax to being a "large" tax. As a result, it is likely that

A. Tax revenue increases, and the deadweight loss increases.

B. Tax revenue increases, and the deadweight loss decreases.

C. Tax revenue decreases, and the deadweight loss increases.

D. Tax revenue decreases, and the deadweight loss decreases.

E. A and D

Key: C

Analysis: As the size of a tax increases, the deadweight loss quickly gets larger. By contrast, tax revenue first rises with the size of a tax, but then, as the tax gets larger, the market shrinks so much that tax revenue starts to fall.

21. A person's tax liability refers to

A. The percentage of income that a person must pay in taxes.

B. The amount of tax a person owes to the government.

C. The amount of tax the government is required to refund to each person.

D. Deductions that can be legally subtracted from a person's income each year.

E. The amount of income tax a person owes to the government.

Key: B

Analysis: It examines the definition of tax liability. With respect to paying income taxes, an individual's tax liability (how much he/she owes) is based on total income.

22. The government taxes corporate income on the basis of

A. Profit.

B. The amount the firm receives for the goods or services it sells.

C. The number of employees.

D. Average profit.

E. All of the above are correct.

Key: A

Analysis: Corporate income tax means taxing each corporation based on its profit. (taxed twice)

23. Corporate profits are

A. Included in payroll taxes.

B. Exempt from taxes.

C. Taxed twice, once as profit and once as dividends.

D. Taxed to pay for medicare.

E. C and D

Key: C

Analysis: It examines the definition of corporate income tax.

24. In the United States, the payroll tax is also called a

    A. Dividend income tax.

    B. Social insurance tax.

    C. Value added tax.

    D. Capital gains tax.

    E. Transfer payments

    Key: B

    Analysis: Revenue from these taxes（the payroll tax）is earmarked to pay for social security and medicare. Payroll Taxes ≈ Social Insurance Taxes.

25. A tax on the wages that a firm pays its workers is called

    A. An income tax.

    B. An excise tax.

    C. A consumption tax.

    D. A payroll tax.

    E. Social insurance taxes.

    Key: D

    Analysis: Tax on the wages that a firm pays its workers is called the payroll taxes.

26. A transfer payment is a government payment

    A. To companies that provide goods or services to government agencies.

    B. Designed to transfer funds from one government agency to another.

    C. Which transfers revenue from the federal government to state government.

    D. Not made in exchange for a good or service.

    E. To individual that lives in the poor condition.

    Key: D

    Analysis: Transfer payments are government payments not made in exchange for a good or a service. Government spending includes transfer payments and the purchase of public goods and services.

On Taxable Income ...	The Tax Rate is ...
Up to $7,000	10%
From $7,000 to $30,000	15
From $30,000 to $76,000	25
From $76,000 to $168,000	28
From $168,000 to $352,000	33
Over $352,000	35

27. Refer to the table above. If Andrea has $85, 000 in taxable income, her marginal tax rate is

    A. 15%.

B. 25%.

C. 28%.

D. 33%.

E. 35%

Key: C

Analysis: The marginal tax rate is the tax rate applied to each additional dollar of income. Higher-income families pay a larger percentage of their income in taxes. $85, 000 is at the stage of "From $76, 000 to $168, 000".

28. Refer to the table above. If Celeste has $47, 000 in taxable income, her average tax rate is

A. 16.8%.

B. 17.9%.

C. 18.3%.

D. 19.4%.

E. 20.3%

Key: B

Analysis: $[7000 \times 10\% + (30000 - 7000) \times 15\% + (47000 - 30000) \times 25\%] \div 47000 = 17.87\%$

29. As government debt increases,

A. Congress will reduce spending by an equal proportion.

B. The government must spend more revenue on interest payments.

C. A tradeoff with government deficits is inevitable.

D. Tax rates must rise to cover the deficit.

E. The budget deficit will appear.

Key: B

Analysis: The government debt has an interest as other debts. In this question, we can eliminate the wrong choices one by one.

30. Suppose a country imposes a lump-sum income tax of $5, 000 on each individual in the country. What is the marginal income tax rate for an individual who earns $40, 000 during the year?

A. 0%

B. 10%

C. More than 10%

D. 12.5%

E. The marginal tax rate cannot be determined without knowing the entire tax schedule.

Key: A

Analysis: A lump-sum tax is a tax that is the same amount for every person, regardless of earnings or any actions that the person might take. So the marginal rate is 0.

31. Country A's tax system is more efficient than Country B's tax system if

A. Country A collects less tax revenue than Country B, and the cost to taxpayers is the same in both countries.

B. Country A collects more tax revenue than Country B, even though the cost to taxpayers is greater in Country A than in Country B.

C. The same amount of revenue is raised in both countries, but the cost to taxpayers is smaller in Country A than in Country B.

D. The same amount of revenue is raised in both countries, but the taxes are collected in a shorter amount of time in Country A than in Country B.

E. None of the above is right.

Key: C

Analysis: One tax system is more efficient than another if it raises the same amount of revenue at a smaller cost to taxpayers.

32. In addition to tax payments, the two other primary costs that a tax system inevitably imposes on taxpayers are

A. Deadweight losses and administrative burdens.

B. Deadweight losses and frustration with the political system.

C. Administrative burdens and tax-preparation costs.

D. Administrative burdens and the risk of punishment for failure to comply with tax laws.

E. Administrative burdens and frustration with the political system.

Key: A

Analysis: The cost of taxes to taxpayers includes 3 aspects: the tax payment itself, deadweight losses, and administrative burdens.

33. Adam, Barb, and Carli all like to read novels. The current bestseller costs $10. Adam values it at $15, Barb at $13, and Carli at $11. Suppose that if the government taxes books at $2 each, the selling price will rise to $12. A consequence of the tax is that

A. Consumer surplus shrinks by $4 and tax revenues increase by $6, so there is a deadweight loss of $2.

B. Consumer surplus shrinks by $6 and tax revenues increase by $6, so there is no deadweight loss.

C. Consumer surplus shrinks by $5 and tax revenues increase by $6, so there is no deadweight loss.

D. Consumer surplus shrinks by $5 and tax revenues increase by $4, so there is a deadweight loss of $1.

E. None of the above is right.

Key: D

Analysis: Now the books' price will be $12, so Carli will not buy. Then we can calculate the surplus change.

2005		2006	
On Taxable Income ...	**The Tax Rate is ...**	**On Taxable Income ...**	**The Tax Rate is ...**
$0 to $15,000	10%	Over $0	20%
$15,001 to $40,000	15%		
$40,001 to $75,000	20%		
$75,001 to $120,000	25%		
Over $120,000			

34. Refer to the table above. Suppose one goal of the tax system was to achieve vertical equity. While people may disagree about what is "equitable", based on the marginal tax rates given for the two years, which of the following statements is true?

    A. Vertical equity is possible in both years.

    B. Vertical equity is possible in 2005 but not in 2006.

    C. Vertical equity is not possible in 2005 but is possible in 2006.

    D. Vertical equity is not possible in either year.

    E. B and C

    Key: A

    Analysis: Vertical equity is the idea that taxpayers with a greater ability to pay taxes should pay larger amounts. For example, people with higher income should pay more than people with lower income.

35. Refer to the table above. Which of the following best describes the tax schedule in 2005?

    A. Proportional tax

    B. Progressive tax

    C. Regressive tax

    D. Vertical tax

    E. Lump-sum tax

    Key: A

    Analysis: Progressive tax means a tax for which high-income taxpayers pay a larger fraction of their income than do low-income taxpayers.

36. The notion that similar taxpayers should pay similar amounts of taxes is known as

    A. Vertical equity.

    B. The benefits principle.

    C. Horizontal equity.

    D. Taxpayer efficiency.

    E. Ability-to-Pay Principle.

    Key: C

    Analysis: The ability-to-pay principle leads to two corollary notions of equity: vertical equity, and horizontal equity. Horizontal equity is the idea that taxpayers with similar abilities to pay taxes should pay the same amounts.

37. If revenue from a gasoline tax is used to build and maintain public roads, the gasoline tax may be justified on the basis of

    A. The benefits principle.

    B. The ability-to-pay principle.

    C. Vertical equity.

    D. Horizontal equity.

    E. Taxpayer efficiency.

    Key: A

    Analysis: The benefits principle is the idea that people should pay taxes based on the benefits they receive from government services. Tax revenues from a gasoline tax are used to finance our highway system. People who drive the most also pay the most for maintaining roads. So a gasoline tax is a typical example of the benefits principle.

38. When a tax is justified on the basis that the taxpayers who pay the tax receive specific government services from payment of the tax, the tax

    A. Is considered horizontally equitable.

    B. Burden is minimized.

    C. Satisfies the benefits principle.

    D. Is considered vertically equitable.

    E. Burden is maximized.

    Key: C

    Analysis: The benefits principle is the idea that people should pay taxes based on the benefits they receive from government services.

39. "A $1, 000 tax paid by a poor person may be a larger sacrifice than a $10, 000 tax paid by a wealthy person" is an argument in favor of

    A. The horizontal equity principle.

    B. The benefits principle.

    C. A regressive tax argument.

    D. The ability-to-pay principle.

    E. The vertical equity principle.

    Key: D

    Analysis: The ability-to-pay principle is the idea that taxes should be levied on a person according to how well that person can shoulder the burden.

40. The flypaper theory of tax incidence

    A. Says that the burden of a tax can freely shift between the consumers and the producers.

    B. Assumes that most taxes should be "stuck on" the rich.

    C. Says that once a tax has been imposed, there is little chance of it changing, so in essence people are stuck with it.

    D. Suggests that taxes are like flies because they are everywhere and will never go away.

    E. Ignores the indirect effects of taxes.

Key: E

Analysis: According to the flypaper theory, the burden of a tax, like a fly on flypaper, sticks wherever it first lands. But just as a tax on a corporation, the corporation is more like a tax collector than a taxpayer. The burden of the tax ultimately falls on people—the owners, customers, or workers of the corporation. Many economists believe that workers and customers bear much of the burden of the corporate income tax. The corporate income tax shows how dangerous the flypaper theory of tax incidence can be.

41. Vaccinations for contagious diseases benefit the consumers as well as others in the community. Assume that vaccines are produced in a competitive market.

(a) Draw a correctly labeled graph of supply and demand, and

    (i) Label the market price "P_m", and label the market output "Q_m".

    (ii) Label the socially efficient level of output "Q_s".

    (iii) Shade the area of the deadweight loss.

(b) Is marginal social cost (MSC) greater than, less than, or equal to marginal social benefit (MSB) at the market output?

(c) How will a tax on producers of the vaccines affect the deadweight loss that you identified in part (a)(iii)? Explain.

Key: 6 points $(3 + 1 + 2)$

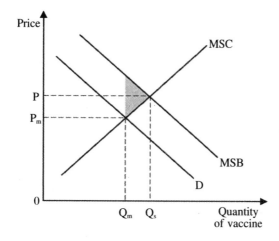

(a) 3 points:

One point is earned for the correctly labeled graph with Q_m and P_m correctly identified.

One point is earned for correctly identifying Q_s.

One point is earned for shading the area of the deadweight loss.

(b) 1 point:

One point is earned for stating that the MSC is less than the MSB.

(c) 2 points:

One point is earned for stating that the tax will increase the deadweight loss.

One point is earned for the explanation that the tax raises the cost and causes output of vaccine to fall.

42. Assume that the market for home security systems is perfectly competitive and currently in equilibrium.

(a) Draw a correctly labeled graph of supply and demand, show each of the following.

(i) The equilibrium price and quantity, labeled as P* and Q*, respectively.

(ii) The area representing consumer surplus, labeled as CS.

(iii) The area representing producer surplus, labeled as PS.

(b) Suppose that the government imposes an effective (binding) price ceiling. Redraw your graph in part (a), and label the ceiling price as P_2. Completely shade the area representing the sum of the consumer surplus and the producer surplus after the imposition of the price ceiling.

(c) Suppose the demand for home security systems decreases and the price ceiling remains binding. Indicate what will happen to each of the following.

(i) Consumer surplus

(ii) Producer surplus

Key: 7 points $(3 + 2 + 2)$

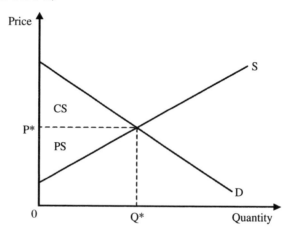

(a) 3 points:

One point is earned for a correctly labeled graph with equilibrium price and quantity.

One point is earned for showing the correct area of consumer surplus.

One point is earned for showing the correct area of producer surplus.

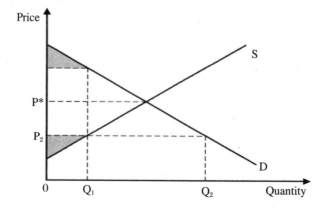

(b) 2 points:

One point is earned for showing the price ceiling below the equilibrium.

One point is earned for shading the correct area of consumer surplus and producer surplus.

(c) 2 points:

One point is earned for indicating that consumer surplus will decrease.

One point is earned for indicating that producer surplus will not change.

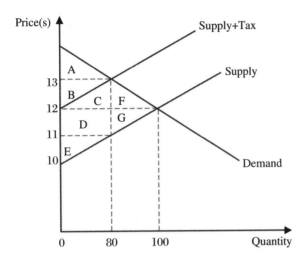

43. The graph above shows the market for a good that is subject to a per-unit tax. The letters in the graph represent the enclosed areas.

(a) Using the labeling on the graph, identify each of the following.

(i) The equilibrium price and quantity before the tax

(ii) The area representing the consumer surplus before the tax

(iii) The area representing the producer surplus before the tax

(b) Assume that the tax is now imposed. Based on the graph, does the price paid by the buyers rise by the full amount of the tax? Explain.

(c) Using the labeling on the graph, identify each of the following after the imposition of the tax.

(i) The net price received by the sellers

(ii) The amount of tax revenue

(iii) The area representing the consumer surplus

(iv) The area representing the deadweight loss

Key: 9 points (3 + 2 + 4)

(a) 3 points:

One point is earned for identifying P=$12 and Q=100 units.

One point is earned for identifying the consumer surplus before the tax=A+B+C+F.

One point is earned for identifying the producer surplus before the tax=D+E+G or $100.

(b) 2 points:

One point is earned for stating that the price paid by the buyers does not rise by the full amount of the tax.

One point is earned for a correct explanation: P increases by $1 and the tax is $2 per unit; or a correct elasticity explanation, such as supply is not perfectly elastic, or demand is not perfectly inelastic, or demand and supply have the same elasticities.

(c) 4 points:

One point is earned for identifying the net price received by the sellers=$11.

One point is earned for identifying the tax revenue=B+C+D or $160.

One point is earned for identifying consumer surplus=A.

One point is earned for identifying the deadweight loss=F+G or $20.

Chapter 10 Application: International Trade
应用：国际贸易

主要内容和概念讲解

随着全球化进程的加快，国与国之间的贸易日益频繁。国际贸易（international trade）也成为我们研究的重要内容之一。那它究竟涉及哪些问题呢？简而言之，这些问题包括：一个国家的进口（import）与出口（export）由什么决定？如果任由这些国家自由贸易，那么哪些国家能够获利，哪些国家将会亏损？人们为什么要采取措施限制国际贸易呢？

要想了解国际贸易，我们不妨先考虑一下在不存在国际贸易的情况下的市场均衡。假设一个国家孤立于世界上其他任何国家，独立生产羊毛。在羊毛市场上仅存在买方与卖方，并且不允许国内任何一个人进口或者出口羊毛。那么，这就达到了前面我们所介绍的自由市场的均衡，如下图所示：

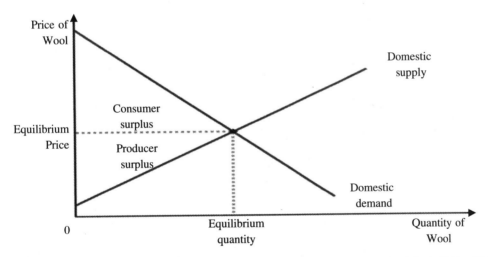

在这种情况下，国内羊毛的价格在市场的作用下自动调节并平衡国内需求和供给。消费者剩余和生产者剩余体现了这个国家的社会总福利。

但是，当允许这个国家参与国际羊毛贸易的时候，我们就不得不考虑这样一个问题：它是充当羊毛进口商的角色还是出口商的角色呢？这里就要引入一个概念——世界价格（world price）。世界价格是指商品在世界范围内的统一价格。当一个国家的国内市场价格低于世界价格时，我们就称这个国家在这个商品市场上具有比较优势（comparative advantage），这时毫无疑问，这个国家在国际商品市场上充当出口商的角色，因为它的售价比其他各国都要便宜。反之，如果这个国家的国内市场价格高于世界价格，那么它就不具有比较优势，在国际市场上充当的就是进口商的角色。我们通过下图来详细说明：

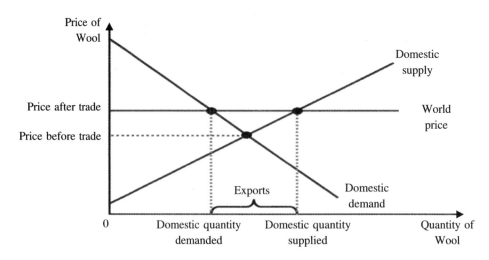

对于一个出口国,在不存在国际贸易且仅考虑国内市场时,市场自动调节到均衡价格和均衡产量。但是当允许一国进行国际贸易时,在国际市场上商品的价格为世界价格(world price),高于国内均衡价格,因此由于价格的上升,国内的商品需求量减少,而商品的供给量增加,这之间的差额即为出口量(exports)。

那么对于这样的一个出口国家,国际贸易对其社会福利会产生怎样的影响呢?我们仍运用第八章所学的福利经济学内容,首先用图形来进行分析:

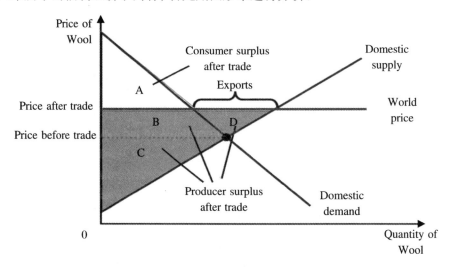

从上图可以很清楚地看到,当不存在国际贸易时,消费者剩余为(A+B),生产者剩余为C,因此社会总剩余为(A+B+C);而国际贸易出现后,价格线变为水平的世界价格线,消费者剩余变为A,而生产者剩余变为(B+C+D),因此社会总福利变为(A+B+C+D)。因此,区域 D 就是一个出口国在国际贸易中获得的总收益(gains from trade)。我们可以用一个表格加以总结:

	Before Trade	**After Trade**	**Change**
Consumer Surplus	A+B	A	−B
Producer Surplus	C	B+C+D	+(B+D)
Total Surplus	A+B+C	A+B+C+D	+D

通过上述对于出口国的分析,我们不难得出关于出口国的两个结论:第一,国内的商品生产者状况变好了,但是同时国内消费者的状况变差了;第二,整个国家的社会总福利,或者说整体社会经济生活,通过国际贸易得到了提高。

对于进口国我们也可以做同样的分析。由于国内市场价格高于世界价格,国内的消费者更倾向于购买国际上更加便宜的商品,而国内的生产者则不得不为世界市场上的低廉价格减少生产量。如下图所示,国内需求量与国内供给量之间的差额就是进口量(imports)。

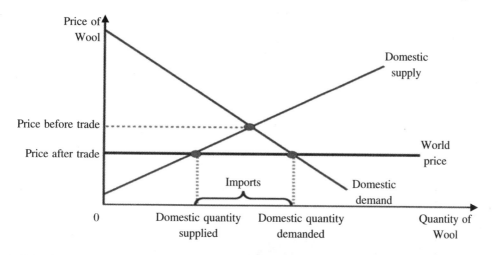

同样我们可以进行福利经济学分析,如下图所示。

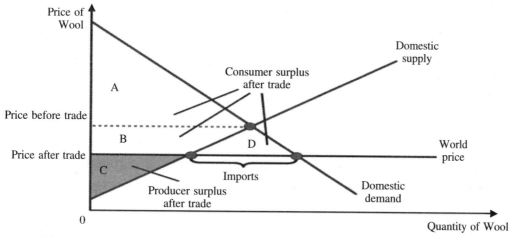

当不存在国际贸易时,消费者剩余为 A,生产者剩余为(B+C),因此社会总剩余为(A+B+C);而国际贸易出现后,价格线变为水平的世界价格线,消费者剩余变为(A+B+D),而生产者剩余变为 C,因此社会总福利变为(A+B+C+D)。因此,区域 D 就是一个出口国在国际贸易中获得的总收益(gains from trade)。我们同样可以用一个表格加以总结:

	Before Trade	**After Trade**	**Change**
Consumer Surplus	A	A+B+D	+(B+D)
Producer Surplus	B+C	C	−B
Total Surplus	A+B+C	A+B+C+D	+D

因此,对于一个进口国家,我们也得出这样两个结论:第一,国内的商品消费者状况变好了,但是同时国内生产者的状况变差了;第二,整个国家的社会总福利,或者说整体社会经济生活,同样通过国际贸易得到了提高。

综上所述,我们可以知道,在自由国际贸易下,不论是进口国还是出口国,受益者得到的利益将会大于受害者遭受的损失。也就是说,从总体上看,社会总剩余是增加的。

这里需要提到的是,我们的上述讨论均属于不设置任何国际贸易壁垒(barrier)的情况,但是在实际生活中,国家总会对进出口商品设置一系列的贸易壁垒。

首先我们考虑一下关税(tariff)的影响。关税就是一个国家对于进口商品征收的税费。由于它的存在,进口商品的价格就会高于世界价格,而其与世界价格的差额就是关税。我们来看下面这幅图:

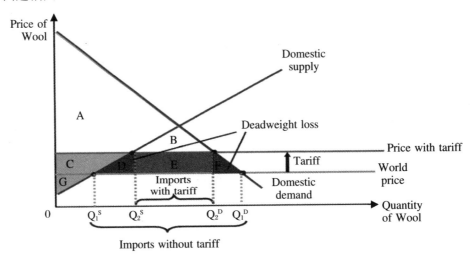

下面那条水平线代表了世界价格线,但是在增加了关税后,价格线水平上移至上面那条水平线。于是进口商品的数量由原先的 $Q_1^D - Q_1^S$ 减少至 $Q_2^D - D_2^S$,而消费者剩余由(A+B+C+D+E+F)减少至(A+B),生产者剩余由 G 增加为(C+G)。我们知道征收的关税最终落到政府手中,而关税收入即为单位关税额与进口商品数量之积,也就是长方形区域 E 的面积。这部分也就是政府的关税税收收入。于是,增加了关税后,社会总剩余由(A+B+C+D+E+F+G)减少至(A+B+C+E+G)。因此社会福利的无谓损失(deadweight loss)为区域(D+F)。具体如下表所示:

	Before Tariff	**After Tariff**	**Change**
Consumer Surplus	A+B+C+D+E+F	A+B	−(C+D+E+F)
Producer Surplus	G	C+G	+C
Government Revenue	None	E	+E
Total Surplus	A+B+C+D+E+F+G	A+B+C+E+G	−(D+F)

由此可见关税对于社会福利的影响是消极的,它减少了更加廉价的商品进口数量,降低了社会总剩余,使得国内市场向着不存在国际贸易的情况靠拢。

讨论完关税之后,接下来我们来考虑另外一种贸易壁垒——进口配额(import quota)。进口配额是为了保护国内生产者,对进口商品购买数量加以限制,即并不是所有人都可以进行国际贸易,只有拥有配额许可证的生产者(license holder)可以按照世界价格购买进口商品,再在国内市场上出售。在这种情况下,供给曲线将发生变化,当供给价格高于世界价格线时,供给曲线向右平移,平移距离为发放的配额数量,并由此得到新的均衡数量和均衡价格,如下图所示:

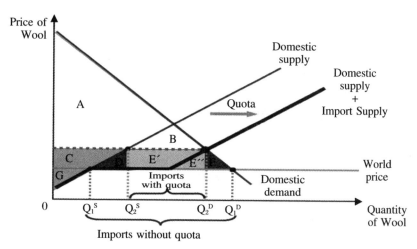

在增加了进口配额后,均衡数量由原先的 Q_1^D–Q_1^S 减少至 Q_2^D–Q_2^S,而消费者剩余由 (A+B+C+D+E'+E''+F) 减少至 (A+B),生产者剩余由 G 增加为 (C+G)。而政府收入(government revenue)即为(E'+E'')。于是,在增加了进口配额后,社会总剩余由(A+B+C+D+ E'+E''+F+G)减少至(A+B+C+ E'+E''+G)。因此社会福利的无谓损失(deadweight loss)为区域(D+F)。具体如下表所示:

	Before Quota	**After Quota**	**Change**
Consumer Surplus	A+B+C+D+E'+E''+F	A+B	−(C+D+E'+E''+F)
Producer Surplus	G	C+G	+C
Government Revenue	None	E'+E''	+E(E'+E'')
Total Surplus	A+B+C+D+E'+E''+F+G	A+B+C+E'+E''+G	−(D+F)

由此可见,进口限额对于社会福利的影响是消极的,它降低了社会总剩余。并且如果采用游说议员(lobbying)这一机制来分配许可证,则会引起更大的无谓损失。

可以看出,如果政府按其全部价值出售进口许可证,且政府收入等于等量关税收入时,进口限额与征收关税的效果是一样的。这两种政策同样都提高了国内市场的商品售价,降低了国内消费者的福利,增加了国内生产者的福利,但也同时都造成了无谓损失。

国际贸易除了可以增加国内社会总剩余,还有其他很多优点,例如使国内商品多样化,通过规模经济(economics of scale)降低成本,增加竞争,并且加强思想交流。

虽然国际贸易有众多优点,但仍然存在很多支持贸易壁垒的依据,比如引入竞争后的工作岗位(jobs)问题、国家安全(national security)问题、幼稚产业(infant industry)成长问题,以及不公平竞争(unfair competition)问题等。

最后我们来介绍一下有关的贸易协定(trade agreements)。贸易协定分为两类:一种是单边协定(unilateral),即一个国家取消自己的贸易壁垒;另一种为多边协定(multilateral),即一个国家与其他国家一起减少贸易壁垒。其中最著名的有两个协定中，一个是北美自由贸易协定(NAFTA)，它是多边协定的典型例子，于1993年制定，旨在削减美国、加拿大和墨西哥之间的贸易壁垒(trade barriers)。另一个则是关贸总协定(GATT)，这是世界上许多国家为了促进自由贸易而进行的一系列连续谈判的结果。

重要名词解释

1. **World price**：prevailing(盛行的) price in the world market
2. **Comparative advantage**：If the domestic price is below the world price, then the country has a comparative advantage.
3. **Tariff**：taxes on imported goods
4. **Import quota**：a limit on the quantity of imports
5. **NAFTA**：The North American Free Trade Agreement
6. **GATT**：The General Agreement on Tariffs and Trade

主要图表

1.

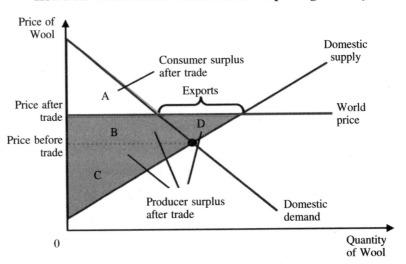

How Free Trade Affects Welfare in an Exporting Country

	Before Trade	**After Trade**	**Change**
Consumer Surplus	A+B	A	−B
Producer Surplus	C	B+C+D	+(B+D)
Total Surplus	A+B+C	A+B+C+D	+D

2.

How Free Trade Affects Welfare in an Importing Country

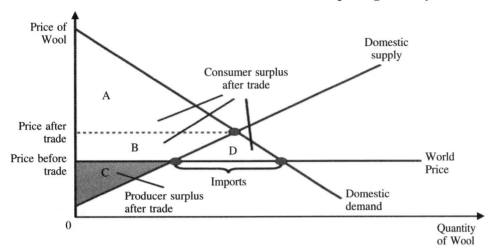

	Before Trade	**After Trade**	**Change**
Consumer Surplus	A	A+B+D	+(B+D)
Producer Surplus	B+C	C	−B
Total Surplus	A+B+C	A+B+C+D	+D

3.

Changes in Welfare from a Tariff

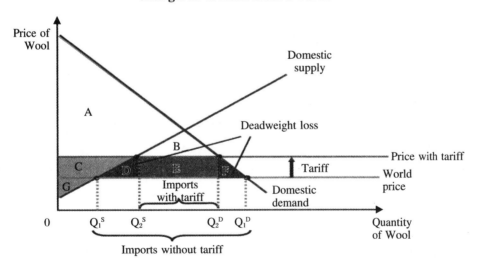

	Before Tariff	**After Tariff**	**Change**
Consumer Surplus	A+B+C+D+E+F	A+B	−(C+D+E+F)
Producer Surplus	G	C+G	+C
Government Revenue	None	E	+E
Total Surplus	A+B+C+D+E+F+G	A+B+C+E+G	−(D+F)

4.

Changes in Welfare from an Import Quota

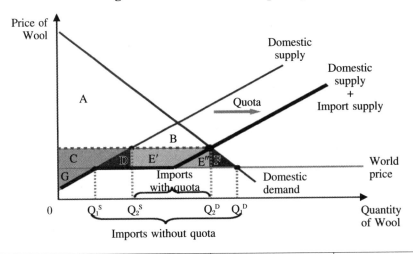

	Before Quota	**After Quota**	**Change**
Consumer Surplus	$A+B+C+D+E'+E''+F$	$A+B$	$-(C+D+E'+E''+F)$
Producer Surplus	G	$C+G$	$+C$
Government Revenue	None	$E'+E''$	$+E(E'+E'')$
Total Surplus	$A+B+C+D+E'+E''+F+G$	$A+B+C+E'+E''+G$	$-(D+F)$

模拟试题

1. An important factor in the decline of the U.S. textile industry over the past 100 years or so is

   A. Foreign competitors that can produce quality textile goods at low cost.

   B. Lower prices of goods that are substitutes for clothing.

   C. A decrease in Americans' demand for clothing, due to increased incomes and the fact that clothing is an inferior good.

   D. The fact that the minimum wage in the U.S. has failed to keep pace with the cost of living.

   E. None of the above.

   Key: A

   Analysis: Gains from trade and specialization.

2. Which of the following tools and concepts is useful in the analysis of international trade?

   A. Total surplus

   B. Domestic supply

   C. Equilibrium price

   D. Domestic demand

   E. All of the above are correct.

   Key: E

Analysis: It examines the understanding of international trade, and we can use lots of tools about the supply and demand.

3. A logical starting point from which the study of international trade begins is

   A. The recognition that not all markets are competitive.

   B. The recognition that government intervention in markets sometimes enhances the economic welfare of the society.

   C. The principle of absolute advantage.

   D. The principle of comparative advantage.

   E. The concept of surplus.

   Key: D

   Analysis: It examines the understanding of comparative advantage.

4. The nation of Pineland forbids international trade. In Pineland, you can get 1 pound of fish for 2 pounds of beef. In other countries, you can get 1 pound of fish for 1.5 pounds of beef. These facts indicate that

   A. Pineland has a comparative advantage, relative to other countries, in producing fish.

   B. Other countries have a comparative advantage, relative to Pineland, in producing beef.

   C. The price of beef in Pineland exceeds the world price of beef.

   D. If Pineland were to allow trade, it would import fish.

   E. If Pineland were to allow trade, it would import beef.

   Key: D

   Analysis: The costs of fish in Pineland are higher$(2>1.5)$. So the country would import fish.

5. When a country that imported a particular good abandons a free-trade policy and adopts a non-trade policy,

   A. Producer surplus increases and total surplus increases in the market for that good.

   B. Producer surplus increases and total surplus decreases in the market for that good.

   C. Producer surplus decreases and total surplus increases in the market for that good.

   D. Producer surplus decreases and total surplus decreases in the market for that good.

   E. A and D are possible.

   Key: B

   Analysis: When the policy change happens, the producer surplus increases and total surplus decreases in the market for that good. The gain from trade will disappear.

6. In analyzing international trade, we often focus on a country whose economy is small relative to the rest of the world. We do so

   A. Because it is impossible to analyze the gains and losses from international trade without making this assumption.

   B. Because then we can assume that world prices of goods are unaffected by that country's participation in international trade.

   C. In order to rule out the possibility of tariffs or quotas.

   D. In order to ignore some political impact.

E. All of the above are correct.

Key: B

Analysis: It examines the understanding of the assumption of model.

7. In analyzing the gains and losses from international trade, to say that Moldova is a small country is to say that

A. Moldova can only import goods; it cannot export goods.

B. Moldova's choice of which goods to export and which goods to import is not based on the principle of comparative advantage.

C. Only the domestic price of a good is relevant for Moldova; the world price of a good is irrelevant.

D. Moldova is a price taker.

E. All of the above are wrong.

Key: D

Analysis: We assume that world prices of goods are unaffected by that country's participation in international trade. A small country in the world market is a price taker.

8. Trade enhances the economic well-being of a nation in the sense that

A. Both domestic producers and domestic consumers of a good become better off with trade, regardless of whether the nation imports or exports the good in question.

B. The gains of domestic producers of a good exceed the losses of domestic consumers of a good, regardless of whether the nation imports or exports the good in question.

C. Trade results in an increase in total surplus.

D. Trade puts downward pressure on the prices of all goods.

E. The domestic price is lower.

Key: C

Analysis: In an exporting country, domestic producers of the good are better off, and domestic consumers of the good are worse off. Trade raises the economic well-being of the nation as a whole, in the sense that the gains of the winners exceed the losses of the losers. In an importing country, similar analysis follows. In short, trade results in an increase in total surplus.

9. When the nation of Worldova allows trade and becomes an exporter of silk,

A. Residents of Worldova who produce silk become worse off; residents of Worldova who buy silk become better off; and the economic well-being of Worldova rises.

B. Residents of Worldova who produce silk become worse off; residents of Worldova who buy silk become better off; and the economic well-being of Worldova falls.

C. Residents of Worldova who produce silk become better off; residents of Worldova who buy silk become worse off; and the economic well-being of Worldova rises.

D. Residents of Worldova who produce silk become better off; residents of Worldova who buy silk become worse off; and the economic well-being of Worldova falls.

E. All of the above are wrong.

Key: C

Analysis: In an exporting country, domestic producers of the good are better off, and domestic consumers of the good are worse off, but total surplus increases.

10. When a country allows trade and becomes an importer of steel,
    A. The losses of domestic producers of steel exceed the gains of domestic consumers of steel.
    B. The losses of domestic consumers of steel exceed the gains of domestic producers of steel.
    C. The gains of domestic producers of steel exceed the losses of domestic consumers of steel.
    D. The gains of domestic consumers of steel exceed the losses of domestic producers of steel.
    E. The gains of domestic consumers of steel exceed or equal the losses of domestic producers of steel.

Key: D

Analysis: In an importing country, domestic producers of the good are worse off, and domestic consumers of the good are better off. Trade raises the economic well-being of the nation as a whole in the sense that the gains of consumers exceed the losses of producers.

11. When a country allows trade and becomes an importer of bottled water, which of the following is not a consequence?
    A. The gains of domestic consumers of bottled water exceed the losses of domestic producers of bottled water.
    B. The losses of domestic producers of bottled water exceed the gains of domestic consumers of bottled water.
    C. The price paid by domestic consumers of bottled water decreases.
    D. The price received by domestic producers of bottled water decreases.
    E. The consumers are better off.

Key: B

Analysis: The losses of domestic producers of bottled water cannot exceed the gains of domestic consumers of bottled water. Trade results in an increase in total surplus.

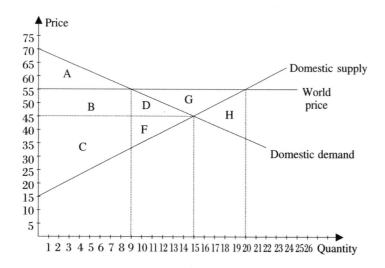

12. Refer to the figure above. With trade, total surplus in the New Zealand wool market amounts to

    A. 312.5

    B. 367.0

    C. 467.5

    D. 495.0

    E. 512.5

    Key: C

    Analysis: A+B+C+D+F+G= (70–15)×15/2+ (20–9)×(55–45)/2= 467.5

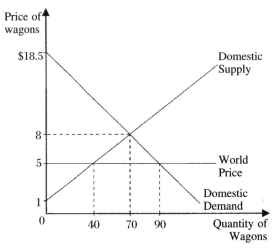

13. Refer to the figure above. The increase in total surplus resulting from trade is

    A. $60, since producer surplus increases by $180 and consumer surplus falls by $240.

    B. $60, since consumer surplus increases by $180 and producer surplus falls by $240.

    C. $75, since consumer surplus increases by $240 and producer surplus falls by $165.

    D. $75, since consumer surplus increases by $300 and producer surplus falls by $225.

    E. $75, since consumer surplus increases by $450 and producer surplus falls by $315.

    Key: C

    Analysis: Consumer surplus increases: (90+70)×(8–5)/2=240. Producer surplus falls: (40+70)×3/2=165. So total surplus increases: 240–165=75.

14. A tariff on a product makes

    A. Domestic sellers better off and domestic buyers worse off.

    B. Domestic sellers worse off and domestic buyers worse off.

    C. Domestic sellers better off and domestic buyers better off.

    D. Domestic sellers worse off and domestic buyers better off.

    E. Domestic sellers better off and domestic buyers stay the same.

    Key: A

    Analysis: It examines the understanding of tariff's effects.

15. A tariff on a product

    A. Enhances the economic well-being of the domestic economy.

    B. Increases the domestic quantity supplied.

C. Increases the domestic quantity demanded.

D. Results in an increase in producer surplus that is greater than the decrease in consumer surplus.

E. Increases domestic consumer surplus.

Key: B

Analysis: Because the tariff raises the domestic price above the world price, the domestic quantity supplied will increase because of higher profit.

16. When a country that imports a particular good imposes a tariff on that good,

A. Consumer surplus increases and total surplus increases in the market for that good.

B. Consumer surplus increases and total surplus decreases in the market for that good.

C. Consumer surplus decreases and total surplus increases in the market for that good.

D. Consumer surplus decreases and total surplus decreases in the market for that good.

E. Consumer surplus increases and total surplus remains the same in the market for that good.

Key: D

Analysis: A tariff will reduce the welfare of domestic consumers and increase the welfare of domestic producers. And in the end, it causes the deadweight loss.

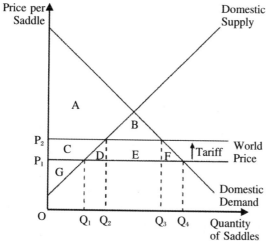

17. Refer to the figure above. As a result of the tariff, there is a deadweight loss that amounts to

A. B.

B. E.

C. D + F.

D. B + D + E + F.

E. D + E + F.

Key: C

Analysis: It examines the understanding of the graph of tariff.

18. The United States has imposed taxes on some imported goods that have been sold here by foreign countries at below their cost of production. These taxes

A. Benefit the United States as a whole, because they generate revenue for the government. In addition, because the goods are priced below the cost, the taxes do not harm domestic consumers.

B. Benefit the United States as a whole, because they generate revenue for the government and increase producer surplus.

C. Harm the United States as a whole, because they reduce consumer surplus by an amount that exceeds the gain in producer surplus and government revenue.

D. Harm the United States as a whole, because they reduce producer surplus by an amount that exceeds the gain in consumer surplus and government revenue.

E. All of the above are wrong.

Key: C

Analysis: A tariff—a tax on imports—moves a market closer to the equilibrium than would exist without trade, and therefore reduces the gains from trade. Although domestic producers are better off and the government raises revenue, the losses to consumers exceed these gains.

19. Some goods can be produced at low cost only if they are produced in large quantities. This phenomenon is called

A. Marginal cost of production.

B. Marginal benefit of size.

C. Economies of scale.

D. Economies of production.

E. Marginal economies of production.

Key: C

Analysis: The definition of economies of scale.

20. The infant-industry argument

A. is based on the belief that protecting industries when they are young will pay off later.

B. is based on the belief that protecting industries producing goods and services for infants is necessary if a country is to have healthy children.

C. has the support of most economists.

D. is an argument that is advanced by advocates of free trade.

E. is based on the belief that protecting industries producing goods and services for infants should by the subsidy and not the tariff.

Key: A

Analysis: We can eliminate the wrong choices one by one. Only A is right.

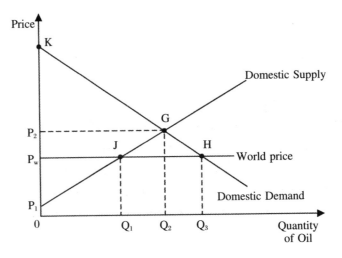

21. The graph above shows the demand for oil by United States residents, the supply of oil by United States producers, and the world price of oil. Use the labeling of the graph to answer the following questions.

(a) Identify the following before international trade occurs.

(i) Price of oil in the United States market

(ii) Quantity of oil produced in the United States

(b) Now assume that the United States begins to import oil at the world price of P_w. Identify the quantity imported by the United States.

(c) Identify the consumer surplus in the United States market for each of the following cases.

(i) Before international trade

(ii) After international trade

(d) Identify the producer surplus in the United States market for each of the following cases.

(i) Before international trade

(ii) After international trade

(e) Identify the net gain in total surplus from trade.

Key:

(a) As shown on the graph, P_2 and Q_2 were the price and quantity of oil before international trade.

(b) The amount of oil imported into the US market after trade would be equal to Q_3–Q_1.
US production drops to Q_1 but quantity demanded rises to Q_3.

(c) The triangle P_2KG represents the consumer surplus before trade, while triangle P_wKH represents the consumer surplus after trade.

(d) The triangle P_1P_2G represents the producer surplus before trade, while triangle P_1P_wJ represents the producer surplus after trade.

(e) The triangle JGH represents the net gain in total surplus from trade.

Scoring Guidelines: 8 points (2+1+2+2+1)

(a) 2 points: (Pre-trade)

1 - Identifying P_2

1 - Identifying Q_2

(b) 1 point: (Imports) Identifying (Q_3-Q_1) or (H–J)

(c) 2 points: (Consumer surpluses)

1 - Identifying P_2KG (before)

1 - Identifying P_wKH (after)

(d) 2 points: (Producer surpluses)

1 - Identifying P_1P_2G (before)

1 - Identifying P_1P_wJ (after)

(e) 1 point: (Net gain in surplus) Identifying JGH

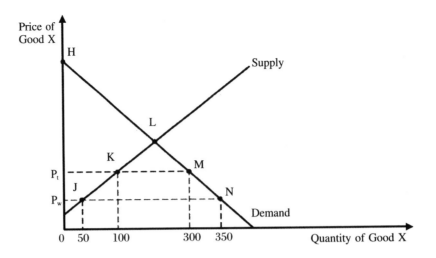

22. The diagram above shows the domestic supply of and demand for good X in the country of Placonia.

(a) If the current world price of good X is P_w, does Placonia export or import good X? Explain.

(b) Given your answer in part (a), indicate the quantity of good X that Placonia exports or imports.

(c) Assume that the government of Placonia imposes a tariff on good X, increasing the price from P_w to P_t. Using the labels in the graph, indicate the change in each of the following in Placonia.

(i) Consumer surplus

(ii) Producer surplus

(d) Indicate how employment in the domestic industry that produces good X is affected by the tariff.

Key: 6 points (2+1+2+1)

(a) 2 points:

1- Placonia imports the good.

1- The domestic opportunity cost of producing good X is higher than the world price (P_w) for unit J–N. Or, they can get it cheaper at the world price.

(b) 1 point: It imports 300 (=350−50) units or J–N units.

(c) 2 points:

1 - Consumer surplus decreases from P_wNH to P_tMH, or a decrease of MN$P_w$$P_t$

1 - Producer surplus increases by JK$P_t$$P_w$

(d) 1 point: Employment would increase because domestic production of good X increases in Placonia.

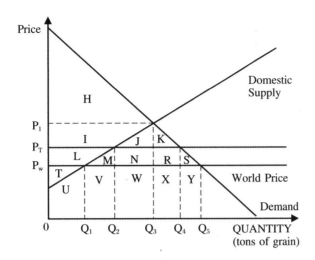

23. The diagram above illustrates the domestic market for grain in Country X before and after international trade. The letters inside the diagram represent areas, not points.

   (a) Using the labeling of the graph, identify each of the following before any trade occurs.

      (i) Equilibrium price and quantity

      (ii) Area of consumer surplus

      (iii) Area of producer surplus

   (b) Using the labeling of the graph, identify the amount of grain that Country X will import if it engages in trade and the world price of grain is at P_W.

   (c) Now assume that Country X imposes a tariff that raises the price of grain from the free-trade case to P_T. Using the labeling of the graph, identify the change in each of the following.

      (i) Domestic production

      (ii) Domestic consumption

      (iii) Consumer surplus

      (iv) Producer surplus

Key:

   (a) Before trade, the relevant curves are the domestic supply curve and the domestic demand curve. The intersection of domestic supply and demand determines the equilibrium price and quantity, which are P_1 and Q_3. Consumer surplus is area H, above the price line and below the demand curve. Producer surplus is area $(I + L + T)$, above the domestic supply curve and below the price line.

   (b) With free trade and a world price of P_W, domestic suppliers are unable to charge more than P_W because consumers can purchase all that they want at the world price. At P_W, domestic suppliers are willing to supply quantity Q_1 and buyers will purchase quantity Q_5. The difference between these quantities, $Q_5 - Q_1$, will be imported by Country X.

   (c) At the post-tariff price P_T, the domestic supply curve indicates that domestic suppliers will produce the quantity Q_2 rather than Q_1, so the change is $Q_2 - Q_1$. The demand curve indicates that domestic consumers will demand the quantity Q_4 rather than Q_5, so the change is Q_4-Q_5. Consumer surplus shrinks from $(H+I+J+K+L+M+N+R+S)$ to $(H+I+J+K)$, a loss of $(L+M+N+R+S)$. Producer surplus increases from T to $(T+L)$, a gain of L.

Scoring Guidelines: 8 points $(3+1+4)$

(a) 3 points:

1 point - for identifying P_1 and Q_3

1 point - for identifying H

1 point - for identifying $(I+L+T)$

(b) 1 point - for identifying Q_5-Q_1

(c) 4 points

1 point–for identifying Q_2-Q_1; Q_2 is acceptable if part (b) is correct.

1 point–for identifying Q_4-Q_5; Q_4 is acceptable if part (b) is correct.

1 point–for identifying the loss: $(L+M+N+R+S)$ $((H+I+J+K)$ is not acceptable — you must identify the CHANGE).

1 for identifying the gain: L $((T + L)$ is not acceptable — you must identify the CHANGE).

The Costs of Production
生产成本

Chapter 11

主要内容和概念讲解

综合第二章至第七章，我们知道供给（supply）与需求（demand）是经济学家们最常使用的词汇，也是支配市场经济发展的动力。我们的现代微观经济学就是研究供给、需求与市场均衡的学科。之前几章研究的都是消费者理论，从本章开始，将利用几章来研究生产者理论，而我们这章的内容就是介绍生产成本（the cost of production）。

那么什么是成本（cost）呢？根据供给定律（law of supply），当一种商品的价格很高时，企业更倾向于生产和销售这种商品，这反映在供给曲线上，表示为供给曲线向上倾斜。对于一个企业而言，毫无疑问，它最终的经济目标就是企业利润最大化。那么利润（profits）等于什么呢？我们知道总利润（total profit）等于总收益（total revenue）减去总成本（total cost）。总收益是一个企业的产品销售所得，而总成本则是企业在生产过程中所耗费资料的市场价值。企业的生产成本包括制造产品和服务过程中的所有机会成本（opportunity costs），而这些成本又可以分为显性成本（explicit costs）和隐性成本（implicit costs）。显性成本是指企业投入生产的直接费用支出，相对地，隐性成本就是指那些不需要费用支出的成本。

关于利润我们首先得区分两个概念——经济利润（economic profit）和会计利润（accounting profit）。经济利润是用企业总收益扣除全部机会成本，包括显性成本和隐性成本，而会计利润是企业总收益扣去显性成本，因此可以看出，在使用会计成本时我们通常忽略了隐性成本。所以显然，经济利润通常来说小于会计利润。用下图可以更形象地理解这两个概念。

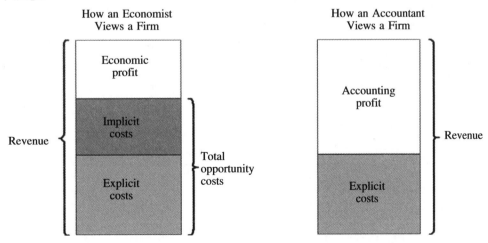

了解了何为成本，我们接下来进入本章的重点——生产函数（production function）。生产函数描述的是商品的投入要素与商品产出之间的关系。某一投入要素的边际产品

（marginal product，亦称边际产量）是指其他变量保持不变，该投入要素增加一单位时，产出数量的增加，可用下面等式表示：

$$\text{Marginal product} = \frac{\text{Additional output}}{\text{Additional input}}$$

由此可见，边际产品就是生产函数的斜率。而对于边际产品我们有一个定理：边际产品随着生产要素的投入而减少，即边际产品递减（diminishing marginal product）原则。例如，随着企业雇佣工人数量的不断增加，在设备数目不变的情况下，每一个工人对于生产的贡献越来越少。因此如下图，随着边际产品的减少，生产函数越来越平坦。

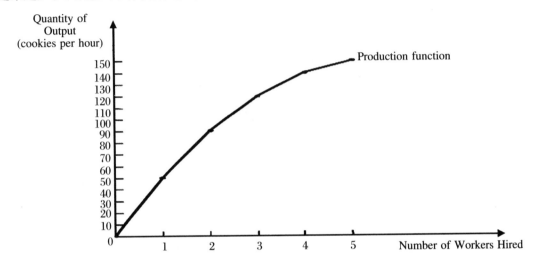

由这条生产函数曲线我们就能得到总成本曲线（total-cost curve）。我们通过一个具体的例子来解释。例如，一家饼干加工厂，它的生产函数以及各投入要素成本分别如下表：

Number of workers	Output（quantity of cookies produced per hour）	Marginal Product of Labor	Cost of Factory	Cost of workers	Total Cost of Inputs（cost of factory+cost of workers）
0	0	50	$30	$0	$30
1	50	40	30	10	40
2	90	30	30	20	50
3	120	20	30	30	60
4	140	10	30	40	70
5	150		30	50	80

由此，我们就得到了这家饼干加工厂的总成本曲线，如下：

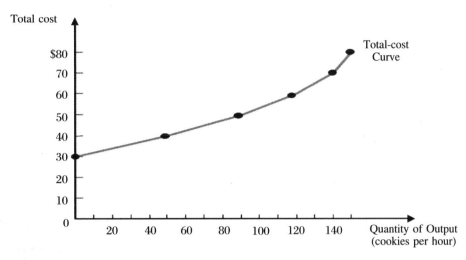

　　上面我们提到过成本可以分为显性成本和隐性成本，其实成本的分类有多种方式。这里再介绍一种，即将其分为固定成本（fixed costs）和可变成本（variable costs）。固定成本指那些不会因为产出数量增加而变动的成本，而可变成本是指当企业变动生产数量时会随之变动的成本。由此，我们可以将总成本（total costs, TC）分为总固定成本（total fixed costs, TFC）和总可变成本（total variable costs, TVC）。即：

$$TC = TFC + TVC$$

　　而平均成本（average costs, AC），即单位产品的成本，也可以划分为平均固定成本（average fixed costs, AFC）和平均可变成本（average variable costs, AVC）。即：

$$AC = AFC + AVC$$

　　且：

$$AFC = \frac{Total\ Fixed\ Cost}{Quantity} = \frac{TFC}{Q}$$

$$AVC = \frac{Total\ Variable\ Cost}{Quantity} = \frac{TVC}{Q}$$

$$ATC = \frac{Total\ Cost}{Quantity} = \frac{TC}{Q}$$

　　边际成本（marginal costs, MC）计算的是额外生产出一单位产所新增加的成本。因此有：

$$MC = \frac{(Change\ in\ total\ cost)}{(Change\ in\ quantity)} = \frac{\Delta TC}{\Delta Q}$$

　　根据边际产品递减原则，我们可以得出：随着产量的增加，边际成本递增。因此边际成本线向上倾斜。而平均总成本线的形状是 U 形的，因为在产出很少时，每个产品分摊的固定成本很高，从而导致平均总成本高，当产出开始增加，平均总成本随着固定成本的摊薄而降低，但是由于边际成本递增，平均可变成本不断增加，当它的增加超过平均固定成本的减少时，平均总成本开始增大。具体可以看下面这幅图：

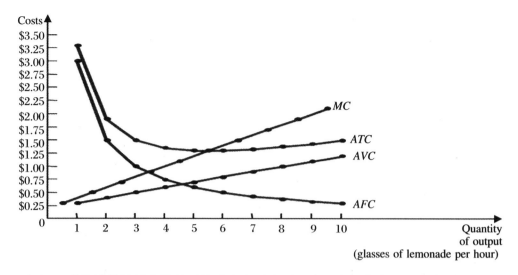

这个 U 形曲线的最低点就是平均总成本最小时的点,我们常称这时的产出为企业有效规模(efficient scale)。

接下来,我们不妨看一下边际成本与平均总成本之间的关系。当边际成本低于平均总成本时,很显然平均总成本会降低,因为新生产一个单位产品的成本会拉低原平均总成本;而反之,当边际成本高于平均总成本时,平均总成本会增加。由此可知,边际成本曲线将通过平均总成本曲线的最低点,也就是有效规模点。如图所示:

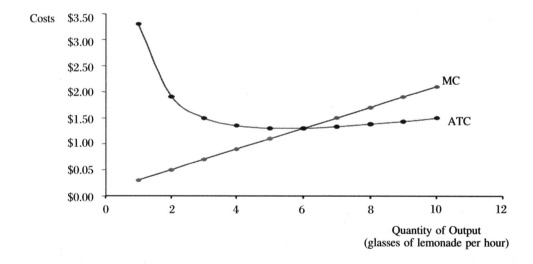

上面讨论了这么多成本曲线,现在我们可以来研究总成本曲线到底是怎样的。

首先我们明确了边际成本曲线和平均总成本曲线的各条性质:第一,边际成本线最终将随着产出的增加而上升;第二,平均总成本线是 U 形的;第三,边际成本线通过平均总成本线的最低点。因此,总成本曲线始终随产出的增加而上升,但在达到有效规模(efficient scale)之前,上升速度不断减小,而超过有效规模之后,上升速度开始不断增大。

下面我们来看看时间期限(time horizon)的问题。因为从固定成本和可变成本的角度来看,有许多成本从短期来看是固定成本,但是从长期来看就变成了可变成本,所以短期平均总成本曲线和长期平均总成本曲线是不同的。从长期来看,可以通过调整固定资本来达到所有短期情况下的最优点。也就是说,长期平均总成本曲线经过所有短期平均总成本曲线的最低点。这就是我们经济学中所说的,长期平均总成本曲线是短期平均总成本曲线的包络线。

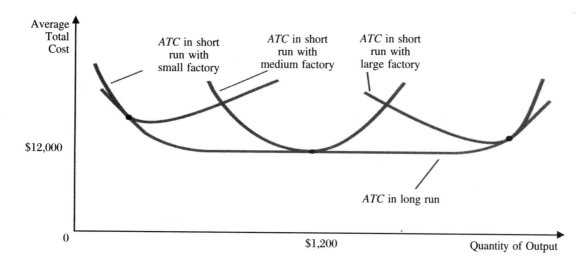

长期平均总成本曲线与产出的关系可分为三类,如下图:第一类为规模经济(economies of scale),即长期平均总成本随着产出的增加而减少;第二类为规模不经济(diseconomies of scale),即长期平均总成本随着产出的增加而增加;第三类为规模报酬不变(constant returns to scale),即长期平均总成本不随产出而变化。

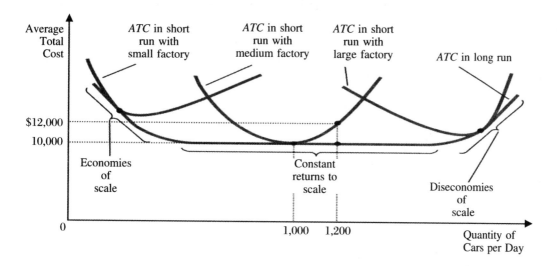

重要名词解释

1. **Total revenue:** the amount that the firm receives for the sale of its output

2. **Total cost:** the market value of the inputs a firm uses in production

3. **Explicit cost:** input costs that require a direct outlay of money by the firm

4. **Implicit cost:** input costs that do not require an outlay of money by the firm

5. **Economic profit:** total revenue minus all the opportunity costs (explicit and implicit)

6. **Accounting profit:** total revenue minus the explicit costs

7. **Production function:** relationship between quantity of inputs used to make a good and the quantity of output of that good

8. **Marginal product** (**MP**): the increase in the quantity of output obtained from an additional unit of that input

9. **Diminishing marginal product:** the marginal product of an input declines as the quantity of the input increases

10. **Fixed costs** (**FC**): costs that do not vary with the quantity of output produced

11. **Variable costs** (**VC**): costs that do change as the firm alters the quantity of output produced

12. **Average costs** (**AC**): the firm's costs divided by the quantity of output produced

13. **Marginal cost** (**MC**): the amount total cost rises when the firm increases production by one unit

14. **Efficient scale:** the quantity that minimizes average total cost

15. **Economies of scale:** occurs when long-run average total cost declines as output increases

16. **Diseconomies of scale:** occurs when long-run average total cost rises as output increases

17. **Constant returns to scale:** occurs when long-run average total cost does not vary as output increases

1.

Cost Curves

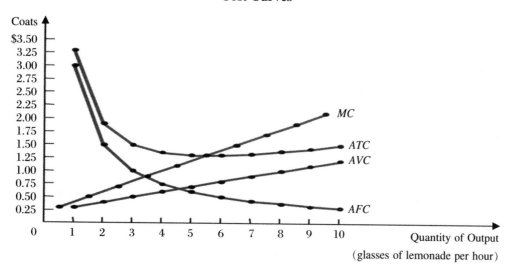

2.

Average Total Cost in the Short and Long Run

(a) Total-Cost Curve

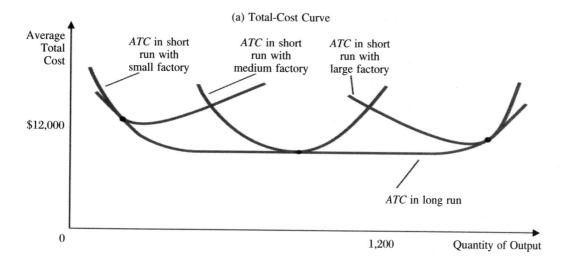

模拟试题

1. Analyzing the behavior of the firm enhances our understanding of

    A. What decisions lie behind the market supply curve.

    B. How consumers allocate their income to purchase scarce resources.

    C. How financial institutions set interest rates.

    D. Whether resources are allocated fairly.

    E. Why market economy work efficiently.

    Key: A

    Analysis: The firm considers supplying according to the costs of production.

2. Economists assume that the typical person who starts his/her own business does so with the intention of

    A. Donating the profits of her business to charity.

    B. Capturing the highest number of sales in her industry.

    C. Realizing personal value.

    D. Minimizing costs.

    E. Maximizing profits.

    Key: E

    Analysis: The economic goal of the firm is to maximize profits.

3. Economists normally assume that the goal of a firm is to

    (i) Sell as much of their products as possible.

    (ii) Set the price of the products as high as possible.

    (iii) Maximize profits.

    A. (i) and (ii) are true.

    B. (ii) and (iii) are true.

    C. They are all true.

    D. (i) and (iii) are true.

    E. Only (iii) is true.

    Key: E

    Analysis: The economic goal of the firm is to maximize profits.

4. The amount of money that a firm receives from the sale of its output is called

    A. Total gross profit.

    B. Total net profit.

    C. Total revenue.

    D. Net revenue.

    E. Total saleroom.

    Key: C

    Analysis: Total revenue is the amount that the firm receives from the sale of its output.

5. Those things that must be forgone to acquire a good are called

   A. Implicit costs.

   B. Opportunity costs.

   C. Explicit costs.

   D. Accounting costs.

   E. Production cost.

   Key: B

   Analysis: A firm's costs of production include all the opportunity costs of making its output of goods and services.

6. A firm's opportunity costs of production are equal to its

   A. Explicit costs only.

   B. Implicit costs only.

   C. Explicit costs + implicit costs.

   D. Explicit costs + implicit costs + total revenue.

   E. Accounting costs.

   Key: C

   Analysis: A firm's opportunity costs of production include explicit costs and implicit costs.

7. An example of an opportunity cost, also an implicit cost, is

   A. A lease payment.

   B. The cost of raw materials.

   C. The value of the business owner's time.

   D. The house rent.

   E. All of the above are correct.

   Key: C

   Analysis: It examines the definition of opportunity cost and implicit cost.

8. Dolores used to work as a high school teacher for $40,000 per year but quit in order to start her own catering business. To invest in her factory, she withdrew $20,000 from her savings, which paid 3 percent interest, and borrowed $30,000 from her uncle, whom she pays 3 percent interest per year. Last year she paid $25,000 for ingredients and had revenue of $60,000. She asked Louis the accountant and Greg the economist to calculate the profit for her.

   A. Louis says her profit is $25,900, and Greg says her profit is $66,500.

   B. Louis says her profit is $35,000, and Greg says she lost $5,900.

   C. Louis says her profit is $34,100, and Greg says she lost $6,500.

   D. Louis says her profit is $34,100, and Greg says her profit is $34,100.

   E. Louis says her profit is $35,000, and Greg says she lost $6,500.

   Key: C

   Analysis: Explicit costs $=25000+30000\times3\%=25900$, so the accounting profit $=60000-25900=34100$. Implicit costs $=40000+20000\times3\%=40600$, so the total costs (opportunity costs) $=$ explicit costs $+$ implicit costs $=66500$. Economic profit $=$ total revenue $-$ opportunity costs =60000–66500=6500.

9. A firm manufactures and sells computer chips. Last year it sold 2 million chips at a price of $10 per chip. For last year, the firm's

   A. Accounting profit amounted to $20 million.

   B. Economic profit amounted to $20 million.

   C. Total revenue amounted to $20 million.

   D. Explicit costs amounted to $20 million.

   E. Implicit costs amounted to $20 million.

   Key: C

   Analysis: It examines the understanding of basic concepts. Note the differences between them.

10. A production function is a relationship between inputs and

    A. Quantity of output.

    B. Revenue.

    C. Costs.

    D. Profit.

    E. Net profit.

    Key: A

    Analysis: The production function shows the relationship between quantity of inputs used to produce a good and the quantity of output of that good.

11. L represents the number of workers hired by a firm and Q represents that firm's quantity of output. Assume two points on the firm's production function are $(L = 12, Q = 122)$ and $(L = 13, Q = 132)$. Then the marginal product of the 13th worker is

    A. 8 units of output.

    B. 10 units of output.

    C. 122 units of output.

    D. 132 units of output.

    E. 120 units of output.

    Key: B

    Analysis: 132–122=10

12. When adding another unit of labor leads to an increase in output that is smaller than the increases in output that resulted from adding previous units of labor, the firm is experiencing

    A. Diminishing labor.

    B. Diminishing output.

    C. Diminishing product.

    D. Negative marginal product.

    E. Diminishing marginal product.

    Key: E

    Analysis: Diminishing marginal product is the property whereby the marginal product of an input declines as the quantity of the input increases.

13. On a 100-acre farm, a farmer is able to produce 3,000 bushels of wheat when he hires 2 workers. He is able to produce 4,400 bushels of wheat when he hires 3 workers. Which of the following possibilities is consistent with the property of diminishing marginal product?

    A. The farmer is able to produce 5,600 bushels of wheat when he hires 4 workers.

    B. The farmer is able to produce 5,800 bushels of wheat when he hires 4 workers.

    C. The farmer is able to produce 6,000 bushels of wheat when he hires 4 workers.

    D. The farmer is able to produce 6,200 bushels of wheat when he hires 4 workers.

    E. Any of the above could be correct.

Key: A

Analysis: Marginal products $\leqslant 4400-3000=1400$, so when he hires 4 workers, the production must be less than $4400+1400=5800$.

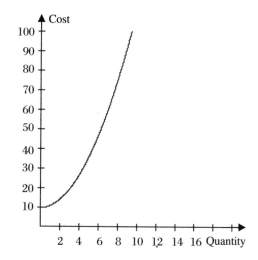

14. Refer to the figure above. It illustrates a typical

    A. Total-cost curve.

    B. Production function.

    C. Production possibilities frontier.

    D. Fixed-cost curve.

    E. Average-cost curve.

Key: A

Analysis: The relationship between the quantity a firm can produce and its costs determines pricing decisions. The total-cost curve shows this relationship graphically.

15. If the total cost curve gets steeper as output increases, the firm is experiencing

    A. Diseconomies of scale.

    B. Economies of scale.

    C. Diminishing marginal product.

    D. Increasing marginal product.

    E. Constant returns to scale.

Key: C

Analysis: It examines the understanding of diminishing marginal product. Diminishing marginal product is the property whereby the marginal product of an input declines as the quantity of the input increases. So it is the same as the property whereby the marginal costs of an output increases as the quantity of the outputs increases.

16. Which of the following is the best example of a variable cost?

    A. Monthly wage payments for hired labor.

    B. Annual property tax payments for a building.

    C. Monthly rent payments for a warehouse.

    D. Annual insurance payments for a warehouse.

    E. Fixed machine maintenance cost.

    Key: A

    Analysis: Variable costs are those costs that do change as the firm alters the quantity of output produced.

17. Average total cost equals

    A. Change in total costs divided by quantity produced.

    B. Change in total costs divided by change in quantity produced.

    C. (Fixed costs + variable costs) divided by quantity produced.

    D. (Fixed costs + variable costs) divided by change in quantity produced.

    E. Total cost – total quantity of output.

    Key: C

    Analysis: Average total cost is the total cost divided by the quantity of output. The total cost = fixed costs + variable costs, so ATC = AFC + AVC.

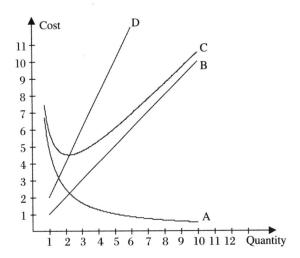

18. Refer to the figure above. Curve D is increasing because of

    A. Diminishing marginal product.

    B. Increasing marginal product.

    C. The fact that increasing marginal product follows decreasing marginal product.

    D. The fact that decreasing marginal product follows increasing marginal product.

E. Diminishing total product.

Key: A

Analysis: Curve D is a marginal cost curve. Diminishing marginal product will cause the marginal cost to increase.

19. Refer to the figure above. Curve D intersects curve C

   A. Where the firm maximizes profit.

   B. At the minimum of average fixed cost.

   C. At the efficient scale.

   D. Where fixed costs equal variable costs.

   E. All of the above are wrong.

Key: C

Analysis: Whenever marginal cost is less than average total cost, average total cost is falling. Whenever marginal cost is greater than average total cost, average total cost is rising. The bottom of the U-shape occurs at the quantity that minimizes average total cost. This quantity is sometimes called the efficient scale of the firm.

20. In the long run,

   A. Inputs that were fixed in the short run remain fixed.

   B. Inputs that were fixed in the short run become variable.

   C. Inputs that were variable in the short run become fixed.

   D. Variable inputs are rarely used.

   E. Variable inputs stay the same.

Key: B

Analysis: Because many costs are fixed in the short run but variable in the long run, a firm's long-run cost curves differ from its short-run cost curves.

Perfectly Competitive Market
完全竞争市场

虽然你去早市买水果的时候会习惯性地货比三家，但却时常发现各个摊位的报价几乎一样。一旦有一家的水果格外贵，在那儿买的人就特别少。但当你买好水果，开车去加油站加油的时候，不幸发现油价涨了，你虽然心有不快，但还是加了油，付了钱。因为你知道即使加油站到处都是，汽油的最终供给者其实只有一家，提价一定是全国统一的行为。换个加油站，价格必然还是一样的。我们可以看到，消费者在这两个市场中所处的地位是不同的，而这种不同其实是由这两个市场的市场结构决定的。什么是市场结构？在不同结构的市场中，消费者和厂商分别扮演着怎样的角色？市场结构对产品的价格和产量又会有怎样的影响？我们将通过接下来的四章来深入地探讨这些问题。

市场结构的划分

首先，我们来看看什么是市场结构。经济活动离不开市场（market），现实中的市场都各有特点，因而也就存在着各种不同的市场结构。所谓市场结构（market structure），通常被定义为对市场内竞争程度及价格形成等产生战略性影响的市场组织的特征，也就是市场竞争或垄断的程度。决定市场结构的因素主要是市场集中程度、产品差别化程度和进入壁垒的高低。在不同市场结构下，即在不同市场竞争或垄断条件下，商品的均衡价格与均衡产量是不同的，厂商行为受到市场结构的制约。要分析厂商行为首先要了解市场结构。

一般来说，划分市场结构的重要标准有以下四个：第一，厂商数量的多少。有的行业厂商数量多，有的则少，也有一家厂商就是一个行业的。厂商数量的多少决定了各厂商间的竞争方法与决策行为，对厂商的市场行为影响很大。第二，产品差别。现实中有些产品无差别或差别极小，称为同质产品。比如，不同农户生产的小麦或大米，可近似认为没有产品差别。但更多的产品是有差别的，比如我们日常所用的各种物品。产品差别程度反映了各厂商的产品之间的相互替代程度，对市场结构有一定的影响。第三，对价格的控制程度。有的行业厂商众多，单个厂商所占市场份额微小，无法控制市场价格，而另一些行业厂商数量少，单个企业所占市场份额大，能操纵和控制商品的市场价格。能否对市场商品的价格进行控制是划分不同市场结构的又一重要标准。第四，进入的难易程度。有的行业，企业可以自由进入或退出，不存在进入限制或进入壁垒。有的行业，新企业根本无法进入，进入壁垒达到最高。也有的行业，新企业可以进入，但有不同程度的难度，存在不同程度的进入限制。一个行业的进入壁垒的高低决定了该行业企业数量的多少。一般来说，能自由进入的行业，企业数量就多。进入限制大、壁垒高的行业，企业数量就少。正是因为如此，进入限制或壁垒也是判断市场结构的一个标准。

根据以上标准，西方经济学将市场结构划分为四种类型，即完全竞争市场、垄断竞争市场、寡头市场和完全垄断市场。关于四种类型市场结构的划分及其相应特征可用下表来概括。

表 12.1　市场类型的划分和特征

市场类型	厂商数目	产品差别程度	对价格的控制程度	进出该行业的难易程度	例子
完全竞争	很多	完全无差别	没有	很容易	一些农产品，如玉米、小麦
垄断竞争	很多	相似但有差别	有一些	比较容易	一些轻工业品，如服装、食品
寡头	几个	有差别或无差别	相当程度	比较困难	汽车、石油、钢铁
完全垄断	一个	唯一的产品，且无相近的替代品	很大程度，但常受管制	很困难，几乎不可能	公共事业，如水、电

完全竞争市场

完全竞争市场（perfectly competitive market）是指丝毫不存在垄断因素的市场结构。完全竞争的市场类型必须同时具备以下四个条件：

第一，市场上有很多的买者和卖者。由于市场上有很多的需求者和供给者，其中每一个成员的购买份额或销售份额相对于整个市场规模来说微不足道，以致谁都不能影响商品的价格。任何一个买者买与不买或买多与买少，以及任何一个卖者卖与不卖或卖多与卖少，都不会对市场的价格水平产生任何影响。在这样的市场中，每一个消费者或每一个厂商对市场价格都没有控制力，他们都是市场价格的接受者（price taker），只能被动地接受既定的市场价格，而不是价格的制定者（price maker）。

第二，市场上每一个厂商提供的产品都是同质的。所谓产品同质是指，所有的厂商生产的产品是完全相同的，厂商提供的产品之间具有完全的替代关系。产品不仅不存在商标、牌号、外观、质量、性能等方面的差别，而且甚至不存在销售地点与销售条件的差别。由于产品无任何差别，消费者购买哪一家厂商的商品是无所谓的，消费者唯一需要关注的就是商品的价格。如果一个厂商稍微提高其产品的价格，所有的顾客就会转而购买其他厂商的产品，这个厂商的商品就会完全卖不出去。

第三，所有的资源具有完全的流动性。这意味着厂商进入或退出一个行业是完全自由和毫无困难的，不存在任何自然的、社会的或法律上的障碍，所有资源可以在各厂商之间和各行业之间完全自由地流动。这样，任何一个资源都可以及时投向能获得最大利润的生产领域，并及时从亏损的生产领域中退出。

第四，经济运行主体具有完全的信息。生产者、消费者等经济运行主体必须具有完全的信息。市场上不存在不确定性。进入市场的每一个消费者和每一个生产者都可以根据自己掌握的完全信息，做出最优的经济决策，从而获得最大的经济利益。不仅如此，完全信息意味着所有的经济运行主体对过去、当前和未来的情况都有准确的了解和把握。完全信息也就排除了由于信息不通畅而可能导致的一个市场同时按照不同的价格进行交易的情况。

严格地讲，只有同时满足上述四个条件才能称得上是完全竞争的市场。但在现实生活中，真正符合以上四个条件的市场是不存在的。通常只是将一些农产品市场，如玉米市场、小麦市场等，看成是比较接近完全竞争市场的。虽然在现实经济生活中并不存在完全竞争市场，但大量经验证明完全竞争市场模型仍然是一个较有用的简化模型。通过对完全竞争市场模型的分析，可以得出关于市场机制及其配置资源的一些基本原理。

完全竞争市场的收益

根据我们前面所需的供给需求理论，在完全竞争的市场中，整个行业面临着一条向右下方倾斜的需求曲线，与此对应的是一条向右上方倾斜的供给曲线。整个行业产品的价格就这样由需求与供给来共同决定。如图 12.1(a)中所示。

但对单个厂商来说情况就不同了。在完全竞争市场中，由于厂商是既定市场价格的接受者，所以，完全竞争厂商所面临的需求曲线是一条由既定市场价格出发的水平线。如图12.1 中(b)所示。水平状的厂商需求曲线意味着：厂商只能被动地接受给定的市场价格 P_e 且厂商不会也无法改变这一价格水平，厂商可以按给定的价格水平卖掉它想卖的任何产量。

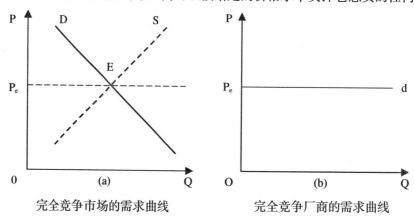

完全竞争市场的需求曲线　　　　　完全竞争厂商的需求曲线

图 12.1　完全竞争市场和完全竞争厂商的需求曲线

知道了完全竞争厂商所面临的需求曲线，我们就能计算出厂商的收益了。厂商的收益（revenue）就是厂商的销售收入。其中，厂商的总收益（total revenue, TR）是指厂商出售产品后所得到的销售收入，即出售产品的总卖价。以 P 表示既定的市场价格，以 Q 表示销售总量，总收益的公式为：

$$TR(Q)=P \times Q$$

平均收益（average revenue, AR）指厂商在平均每一单位的产品销售中所获得的收入，定义公式为：

$$AR(Q)=TR(Q)/Q$$

在完全竞争市场中，平均收益为：

$$AR(Q)=TR(Q)/Q=P*Q/Q=P$$

边际收益(marginal revenue, MR)指厂商每增加或减少一单位产品销售所引起的总收益的变化。边际收益的定义公式为:

$$MR(Q)=\Delta TR(Q)/\Delta Q$$

或者,

$$MR(Q)=\lim_{\Delta Q\to 0}\frac{\Delta TR(Q)}{\Delta Q}=\frac{dTR(Q)}{d(Q}$$

容易看出,在完全竞争市场中,边际收益也是商品的市场价格 P。

我们来看下表中的例子。在啤酒市场有众多的啤酒生产厂商,这个市场可以看做是完全竞争的市场。对于某个生产商来说,市场均衡时,啤酒价格为每加仑 6 美元,由于这个厂商是一个价格接受者,因此,它也必须以 6 美元/加仑的价格出售啤酒。这样我们就能分别算出它的总收益、平均收益和边际收益。正像我们之前计算的那样,它的平均收益和边际收益都等于啤酒的均衡价格。

表 12.2　**Total, Average, and Marginal Revenue for a Competitive Firm**

Quantity (Q)	Price (P)	Total Revenue $(TR=P\times Q)$	Average Revenue $(AR=TR/Q)$	Marginal Revenue $(MR)=\Delta TR/\Delta Q$
1 gallon	$6	$6	$6	
				$6
2	6	12	6	
				6
3	6	18	6	
				6
4	6	24	6	
				6
5	6	30	6	
				6
6	6	36	6	
				6
7	6	42	6	
				6
8	6	48	6	

根据表 12.2 可画出图 12.2:

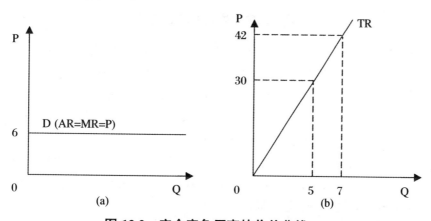

图 12.2　**完全竞争厂商的收益曲线**

图 12.2 体现了完全竞争厂商的收益曲线特征。由图 12.2(a)可以看出，完全竞争厂商的平均收益 *AR* 曲线，边际收益 *MR* 曲线和需求曲线 *d* 是完全重叠、三线合一的，它们都用同一条由既定价格出发的水平线来表示。这是由于在厂商的每一个销售量水平都有 *AR=MR=P*，且厂商的需求曲线本身就是一条由既定价格出发的水平线。此外，完全竞争厂商的总收益 *TR* 曲线是一条由原点出发的斜率不变的直线，且 *MR* 值等于固定不变的价格水平，见图 12.2(b)。

完全竞争厂商的短期均衡

企业的目标是利润最大化，利润等于总收益减去总成本。我们刚刚给出了企业收益的计算方法，而成本我们也在前面的章节中详细地讨论过了。下面我们就来看一下，企业是如何在短期内使自己的利润最大化的，以及这种决策如何得出短期的供给曲线。

我们利用图 12.3 来寻找厂商实现利润最大化的生产均衡点。正如我们前几章讲的那样，生产厂商的边际成本曲线(*MC*)向右上倾斜；平均总成本曲线(*ATC*)是 U 型的；边际成本曲线与平均总成本曲线相交于平均总成本曲线的最低点。市场价格(*P*)是一条水平线。要记住，对一个竞争厂商来说，企业产品的价格既等于其平均收益（*AR*），又等于其边际收益(*MR*)。

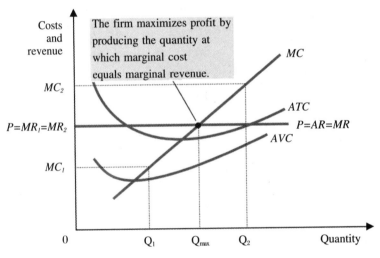

图 12.3　完全竞争企业的利润最大化

当厂商的决定产量小于 Q_{max}，例如为 Q_1 时，厂商的边际收益大于边际成本，即有 *MR>MC*。这表明厂商增加一单位产量所带来的总收益的增加量大于所付的总成本的增加量，也就是说，厂商增加产量是有利可图的，可以使利润得到增加。所以，只要 *MR>MC*，厂商就会增加产量，获得更大的利润（或更小的亏损）。相反，当产量大于均衡产量 *QMAX* 时，例如为 Q_2，厂商的边际收益小于边际成本，即有 *MR<MC*。这表明厂商每增加一单位产量所带来的总收益的增加量小于总成本的增加量，也就是说，增加产量是不利的，它会使利润减少。而这时减小产量是有利的，所以只要 *MR<MC*，厂商就会减少产量，直到 *MR=MC* 为止。这样，厂商的利润就会逐步达到最高的水平。

由此可见，厂商只有调整产量使 *MR=MC* 时，才能获得利润最大化。所以说，边际收益

MR 等于边际成本 *MC* 是厂商实现利润最大化的均衡条件。

在完全竞争厂商的短期生产中，市场价格是给定的，而且，生产中的不变要素的投入量是无法变动的，即生产规模也是给定的。因此，在短期，厂商在既定的生产规模下，只有通过对产量的调整才能实现 *MR=SMC* 这一利润最大化的均衡条件。

必须指出，完全竞争厂商在短期内依据 *MR=SMC* 的原则决定产量水平，并非一定能赢利，有的厂商能获得超额利润，有的只能获取正常利润，有的甚至还会亏损。究竟处于哪一种情况，既取决于由整个行业(或市场)的供求状况所决定的市场均衡价格水平，又取决于各厂商因管理水平等因素的差异而导致的平均成本和边际成本的不同。具体地说，完全竞争厂商在短期内有以下四种可能性。

1. 经济利润大于零

在市场均衡价格既定的情况下，由于厂商的技术和管理水平较高，从而使得其平均成本较低，在某些特别的情况下，厂商的平均成本曲线的最低点位于需求曲线以下，如图 12.4 (a)所示。

根据 *MR=SMC* 的利润最大化的均衡条件，厂商利润最大化的均衡点为 *MR* 曲线和 *SMC* 曲线的交点 *E*，相应的产量为 Q_e，在 Q_e 的均衡产量上，平均收益为 EQ_e，平均成本为 FQ_e。由于平均收益大于平均成本，厂商获得经济利润，其总量相当于图 12.4 (a)中阴影部分的面积。

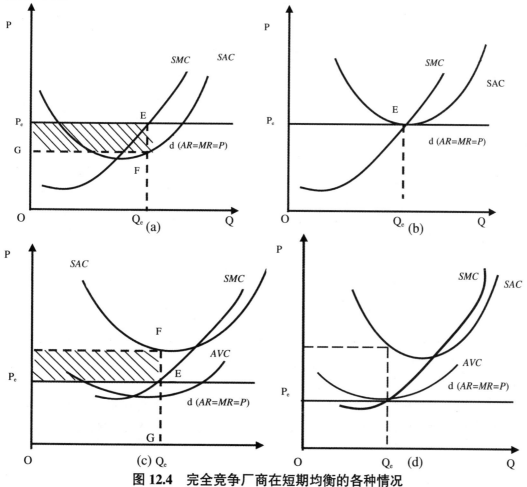

图 12.4 完全竞争厂商在短期均衡的各种情况

2. 经济利润为零

如果完全竞争厂商所面对的需求曲线与平均成本曲线的最低点相切,那么,该厂商只能赚取正常利润,经济利润为零,如图 12.4(b)所示。

在图 12.4(b)中,厂商的需求曲线 d 相切于 SAC 曲线的最低点。这一点是 SAC 曲线和 SMC 曲线的交点。这一点恰好也是由 MR=SMC 所确定的利润最大化的均衡点 E。在均衡产量 Q_e 上,平均收益等于平均成本,厂商的经济利润为零。但厂商的正常利润实现了,因为在均衡点 E 上,厂商既无利润,也无亏损。因此,SAC 曲线和 SMC 曲线的交点,也即平均成本曲线的最低点,又称为厂商的收支相抵点。

3. 亏损最小化的产量决策

如果厂商所面临的需求曲线低于平均成本曲线的最低点,且高于平均可变成本曲线的最低点时,厂商虽然遭受亏损,但仍应继续生产,如图 12.4(c)所示。

在图 12.4(c)中,由均衡点 E 和均衡产量 Q_e 可知,厂商的平均收益小于平均成本,厂商出现亏损,其亏损量相当于图 12.4(c)中阴影部分的面积。但由于在 Q_e 的产量上,厂商的平均收益大于平均可变成本 AVC,所以,厂商虽然亏损,但仍应该继续生产。这是因为,厂商用全部收益弥补全部可变成本以后还有剩余,可以弥补在短期内总是存在的固定成本的一部分,从而使亏损最小化。

4. 关闭政策

如果厂商所面对的需求曲线与平均可变成本的最低点恰好相切时,厂商亏损,处于生产与不生产的临界点,如图 12.4(d)所示。

在图 12.4(d)中,厂商的需求曲线相切于 AVC 曲线的最低点,这一点是 AVC 曲线和 SMC 曲线的交点,同时也是 MR=SMC 的利润最大化的均衡点。在均衡产量 Q_e 上,厂商是亏损的,其亏损相当于图中的阴影部分。此时,厂商的平均收益 AR 等于平均可变成本 AVC,无论生产或不生产,其结果都是一样的。如果厂商生产的话,则全部收益只能弥补全部可变成本,不变成本得不到任何弥补;如果厂商不生产的话,厂商虽然可以不必支付可变成本,但是全部不变成本仍然存在。因此,AVC 曲线和 SMC 曲线的交点,即 AVC 曲线的最低点,又被称为停止营业点或关闭点。当然,如果 AVC 曲线的最低点高出厂商的需求曲线,生产的全部收益都不足以弥补可变成本,不考虑其他因素,厂商的最佳选择是停产。

知道了这些之后,我们就可以推导出完全竞争厂商的短期供给曲线了。在完全竞争市场的条件下,只要市场价格确定,厂商不管出售多少数量的产品,都要按照这一价格出售,即需求曲线是水平的。在厂商面临的需求曲线为水平的情况下,厂商的边际收益 MR 等于厂商所面临的市场价格 P,按照利润最大化原则,厂商的价格 MR(等于边际收益 MR)等于边际成本 MC 时达到利润最大化。因此,当商品价格为 P 时,厂商会按照 MC 曲线在 P 处所对应的产量进行生产,因此,短期供给曲线与厂商的边际成本曲线(MC)是重合的。如图 12.5 所示。

但要注意的是,由于厂商短期生产只有在价格高于平均可变成本时($P \geq AVC$)才会进行。因此,厂商的短期供给曲线应该用 MC 曲线上的高于和等于 AVC 曲线最低点的部分来表示。

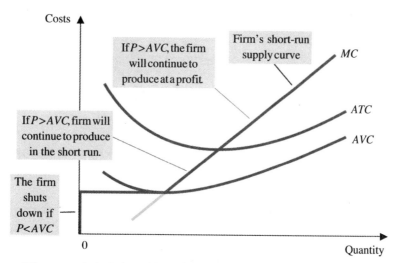

图12.5　完全竞争厂商的短期边际成本曲线及短期供给曲线

在完全竞争市场条件下，一个行业是由许多生产同样产品的厂商组成的，因而一个行业短期的供给曲线就是许多单个厂商的供给曲线的总和，即该行业中所有厂商高于平均可变成本的边际成本曲线部分的横向总和。

完全竞争厂商的长期均衡

根据前面的分析我们知道，完全竞争厂商在短期内可能出现以下三种情况：经济利润大于零、经济利润等于零和亏损。但在长期内只有一种可能性：在该市场的所有厂商只能获得正常利润也就是经济利润为零。

在长期生产中，所有的生产要素投入量都是可变的，完全竞争厂商可以做出两类选择。第一，厂商可以调整生产要素的使用量，进而选择最优的生产规模以实现利润最大化；第二，厂商可以决定继续停留于该产业或退出而进入其他产业。正是因为这两类选择活动使完全竞争厂商实现了长期均衡并且只能获取零经济利润。

如果市场上现有的企业是盈利的［如图12.6（a）］，新的企业就有动力进入这个行业。这种进入将增加企业数量，增加商品的供给量，从而导致商品价格下降，利润减少。相反，如果市场上的企业有亏损［如图12.6（b）］，那么一些现有的企业将退出市场。它们的退出将减少企业的数量，减少商品的供给量，从而促使价格提高，利润增加。在这种进入和退出过程结束后，仍然留在市场中的企业的经济利润必定是零。

我们可以把企业的利润写成：

$$\pi=(P-ATC) \times Q$$

从这个等式我们就能看出，当且仅当商品的价格等于它的平均总成本时，一个正在经营的厂商才能获得零利润。如果价格高于平均总成本，利润为正，这就鼓励了新企业的进入；如果价格低于平均总成本，利润为负，这就使得一些企业退出。只有当价格与平均总成本相等时，进入和退出的过程才会结束。

根据对企业行为的分析，我们可以进一步确定市场的长期供给曲线。在可以自由进入和退出的市场中，只有一种价格与零利润一致，那就是最低平均总成本的价格。因此，长期

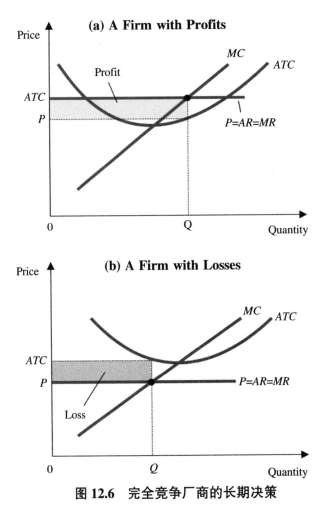

图 12.6　完全竞争厂商的长期决策

市场供给曲线必然是这种价格的水平线，如图 12.7（b）所示，是一条完全富有弹性的供给曲线。任何高于这种水平的价格都会引起正的利润，导致企业进入，并增加总供给量；任何低于这种水平的价格都会引起亏损，导致企业退出，并减少总供给量。最后，市场中的企业数量必须做出调整，以使价格等于最低的平均总成本，而且，在这种价格时，有足够的企业可以满足所有需求。

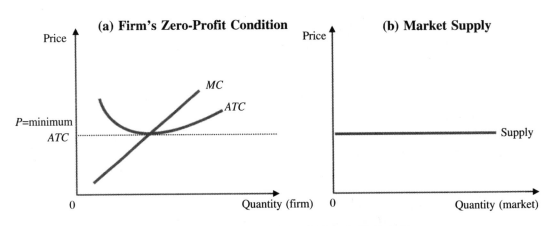

图 12.7　完全竞争厂商的长期供给曲线

这里，我们必须来说明一个乍一看很荒唐的问题。为什么竞争企业从长期看来只能获得零利润呢？如果真是这样，那么企业家为什么还要开工厂呢？这也和我们在现实中看到的似乎有所出入。

这里，我们必须界定清楚经济利润这个概念，它和我们在生活中经常看到的会计利润有所不同。我们也在前面说过这个问题，会计师们只关注显性成本，不关注隐形成本。这就是说，他们衡量的是使货币流出企业的成本，但没有包括不涉及货币流出的机会成本。举个例子，一个人投资 20 万经营一个面包店，这样他就放弃了把 20 万存入银行可以获得的每年 1 万的利息收入，同时，他还必须放弃一份年薪 3 万的工作。这 4 万元其实并不会计入到他的会计成本中，而会作为机会成本计入到他的经济成本中。因此，即使他最终的经济利润为零，他也可以从这个面包店中获得 4 万元的会计利润。

我们再来进一步探讨完全竞争市场的长期供给曲线。前面的分析中，我们得到了一条水平的长期供给曲线，这与我们现实看到的情况似乎也有所不同。原因就在于我们假设了长期内，当厂商进入或退出一个行业时，整个行业产量的变化对生产要素的需求和价格不会产生影响，所以厂商的长期平均成本不变。我们用图 12.8 来进行分析。

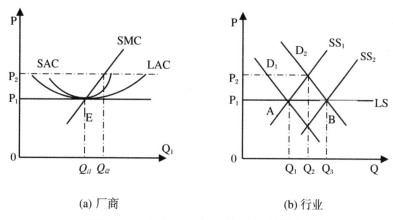

(a) 厂商　　　　　　　(b) 行业

图 12.8　成本不变行业的长期供给曲线

图(a)中单个厂商在 LAC 曲线的最低点 E 实现长期均衡，单个厂商的利润为零。相应地，在图(b)中，表示市场供求相等的市场需求曲线 D_1 和短期供给曲线 SS_1 的交点 A，是行业的一个长期均衡点。在长期均衡状态中，市场均衡的价格为 P_1，它等于单个厂商的最低长期平均成本，产品的均衡产量为 Q_1。

现假定市场需求增加，市场需求曲线由 D_1 移到 D_2，形成新的市场均衡价格 P_2，厂商按照现有的生产规模沿着短期供给曲线，即 SMC 曲线，将产量调整到 Q_{i2}。单个厂商的供给量 Q_{i2} 之和便构成了行业的总供给量 Q_2，它满足了市场上增加的需求，同时单个厂商也获得了利润。

从长期来看，利润的存在会将新的厂商吸引到该行业的生产中来，从而使行业的供给进一步增加。假定在供给不断增加的过程中，生产要素的价格不发生变化，那么厂商在每一个产量的投入要素的支出成本既不会增加，也不会减少，企业的成本曲线位置不发生任何变化。随着新厂商的进入所引起的行业供给的增加，行业的短期供给曲线 SS_1 不断向右下方平移，这个过程一直持续到市场的均衡价格下降到使单个厂商的利润消失为止，即市场短期供给曲线移到 SS_2 位置。于是整个行业在 SS_2 曲线和 D_2 曲线的交点 B 实现了长期均衡。在行业新的长期均衡点 B 上，市场的均衡价格又回到了原来长期均衡价格 P_1 的水平。同时，单个厂商又在 LAC 曲线的最低点 E 实现了长期均衡。市场的长期供给量由原来的 Q_1 增加到 Q_3，其增加量 Q_1Q_3 是新加入的厂商提供的。行业内每个厂商的供给量仍为 Q_{i1}。

连接图 (b) 中 A、B 这两个行业的长期均衡点的直线 LS，就是行业的长期供给曲线。成本不变行业的长期供给曲线是一条水平线，它表示在长期内，成本不变行业是在不变的均衡价格水平的提供产量，这个均衡价格水平等于单个厂商不变的最低长期平均成本。整个行业的均衡产量，会因市场需求的增减而增减。而长期的均衡价格却不会发生变化。

然而在现实中，整个行业产量的变化是可以对生产要素的需求和价格产生影响的，进而影响厂商的长期平均成本。除了成本不变行业，还有成本递增行业和成本递减行业。

1. 成本递增行业的长期供给曲线

成本递增行业是这样一种行业，它的产量的增加所引起的生产要素的增加会导致生产要素价格的上升。在这种情况下，行业的长期供给曲线是一条向右上方倾斜的曲线。我们以图 12.9 为例进行分析。

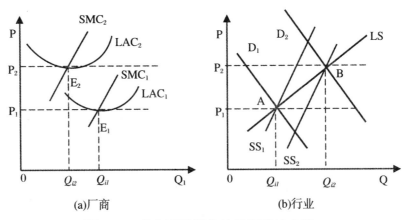

图 12.9　成本递增行业的长期供给曲线

最初，完全竞争厂商的生产成本以 LAC_1 和 SMC_1 曲线表示。图 (a) 中 LAC_1 曲线的最低点 E_1 和图 (b) 中的市场供求曲线 D_1 和 SS_1 的交点 A，分别是完全竞争厂商和行业的长期均衡点。此时，市场的均衡价格为 P_1，它等于厂商的最低长期平均成本 E_1Q_{i1}；市场的均衡产量为 Q_1，它等于行业内每个厂商提供的均衡产量 Q_{i1} 之和，行业内每个厂商的利润为零。

如果市场需求增加，市场需求曲线移至 D_2，市场均衡价格水平上升，从而给单个厂商带来了利润，并将新的厂商吸引到该行业的生产中来。假定行业产量的扩张，使生产要素的价格上升，于是厂商生产每一产量水平的要素的成本支出增加，企业的整个成本曲线的位置向上移动。最后行业的短期供给曲线移至 SS_2，单个厂商的成本曲线上升至 LAC_2 和 SMC_2 单个厂商在 LAC_2 曲线的最低点 E_2 实现长期均衡，整个行业在 SS_2 曲线和 D_2 曲线的交点 B 实现长期均衡。此时市场的长期均衡价格为 P_2，等于企业的最低长期平均成本 E_2Q_{i2}；行业的供给量为 Q_2，等于行业内每个厂商的供给量 Q_{i2} 之和；行业内每个厂商的利润为零。顺便需指出的是,图中单个厂商的长期均衡产量 Q_{i2} 小于原来的长期均衡产量 Q_{i1}。实际上,Q_{i2} 可以小于、大于或等于 Q_{i1},这要视具体情况而定。

连接图 (b) 中 A、B 这两个行业的长期均衡点的直线 LS,就是行业的长期供给曲线。成本递增行业供给曲线是向右上方倾斜的,它表示随着成本递增行业长期供给量的增加,长期供给价格是不断上升的。市场需求的变化不仅引起行业长期均衡产量的同方向变化,还引起市场长期均衡价格的同方向变化。

2. 成本递减行业的长期供给曲线

成本递增行业是这样一种行业,它的产量的增加引起生产要素需求的增加,反而使生产要素的价格下降了。行业成本递减的是由于外在经济的作用,这主要可能是因为生产要素行业的产量增加,使得行业内单个企业的生产效率提高,从而使得所生产出来的要素的价格下降。成本递减行业的长期供给曲线是向右下方倾斜的。我们以图 12.10 为例进行分析。

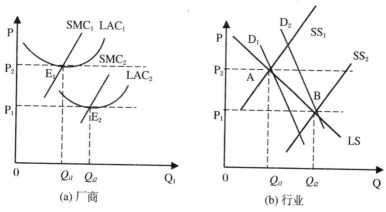

图 12.10　成本递减行业的长期供给曲线

图 (a) 中的 E_1 点和图 (b) 中的 A 点,分别是初始完全竞争厂商和行业的长期均衡点。

当市场的需求增加时,市场的需求曲线移至 D_2,市场的均衡价格升高,单个厂商获得利润。此时,新厂商会进入,行业的供给会增加,行业的短期供给曲线 SS_1 会向右移动。假定行业产量的增加反而使生产要素的价格下降,单个厂商的成本曲线位置就会向下移动,最后行业的短期供给曲线移至 SS_2 的位置,厂商成本下降到 LAC_2 和 SMC_2 曲线的位置,单个厂商在 LAC_2 曲线的最低点 E_2 实现长期均衡,整个行业在市场供求曲线 D_2 和 SS_2 的交点 B 实现长期均衡。此时市场的长期均衡价格由 P_2 下降为 P_1,它等于企业的最低长期成本 E_2Q_{i2};行业的供给量为 Q_2,它等于行业内所有厂商的供给量 Q_{i2} 之和;行业内的每个厂商的利润都为零。

连接图 (b) 中 A、B 这两个行业的长期均衡点的直线 LS,便是行业的长期供给曲线。成本递减行业的长期供给曲线是向右下方倾斜的。它表示该行业的长期供给价格随行业长期供给量的增加而下降。市场需求的变化会引起行业长期均衡产量的同方向变化和市场长期均衡价格的反方向变化。

大多数西方经济学家认为,就以上三种类型的行业来说,在经济生活中成本递增行业是比较普遍的,成本递减行业则较少。在大多数情况下,行业的长期供给曲线是向右上方倾斜的。

重要名词解释

1. **Perfect competition**: markets such that no participants are large enough to have the market power to set the price of a homogeneous product

2. **Marginal revenue**: the extra revenue that an additional unit of product will bring. It is the additional income from selling one more unit of a good

3. **Average revenue**: the revenue received for selling a good per unit of output sold, found by dividing total revenue by the quantity of output

4. **Price taker**: a firm that can alter its rate of production and sales without significantly affecting the market price of its product

5. **Total revenue**: the total receipts of a firm from the sale of any given quantity of output. It can be calculated as the selling price of the firm's product times the quantity sold

主要图表

1.

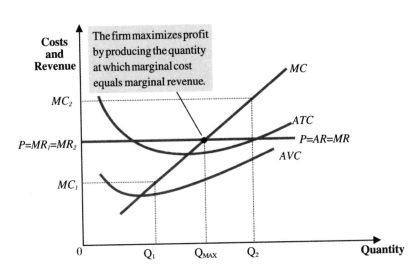

2.

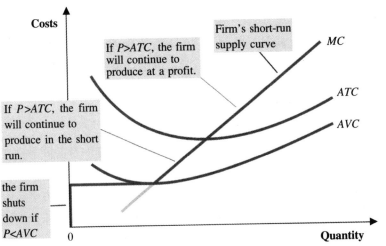

3.

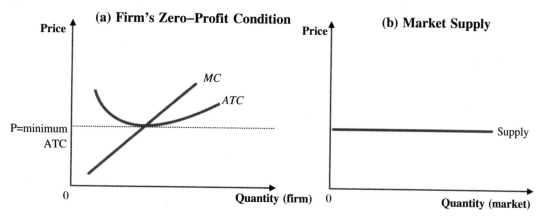

(a) Firm's Zero–Profit Condition

Price

MC

ATC

P=minimum
ATC

0   Quantity (firm)

(b) Market Supply

Price

Supply

0   Quantity (market)

模拟试题

1. A firm has market power if it can

A. Maximize profits.

B. Minimize costs.

C. Influence the market price of the good it sells.

D. Hire as many workers as it needs at the prevailing wage rate.

E. Produce a lot of goods.

Key: C

Analysis: If a firm can influence the market price of the good it sells, it is said to have market power.

2. The analysis of competitive firms sheds light on the decisions that lie behind the

A. Demand curve.

B. Supply curve.

C. Way firms make pricing decisions in the not-for-profit sector of the economy.

D. Way financial markets set interest rates.

E. Average cost curve.

Key: B

Analysis: Buyers and sellers in competitive markets are said to be price takers. So we care more about the supply curve.

3. A key characteristic of a competitive market is that

A. Government antitrust laws regulate competition.

B. Producers sell nearly identical products.

C. Firms minimize total costs.

D. Firms have price setting power.

E. Free entry is unlimited.

Key: B

Analysis: Producers sell nearly identical products. This is the key and basic characteristic. So firms can freely enter or exit the market.

4. A market is competitive if

(i) Firms have the flexibility to price their own product.

(ii) Each buyer is small compared to the market.

(iii) Each seller is small compared to the market.

A. (i) and (ii) only

B. (i) and (iii) only

C. (ii) and (iii) only

D. (i), (ii), and (iii)

E. (i) only

Key: C

Analysis: In a perfectly competitive market, each buyer and seller takes the market price as given.

5. Suppose that a firm operating in perfectly competitive market sells 100 units of output. Its total revenues from the sale are $500. Which of the following statements is correct?

(i) Marginal revenue equals $5.

(ii) Average revenue equals $5.

(iii) Price equals $5.

A. (i) only

B. (iii) only

C. (i) and (ii) only

D. (ii), and (iii) only

E. (i), (ii), and (iii)

Key: E

Analysis: In the perfectly competitive market, P=MR=AR.

6. Which of the following statements is correct?

A. For all firms, marginal revenue equals the price of the good.

B. Only for competitive firms does average revenue equal the price of the good.

C. Marginal revenue can be calculated as total revenue divided by the quantity sold.

D. Only for competitive firms does average revenue equal marginal revenue.

E. For all firms, average revenue is always less than the marginal revenue.

Key: D

Analysis: In the competitive markets, average revenue equals marginal revenue, and they both equal P.

7. Comparing marginal revenue to marginal cost

(i) Reveals the contribution of the last unit of production to total profit.

(ii) Is helpful in making profit-maximizing production decisions.

(iii) Tells a firm whether its fixed costs are too high.

A. (i) only

B. (i) and (ii) only

C. (ii) and (iii) only

D. (i) and (iii) only

E. (i) , (ii) and (iii)

Key: B

Analysis: It examines the cost-benefit analysis method and marginal thinking. Profit maximization occurs at the quantity where marginal revenue equals marginal cost.

8.　At the profit-maximizing level of output,

A. Marginal revenue equals average total cost.

B. Marginal revenue equals average variable cost.

C. Marginal revenue equals marginal cost.

D. Average revenue equals average total cost.

E. Average revenue equals marginal cost.

Key: C

Analysis: When MR = MC, profit is maximized.

9.　When profit-maximizing firms in competitive markets are earning profits,

A. Market demand must exceed market supply at the market equilibrium price.

B. Market supply must exceed market demand at the market equilibrium price.

C. New firms will enter the market.

D. The most inefficient firms will be encouraged to leave the market.

E. The most efficient firms will decrease the production.

Key: C

Analysis: A firm will enter the industry if such an action would be profitable. Firms will enter or exit the market until profit is driven to zero.

10.　The accountants hired by Davis Golf Course have determined total fixed cost to be $75,000, total variable cost to be $130,000, and total revenue to be $145,000. With this information, in the short run, Davis Golf Course should

A. Shut-down.

B. Exit the industry.

C. Stay open because shutting down would be more expensive.

D. Stay open because the firm is making an economic profit.

E. Stay opens because of the sunk cost.

Key: C

Analysis: The firm shuts down if the revenue it gets from producing is less than the variable cost of production. But 145,000>130,000, so it stays open.

11.　Which of the following expressions is correct for a competitive firm?

A. Profit = (Quantity of output) × (Price – Average total cost)

B. Marginal revenue = (Change in total revenue)/(Quantity of output)

C. Average total cost = Total variable cost/Quantity of output

D. Average revenue = (Marginal revenue) × (Quantity of output)

E. All of the above are false.

Key: A

Analysis: It examines the understanding of some important concepts and calculation related to competitive firms.

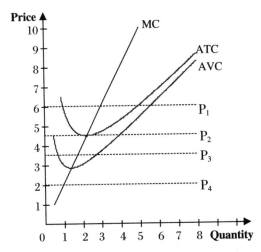

12. Refer to the figure above. If the market price is P2, in the short run, the perfectly competitive firm will earn

A. Positive economic profits.

B. Negative economic profits but will try to remain open.

C. Negative economic profits and will shut down.

D. Zero economic profits.

E. Negative economic profits and will exit.

Key: D

Analysis: At this point, P=MR=ATC, and the economic profit is 0.

13. Refer to figure above. If the market price is P3, in the short run, the perfectly competitive firm will earn

A. Positive economic profits.

B. Negative economic profits but will try to remain open.

C. Negative economic profits and will shut down.

D. Zero economic profits.

E. Zero economic profits and will exit.

Key: B

Analysis: At this point, AVC<P=MR<ATC, the economic profit is negative, but still can recover the fixed costs.

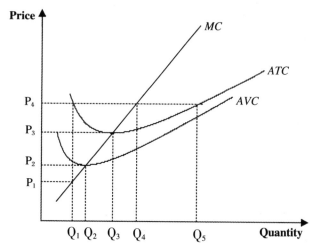

14. Refer to the figure above. When price falls from P_3 to P_1, the firm finds that it

   A. Decreases its fixed costs.

   B. Should produce Q_1 units of output.

   C. Should produce Q_3 units of output.

   D. Should shut down immediately.

   E. Should produce Q_2 units of output.

Key: D

Analysis: P1<AVC, so it should shut down.

15. Refer to the figure above. When price rises from P_3 to P_4, the firm finds that

   A. Fixed costs decrease as output increases from Q_3 to Q_4.

   B. It can earn a positive profit by increasing production to Q_4.

   C. Profit is still maximized at a production level of Q_3.

   D. Average revenue exceeds marginal revenue at a production level of Q_4.

   E. A and B

Key: B

Analysis: P=MC>ATC, so it can earn a positive profit by increasing production to Q_4. MC curve（above AVC curve）is the supply curve.

16. In the short-run, a firm's supply curve is equal to the

   A. Marginal cost curve above its average variable cost curve.

   B. Marginal cost curve above its average total cost curve.

   C. Average variable cost curve above its marginal cost curve.

   D. Average total cost curve above its marginal cost curve.

   E. Average variable cost curve below its average total cost curve.

Key: A

Analysis: The competitive firm's long-run supply curve is the portion of its marginal-cost curve that lies above its average total cost.

17. In the long run, assuming that the owner of a firm in a competitive industry has positive opportunity costs, she

A. Should exit the industry unless her economic profits are positive.

B. Will earn zero accounting profits but positive economic profits.

C. Will earn zero economic profits but positive accounting profits.

D. Should ignore opportunity costs because they are a type of sunk cost that disappears in the long run.

E. Will earn positive economic profits and positive accounting profits.

Key: C

Analysis: In the long run, the economic profits must be 0. When a firm gets 0 economic profit, it has the positive accounting profits.

18. Regardless of the cost structure of firms in a competitive market, in the long run

A. Firms will experience rising demand for their products.

B. The marginal firm will earn zero economic profit.

C. Firms will experience a less competitive market environment.

D. Exit and entry is likely to lead to a horizontal long-run supply curve.

E. None of the above is right.

Key: B

Analysis: If firms have different costs, some firms earn profit even in the long run. In this case, the price in the market reflects the average total cost of the marginal firm—the firm that would exit the market if the price were any lower.

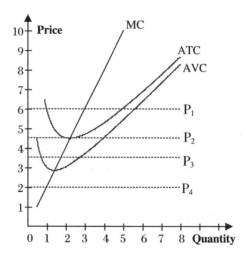

19. Refer to the figure above. If the price is P_1 in the short run, what will happen in the long run?

A. Nothing. The price is consistent with zero economic profits, so there is no incentive for firms to enter or exit the industry.

B. Individual firms will earn positive economic profits in the short run, which will entice other firms to enter the industry.

C. Individual firms will earn negative economic profits in the short run, which will cause some firms to exit the industry.

D. Because the price is below the firm's average variable costs, the firms will shut down.

E. Because the price is below the firm's average total costs, the firms will shut down.

Key: B

Analysis: At that point, P_1>ATC, and there will be positive economic profits. So some new firms will enter the market.

20. The production decisions of perfectly competitive firms follow one of the Ten Principles of Economics, which states that rational people

　A. Consider sunk costs.

　B. Equate prices to the average costs of production.

　C. Will eventually leave markets that experience zero profit.

　D. Think at the margin.

　E. People face tradeoffs.

Key: D

Analysis: In the analysis, we compare the marginal revenue with the marginal cost. When MR=MC, the profit is maximized.

21. Cathy's Orchard grows oranges and operates in a constant-cost and perfectly competitive orange industry. Cathy's Orchard is currently in long-run equilibrium.

　(a) Draw correctly labeled side-by-side graphs for the apple market and Cathy's Orchard, and show each of the following.

　　(i) Market output and price, labeled as "Q_M" and "P_M", respectively.

　　(ii) Cathy's output and price, labeled as "Q_F" and "P_F", respectively.

　(b) Assume that the government provides farm support to orange growers by granting an annual lump-sum subsidy to all orange growers. Indicate the effect the subsidy would have on each of the following in the short run.

　　(i) Cathy's quantity of output. Explain.

　　(ii) Cathy's profit

　　(iii) The number of firms in the industry

　(c) Indicate how each of the following will change in the long run as a result of the lump-sum subsidy.

　　(i) The number of firms in the industry. Explain.

　　(ii) Price

　　(iii) Industry output

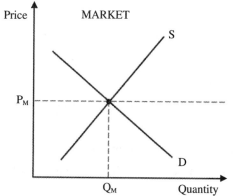
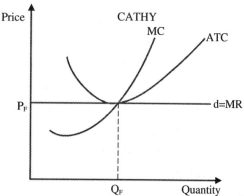

Key: 12 points $(4 + 4 + 4)$

(a) 4 points:

One point is earned for a correctly labeled graph of the apple market, with P_M and Q_M properly indicated.

One point is earned for showing that the firm's price equals the market price.

One point is earned for the tangency of flat firm demand (P_F) and ATC.

One point is earned for Q_F where MR $(P) =$ MC.

(b) 4 points:

One point is earned for concluding that the lump-sum subsidy will have no impact on Cathy's output.

One point is earned for explaining that the lump-sum subsidy will not affect MC (or MR).

One point is earned for concluding that Cathy's profit will increase.

One point is earned for concluding that the number of firms in the industry will not change.

(c) 4 points:

One point is earned for concluding that the number of firms in the industry will increase.

One point is earned for explaining that the existence of profits attracts new firms.

One point is earned for concluding that the price will fall.

One point is earned for concluding that industry output will increase.

Short-Run Total Cost Function

Quantity Produced	Total Cost (in dollars)
0	20
1	27
2	38
3	53
4	72
5	95
6	122

22. The table above gives the short-run total cost function for a typical firm in a perfectly competitive industry.

(a) What is the dollar value of the firm's total fixed cost?

(b) Calculate the marginal cost of producing the first unit of output.

(c) If the price the firm receives for its product is $20, indicate the firm's profit-maximizing quantity of output and explain how you determined your answer.

(d) Given your results in part (c), explain what will happen to the number of firms in the industry in the long run.

(e) Assume that this firm operates in a constant-cost industry and has reached long-run equilibrium. If the government imposes a per-unit tax of $2, indicate what will happen to the firm's profit-maximizing output in the long run.

Key: 7 points（1+1+2+ 2+1）

（a）1 point:

One point is earned for indicating that TFC is $20.

（b）1 point:

One point is earned for indicating that MC of the first unit is $7.

（c）2 points:

One point is earned for indicating that the profit-maximizing output=4 units（or between 4 and 5 units）.

One point is earned for explaining that MR>MC for all units until Q=5（or direct calculation of TR–TC）.

（d）2 points:

One point is earned for concluding that the number of firms will increase.

One point is earned for explaining that profits will attract new firms to enter.

（e）1 point:

One point is earned for stating that there is no change in the profit-maximizing output.

23. AmeriDairy, a typical profit-maximizing dairy firm, is operating in a constant-cost, perfectly competitive industry that is in long-run equilibrium.

（a）Draw correctly labeled side-by-side graphs for the dairy market and for AmeriDairy and show each of the following.

（i）Price and output for the industry

（ii）Price and output for AmeriDairy

（b）Assume that milk is a normal good and that consumer income falls. Assume that AmeriDairy continues to produce. On your graphs in part（a）, show the effect of the decrease in income on each of the following in the short run.

（i）Price and output for the industry

（ii）Price and output for AmeriDairy

（iii）Area of loss or profit for AmeriDairy

（c）Following the decrease in consumer income, what must be true for AmeriDairy to continue to produce in the short run?

（d）Assume that the industry adjusts to a new long-run equilibrium. Compare the following between the initial and the new long-run equilibrium.

（i）Price in the industry

（ii）Output of a typical firm

（iii）The number of firms in the dairy industry

Key: 12 points（4 + 4 + 1 + 3）

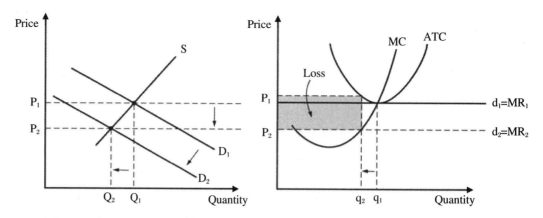

(a) 4 points:

One point is earned for a correctly labeled market graph of the dairy industry.

One point is earned for correctly labeled equilibrium industry price and quantity.

One point is earned for drawing a horizontal demand curve for AmeriDairy at the market price.

One point is earned for showing the equilibrium quantity for AmeriDairy where price equals marginal cost and the minimum of average total cost (P=MC=ATC).

(b) 4 points:

One point is earned for showing a decrease in market demand.

One point is earned for showing a decrease in equilibrium market price and quantity.

One point is earned for showing the change to a new lower profit-maximizing price and quantity for AmeriDairy.

One point is earned for shading the area of loss for AmeriDairy.

(c) 1 point:

One point is earned for stating that P>AVC, TR>TVC, or losses are less than total fixed cost.

(d) 3 points:

One point is earned for stating that industry price returns to the original long-run equilibrium price.

One point is earned for stating that the output of a typical firm returns to the original profit-maximizing quantity.

One point is earned for stating that there is a decrease in the number of firms.

24. J & P Company operates in a perfectly competitive market for smoke alarms. J & P is currently earning short-run positive economic profits.

(a) Using correctly labeled side-by-side graphs for the smoke alarm market and J & P Company indicate each of the following for both the market and the J & P Company.

(i) Price

(ii) Output

(b) In the graph in part(a) for J & P, indicate the area of economic profits that J & P

Company is earning in the short run.

(c) Using a new set of correctly labeled side-by-side graphs for the smoke alarm market and J & P Company, show what will happen in the long run to each of the following.

(i) Long-run equilibrium price and quantity in the market

(ii) Long-run equilibrium price and quantity for J & P Company

(d) Assume that purchases of smoke alarms create positive externalities. Draw a correctly labeled graph of the smoke alarm market.

(i) Label the market equilibrium quantity as Q_M

(ii) Label the socially optimum equilibrium quantity as Q_S

(e) Identify one government policy that could be implemented to encourage the industry to produce the socially optimum level of smoke alarms.

Key:

Part a: The market graph should have a downward-sloping demand curve and an upward-sloping supply curve with an equilibrium price and quantity clearly labeled. The firm graph should have a perfectly elastic (or horizontal) demand curve at the equilibrium market price. The firm's profit-maximizing quantity is found at the intersection of this demand or marginal revenue curve with the firm's marginal cost curve.

Part b: The firm's profits are represented by the rectangle that has a height (or vertical distance) of (P–ATC) multiplied by the firm's profit-maximizing output or q.

Part c: With profits being earned, new firms will enter the smoke alarm market. The market supply will increase (shift out to the right) and the equilibrium price will fall and quantity will increase. As the market price falls, the firm has a downward shift in its horizontal demand curve. The process continues until price of output has fallen to the minimum of the average total cost of the firm.

Part d: With a positive consumption externality in the market for smoke alarms, the demand curve with marginal social benefits should lie above the demand curve with only marginal private benefits. Thus, the socially optimal output level will exceed the output level produced by an unregulated private market.

Part e: To increase the market output to the socially optimal output, the government could subsidize the consumption or production of smoke alarms.

Point allocations: (12 points: 4+1+4+2+1)

(a) 4 points:

1 point for the market graph (S, D) with a downward-sloping demand curve and an upward sloping supply curve.

1 point for correctly labeling equilibrium P and Q for the market.

1 point for the firm graph (horizontal D or P curve).

1 point for applying MR=MC to find equilibrium quantity.

MR must be logically consistent with demand curve

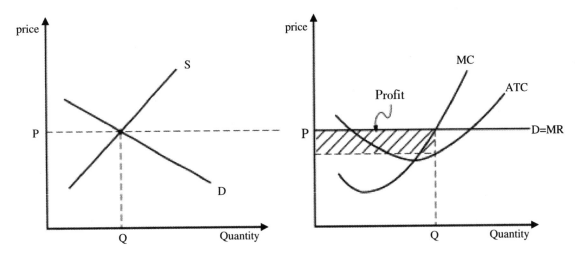

(b) 1 point for showing the AREA of economic profit for the firm. Must use P, ATC, and q.

(c) 4 points: (2 +2)

(i) 2 points:

1 point for showing an increase in supply on market graph (resulting from the entry of new firms).

1 point for showing both a lower P and higher Q due to an increase in supply.

(ii) 2 points:

1 point for the downward shift in the firm's demand curve (P or MR or D).

1 point for q (for firm) where P = min ATC for firm.

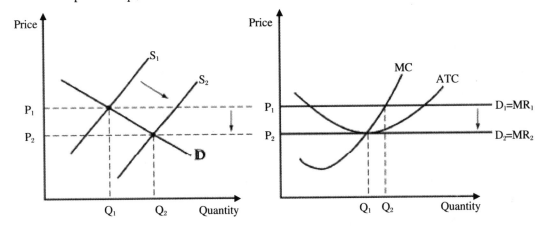

(d) 2 points:

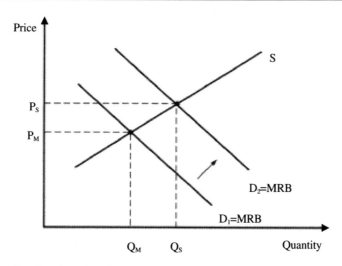

1 point for showing that $Q_S > Q_M$.

1 point for having two marginal benefit curves: one with and the other without the positive externality.

(e) 1 point for any of the following: subsidize sellers or buyers, mandatory smoke alarm system, or tax relief.

主要内容和概念讲解

　　打开一台电脑，它的操作系统十有八九是微软公司研发生产的视窗系统。对于类似的科技公司而言，专利保护使得它们在相应的市场上享有一定的市场势力，能够影响市场价格与产量。相对于上一章的价格接受者(price taker)而言，这些企业则被认为是价格制定者(price maker)。

　　对于完全竞争市场中企业行为的描述，已经不能够准确地描绘不完全竞争市场中的企业模式，所以我们还需要再引入完全垄断、垄断竞争、寡头这三种市场结构的概念。它们都属于不完全竞争市场，可以用市场中企业的个数以及市场势力的程度来加以区分。完全竞争市场和完全垄断市场就如同相对的两极，下面我们先从完全垄断市场来探讨不完全竞争市场的特征。

完全垄断市场的形成

　　完全垄断通常简称为垄断(monopoly)，它包括卖方垄断和买方垄断。但是，在无特殊说明的情况下，完全垄断(或垄断)常指卖方垄断。本章主要研究的是卖方垄断的商品市场。完全垄断市场是指整个行业中只有唯一一家厂商的市场组织形式。完全垄断市场必须具备以下三个条件：第一，市场上只有唯一一家厂商生产和销售商品；第二，该厂商生产和销售的商品只有一种，且没有任何相近的替代品；第三，新厂商不能进入该市场。这样的市场排除了任何的竞争因素，独家垄断厂商控制了整个行业的生产和销售。所以，垄断厂商可以控制和操纵市场价格。完全垄断市场与完全竞争市场一样，也是市场结构的一种极端，在现实经济生活中是不常见的。垄断厂商不存在直接的竞争者，但是并非不存在潜在或间接的竞争者，因为许多商品之间都存在一定程度的替代关系。尽管如此，完全垄断同样是一个非常有用的模型，它向我们揭示了不完全竞争市场最根本的特征。

　　在这三个特征中，最重要的就是行业壁垒。正是由于行业壁垒的存在，才使得垄断厂商能够长期维持自己的垄断地位。形成这种行业壁垒的原因主要有以下几个：第一，独家厂商控制了生产某种商品所必需的原材料的全部供给。这种对生产资源的独占，排除了其他厂商生产同种商品的可能性。例如，一直到二战之前，美国的 Alcoa 公司(铝业公司)都拥有和控制着制铝所必需的原料即铝土矿的所有来源，这也是该公司能够长期独霸美国制铝业的一个重要原因。

　　第二，独家厂商拥有某种商品生产的专利权。各国政府和国际组织为鼓励发明创造，保护发明者的利益，都制定了许多有关专利权的法律。这样，只要拥有了专利权就可以形成垄断。例如当玻璃纸刚刚发明出来时，美国的 DUPONT 公司(杜邦公司)就是依靠专利权垄断了全部玻璃纸的生产。

第三，政府的特许经营权。政府往往通过授予某个厂商经营某种商品的特许权，垄断某行业的生产，从而实现特定的社会目标。许多国家的铁路运输部门，供电、供水部门，以及邮政业等都是政府给予某个厂商特许的垄断经营权，从而使该独家厂商成为这些行业的垄断者。

第四，自然垄断，即由于规模经济的需要而形成的垄断。自然垄断是指由于一个企业能够以低于两个或更多企业的成本向整个市场供给一种产品或劳务而产生的垄断。某些行业在相关产量范围内存在着规模报酬递增的特征，并且市场规模正好处于这一范围之内。此时，在这些行业中只需要一家厂商生产经营就可以满足整个市场的需求，并可获取规模经济的好处。若有两家或两家以上的厂商生产则会产生较高的平均成本，造成社会资源的浪费。通过竞争，行业内总会有某个厂商最先达到规模经济所要求的最佳生产规模，从而垄断整个行业的生产和销售，这样，自然垄断就产生了。例如，铁路和城市的公共事业就属于自然垄断。

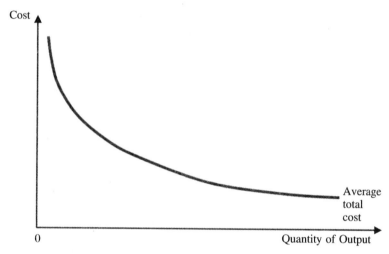

图 13.1　规模经济导致的垄断的形成

自然垄断的形成与技术条件、市场规模等因素密切相关，同时也是政府根据成本收益分析实施进入管制的结果。随着技术的进步、市场规模的扩大及政府进入管制的放松，一些部门的自然垄断正在逐步失去其合理性，可能会演变成寡头垄断、垄断竞争甚至完全竞争。

垄断厂商的需求曲线和收益曲线

1、垄断厂商的需求曲线

与完全竞争市场不同，完全垄断市场中只有一个厂商，或者说，一个厂商就是整个行业。因此，市场的需求曲线就是垄断厂商所面临的需求曲线，它是一条向右下方倾斜的曲线，垄断厂商的需求曲线可由图 13.2(b)来表示，垄断厂商可以用减少销售量的方法来提高市场价格，也可以用增加销售量的方法来压低市场价格。也就是说，垄断厂商可以通过改变销售量来控制市场价格，而且，垄断厂商的销售量与市场价格的变动成反比。

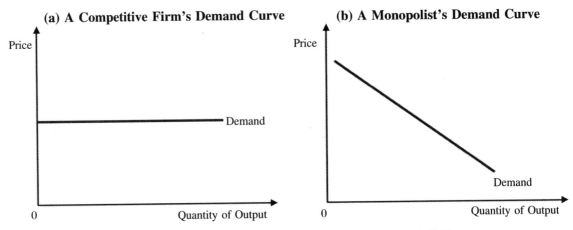

图 13.2　完全竞争市场和完全垄断市场厂商的需求曲线

2、垄断厂商的收益曲线

在完全竞争市场中，厂商的需求曲线、平均收益曲线和边际收益曲线三线重叠。而在完全垄断市场中，垄断厂商的收益曲线与完全竞争市场有较大的差异。

我们通过表 13.1 中给出的例子来看一下垄断厂商的收益情况。

表 13.1　垄断厂商的总收益、平均收益和边际收益

Quantity of Gasoline	Price	Total Revenue	Average Revenue	Marginal Revenue
(Q)	(P)	$(TR=P\times Q)$	$AR=TR/Q$	$(MR=\Delta TR/\Delta Q)$
0 gallon	$11	$0	–	
1	10	10	$10	$10
2	9	18	9	8
3	8	24	8	6
4	7	28	7	4
5	6	30	6	2
6	5	30	5	0
7	4	28	4	−2
8	3	24	3	−4

前两栏表示垄断厂商所面临的需求曲线。如果生产 1 加仑的汽油，它可以把这 1 加仑的汽油卖到 10 美元；如果生产 2 加仑，价格就得下降到 9 美元，以此类推。表的第三栏代表垄断厂商的总收益，它等于销售量乘以价格。第四栏代表企业的平均收益，即企业每售出一单位产品得到的收益量。我们可以用第三栏中总收益的数字除以第一栏中的产量来计算平均收益。

表的最后一栏表示企业的边际收益，即企业每增加一单位产量所得到的收益。例如，当企业生产 3 加仑汽油时，它得到的总收益是 24 美元；当生产量增加到 4 加仑时，总收益增加到了 28 美元。因此，边际收益为 28 美元-24 美元=4 美元。

从表中我们可以发现垄断厂商的一些很重要的特征：垄断厂商的平均收益与产品的价格总是相等的（这一点与完全竞争厂商一致），边际收益却总是小于产品的价格。下面，我们就来看看垄断厂商的收益情况。

平均收益曲线： 由于垄断厂商的平均收益 AR 等于总收益 TR 除以产量 Q，即

$$AR=TR(Q)/Q=P(Q) \cdot Q/Q=P(Q)。$$

因此，垄断厂商的平均收益曲线和需求曲线重叠，都是同一条向右下方倾斜的曲线。如图 13.3 所示。

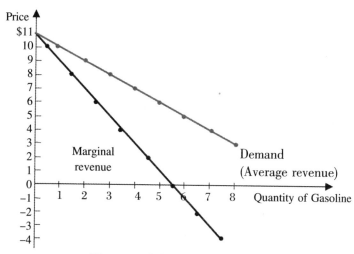

图 13.3　垄断厂商的收益曲线

边际收益曲线： 在完全垄断市场中，垄断厂商的需求曲线是一条向右下方倾斜的曲线，这意味着增加销售量就会降低商品的价格，减少销售量就会使价格上升。而价格又和平均收益相同，由此可推知垄断厂商的边际收益总是小于平均收益 。因此，如图 13.3 所示，完全垄断厂商的边际收益曲线位于平均收益曲线的左下方，且也向右下方倾斜。

总收益曲线： 由于每一销售量上的边际收益 MR 值就是相应的总收益 TR 曲线的斜率，因此，当 $MR>0$ 时，TR 曲线的斜率为正；当 $MR<0$ 时，TR 曲线的斜率为负；当 $MR=0$ 时，TR 曲线达到最大值。

完全垄断厂商的短期均衡

垄断厂商为了获取最大的利润，也必须遵循 $MR=MC$ 原则。在短期内，垄断厂商无法改变不变生产要素的投入量，只能在既定的生产规模下通过对产量和价格的调整来实现利润最大化。下面通过图 13.4 来说明。

图 13.4 中的 SMC 曲线和 SAC 曲线代表垄断厂商在短期内既定的生产规模，D 曲线和 MR 曲线代表厂商的需求和边际收益状况。垄断厂商根据 $MR=MC$ 这一利润最大化的均衡条件，将产量和价格调整为 Q_1 和 P_1 的水平，在短期均衡点 E 上，垄断厂商的平均收益为 FQ_1，平均成本为 GQ_1。平均收益大于平均成本，垄断厂商获得利润。单位利润为 FG，总利润量相当于图中矩形 $FGHP_1$ 的面积。

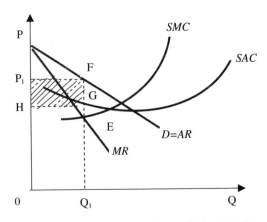

图 13.4　垄断厂商获得经济利润的短期均衡

由于在短期内不能调整生产规模，垄断厂商并非总能获得利润。垄断厂商在短期内能否获得利润要看商品市场价格的高低与垄断厂商平均成本的高低。若在均衡的产出水平商品价格低于平均成本，则垄断厂商就会亏损。图 13.5 所示的就是垄断厂商短期内亏损的情况。

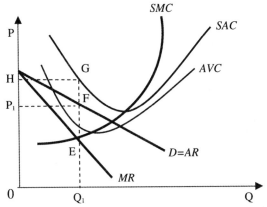

图 13.5　垄断厂商亏损状态下的短期均衡

在图 13.5 中，厂商遵循 $MR=SMC$ 原则，将产量和价格调整为 Q_1 和 P_1 的水平。在短期均衡点 E 上，垄断厂商是亏损的，单位产品的平均亏损额为 FG。总亏损额相当于矩形 HP_1FG 的面积。

与完全竞争厂商相同，在亏损的情况下，若 $AR>AVC$，垄断厂商就继续生产；若 $AR=AVC$，对垄断厂商来说生产或不生产都是一样的；若 $AR<AVC$，垄断厂商就停止生产。图 13.5 中 $AR>AVC$，所以垄断厂商应继续生产。

由此可以得出，垄断厂商短期均衡的条件为 $MR=SMC$。垄断厂商在短期均衡点上可以获得最大利润，可以利润为零，也可以蒙受最小亏损。

完全垄断厂商的长期均衡

由于垄断行业只有唯一一家厂商经营该行业的全部商品，不存在其他厂商的竞争，所以即使垄断厂商存在超额利润(经济利润)，在长期内也不可能像完全竞争行业那样通过新厂商的进入或厂商之间的竞争使超额利润消失。因此，完全垄断厂商的长期均衡是指垄断厂商在长期内通过自行调整而达到利润最大化的均衡。

　　垄断厂商在长期内对生产进行调整一般会有两种情况。一种情况是垄断厂商在短期内发生了亏损（如图 13.5 所示），厂商通过调整生产规模改变了亏损状况。如果厂商通过选择最优的生产规模仍然摆脱不了亏损，那么垄断厂商就将退出该行业。另一种情况是，垄断厂商在短期内利用既定的生产规模获得了利润，在长期内它通过调整生产规模，使自己获得了更多的利润。下面我们利用图 13.6 来分析第二种情况。

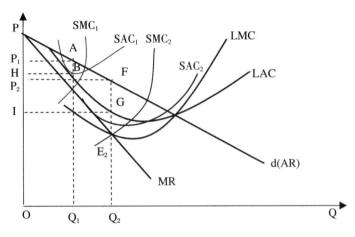

图 13.6　垄断厂商的长期均衡

　　图中 $d(AR)$ 曲线和 MR 曲线分别表示垄断厂商面临的市场需求曲线（平均收益曲线）和边际收益曲线，LAC 曲线和 LMC 曲线分别为垄断厂商的长期平均成本曲线和长期边际成本曲线。

　　假定垄断厂商开始时在由 SAC_1 曲线和 SMC_1 曲线所代表的生产规模上进行生产。在短期内厂商只能遵循 $MR=SMC$ 原则，在现有的生产规模上将均衡产量和均衡价格调整为 Q_1 和 P_1。在短期均衡点 E 上，垄断厂商所获得的利润只相当于图中较小的矩形 HP_1AB 的面积。

　　在长期内垄断厂商可以调整生产规模进一步增大利润。按照 $MR=LMC$ 长期均衡原则，垄断厂商的长期均衡为 E_2，均衡产量和均衡价格分别为 Q_2 和 P_2，垄断厂商所选择的相应的最优生产规模由 SAC_2 曲线和 SMC_2 曲线表示，此时垄断厂商获得了比短期更大的利润，其利润量相当于图中较大的矩形 IP_2FG 的面积。

　　显然，垄断厂商利用能够产生平均成本 SAC_2 曲线的生产规模比利用能够产生平均成本 SAC_1 曲线的生产规模获得了更多的经济利润，所以垄断厂商进行长期调整是有利的。由于不存在直接的竞争对手，垄断厂商的经济利润可以长期保持。在达到长期均衡时，长期边际成本 LMC 等于边际收益 MR，并且与短期边际成本 SMC_2 相等，长期平均成本 LAC 曲线与短期平均成本 SAC_2 曲线相切。因此，垄断厂商长期均衡条件可表示为：$MR=LMC=SMC$。

垄断市场的福利损失

　　在完全垄断市场中，垄断厂商为了获取长期超额利润，通常在产品价格高于边际成本的条件下进行生产。价格高于边际成本导致资源配置效率较低，这样垄断厂商通过减少消费者剩余与生产者剩余对社会福利造成无谓损失。我们利用图 13.7 对两种完全垄断竞争市场的长期均衡情况进行比较,通过这种比较来分析垄断所造成的社会福利水平下降的情况。

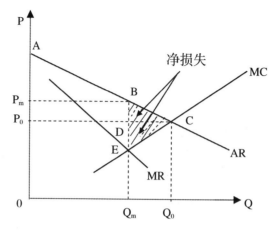

图 13.7　垄断的社会成本

在图 13.7 中,我们假定由一家垄断厂商来生产完全竞争行业中所有厂商所生产的商品,且假定完全垄断与完全竞争这两种市场的成本曲线完全相同。图中 P_0 和 Q_0 分别代表完全竞争市场的均衡价格和均衡产量;P_m 和 Q_m 分别代表完全垄断市场的均衡价格和均衡产量。对于完全竞争市场中的厂商来讲,按照 P_0 的价格和 Q_0 的产量生产可以使每一个厂商都获得最大化的利润。对于垄断厂商来讲,按照 P_m 的价格和 Q_m 的产量生产可以获得最大化的利润。在两种市场都分别使厂商的利润达到最大化并处于均衡的情况下,垄断市场的均衡价格 P_m 高于完全竞争市场的均衡价格 P_0,垄断市场的均衡产量 Q_m 低于完全竞争市场的产量 Q_0。也就是说,消费者支付了较高的价格,却消费了较少的商品数量。由于完全竞争市场是在平均成本最低点生产 Q_0 的产量,而垄断市场不是在平均成本最低点生产 Q_m 的产量,所以垄断市场中厂商的生产能力没有得到充分的发挥。

由图 13.7 还可以看出,因完全垄断造成的消费者剩余的损失为长方形 P_0P_mBD 的面积加上三角形 BCD 的面积。生产者剩余的增加等于长方形 P_0P_mBD 的面积减去三角形 CDE 的面积。综合考虑可知,三角形 BCE 就是社会福利的净损失,这种损失是非效率的社会成本,也叫做无谓损失(deadweight loss)。其中,三角形 BCD 的面积代表着消费者剩余的净损失。垄断使社会福利发生了净损失,这就是垄断造成的社会成本。

正因为垄断会造成效率上的一定损失,所以政府应该采取一定的措施来规范商品的定价。

自然垄断(natural monopoly)的一个主要特征是厂商的平均成本在很高的产量水平上仍随着产量的增加而递减,也就是存在着规模经济。由于自然垄断根源于规模经济,所以从理论上来讲,其经济效率肯定要比几家厂商同时经营时要高。但这仅是问题的一方面。而引起经济学家注意的另一方面是,自然垄断作为垄断的一种形式,同样存在着因缺乏竞争所造成的垄断厂商的高价格、高利润、低产出等经济效率的损失。所以,在大多数西方国家,一些公共事业、通讯业和运输业都处于政府的管制(regulation)之下。

垄断厂商获取的价格一般要高于边际成本,而很多经济学家认为,垄断厂商不应将价格定得过高,价格应能正确地反映生产的边际成本,因此便有了边际成本定价法。

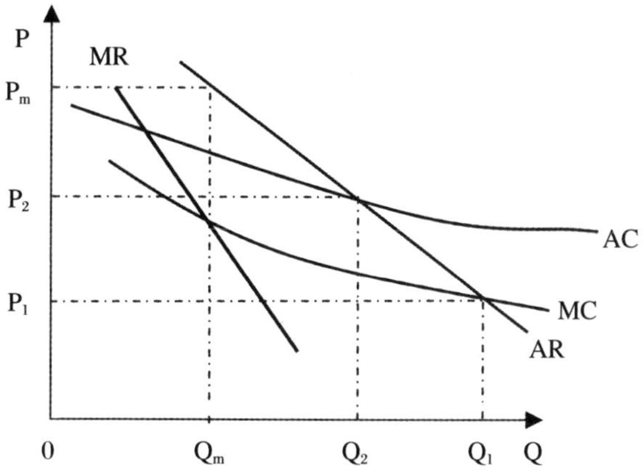

图 13.8　对自然垄断的价格管制

图 13.8 中,在无管制的情况下,垄断厂商依据 $MR=MC$ 的原则将价格定为 P_m,产量为 Q_m,价格显然高于边际成本。在政府管制的情况下,理想的状况是按照边际成本定价,即 $P=MC$。这时,厂商价格下降为 P_1,产量增加为 Q_1,但由于自然垄断厂商是在 AC 曲线下降的规模经济段进行生产,即自然垄断厂商的平均成本曲线一直是下降的,因此 MC 曲线必定位于 AC 曲线的下方,也就是说,按照边际成本 MC 所决定的价格 P_1 一定小于平均成本 AC。因此,在管制下若将价格压低至 P_1,厂商肯定会因亏损而退出生产。这样一来,管制机构陷入困境,要么放弃边际成本定价法,要么政府资助被管制的企业。

从控制价格的角度来说,可以采取另外的定价方法来代替边际成本定价法,从而走出边际成本定价法的困境。其中最主要的方法是平均成本定价法。平均成本定价法是使价格等于平均成本。仍以图 13.8 为例,根据平均成本定价法 $P=AC$,管制价格确定为 P_2,相应的产量为 Q_2。此时,由于 $P_2=AC$,厂商没有垄断利润但也不再亏损,且产出已尽可能大到正好使垄断厂商不退出经营的程度。

在传统的价格管制中,价格是由生产成本加投资回报来决定的。这种方法对经济的激励性相对较弱,而且诱使企业采用资本密集型生产技术,因为价格等于平均成本,厂商可以通过降低成本来提高利润。

价格歧视

由于垄断厂商具有一定的市场势力从而能够控制商品的市场价格,因此对于出售的相同商品,它们可以通过收取不同的价格,以使自己的利润最大化,这就属于价格歧视(price discrimination)。要准确定义价格歧视并不容易,通常来说,价格歧视是指一家厂商出售完全相同或很相似的商品时,以不同的净价格销售商品的行为。理解这一定义应该把握如下三点:第一,价格歧视的实施者必须是同一卖者,针对不同买者对同一产品与劳务收取不同价格;第二,净价格是指剔除了商品差异而得到的价格;第三,收取不同价格时的对象可以是不同消费者,也可以是同一消费者。从严格的经济学意义上来说,并非所有的价格差异都被视为价格歧视,如果价格差异反映了商品质量或生产经营成本的差异,就不应划归为价格歧视。

庇古(Pigou, 1963)将价格歧视主要划分为三种不同的类型,即一级价格歧视、二级价格歧视和三级价格歧视,其中三级价格歧视是最常见的价格歧视。有时人们就把三级价格歧视称之为价格歧视。下面,我们来分别讨论这三种价格歧视。

1、一级价格歧视(first degree price discrimination)

一级价格歧视又叫做完全价格歧视（perfect price discrimination），是指垄断厂商在销售商品时,将每单位商品以不同的价格出售以获得最大可能的利润。一级价格歧视如图13.9 所示。

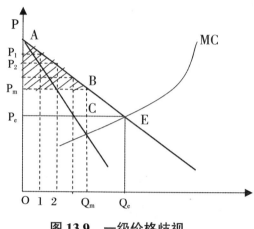

图 13.9　一级价格歧视

垄断厂商出售第一单位商品时,消费者愿意支付的最高价格为 P_1,于是厂商就按照此价格出售第一单位商品。当厂商销售第二单位产品时消费者愿意支付的最高价格为 P_2,于是厂商又按照消费者愿意支付的价格 P_2 出售。依次类推,直到厂商销售完 Q_m 为止。这时厂商得到的总收益相当于图 13.9 中的阴影部分面积(即垄断厂商实行同一定价时的消费者剩余)加上 OP_mBQ_m 的面积。若不实行价格歧视,都按照同一价格 P_m 出售 Q_m 的产量,则总收益为 OP_mBQ_m 的面积。

我们从图 13.9 中可知,垄断厂商若实行同一定价,则根据 $MR=MC$ 原则所确定的均衡价格为 P_m,均衡产量为 Q_m。如果实行一级价格歧视,在产量达到 Q_m 以后,消费者愿意支付的价格仍大于 MC,所以增加产量还可以增加利润。厂商一直将产量增加到 Q_e 水平为止,此时,厂商的总收益相当于图 13.9 中的 $OAEQ_e$ 的面积,与按同一价格销售商品相比,厂商获得了更多的利润,此时产量为 Q_e。在 Q_e 的产量水平上,有 $P=MC$,这说明 P_e 和 Q_e 等于完全竞争时的均衡价格和均衡产量。所以,一级价格歧视不影响资源配置的效率(产量仍然为 Q_e),但是会改变消费者与垄断者之间的收入分配结构。

总之,一级价格歧视是:垄断者明确知道消费者购买商品时愿意支付的最高价格,对每个单位商品收取的价格都不一样,最低的价格取决于成本。在一级价格歧视的情况下,每一单位商品都卖给对其评价最高,并愿意按最高价格支付的买者,因此,在这样的市场上不会产生消费者剩余。此时,相当于图中三角形 $\triangle P_eAE$ 的面积的剩余全部被垄断厂商占有,转化为厂商的收益(或利润)增加量。

注意:一级价格歧视只有在垄断者面临少数消费者以及垄断者能够清楚地了解消费者愿意支付的最高价格时,才可能实行。

2、二级价格歧视(second degree price discrimination)

二级价格歧视是指垄断厂商对一定数量的同种商品收取一种价格,而对于另外一定数量的该商品收取另一种价格,二级价格歧视也被称为成批定价。此时,消费者购买某商品的支出不随购买数量的增加而呈成比例的线性增加。

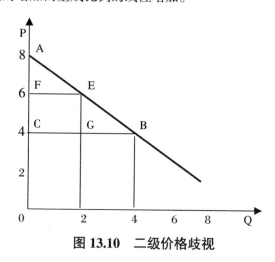

图 13.10   二级价格歧视

假如某垄断厂商所面临的需求函数为 $Q_d=8-P$,垄断厂商共销售 4 个单位商品,前两个单位按单价 6 出售,后两个单位按单价 4 出售,4 个单位商品得到的总收益为 20。如果不实行二级价格歧视,4 个单位产品都按同一价格 4 来出售。消费者只需支出 16 单位的成本。显然,在二级价格歧视下垄断厂商剥夺了部分消费者剩余。图 13.10 显示了厂商实行二级价格歧视的情况。

若不存在价格歧视,消费者得到的消费者剩余是图 13.10 中 $\triangle ABC$ 的面积。在实行二级价格歧视的情况下,消费者得到的消费者剩余仅相当于图中 $\triangle AEF$ 的面积与 $\triangle EGB$ 的面积之和,被垄断厂商剥夺的消费者剩余相当于图中矩形 $CFEG$ 的面积。

二级价格歧视面对的是很多消费者,不需要垄断厂商准确知道消费者愿意支付的最高价格,只需要对需求情况与支付意愿有大致的了解就可以实行,此时消费者有选择的自由,故实行二级价格歧视比实行一级价格歧视要容易得多。

3、三级价格歧视(third degree price discrimination)

三级价格歧视是指垄断厂商将顾客分为两个或两个以上的群体(或市场),针对不同群体(或市场)同一商品的销售价格却不同。此时,不同群体购买同一商品的价格不同,同一群体的不同顾客购买同一产品的价格相同。例如,同种商品在富人区的价格高于贫民区的价格;电影院对学生减价;药房对老年人减价;同样的学术刊物,图书馆购买的价格高于学生购买的价格等。我们最常见的例子是,对于同种商品,国内市场和国外市场的价格不一样,城市市场和农村市场的价格不一样等。

重要名词解释

1. **Monopoly**: exists when a specific individual or an enterprise has sufficient control over a particular product or service to determine significantly the terms on which other individuals shall have access to it

2. **Deadweight loss**: a loss of economic efficiency that can occur when equilibrium for a good or service is not Pareto optimal. People who have more marginal benefit than marginal cost are not buying the product, while people who have more marginal cost than marginal benefit are buying the product.

3. **Natural monopoly**: arises when the largest supplier in an industry, often the first supplier in a market, has an overwhelming cost advantage over other actual and potential competitors. This tends to be the case in industries where capital costs predominate, creating economies of scale that are large in relation to the size of the market, and hence having high barriers to entry.

4. **Price discrimination**: exists when sales of identical goods or services are transacted at different prices from the same provider. In a theoretical market with perfect information, perfect substitutes, and no transaction costs or prohibition on secondary exchange (or reselling) to prevent arbitrage, price discrimination can only be a feature of monopolistic and oligopolistic markets, where market power can be exercised.

主要图表

1.

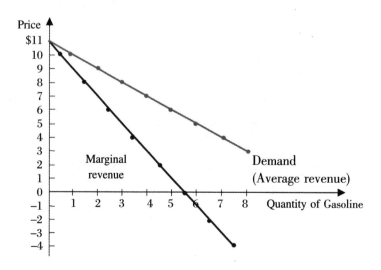

2.

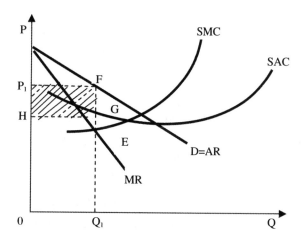

模拟试题

1. Which of the following statements is correct?

   A. Both a competitive firm and a monopolist are price takers.

   B. Both a competitive firm and a monopolist are price makers.

   C. A competitive firm is a price taker, whereas a monopolist is a price maker.

   D. A competitive firm is a price maker, whereas a monopolist is a price taker.

   E. A competitive firm sometimes is both a price taker and a price maker.

   Key: C

   Analysis: While a competitive firm is a price taker, a monopolist is a price maker.

2. One difference between a perfectly competitive firm and a monopoly firm is that a perfectly competitive firm produces when

   A. Marginal cost equals price, while a monopoly firm produces when price exceeds marginal cost.

   B. Marginal cost equals price, while a monopoly firm produces when marginal cost exceeds price.

   C. Price exceeds marginal cost, while a monopoly firm produces when marginal cost equals price.

   D. Marginal cost exceeds price, while a monopoly firm produces when marginal cost equals price.

   E. Marginal cost equals price, while a monopoly firm produces when marginal cost equals price.

   Key: A

   Analysis: In the perfectly competitive market, marginal cost equals price. In the monopoly market, the price exceeds marginal cost.

3. A perfectly competitive market

   A. May not be in the best interests of society, whereas a monopoly market promotes general economic well-being.

   B. Promotes general economic well-being, whereas a monopoly market may not be in the best interests of society.

   C. And a monopoly market is equally likely to promote general economic well-being.

   D. Is less likely to promote general economic well-being than a monopoly market.

   E. Sometimes will cause the deadweight loss.

Key: B

Analysis: Because a monopoly market sets its price above marginal cost, it places a wedge between the consumer's willingness to pay and the producer's cost. The deadweight loss caused by a monopoly market is similar to the deadweight loss caused by a tax.

4. The fundamental source of monopoly power is

   A. Barriers to entry.

   B. Profit.

   C. Decreasing average total cost.

   D. A product without close substitutes.

   E. Natural monopoly.

Key: A

Analysis: The fundamental cause of monopoly is barriers to entry.

5. For a single firm, the simplest way to form monopoly is to

   A. Decrease its price to make it lower than its competitors' prices.

   B. Decrease production to increase demand for its product.

   C. Make pricing decisions jointly with other firms.

   D. Use the force to control the market.

   E. Own a key resource.

Key: E

Analysis: Exclusive ownership of a key resource is a potential source of monopoly.

6. Which of the following is an example of a barrier to entry?

   A. Tom charges a higher price than his competitors for his house-painting service.

   B. Dick obtains a copyright for the new computer game that he invented.

   C. Harry offers free concerts on Sunday afternoons as a form of advertising.

   D. Larry charges a lower price than his competitors for his lawn-mowing service.

   E. Matthew offers free samples of his latest flavored coffee drink to entice customers to buy a cup.

Key: B

Analysis: Barriers to entry have three sources: A key resource is owned by a single firm; The government gives a single firm the exclusive right to produce some good or service; The costs of production make a single producer more efficient than a large number of producers.

7. Which of the following statements is true about patents and copyrights?

(i) They have benefits and costs.

(ii) They lead to higher prices.

(iii) They enhance the ability of monopolists to earn above-average profits.

A. (i) and (ii).

B. (ii) and (iii).

C. (ii) only.

D. (iii) only.

E. (i), (ii), and (iii).

Key: E

Analysis: The patent and copyright laws are two important examples of how the government creates a monopoly to serve the public interests.

8. Which of the following is a characteristic of a natural monopoly?

A. Marginal cost declines over large regions of output.

B. Average total cost declines over large regions of output.

C. The product sold is a natural resource such as diamonds or water.

D. One firm can supply output at a higher cost than two firms.

E. Increasing the number of firms decreases each firm's average total cost.

Key: B

Analysis: It examines the understanding of natural monopoly. We can eliminate the wrong choices one by one.

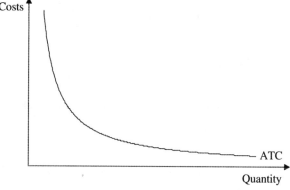

9. Refer to the figure above. The shape of the average total cost curve reveals information about the nature of the barrier to entry that might exist in a monopoly market. Which of the following monopoly types coincides with the figure best?

A. Ownership of a key resource by a single firm.

B. Natural monopoly.

C. Government-created monopoly.

D. A patent or copyright monopoly.

E. Economies of scale.

Key: B

Analysis: An industry is a natural monopoly when a single firm can supply a good or service to an entire market at a smaller cost than two or more firms could do. A natural monopoly arises when there are economies of scale over the relevant range of output.

10. If government officials break a natural monopoly up into several smaller firms, then
    A. Competition will force firms to attain economic profits rather than accounting profits.
    B. Competition will force firms to produce surplus output, which drives up price.
    C. The average costs of production will increase.
    D. The average costs of production will decrease.
    E. A and C

    Key: C

    Analysis: An industry is a natural monopoly when a single firm can supply a good or service to an entire market at a smaller cost than two or more firms could do.

11. The market demand curve for a monopolist is typically
    A. Unit price elastic.
    B. Downward sloping.
    C. Horizontal.
    D. Vertical.
    E. Upward sloping.

    Key: B

    Analysis: Because a monopoly firm is a price maker, it directly faces the total market. Its demand curve is then downward sloping.

12. In order to sell more of its product, a monopolist must
    A. Sell it to the government.
    B. Sell it in international markets.
    C. Lower its price.
    D. Use its market power to force up the price of complementary products.
    E. Possess more natural resources.

    Key: C

    Analysis: The market demand curve for a monopolist is typically downward sloping. So it must lower its price to sell more of its products.

13. The supply curve for the monopolist
    A. Is horizontal.
    B. Is vertical.
    C. Is upward sloping.
    D. Is downward sloping.
    E. Does not exist.

    Key: E

    Analysis: A monopoly firm maximizes its profit by producing the quantity at which marginal revenue equals marginal cost (MR=MC). It then uses the demand curve to find the price that will induce consumers to buy that quantity.

14. The profit-maximization problem for a monopolist differs from that of a competitive firm in which of the following ways?

   A. A competitive firm maximizes its profit at the point where marginal revenue equals to marginal cost; a monopolist maximizes its profit at the point where marginal revenue exceeds marginal cost.

   B. A competitive firm maximizes its profit at the point where average revenue equals to marginal cost; a monopolist maximizes its profit at the point where average revenue exceeds marginal cost.

   C. For competitive firm, marginal revenue at the profit-maximizing level of output is equal to marginal revenue at all other levels of output; for a monopolist, marginal revenue at the profit-maximizing level of output is smaller than it is for larger levels of output.

   D. For a profit-maximizing competitive firm, thinking about the margin is much more important than it is for a profit-maximizing monopolist.

   E. None of the above is right.

   Key: B

   Analysis: For a competitive firm, price equals marginal cost, P = MR = MC. For a monopoly firm, price exceeds marginal cost, P > MR = MC.

15. A monopolist maximizes profits by

   A. Producing an output level where marginal revenue equals to marginal cost.

   B. Charging a price that is greater than marginal revenue.

   C. Earning a profit of (P–MC)×Q.

   D. Both A and B are correct.

   E. Both A and C are correct.

   Key: D

   Analysis: For a monopoly firm, price exceeds marginal cost, P > MR = MC, so it earns a profit of (P–AC)×Q.

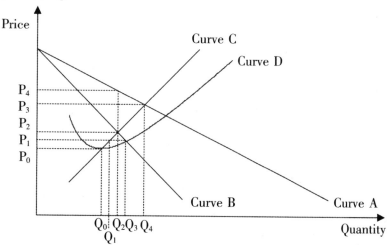

16. Refer to the figure above. Profit can always be increased by increasing the level of output by one unit if the monopolist is currently operating at

(i) Q_0.

(ii) Q_1.

(iii) Q_2.

(iv) Q_3.

A. (ii) only.

B. (i) or (ii).

C. (i) only.

D. (i), (ii), or (iii).

E. (i), (ii), and (iii).

Key: B

Analysis: In the graph, the quantity should be less than Q_2 because Q_2 is the profit maximization quantity.

17. Suppose a monopolist chooses the price and production level that maximizes its profit. From that point, to increase society's economic welfare, output would need to be increased as long as

A. Average revenue exceeds marginal cost.

B. Average revenue exceeds average total cost.

C. Marginal revenue exceeds marginal cost.

D. Marginal revenue exceeds average total cost.

E. Average revenue exceeds marginal revenue.

Key: A

Analysis: Because a monopoly sets its price(=average revenue) above marginal cost, it places a wedge between the consumer's willingness to pay and the producer's cost. This wedge causes the quantity sold to fall short of the social optimum.

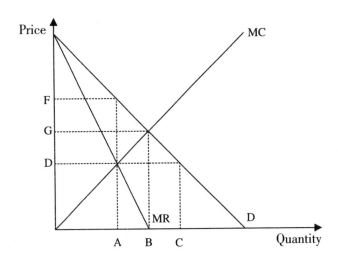

18. Refer to the figure above. Which area represents the total surplus lost due to monopoly pricing?

    A. The rectangle FDIE

    B. The triangle EIJ

    C. The triangle EHJ

    D. The rectangle FDIE plus the triangle EIJ

    E. The rectangle FGHE

    Key：B

    Analysis: Because a monopoly sets its price above marginal cost, it places a wedge between the consumer's willingness to pay and the producer's cost.

19. When a monopolist is able to sell its product at different prices, it is engaging in

    A. Distribution pricing.

    B. Quality-adjusted pricing.

    C. Price differentiation.

    D. Price discrimination.

    E. Price segregation.

    Key：D

    Analysis: Price discrimination is the practice of selling the same good at different prices to different customers, even though the costs for producing for customers are the same.

20. For a long while, electricity producers were thought to be a classic example of a natural monopoly. People held this view because

    A. The average cost of producing units of electricity by one producer in a specific region was lower than that if the same quantity was produced by two or more producers in the same region.

    B. The average cost of producing units of electricity by one producer in a specific region was higher than that if the same quantity was produced by two or more produced in the same region.

    C. The marginal cost of producing units of electricity by one producer in a specific region was higher than that if the same quantity was produced by two or more producers in the same region.

    D. Electricity is a special non-excludable good that could never be sold in a competitive market.

    E. Electricity is a special rival good that one person's use diminishes other people's use.

    Key：A

    Analysis: An industry is a natural monopoly when a single firm can supply a good or service to an entire market at a smaller cost than two or more firms could do.

21. XYZ Company is a profit-maximizing firm. It has a patent for a unique antispyware computer program called Aspy that gives XYZ the exclusive right to produce and market it for a period of time.

(a) Assume that XYZ is making economic profit. Draw a correctly labeled graph and show the profit-maximizing price and quantity.

(b) Assume that the government imposes a lump-sum tax on XYZ.

(i) What will happen to output and market price? Explain.

(ii) What will happen to XYZ's profits?

(c) Assume that the government grants a per-unit subsidy to XYZ for Aspy instead.

(i) What will happen to output and market price? Explain.

(ii) What will happen to XYZ's profits?

(d) Now assume that XYZ's patent on Aspy expires. What will happen to XYZ's economic profits in the long run? Explain.

Key: 12 points $(4 + 3 + 3 + 2)$

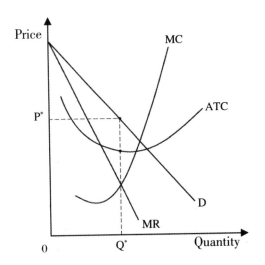

(a) 4 points:

One point is earned for correctly labeled axes and an MR curve below a downward-sloping demand curve.

One point is earned for showing profit-maximizing Q^* at MC=MR.

One point is earned for identifying P^* on the demand curve above Q^*.

One point is earned for showing that P>ATC at Q^*.

(b) 3 points:

One point is earned for concluding that profit-maximizing Q^* and P^* will not change.

One point is earned for correctly explaining that the lump-sum tax will not affect MC.

One point is earned for concluding that profits will decrease.

(c) 3 points:

One point is earned for concluding that profit-maximizing Q^* will increase and P^* will decrease.

One point is earned for explaining that the MC curve shifts down.

One point is earned for concluding that profits will increase.

（d）2 points:

　　One point is earned for concluding that XYZ's profits will fall in the long run.

　　One point is earned for stating that new firms will enter the market.

22. Social efficiency is affected by government policy and the structure of markets.

　（a）For a competitive market, there is a binding（effective）price ceiling. Draw a correctly labeled graph and label the price ceiling P_c, the quantity sold Q_A, and the socially efficient output Q_B.

　（b）The graph below shows a natural monopoly.

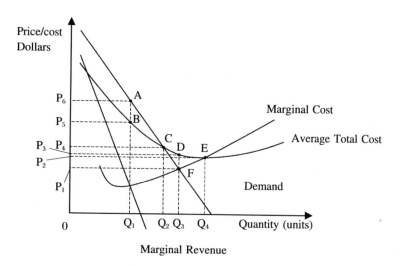

（i）Using the labeling in the graph, identify each of the following.

　（1）The profit-maximizing output

　（2）The socially efficient output

（ii）At the socially efficient output, is the monopoly making a profit or incurring a loss? Using the labeling on the graph, identify the area of profit or loss.

Key: 7 points（3 + 4）

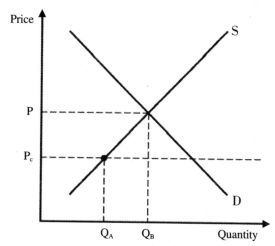

(a) 3 points:

One point is earned for a correctly labeled supply and demand graph with a price ceiling indicated below the market equilibrium.

One point is earned for correctly labeled Q_A.

One point is earned for correctly labeled Q_B.

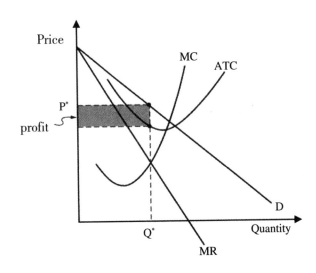

(b) 4 points:

(i) 2 points:

One point is earned for identifying Q_1 as the profit-maximizing output.

One point is earned for identifying Q_3 as the socially efficient output.

(ii) 2 points:

One point is earned for recognizing that at Q_3, the monopolist incurs a loss.

One point is earned for identifying the area of loss, P_1P_3DF.

23. Assume that Clark Electronics has a monopoly in the production and sale of a new device for detecting and destroying a computer virus. Clark Electronics currently incurs short-run losses, but it continues to operate.

(a) What must be true for Clark to continue to operate in the short run?

(b) Draw a correctly labeled graph, and show each of the following for Clark.

(i) The profit-maximizing price and output

(ii) Area of loss

(c) Assume Clark is maximizing profit. What will happen to its total revenue if Clark raises its price? Explain.

(d) If demand for the new device increases, explain what will happen to each of the following in the short run.

(i) Profit-maximizing output

(ii) Total cost

Key: 11 points $(1 + 4 + 2 + 4)$

(a) 1 point:

One point is earned for stating that the firm must be covering its AVC (or TVC), or P>AVC.

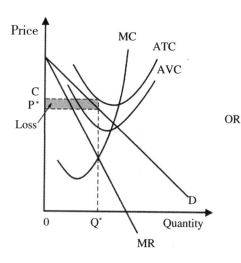　OR　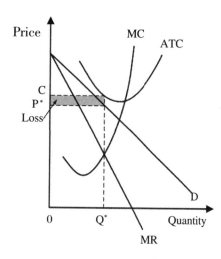

(b) 4 points:

One point is earned for a correctly labeled graph with MR below the demand curve.

One point is earned for identifying profit-maximizing quantity at MR=MC.

One point is earned for identifying price on the demand curve above equilibrium quantity and below ATC.

One point is earned for showing the correct loss area.

(c) 2 points:

One point is earned for indicating that total revenue will fall.

One point is earned for explaining that demand is elastic or MR is positive.

(d) 4 points:

One point is earned for indicating that the profit-maximizing output will increase.

One point is earned for explaining that the marginal revenue curve will shift to the right.

One point is earned for concluding that total cost will increase.

One point is earned for explaining that output increases.

24. PetsCo is a profit-maximizing monopolist. It sells a patented rabies vaccine for pets and earns economic profits.

(a) Draw a correctly labeled graph that shows each of the following for PetsCo.

(i) Output and price of the vaccine

(ii) Area of economic profits

(b) Assume that PetsCo hires its production workers in a perfectly competitive labor market at the wage rate of $20 per hour.

(i) State the marginal conditions for hiring the profit-maximizing amount of labor.

(ii) Draw a correctly labeled graph that shows the labor supply and demand curves for PetsCo and indicate the profit-maximizing quantity of labor.

(c) Suppose that the market wage rate now falls to $15 per hour. Show on your diagram in

(b) (ii) how each of the following would be affected.

(i) The supply of labor to PetsCo

(ii) The amount of labor PetsCo would hire

(d) Given the lower wage rate in (c), indicate how each of the following would change.

(i) Total fixed cost

(ii) Marginal cost

(iii) Price of the product

Key: 13 points $(4 + 4 + 2 + 3)$

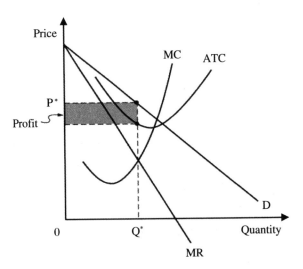

(a) 4 points:

One point is earned for a graph with downward sloping demand curve with *MR* below.

One point is earned for showing output at MR=MC.

One point is earned for showing price on the demand curve above MR=MC.

One point is earned for showing the area of profit, shaded or labeled.

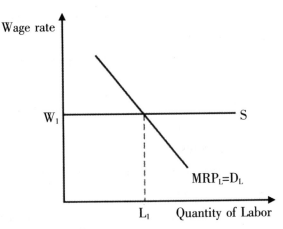

（b）4 points:

One point is earned for stating that MRP=MFC or MRP=Wage or MRP=MRC.

One point is earned for drawing a correct graph with downward sloping labor-demand curve.

One point is earned for drawing a horizontal labor-supply curve at the wage rate.

One point is earned for indicating the profit-maximizing quantity of labor.

（c）2 points:

One point is earned for showing that labor-supply curve shifts down.

One point is earned for showing that the amount of labor hired increases.

（d）3 points:

One point is earned for indicating that the total fixed cost would not change.

One point is earned for indicating that the marginal cost would fall.

One point is earned for indicating that the product price would fall.

25. Due to a new technology, Brunelle Inc. enjoys monopoly power. Brunelle does not engage in price discrimination.

（a）Explain why the demand curve lies above the marginal revenue curve for Brunelle.

（b）Assume that Brunelle is earning short-run economic profits. Using a correctly labeled graph, show the following for Brunelle.

（i）Profit-maximizing level of output, labeled as Q^*

（ii）Profit-maximizing price, labeled as P^*

（iii）Economic profits, as a shaded area

（c）If Brunelle wants to maximize its total revenue instead of profits, using the graph from （b）to show the following.

（i）Revenue-maximizing level of output, labeled as Q^r

（ii）Revenue-maximizing price, labeled as P^r

（d）Given your answer in （b）, indicate whether Brunelle is producing the allocatively efficient level of output. Explain.

（e）Explain what will happen to Brunelle's demand curve as other firms adopt the same technology.

Key: 9 points（1+4+2+1+1）

（a）1 point:

Brunelle must lower its price on all units to sell additional units. Thus, the additional revenue from the last unit sold is the price minus the loss on units that would otherwise sell at a higher price.

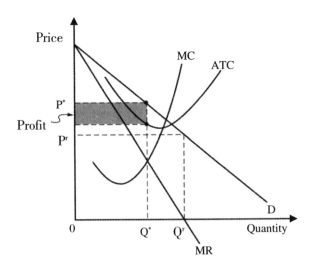

(b) 4 points:

One point is earned for a correctly labeled graph with downward-sloping demand curve and marginal revenue curve below demand.

One point is earned for Q^* at MC=MR.

One point is earned for P^* at the height of the demand curve above MC=MR.

One point is earned for shading the correct area of profit $(P^*-ATC)\,Q^*$

(c) 2 points:

One point is earned for identifying O^r at MR =0.

One point is earned for identifying P^r at the height of the demand curve above O^r.

(d) 1 point:

Brunelle is not producing the allocatively efficient level of output because $P<MC$ ($MSB < MSC$)

(e) 1 point:

Brunelle's demand curve will shift inward to the left.

26. Market structures differ from one another in many respects. Consider two profit-maximizing firms that earn short-run economic profits. One is a perfectly competitive firm and the other is a monopoly.

    (a) For each firm, draw a correctly labeled graph showing the following.

        (i) Price

        (ii) Quantity of output

        (iii) Area of economic profits

    (b) For each firm, explain the relationship between price and marginal revenue.

    (c) For each firm, explain how the economic profits would most likely change in the long run.

    (d) Label the area that represents the deadweight loss on the graph for the monopoly firm drawn in (a). Explain what this deadweight loss represents.

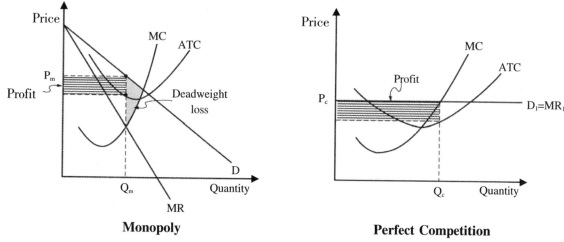

Monopoly   **Perfect Competition**

Key:

(a) The diagram above illustrates the graphs for a monopoly and a competitive firm earning short-run economic profits. The areas of economic profits are shaded with horizontal lines.

(b) The competitive firm is a price taker with a horizontal demand curve determined by the market equilibrium price. It can sell as many units as it wants at the market price, so it takes that price as its marginal revenue for each good. Price and marginal revenue are therefore the same. The monopoly faces a downward-sloping demand curve, meaning that it must lower its price in order to sell more units. When it lowers its price to sell another unit, its marginal revenue is the new price minus the loss it incurs by lowering its price on units previously sold at a higher price. Thus, marginal revenue is below price for a monopoly.

(c) Under perfect competition there are no barriers to entry, so in the long run new firms will enter when economic profits are being made. The entry of new firms increases market supply and lowers market price until the price falls to the level of minimum average total cost and zero economic profits are being made. Barriers to entry allow the monopoly to continue to earn economic profits even in the long run.

(d) The triangular shaded area in the monopoly graph represents the deadweight loss caused by the monopoly firm. The deadweight loss represents the loss of consumer and producer surplus caused by a suboptimal level of production at which marginal cost is below the price level.

Key: 14 Points

(a) 8 points

Monopoly	Perfectly Competitive Firms
1 point: Graph with downward D and MR below D	1 point: Graph with horizontal D
1 point: P from the demand curve	1 point: P at intersection of D and MC
1 point: Q at MR=MC	1 point: Q at MR=MC
1 point: Area of profit	1 point: Area of profit

（b）2 points:（1/2 for each relationship and 1/2 for each explanation）

1/2 point: P_c is the same as MR.

1/2 point: Because Po is constant and the perfectly competitive firm is a price taker.

1/2 point:

1/2 point: Because the monopoly firm must lower price（on all units）to sell more output.

（c）2 points:（one for competitive firm and one for monopoly firm）

1 point: With perfect competition, the entry of new firms increases supply and decreases price to the level of minimum average total cost, resulting in zero economic profits.

1 point: For the monopoly, economic profits can continue in the long run due to barriers to entry.

（d）2 points:

1 point: Correct area, including lost consumer surplus and lost producer surplus.

1 point: Lost consumer and producer surplus due to suboptimal quantity/production where $P>MC$.

Chapter 14 Oligopoly Market 寡头垄断市场

主要内容和概念讲解

美国的汽车行业是由为数不多的几个主要制造商组成的，比如通用、福特、克莱斯勒、丰田、本田等汽车公司；其电器设备零配件业一直受到通用电气和西屋电气的控制。寡头垄断在西方发达国家是一种常见的市场结构。寡头垄断的形成是竞争的必然结果，也是某些产业部门的技术经济特点使然，是客观的经济现象。造成一些产业部门呈现寡头垄断特征的原因主要有：长期竞争的作用；规模经济与范围经济的作用；对基本生产资源供给的控制；政府的特许、扶植和支持等。

寡头市场的含义及特征

寡头垄断(oligopoly)市场，又称寡占市场，是指少数几家厂商控制着整个市场的产品生产和销售的一种市场结构。寡头垄断市场既包含垄断因素又包含竞争因素，但更接近于完全垄断市场。寡头垄断市场的特征是市场中只有很少几家厂商，这些厂商之间存在着高度的相互依存关系，一家厂商在产量或价格方面的任何变化都将影响市场价格，从而影响竞争对手的利润。由于寡头间的相互依存性，任何一个寡头垄断厂商的最佳决策都不仅取决于自身，也取决于其他寡头垄断厂商的决策。因此，寡头垄断厂商在决定自己的最佳策略时必须考虑竞争对手的行为和反应，必须意识到自己策略的调整可能会诱发竞争对手策略的改变。

如果寡头垄断产业的每个寡头所生产的产品是同质的，例如从事钢铁、水泥、铜等产品生产的寡头，则称为纯粹寡头(pure oligopoly)。如果寡头所生产的产品是有差别的，例如从事汽车、电脑产品生产的寡头，则称为差别寡头(differentiation oligopoly)。此外，寡头产业还可按厂商的行动方式，分为有勾结行为的和独立行动的两种类型。

在完全竞争、完全垄断、垄断竞争三种市场上，厂商的行为是相互独立的，每个厂商在作决策时都无须考虑其他厂商会作出什么反应。而在寡头垄断市场上，少数几个厂商生产一个产业的全部或绝大部分产量，因此每一个厂商的行为都会对其他寡头产生举足轻重的影响。一个厂商通过产品降价或新式产品的推出扩大自己产品的市场份额，同时就会使得其他寡头厂商的产品需求量下降。正因为如此，一个厂商采取某种对策扩大自己的产量时就会遭遇到对手的策略性行为。厂商之间的竞争行为是不确定的，一个厂商通过降价来扩大自己的市场份额可能会导致对手的如法炮制。一个寡头通过广告战争夺市场也会引起对手用相同手法来遏制它的行为。有时，寡头之间也可能不通过竞争而通过合作的方式共同谋取利益。

由于寡头间的博弈行为存在相互依赖性和不确定性,所以寡头厂商对产品价格和产量的决定是一个很复杂的问题。一般来说,有多少关于竞争对手的反应方式的假定,就有多少寡头厂商的模型,也就可以得到多少不同的结论。寡头模型是厂商定价理论中最不定型的模型。模型的种类很多,但是至今仍找不到一种模型可以对寡头市场的价格和产量的决定做出一般的理论总结。

双寡头(duopoly)模型的例子

在一个只有少数几个卖者的寡头垄断市场上,一个寡头垄断厂商的决策会直接影响到其他的厂商,所以,寡头的关键特征就是合作与利己之间的冲突。它们可以进行合作,像一个垄断厂商那样进行决策。这样做所有的厂商都获得更大的利益。但每个寡头都更加关心自己的利益,对更大利益的追求驱使这些寡头垄断厂商打破合作。所以,垄断集团其实是很难维持的。

为了理解寡头垄断市场的基本特征,我们先只考虑两个卖者的双寡头模型,也称古诺双头模型。这是一个最基本的模型,不过,即使有第三家或是更多的寡头,它们所面临的问题也和双寡头模型的情形是相同的。下面我们就来看看这个模型。

假定市场上只有 A、B 两个厂商生产和销售饮用水(水是同质的),它们的生产成本为零;它们共同面临的市场的需求曲线是线性的(如表 14.1 所示);A、B 两个厂商都准确地了解市场的需求曲线;A、B 两个厂商都是在已知对方产量的情况下,各自确定能够给自己带来最大利润的产量。

表 14.1 饮用水的需求表

Quantity (in gallons)	Price	Total Revenue (and total profit)
0 gallon	$120	$0
10	110	1,100
20	100	2,000
30	90	2,700
40	80	3,200
50	70	3,500
60	60	3,600
70	50	3,500
80	40	3,200
90	30	2,700
100	20	2,000
110	10	1,100
120	0	0

现在我们来考虑饮用水行业组织是如何影响水的价格和产量的。从表中我们可以看出当饮用水的产量为 60 加仑时，A 与 B 的利润和最大，为 3600 美元。也就是说，如果只有一个厂商，它一定会选择生产 60 加仑的饮用水。但当市场上出现了两个寡头厂商时又会发生什么事情呢？

一种可能是 A 与 B 结合在一起，并就水的生产量和收取的价格达成一致。企业之间的这种对生产和价格等达成协议的行为被称为勾结（collusion），联合起来行事的企业集团被称为卡特尔（cartel）。一旦形成了卡特尔，市场实际上就只有一个垄断厂商提供服务，此时我们可以运用上一章提到的分析方法。一个典型的卡特尔的例子是 OPEC。

形成卡特尔的结果是生产者能从市场上得到最大的总利润，此时的价格为 60 美元，远高于饮用水的边际成本，所以从社会的角度来看，结果是无效率的。

卡特尔不仅必须就总产量达成一致的协议，而且还要就每个成员的产量达成一致。在这个例子中，A 和 B 还要就如何分配这 60 加仑水的垄断性生产达成一致。卡特尔的每个成员都想有较大的市场份额，因为市场份额越大，利润就越大。如果 A 和 B 同意平均划分市场，那么，每个厂商将生产 30 加仑水，价格为 60 美元/加仑，各厂商分别获得 1800 美元的利润。

虽然寡头希望形成卡特尔并赚得垄断利润，但这往往是很难实现的。反托拉斯法把禁止寡头之间的公开协议作为公共政策的重点。卡特尔在美国是非法的，在其他国家有的属于非法的，有的属于合法的。在美国，虽然早在 1890 年就产生了"谢尔曼反托拉斯法"，但卡特尔组织仍然存在，例如在上世纪 50 年代的美国电力设备制造商中，就普遍存在着这一情况。此外，有些贸易协会和专业组织有时表现出类似于卡特尔性质的职能。有的卡特尔形式甚至还得到美国政府的正式认可，例如，某些飞越大西洋航线的航空公司是国际航空交通运输协会的成员，该协会能够规定该航线的统一价格。然而，有时卡特尔成员之间对如何瓜分利润的争斗也使它们之间的协议无法实现。下面我们来分析一下双寡头模型中出现的利益冲突。

对于厂商 A 来说，现在生产 30 加仑的饮用水是不是最优的呢？当它生产 30 加仑水时，市场上的总供给量为 60 加仑，价格为 60 美元/加仑。这时 A 的总利润为 1800 美元。但如果 A 再多生产 10 加仑的饮用水，此时，市场上的总供给量变成了 70 加仑，饮用水的价格降至 50 美元/加仑，两个寡头厂商的总利润下降到了 3500 美元。但是此时 A 厂商的利润上升到了 2000 美元。可以看出，虽然市场的总利润下降了，但 A 的利润却上升了，因为 A 占据了更大的市场份额。所以，在 A、B 双方并没有达成一个强制性协议的情况下，A 是不会把产量定在 30 加仑的。它会增加产量以占据更大的市场份额，提高利润。

同样，厂商 B 也会面临着相同的选择。如果 A 和 B 都将各自的产量提升到 40 加仑的话，市场上饮用水的总供给量提高到了 80 加仑，价格下降到了 40 美元/加仑，两个寡头各自的利益变成了 1600 美元。这个利润水平要低于它们联合起来的水平，也就是说，如果寡头厂商都在决定生产时追逐私利，那么它们最终获得的利润将低于它们合作所获得的垄断利润。

现在我们来看看，这种较低的利润水平又是否能维持下去呢？

对 A 来说，如果将产量提高到 50 加仑，此时，市场上的总供给量变成了 90 加仑，饮用水的价格降至 30 美元/加仑，A 厂商的利润为 1500 美元。这要低于生产 40 加仑水所获得的 1600 美元的利润。相反，如果将产量减少到 30 加仑，此时，市场上的总供给量变成了 70 加仑，饮用水的价格降至 50 美元/加仑，A 厂商的利润也为 1500 美元。同样低于生产 40 加仑水所获得的 1600 美元的利润。

其实，在数学上我们可以证明，在 B 厂商生产 40 加仑的饮用水时，如果 A 厂商也生产 40 加仑水，则自己的利润达到最大。所以 A 厂商其实是没有动力改变自己的产量的。

同样，B 厂商也不会在产量上做出进一步的改变。这样 A、B 厂商各自生产 40 加仑的饮用水就达成了一种均衡的状态。这就是我们经常听到的纳什均衡（Nash equilibrium）。纳什均衡指的是相互作用的经济主体假定其他主体所选择的战略为既定时，选择自己的最优战略的状态。在这个例子中，A 和 B 厂商各自生产 40 加仑饮用水就是纳什均衡状态。一旦双方达到了这一状态，它们就都不会做出任何改变来打破这种均衡。

从这个例子中，我们看到了合作与利己之间的冲突。合作并达成垄断的结果会使寡头的状态最好。但由于它们追求自己的私利，最后不能达成垄断的结果，并且不能使双方的共同利润最大化。每一个寡头都有扩大生产并攫取更大市场份额的动力，当它们这么做时，总的产量会增加，价格会下降。

由于市场上存在着一定的竞争性，寡头垄断实际上在效率上要优于完全垄断市场。但同时，利己也不能总使市场达到竞争的结果。和垄断厂商一样，寡头厂商认识到，它们生产的产品数量的增加会降低其产品的价格。因此，它们不会让价格等于边际成本。

总之，当寡头企业各自进行利润最大化的选择时，它们的产量会大于垄断市场但小于完全竞争的产量水平；它们的价格会低于完全垄断价格，同时高于完全竞争市场和垄断竞争市场的价格。

博弈论与信息经济学

在现实经济中，各个经济主体的选择是相互影响、相互依赖的。无论是消费者还是厂商，在进行效用最大化决策或利润最大化决策时，必然都会对其他消费者的效用或厂商的利润产生影响，其他消费者或厂商也一定会将这一因素考虑到自己的效用函数或利润函数中去，进而进行自己最优的决策。我们上面讲到的寡头垄断的例子就是一个典型的范例。

博弈论（game theory），又译为对策论，就是研究发生直接相互作用时决策主体的行为决策以及这种决策的均衡问题。实际上，博弈是一种日常现象，例如下棋，双方棋手都要根据对手的行动来决定自己的下一步行动，双方的目的都是要战胜对手，彼此之间互相影响，互相制约，互不相容。一般而言，博弈表现为两个或两个以上具有利害冲突的参与人或当事人处于一种互不相容的状态中，一方的行动取决于对方的行动，每个参与人的收益都取决于所有参与人的行动。当所有参与人都作出了自己的决策时，博弈的结果就暂时确定了下来。在经济学中，博弈论是研究当某一经济主体的决策受到其他经济主体决策的影响时，该经济主体的相应决策又反过来影响其他经济主体在作出选择时的决策问题和均衡问题。

严格地说，博弈论并不是经济学的一个分支，而是一种方法论，广泛应用于经济学、政治学、军事、外交、国际关系、公共选择、犯罪学等。实际上，许多人把博弈论看成是数学的一个分支。但是由于博弈论在经济学中应用最广泛、最成功，经济学家对博弈论的贡献也最大，而且经济学和博弈论的研究模式是一样的，都强调个人理性，也都是在给定的约束条件下追求利益最大化，因此，1994 年的诺贝尔经济学奖同时授予三位博弈论专家就不足为奇了。

博弈论中最为著名的例子是囚徒困境(prisoner's dilemma)，我们以此为例来说明一下博弈论的基本原理。

故事是这样的，两个合伙作案的犯罪嫌疑人(A 和 B)被警方抓获。警方虽然怀疑他们作案，但手中并没有掌握他们作案的确凿证据。因此，对两个犯罪嫌疑人犯罪事实的认定及相应的量刑完全取决于他们自己的供认。假定警方对两名犯罪嫌疑人实行隔离关押、隔离审讯，每个犯罪嫌疑人都无法观察到对方的选择。同时，警方分别明确地告知两名犯罪嫌疑人，他们面临着以下几种后果：

如果 2 名犯罪嫌疑人都不招供，警方只能根据掌握的证据，判处两名犯罪嫌疑人各 2 年徒刑。

如果 2 名犯罪嫌疑人供认其犯罪事实，2 人将各被判处 8 年徒刑。

如果 1 名犯罪嫌疑人供认犯罪事实，而其同伙拒不供认，则招供者将从轻被判处 1 年徒刑，拒不招供者将被判处 20 年徒刑。

2 名犯罪嫌疑人所面临的后果(策略选择)可以用图 14.1 表示。该表又被称为"收益矩阵"或"得益矩阵"(payoff matrix)。

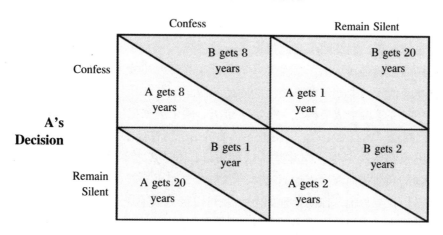

图 14.1   囚徒困境的收益矩阵

从图 14.1 中可以看出，每个犯罪嫌疑人都有 2 种可供选择的策略：供认或不供认。而且，每个犯罪嫌疑人选择的最优策略不依赖于其同伙的策略选择，即不论其同伙选择什么策略，每个犯罪嫌疑人选择的最优策略都是供认。以犯罪嫌疑人 A 为例：(1)当犯罪嫌疑人 B 选择供认时，犯罪嫌疑人 A 如果也选择供认，则将被判处 8 年徒刑；A 如果选择不供认，则将被判处 20 年徒刑。显然，在同伙 B 选择供认策略时，犯罪嫌疑人 A 选择供认是他的最优策略；(2)当犯罪嫌疑人 B 选择不供认时，犯罪嫌疑人 A 如果选择供认，则将被判处 1 年徒刑，B 将被判处 20 年徒刑；犯罪嫌疑人 A 如果也选择不供认，则 A、B 都将被判处 2 年徒刑。同样，在同伙 B 选择不供认的条件下，犯罪嫌疑人 A 选择供认仍然是他的最优策略。

同理可以推出,无论犯罪嫌疑人 A 选择什么样的策略,犯罪嫌疑人 B 的最优策略也都是供认。因此,无论同伙选择什么策略,犯罪嫌疑人 A 或 B 的最优策略都是供认。

也许有人会说,如果两名犯罪嫌疑人都选择不供认,两人将都被判处 2 年徒刑,这显然比每人被判处 8 年徒刑的均衡解要好。那么,为什么两名犯罪嫌疑人都选择不供认不是每个犯罪嫌疑人的最优策略呢? 这是因为犯罪嫌疑人 A 与 B 都是理性的人,他们都知道,每个人在作选择时都是从个人利益的角度出发。即使事先两人达成都不供认的协议,但是由于不存在某种有效约束,每个人在履行协议时都要承担着对方违约的巨大风险。在上述的囚徒困境中,如果两个犯罪嫌疑人之间事先有过不供认的协议,某个犯罪嫌疑人坚持履行协议,一旦另一方违约,他就将被判处 20 年徒刑。因此,图 14.1 中的"A 不供认,B 不供认"不可能是均衡解。

还应当指出的是,占优策略(dominant strategy)均衡虽然要求每个参与人是理性的,但并不要求每个参与人知道其他参与人也是理性的。因为,所有参与人的理性假定虽然影响均衡解,但是不论其他参与人是否理性,都不会影响理性参与人的最优选择。假如囚徒困境中的 A 是理性的,B 是非理性的,B 既可能选择供认,也可能选择不供认。但是,无论 B 如何选择,对 A 来说,选择供认都是其最优策略。当然,均衡解有可能就不一定是"A 供认,B 供认"了。

囚徒困境的问题是博弈论中的一个基本的、典型的事例,类似问题在许多情况下都会出现,如寡头竞争、军备竞赛、团队生产中的劳动供给、公共产品的供给等等。同时,囚徒困境反映了一个深刻的问题,这就是个人理性与集体理性的冲突。例如,微观经济学的基本观点之一是通过市场机制这只"看不见的手",在人人追求自身利益最大化的基础上达到全社会资源的最优配置。囚徒困境对此提出了新的挑战。

囚徒的两难处境与市场的不完全竞争有什么关系呢? 事实上,寡头在力图达到垄断结果时的博弈也类似于两个处于两难处境的囚徒的博弈。

伊朗和伊拉克这两个成员构成一个寡头市场。两个国家都出售原油。在公开的谈判之后,两国一致同意降低石油生产,以使世界石油价格维持在高水平上。在对生产水平达成协议后,两个国家都要决定是合作并坚持这种协议,还是置之不管并生产更多的石油。图 14.2 表示两国的利润如何取决于他们选择的战略。

假设你是伊拉克总统。你的推理如下:"我可以像协议中提到的那样保持低产量,也可以增加产量并在世界市场上出售更多的石油。如果伊朗坚持协议并保持低产量,那么,我国在高产量时可赚利润 600 亿美元,在低产量时赚利润 500 亿美元。在这种情况下,高产量使我国状况更好。如果伊朗不遵守协议并生产高产量,那么,我国在高产量时可以赚 400 亿美元,而在低产量时只赚 300 亿美元。我国在高产量时状况更好。因此,无论伊朗选择怎么做,我国违背协议并提交产量,状况会更好。"在高水平时生产是伊拉克的优势战略。当然,伊朗的推理也是一样。最后会导致不良结果(从伊拉克和伊朗各自的角度看),即每国都是低利润。

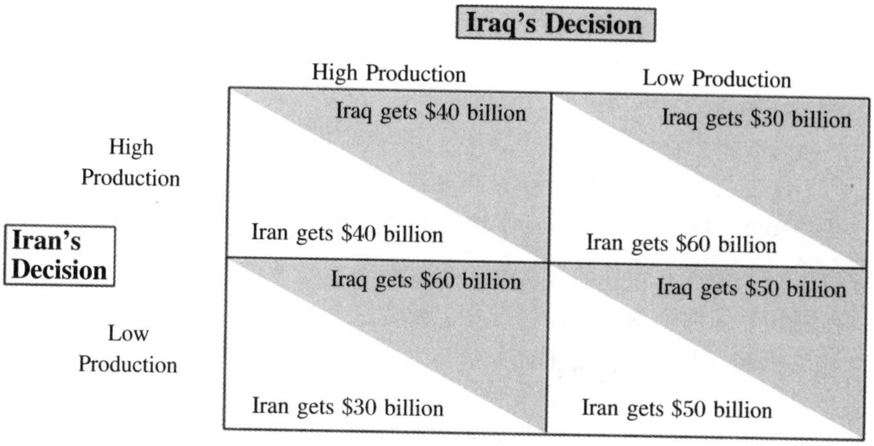

Iraq's Decision

	High Production	Low Production
High Production	Iraq gets $40 billion / Iran gets $40 billion	Iraq gets $30 billion / Iran gets $60 billion
Low Production	Iraq gets $60 billion / Iran gets $30 billion	Iraq gets $50 billion / Iran gets $50 billion

图 14.2 寡头博弈

这个例子说明了为什么寡头维持垄断利润很困难。合作垄断的结果对寡头是有好处的，但每个寡头都有违背协议的激励。正如利己使处于两难困境中的囚徒选择坦白一样，利己也使寡头难以维持低产量、高价格和垄断利润的合作结果。

我们再来看一个关于共有资源的例子。日常生活中，我们会发现人们倾向于过度使用共有资源。可以把这个问题作为囚徒两难处境的一个应用。

设想两个石油公司——埃克森与阿尔科——拥有相邻的油田。这块油田下价值1200万美元的石油为他们共有。钻一口井要花100万美元。如果每个公司钻一口井，每个公司就将得到一半石油，并赚500万美元的利润（收益600万美元减去成本100万美元）。由于油田是共有资源，各公司都不能有效率地使用。假设两个公司都可以钻第二口井。如果一家公司在三口井中有两口，这个公司就将得到三分之二的石油，这就会带来600万美元的利润。但如果每个公司都钻第二口井，那么，两个公司又是平分油田。在这种情况下，每家都要承担第二口井的成本，因此，每家公司的利润都只有400万美元。

可以用图14.3来表示这个博弈。钻两口井是每个公司的优势战略。这两个博弈者的利己心理又使它们得到了不利的结果。

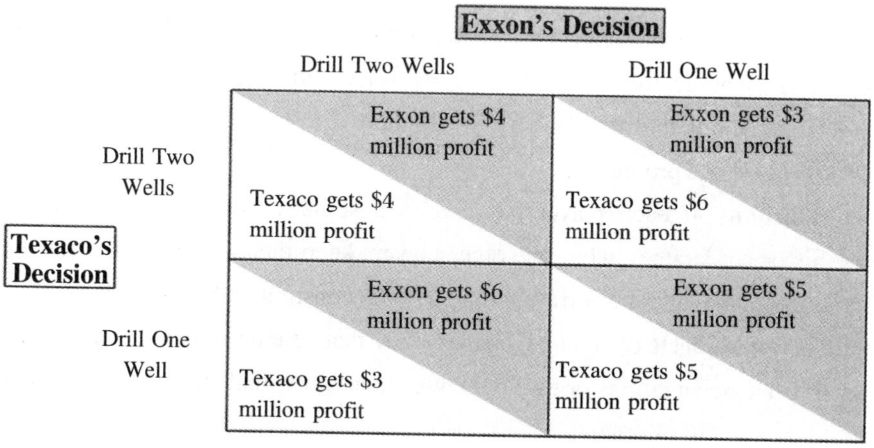

Exxon's Decision

	Drill Two Wells	Drill One Well
Drill Two Wells	Exxon gets $4 million profit / Texaco gets $4 million profit	Exxon gets $3 million profit / Texaco gets $6 million profit
Drill One Well	Exxon gets $6 million profit / Texaco gets $3 million profit	Exxon gets $5 million profit / Texaco gets $5 million profit

图 14.3 共有资源的博弈

在这个共有资源博弈中，阿尔科和埃克森公司额外打的井完全属于浪费。在这种情况下，如果两个参与者能达到合作的结果，社会的福利水平会变得更好。与此相比，在企图维持垄断利润的寡头情况下，从整个社会的角度来看，缺乏合作是合意的。垄断结果对寡头是有利的，但对商品的消费者是不利的。正如我们最早在第八章中说明的，竞争结果对社会是最有利的，因为这个结果使总剩余最大化。当寡头不能合作时，他们生产的数量接近于这个最优水平。换个说法，只有在市场竞争时，"看不见的手"才能引导资源进行有效地配置，而只有市场上的企业不能相互合作时，市场才是竞争的。

同样，在警察审问两个嫌疑犯的情况中，嫌疑犯之间缺乏合作是合意的，因为它使警察可以制止更多的犯罪行为。囚徒的两难处境对囚徒来说是一种两难处境，但对其他每一个人来说是一种福音。

为什么人们有时能合作呢？囚徒的两难处境表明合作是困难的。但并不是不可能合作。在被警察审问的时候，并不是所有囚犯都决定出卖他们的犯罪同伙。有时尽管卡特尔的个别成员有违规的行为，卡特尔也能维持勾结性的协议。通常情况下，参与者可以解决囚徒两难处境的原因是他们的博弈不是一次性的，而是多次的。

政策限制合作的一种方法是通过习惯法。一般来说，合约自由是市场经济的一个基本组成部分。企业和家庭用合约来安排相互有利的贸易。在这样做时，他们依靠司法制度来履行合约。但几百年来，英国和美国法官都认定竞争者之间通过协议来减少产量并提高价格是违背公共利益的。因此，他们拒绝执行这类协议。

现在，美国司法部和私人团体都有权提出法律诉讼来履行反托拉斯法。这些法律被用来防止任何一个企业过大的市场势力的合并。此外，这些法律也用于防止寡头的形成，从而使市场以一种不太垄断的方式进行运作。

重要名词解释

1. **Oligopoly**：a market form in which a market or industry is dominated by a small number of sellers (oligopolists)

2. **Cartel**：a formal (explicit) agreement among competing firms. It is a formal organization of producers and manufacturers that agree to fix prices, marketing, and production. Cartels usually occur in an oligopolistic industry, where there is a small number of sellers and usually involves homogeneous products.

3. **Nash equilibrium**：If each player has chosen a strategy and no player can benefit by changing his or her strategy while the other players keep theirs unchanged, then the current set of strategy choices and the corresponding payoffs constitute a Nash equilibrium.

4. **Game theory**：a branch of applied mathematics that attempts to mathematically capture behavior in strategic situations or games, in which an individual's success in making choices depends on the choices of others

5. **Collusion**：takes place within an industry when rival companies cooperate for their mutual benefit

6. **Prisoner's dilemma:** a fundamental problem in game theory that demonstrates why two people might not cooperate even if it is in both of their best interests to do so. It was originally framed by Merrill Flood and Melvin Dresher working at RAND in 1950.

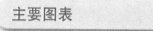

主要图表

1.

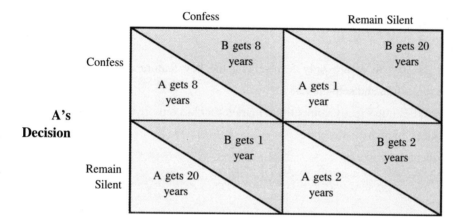

模拟试题

1. In game theory, a situation in which each person must consider how others might respond to his or her own action is called a
   A. Quantifiable situation.
   B. Cooperative situation.
   C. Strategic situation.
   D. Tactical situation.
   E. Tactics situation.
   Key: C
   Analysis: Strategic situations are those in which each person, in deciding what action to take, must consider how others might respond to that action.

2. In general, game theory is the study of
   A. How people behave in strategic situations.
   B. How people behave when the possible actions of other people are irrelevant.
   C. Oligopolistic markets.
   D. All types of markets, including competitive markets, monopolistic markets, and

oligopolistic markets.

E. How people behave in certain business decisions.

Key: A

Analysis: Do not understand game theory as a theory that is applicable to ordinary games such as chess or tic-tac-toe.

3. A distinguishing feature of an oligopolistic industry is the tension between

    A. Profit maximization and cost minimization.

    B. Cooperation and self interest.

    C. Producing a small amount of output and charging a price above marginal cost.

    D. Short-run decisions and long-run decisions.

    E. Higher price and smaller market.

Key: B

Analysis: Because there are only few sellers, the key feature of oligopoly is the tension between cooperation and self-interest.

4. A special kind of imperfectly competitive market that has only two firms is called

    A. A two-tier competitive structure.

    B. An incidental monopoly.

    C. A doublet.

    D. A duopoly.

    E. Cartel.

Key: D

Analysis: A duopoly is an oligopoly with only two members. It is the simplest type of oligopoly.

5. Which of the following statements is correct?

    A. If duopolists successfully collude, their combined output will be equal to the output that would be observed if the market were a monopoly.

    B. Although the logic of self-interest decreases a duopoly's price below the monopoly price, it does not push the duopolists to reach the competitive price.

    C. Although the logic of self-interest increases a duopoly's level of output above the monopoly level, it does not push the duopolists to reach the competitive level.

    D. All of the above are correct.

    E. Both A and B.

Key: D

Analysis: When firms in an oligopoly individually choose to increase production to maximize profit, they produce a quantity of output greater than the level produced by monopoly and less than the level produced by competition. The oligopoly price is less than the monopoly price but greater than the competitive price (which equals marginal cost).

The information in the table below shows the total demand for premium-channel digital cable TV subscriptions in a small urban market. Assume that each digital cable TV operator pays a fixed cost of $200, 000 per year to provide premium digital channels in the market area, then the marginal cost of providing the premium channel service to a household is zero.

Quantity	Price(per year)
0	$180
3, 000	$150
6, 000	$120
9, 000	$90
12, 000	$60
15, 000	$30
18, 000	$0

6. Refer to the table above. Assume there are two profit-maximizing digital cable TV companies operating in this market, and they are able to collude on the quantity of subscriptions that will be sold and on the price that will be charged for subscriptions. How much profit will each company earn?

A. $610, 000

B. $550, 000

C. $410, 000

D. $405, 000

E. $360, 000

Key: D

Analysis: For the monopolistic firm, it must pursue the profit-maximizing. Only in the combination(9000, $90), it will earn the maximal profit (9000×90)/2.

7. Refer to the table again. Assume there are two profit-maximizing digital cable TV companies operating in this market, and they are not able to collude on the price and quantity of premium digital channel subscriptions to sell. How many premium digital channel cable TV subscriptions will be sold altogether when this market reaches a Nash equilibrium?

A. 6, 000

B. 9, 000

C. 12, 000

D. 15, 000

E. 18, 000

Key: C

Analysis: Theoretically, a Nash equilibrium is a situation in which economic actors interact with one another and each chooses his or her best strategy given the strategies that all the other actors have chosen. In actual calculation, each company's output is about one third of the maximal quantity. The profit each company will earn is 2×1/3×18, 000.

8. Continue referring to the table above. Assume there are two profit-maximizing digital cable TV companies operating in this market. Further assume that they are not able to collude on

the price and quantity of premium digital channel subscriptions to sell. What price will premium digital channel cable TV subscriptions be sold at when this market reaches Nash equilibrium?

A. $30

B. $60

C. $90

D. $120

E. $150

Key: B

Analysis: It will choose to sell $1/3 \times 18000$, and the total quantity supplied is 12000, so the price is $60.

9. Continue referring to the table above. Assume that there are two profit-maximizing digital cable TV companies operating in this market. Further assume that they are not able to collude on the price and quantity of premium digital channel subscriptions to sell. How much profit will each firm earn when this market reaches Nash equilibrium?

A. $25, 000

B. $90, 000

C. $160, 000

D. $215, 000

E. $180, 000

Key: C

Analysis: $6000 \times 60 - 200,000 = 160, 000$

10. There are two types of market in which firms face some competition yet are still able to have some control over the prices of their products. Those two types of market are

A. Monopolistic competition and oligopoly.

B. Duopoly and triopoly.

C. Perfect competition and monopolistic competition.

D. Duopoly and imperfect competition.

E. Oligopoly and monopoly.

Key: A

Analysis: Types of imperfectly competitive markets: oligopoly and monopolistic competition.

11. Once a cartel is formed, the market is in effect served by

A. A monopoly.

B. An oligopoly.

C. Imperfect competition.

D. Monopolistic competition.

E. Duopoly.

Key: A

Analysis: Cartel is a group of firms acting in unison.

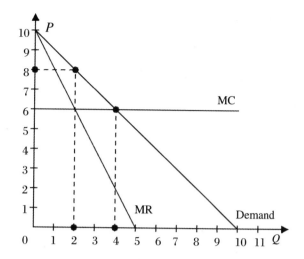

12. Consider the diagram above, which shows the market demand curve for a particular product. Suppose this market is served by two duopolists each of who faces the marginal cost curve shown in the diagram. The marginal revenue curve that a monopolist would face in this market is also shown. Which of the following statements is true?

   A. The total output in this market will likely be 2 units when the market is served by a duopoly.

   B. The price in this market will likely be $6 when the market is served by a duopoly.

   C. The total revenue to each firm will likely be more than $16 when the market is served by a duopoly.

   D. The total output in this market will likely be less than 4 units when the market is served by a duopoly.

   E. None of above is right.

   Key: D

   Analysis: 6<P (the duopoly's price) <8, 2<Q (total quantity) <4

13. When firms are faced with making strategic choices in order to maximize profit, economists typically use

   A. The theory of monopoly to model their behavior.

   B. The theory of aggressive competition to model their behavior.

   C. Game theory to model their behavior.

   D. Cartel theory to model their behavior.

   E. The theory of collusion to model their behavior.

   Key: C

   Analysis: Game theory is not necessary for understanding competitive or monopoly markets.

14. The prisoners' dilemma is an important game to study because

   A. Most games present zero-sum alternatives.

   B. It identifies the fundamental difficulty in maintaining cooperative agreements.

   C. Strategic decisions faced by prisoners are identical to those faced by firms engaged in competitive agreements.

D. All interactions among firms are represented by this game.

E. It provides insight into why cooperation is individually rational.

Key: B

Analysis: The prisoners' dilemma provides insights into the difficulty in maintaining cooperation. People (firms) often fail to cooperate with one another even when cooperation would make them better off.

15. In a game, a dominant strategy is

A. The best strategy for a player to follow only if other players are cooperative.

B. The best strategy for a player to follow, regardless of the strategies followed by other players.

C. A strategy that must appear in every game.

D. A strategy that leads to one player's interests dominating the interests of the other players.

E. A strategy that must make every player better off.

Key: B

Analysis: The definition is that, the dominant strategy is the best strategy for a player to follow regardless of the strategies pursued by other players.

Two companies, ABC and XYZ, are considering whether to produce a high level of output or a low level of output. In the figure, the dollar amounts are payoffs and they represent annual profits for the two companies.

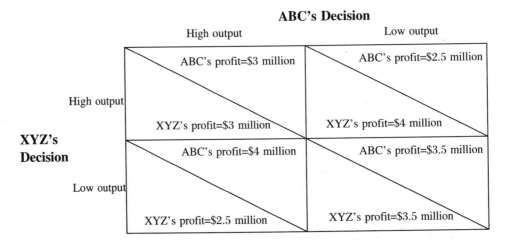

16. Refer to the figure above. The dominant strategy

A. For both companies is to produce high output.

B. For ABC is to produce high output, and the dominant strategy for XYZ is to produce low output.

C. For ABC is to produce low output, and the dominant strategy for XYZ is to produce high output.

D. For both companies is to produce low output.

E. A or C.

Key: A

Analysis: For ABC, whatever XYZ's output is high or low, producing high output is the optimal choice. For XYZ, it is the same.

17. Continue referring to the figure above. Which of the following statements is correct?

    A. ABC can potentially earn its highest possible profit if it produces a high level of output, and for that reason it is a dominant strategy for ABC to produce a high level of output.

    B. The highest possible combined profit for the two firms occurs when both produce a low level of output, and for that reason producing a low level of output is a dominant strategy for both firms.

    C. Regardless of the strategy pursued by ABC, XYZ's best strategy is to produce a high level of output, and for that reason producing a high level of output is a dominant strategy for XYZ.

    D. Our knowledge of game theory suggests that the most likely outcome of the game, if it is played only once, is for one firm to produce a low level of output and for the other firm to produce a high level of output.

    E. None of above is right.

Key: C

Analysis: The dominant strategy is the best strategy for a player to follow regardless of the strategies pursued by other players. To apply this principle, regardless of the strategy pursued by ABC, XYZ's best strategy is to produce a high level of output, and for that reason producing a high level of output is a dominant strategy for XYZ.

18. Continue referring to the figure above. If this game is played only once, then the most likely outcome is that

    A. Both firms produce a low level of output.

    B. ABC produces a low level of output and XYZ produces a high level of output.

    C. ABC produces a high level of output and XYZ produces a low level of output.

    D. Both firms produce a high level of output.

    E. A or D

Key: D

Analysis: Producing a high level of output is a dominant strategy for XYZ, and it is the same for ABC.

19. Games that are played more than once generally

    A. Lead to outcomes dominated purely by self-interest.

    B. Lead to outcomes that do not reflect joint rationality.

    C. Encourage cheating on cartel production quotas.

    D. Make collusive arrangements easier to enforce.

    E. Make the market more efficient.

Key: D

Analysis: It examines the understanding of game theory. The prisoners' dilemma shows that self-interest can prevent people from maintaining cooperation, even when cooperation is in their mutual interests.

20. Consider a game of the "Jack and Jill" type in which a market is a duopoly and each firm decides to produce either a high quantity of output or a low quantity of output. If the two firms successfully reach and maintain the cooperative outcome of the game, then

    A. Both the combined profit of the firms and the total surplus are maximized.

    B. The combined profit of the firms is maximized but the total surplus is not maximized.

    C. The combined profit of the firms is not maximized but the total surplus is maximized.

    D. Neither the combined profit of the firms nor the total surplus is maximized.

    E. Either the combined profit of the firms or the total surplus is maximized.

    Key: B

    Analysis: That circumstance is similar to monopoly, so the combined profit of the firms is maximized but the total surplus is not maximized.

21. A store and B store are two competing retail stores. They are both studying potential store locations in the suburbs of City W. Each store must choose between a location in the east of the city and a location in the west of the city. The payoff matrix is shown below, with the first entry in each cell indicating A Store's daily profit and the second entry indicating B store's daily profit. Both stores know all of the information in the payoff matrix.

B store

		East		West	
	East	$900,	$1,800	$3,000,	$3,500
A Store					
	West	$5,000,	$4,000	$1,500,	$1,000

   (a) If A store chooses a location in the west of the city, which location is better for B store? Explain.

   (b) Is choosing a location in the west of the city a dominant strategy for A store? Explain.

   (c) If the two stores cooperate in choosing locations, where will each firm locate?

   (d) Assume that the west suburb has enacted an incentive package to attract new business. Any store that locates in the west of the city will receive a subsidy of $2,000 per day. Redraw the payoff matrix to include the subsidy.

   Key: 6 points $(2 + 2 + 1 + 1)$

   (a) 2 points:

       One point is earned for stating that the east will be better for B store.

       One point is earned for explaining that B store earns a higher profit by locating in the east than in the west ($4,000 versus $1,000).

   (b) 2 points:

       One point is earned for stating that choosing the west is not a dominant strategy for A store.

One point is earned for explaining that if B store chooses the west, it is better for A store to choose the east. (A store's best strategy depends on B store's move.)

(c) 1 point:

The point is earned for stating that A store chooses the west and B store chooses the east.

(d) 1 point:

The point is earned for redrawing the table with the correct entries:

B store

	East	West
A store East	$900, $1,800	$3,000, $5,500
West	$7,000, $4,000	$3,500, $3,000

22. Two interdependent bus companies—City Ride and Easy Ride—provide transportation services in the same city. Following a change in costs that affects both companies, both companies must decide whether to lower their fare or maintain their current fare. In the payoff matrix below, the first entry in each cell indicates the daily profit for Easy Ride and the second entry indicates the daily profit for City Ride. Both companies know all of the information in the matrix.

City Ride

	Maintain Fare	Lower Fare
Easy Ride Maintain Fare	$150, $180	$130, $120
Lower Fare	$120, $130	$140, $110

(a) If Easy Ride chooses to maintain its current fare, which strategy is better for City Ride? Explain.

(b) Is there a dominant strategy for Easy Ride? Explain.

(c) Assume that the companies must make their decisions simultaneously and do not cooperate. What will be the daily profit for them?

(d) If these two companies could cooperate, which strategy would each of them choose?

(e) Suppose that the local government decides to provide a subsidy of $40 per day to the bus companies. However, only the company that agrees to lower its fare is eligible to receive the subsidy. Draw a new payoff matrix to reflect the change in government policy.

Key: 6 points (1 + 2 + 1 + 1 + 1)

(a) 1 point:

The point is earned for concluding that it is better for City Ride to maintain its current fare, since $180 > $120.

(b) 2 points:

　　One point is earned for stating that Easy Ride does not have a dominant strategy.

　　One point is earned for explaining that Easy Ride's best move depends on City Ride's move.

(c) 1 point:

　　The point is earned for stating that the profit for Easy Ride is $150 and the profit for City Ride is $180.

(d) 1 point:

　　The point is earned for stating that the cooperative solution is for both to maintain their current fares.

(e) 1 point:

　　The point is earned for showing the correct entries in the new payoff matrix as follows:

City Ride

	Maintain Fare	Lower Fare
Easy Ride Maintain Fare	$150, $180	$130, $160
Easy Ride Lower Fare	$160, $130	$180, $150

23. Two bus companies, R1 and R2, operate a route from A city to B city, transporting a mix of passengers and freight. They must file their schedules with the local transportation board each year and cannot alter them during that year. Those schedules are revealed only after both companies have filed. Each company must choose between an early and a late departure. The relevant payoff matrix appears below, with the first entry in each cell indicating R1's daily profit and the second entry in each cell indicating R2's daily profit.

R2

	Early	Late
R1 Early	$1,000, $900	$950, $850
R1 Late	$750, $650	$700, $800

(a) In which market structure do these firms operate? Explain.

(b) If R1 chooses an early departure, which departure time is better for R2?

(c) Identify the dominant strategy for R1.

(d) Is choosing an early departure a dominant strategy for R2? Explain.

(e) If both firms know all of the information in the payoff matrix but do not cooperate, what will be R2's daily profit?

Key: 6 points $(1+1+1+2+1)$

(a) 1 point:

　　The point is earned for identifying the market as an oligopoly, since there are only two firms and their actions are mutually interdependent.

(b) 1 point:

　　The point is earned for stating that R2 will choose early departure.

(c) 1 point:

　　The point is earned for stating that R1's dominant strategy is early departure.

(d) 2 points:

　　One point is earned for stating that early departure is not a dominant strategy for R2.

　　One point is earned for reasoning that if R1 chooses a late departure, R2 is better off choosing a late departure.

(e) 1 point:

　　The point is earned for identifying $900 as R2's daily profit.

24. Airline 1 and Airline 2 are two airline companies that operate a route from City X to City Y, transporting a mix of passengers and freight. They must file their schedules with the National Transportation Board each year and cannot alter them during that year. Those schedules are revealed only after both companies have filed. Each airline must choose between a morning and an evening departure. The relevant payoff matrix appears below, with the first entry in each cell indicating Airline 1's daily profit and the second entry in each cell indicating Airline 2's daily profit.

Airline 2

		Morning	Evening
	Morning	$1,000,　$700	$700,　$600
Airline 1			
	Evening	$750,　$950	$900,　$800

(a) In which market structure do these firms operate? Explain.

(b) If Airline 2 chooses an evening departure, which departure time is better for Airline 1?

(c) Identify the dominant strategy for Airline 1.

(d) Is choosing an evening departure a dominant strategy for Airline 1? Explain.

(e) If both firms know all of the information in the payoff matrix but do not cooperate, what will be Airline 2's daily profit?

Key: 6 points (1 + 1 + 1 + 2 + 1)

(a) 1 point:

　　The point is earned for identifying the market as an oligopoly because there is mutual interdependence—the behavior of each firm affects the other.

(b) 1 point:

　　The point is earned for stating that an evening departure will be best for Airline 1.

(c) 1 pont: The point is earned for stating that Airline's dominant strategy is a morning departure.

(d) 2 points:

One point is earned for stating that choosing an evening departure is not a dominant strategy for Airline 1.

One point is earned for correctly reasoning that Airline 1 does not have a dominant strategy because its best payoff depends on Airline 2's choice (Or, more specifically, if Airline 2 chooses a morning departure, it is best for Airline 1 to choose a morning departure).

(e) 1 point:

The point is earned for identifying $700.

Chapter 15 Monopolistically Competitive Market
垄断竞争市场

主要内容和概念讲解

完全竞争市场和完全垄断市场是理论分析中的两种极端的市场组织。在现实经济生活中，通常存在的是上一章讲过的寡头垄断市场以及本章要分析的垄断竞争市场（monopolistically competitive market）。

垄断竞争是介于完全竞争与完全垄断之间，更接近于完全竞争市场的一种较为现实的市场结构。它既包含竞争因素又包含一定的垄断成分。具体来讲，垄断竞争市场主要具备以下三个条件：

第一，市场中存在大量的厂商（少于完全竞争厂商的数目），单个厂商所占的市场份额比例较小，对市场价格的影响力十分有限。厂商之间存在着激烈的竞争，但不会相互勾结，也不相互依赖。任何一家厂商在进行决策时无需考虑其他对手的可能反应。同时，进入或退出市场比较容易，接近于完全竞争。

第二，垄断竞争厂商所生产的产品是有差别的同类产品，且这些产品彼此之间都非常近似。完全竞争厂商生产的产品都是同质的或标准的，而垄断竞争厂商所生产的产品存在着产品差别（product differentiation）。所谓产品差别就是同类产品由买方偏好而形成的具有不完全替代关系的状态。产品差别可能来自产品实质上的不同，如质量、性能、设计、颜色、款式和包装等，也可能来自购买者主观感觉上的差别。另外，销售条件、专利、商标、厂商名称及信誉等也会造成产品差别。正是因为这些差别，每个厂商都具备不同程度的垄断势力（market power），其大小取决于产品的差别程度。产品的差别越大，垄断势力越强。反之，垄断势力则越弱。注意，垄断竞争市场中的产品首先是同类产品，其次才是有差别的产品。所以，每个厂商既是垄断者又是竞争者，故称为垄断竞争。

第三，厂商进入与退出市场比较容易。厂商的生产规模在技术上要求不太大，资本要求也不太多，进入和退出的壁垒较小。

在垄断竞争理论中，把市场上生产非常接近的同类产品的厂商的全体称为生产集团。垄断竞争是现实经济中的普遍现象。大城市的零售业、加油站、杂货店、餐馆、干洗店、美容美发店等，一般都具有垄断竞争的特征。

由于垄断竞争厂商可以在一定程度上控制自己产品的价格，即通过改变自己生产的有差别产品的销售量来影响产品的价格。所以，如同垄断厂商一样，垄断竞争厂商所面临的需求曲线也是向右下方倾斜的。不同的是，由于各垄断竞争厂商的产品相互之间都是很近似的，市场竞争因素使得垄断竞争厂商的需求曲线具有较大的弹性，因此，垄断竞争厂商向右下方倾斜的需求曲线是比较平坦的，相对而言比较接近完全竞争厂商水平形状的需求曲线。

垄断竞争市场上厂商面临的需求曲线有两种：d需求曲线和D需求曲线。两者的区分涉及每个厂商与本行业（产业）其他厂商的关系。d需求曲线表示的是，当某个厂商改变自己产品的价格，而该行业中与之竞争的其他厂商保持产品价格不变时，该厂商的产品价格与销售量之间的关系。d需求曲线也称为预期需求曲线（expectation demand curve）。在这种情况下，产品价格较小的变动，会导致该厂商的销售量大幅度的变动，因此，这条需求曲线比较平坦，如图15.1所示。

图中d所表示的就是一家厂商价格变动而其他厂商价格保持不变时的需求曲线。当某厂商价格为P_0时销售量为Q_0。当价格由P_0降至P_1时，在其他厂商价格不变的条件下其销售量由Q_0增至Q_1。

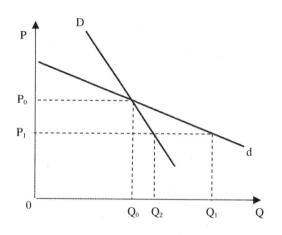

图15.1　垄断竞争厂商的需求曲线

另一条需求曲线D表示的是，当一个厂商改变自己产品的价格，该行业中其他与之竞争的厂商也随之改变价格时，该厂商的产品价格与销售量之间的关系。D需求曲线又称为比例需求曲线或客观需求曲线。

在图15.1中，D所表示的就是这样一条需求曲线，当某垄断厂商价格为P_0时，该厂商的销售量为Q_0；当其价格降至P_1时，该行业其他厂商也随之降价，他的销售量增至Q_2。显然，价格的下降幅度相同，但销售量的增加幅度却不一样。D需求曲线和d需求曲线的一般关系有：（1）当所有垄断竞争厂商都以相同的方式改变产品价格时，整个市场价格的变化会使单个厂商的d需求曲线的位置沿着D需求曲线上下平移。如果市场价格下跌，则d需求曲线沿着D需求曲线向下平移；如果市场价格上升，则d需求曲线沿着D需求曲线向上平移。（2）由于d需求曲线表示的是单个垄断竞争厂商单独改变价格时所预期的需求量，D需求曲线表示的是每个垄断竞争厂商在每一价格水平实际所面临的需求量，所以，d需求曲线和D需求曲线相交意味着垄断竞争市场供求相等的均衡状态。（3）d需求曲线的弹性大于D需求曲线的弹性。

垄断竞争市场的短期均衡

我们以垄断竞争市场的代表性厂商为例来分析垄断竞争条件下的均衡。在短期内，垄断竞争市场的代表性厂商在现有的生产规模下通过产量和价格的同时调整，来实现$MR=$

SMC 的均衡条件。如图 15.2 所示。

在图 15.2 中，SAC 曲线和 SMC 曲线分别表示代表性厂商现有生产规模的平均成本曲线和边际成本曲线，MR_1 与 MR_2 是分别对应于 d_1 曲线和 d_2 曲线的边际收益曲线。我们假定代表性厂商最初在 d_1 曲线和 D 曲线相交的 A 点进行生产，此时，市场价格为 P_0，产量为 Q_0。这一价格和产量与实现最大利润的 $MR_1 = SMC$ 的均衡点 E_1 所要求的产量 Q_1 和价格 P_1 相差很远。于是，该厂商决定将生产由 A 点沿着 d_1 需求曲线调整到 B 点，即将价格降低为 P_1，将产量增加为 Q_1。

然而，由于每个垄断竞争厂商面对的情况都是相同的，而且，每个企业都是在假定自己改变价格而其他企业不会改变价格的情况下采取相同的行动的，即都把价格降为 P_1，并都计划生产 Q_1 的产量。于是，当整个市场的价格下降为 P_1 时，每个厂商的产量实际上都是 Q_2，而不是 Q_1。相应地每个厂商的 d_1 需求曲线也都沿着 D 需求曲线向下平移到了 d_2 需求曲线的位置。所以，首次降价的结果是使代表性厂商的经营位置由 A 点沿着 D 需求曲线移动到了 C 点。

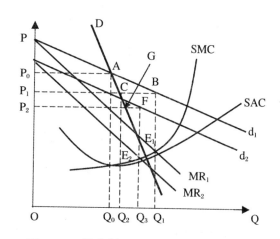

图 15.2　代表性厂商的生产调整过程

在 C 点位置上，d_2 需求曲线与 D 需求曲线相交，相应的边际收益曲线为 MR_2。显然，C 点对应的产品价格 P_1 和产量 Q_2，仍然不符合在新的市场价格水平下的 $MR_2 = SMC$ 的均衡点 E_2 上的价格 P_2 和产量 Q_3 的要求。

因此，该企业又会再一次降价。与第一次降价相似，企业将沿着 D 需求曲线由 C 点移动到 G 点。相应地，d_2 曲线将向下平移，并与 D 曲线相交于 G 点（图中没有画出）。依此类推，代表性厂商为实现利润最大化，会继续降低价格，d 需求曲线会沿着 D 需求曲线不断向下平移，并在每一个新的价格水平与 D 曲线相交。

上述过程一直要持续到代表性厂商没有理由再降价为止，即代表性厂商所追求的 $MR = SMC$ 的均衡条件实现为止。如图 15.3 所示，代表性厂商连续降价行为的最终结果将是 d 曲线和 D 曲线相交点 H 上的产量和价格恰好是 $MR = SMC$ 时的均衡点 E 上所要求的产量 Q_e 和价格 P_e。此时，就实现了垄断竞争厂商的短期均衡，Q_e 和 P_e 分别是垄断竞争厂商的短期均衡产量和价格。

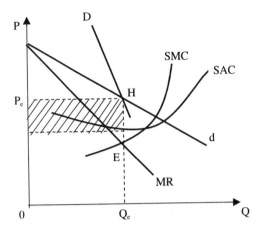

图 15.3　垄断竞争厂商的短期均衡

　　除了有两条需求曲线之外，垄断竞争厂商的短期均衡条件也是 *MR=SMC*。在短期均衡的产量上，必定存在一个 *d* 曲线和 *D* 曲线的交点，它意味着市场上的供求是相等的。此时，垄断竞争厂商可能获得最大利润，可能利润为零，也可能受到最小的亏损。但只要均衡价格在平均可变成本曲线之上，该厂商在短期内就会继续生产。图 15.3 说明了厂商获得经济利润的短期均衡状况，经济利润为图中阴影部分的面积。

垄断竞争厂商的长期均衡

　　在短期内，垄断竞争厂商可能获得超额利润，也可能亏损。出现亏损时，如果垄断竞争厂商通过调整生产规模和产量仍不能摆脱亏损，他就会和完全竞争厂商一样退出该行业。如果垄断竞争厂商在短期内存在超额利润，就必然会引起其他厂商进入垄断竞争市场，这就意味着通过调整生产规模、进入或退出行业，垄断竞争厂商达到长期均衡时的经济利润必定为零。即在垄断竞争长期均衡点上，*d* 需求曲线必定与 *LAC* 曲线相切。

　　图 15.4 所表示的就是垄断竞争厂商的长期均衡。在长期均衡产量 Q_0 上，垄断竞争厂商的经济利润为零。这是因为在均衡状态下，价格和平均成本高于该商品生产可以达到的最小的平均成本，价格高于边际成本，从而导致在更高的价格水平上生产出了更少的产品。因此，一般认为垄断竞争天生是低效率的。不过，也许这就是人类为了获取多样化的产品而必须付出的代价吧！

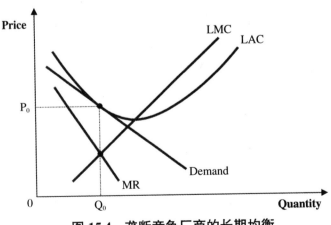

图 15.4　垄断竞争厂商的长期均衡

不同市场经济效率的比较

我们先来比较一下垄断竞争市场与完全竞争市场。如图 15.5 所示，垄断竞争市场和完全竞争市场之间有两个值得注意的差别——生产能力过剩与价格加成。

正如我们刚刚说明的，进入与退出使得垄断竞争市场上的每个企业都达到需求曲线与平均总成本曲线相切的一点上。图 15.5(a)表示，在这一点上的产量小于使平均总成本最小化时的产量。因此，在垄断竞争市场中，企业的生产在其平均总成本曲线向右下方倾斜的那一部分上。在这方面，垄断竞争市场与完全竞争市场形成了鲜明对照。正如图 15.5(b)所示，完全竞争市场上的自由进入使企业能够生产使平均总成本最小的产量。

使平均总成本最小的产量称为企业的有效规模。在长期中，完全竞争厂商生产有效规模，而垄断竞争厂商的生产低于这一水平。可以说厂商在垄断竞争之下有过剩生产能力。换句话说，与完全竞争厂商不同，垄断竞争厂商可以增加其产量并降低生产的平均总成本。

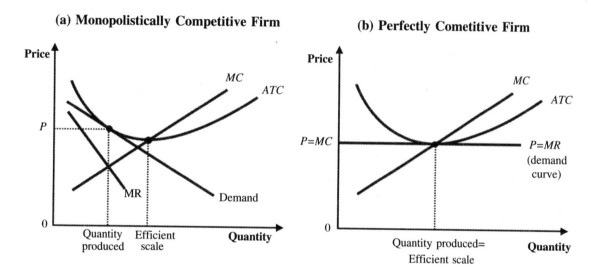

图 15.5   垄断竞争与完全竞争的比较

完全竞争厂商和垄断竞争厂商之间的第二个差别是价格和边际成本之间的关系。对一个如图 15.5(b)所示的完全竞争厂商来说，价格等于边际成本。对于一个如图 15.5(a)所示的垄断竞争厂商来说，价格高于边际成本，因为垄断竞争厂商总有某种市场势力。这种高于边际成本的价格加成如何与自由进入和零利润一致呢？零利润状况只能保证价格等于平均总成本，而不能保证价格等于边际成本。实际上，在长期均衡时，垄断竞争企业在其平均总成本曲线向下的部分运营，因此，边际成本低于平均总成本。这样，在价格等于平均总成本时，价格必定高于边际成本。

经济效率是指利用经济资源的有效性。高的经济效率表示对资源的充分利用或能以最有效的生产方式进行生产；低的经济效率表示对资源的利用不充分或没有以最有效的方式进行生产。不同市场结构的经济效率是不同的，市场结构直接影响经济效率的高低。西方经济学者通过对不同市场条件下厂商的长期均衡状态进行分析得出结论：完全竞争市场的经济效率最高，垄断竞争市场较高，寡头垄断市场较低，完全垄断市场最低。可见，市场的竞争程度越高，其经济效率越高；反之，市场的垄断程度越高，其经济效率越低。具体分析如下：

完全竞争市场是经济效率最高的市场，因为当完全竞争厂商达到长期均衡时，水平的需求曲线相切于长期平均成本曲线的最低点。该厂商不仅是在长期平均成本最低点生产，而且也是在短期平均成本最低点生产。此时，产品的均衡价格最低且等于最低的生产平均成本，产品的均衡产量最高。这说明，在完全竞争情况下的生产规模是适度的生产规模，因为它能够使长期生产成本最小化。同时，在这个适度规模上进行生产，其生产量也是适度的生产量，因为其短期平均成本是最小化的。厂商在这种状态下从事生产活动，只能获得正常的利润，因此社会资源能够得到最佳配置并获得最充分的利用。另外，完全竞争的作用可以使均衡价格降到最低点，从而使消费者也可以从中获得福利，所以完全竞争市场模型被认为是一种理想的经济模型。

在不完全竞争市场条件下，厂商的需求曲线是向右下方倾斜的。厂商的垄断程度越高，需求曲线越陡峭；垄断程度越低，需求曲线越平坦。在垄断竞争市场上，厂商的长期经济利润为零，所以在垄断竞争厂商达到长期均衡时，向右下方倾斜的、相对比较平坦的需求曲线相切于长期平均成本曲线的最低点的左边；产品的均衡价格比较低，且等于生产的平均成本；产品的均衡产量也比较高，但厂商仍存在多余的生产能力。虽然垄断竞争市场的均衡价格高于边际成本，但是该市场与完全竞争市场相比在服务和质量方面具有更大的多样性。在完全垄断市场上，厂商在长期内获得利润，所以，垄断厂商在达到长期均衡时，向右下方倾斜的、相对比较陡峭的需求曲线与长期平均成本曲线相交；产品的均衡价格最高，且大于生产的平均成本；产品的均衡产量最低。垄断厂商若肯放弃一些利润，价格就可以下降一些，产量也可以增加一些。在寡头垄断市场上，厂商的需求曲线不太确定，一般认为，寡头垄断市场是与完全垄断市场比较接近的市场组织形式，在达到长期均衡时，产品的均衡价格比较高，均衡产量比较低。另外，经济学家常利用长期均衡时的价格 P 与长期边际成本 LMC 的关系来判断一个行业是否实现了有效的资源配置。当 $P=LMC$ 时，商品的边际社会价值等于商品的边际社会成本，它表示资源在该行业得到了最有效的配置。

垄断竞争与广告

在现代经济生活中，要想在没有广告轰炸下度过普通的一天几乎是不可能的。无论你是在读报、看电视，或在高速公路上开车，总有一些企业会力图说服你购买它的产品。这种行为是垄断竞争市场的一个自然而然的特征。当企业销售有差别产品并收取高于边际成本的价格时，每个企业都有以广告来吸引更多自己特殊产品的买者的动力。

各种产品之间的广告量差别很大。销售略有差别消费品的企业，例如成药、香水、软饮料、刮胡刀片、早餐玉米片和热狗的企业，通常都把收益的10%~20%用于广告。出售工业品的企业，例如，钻探机与通讯卫星企业，一般用于广告的支出很少。而出售同质产品的企业，例如，小麦、花生或原油企业，根本没有广告支出。就整体经济而言，广告支出占企业总收益的2%左右，或者在1000亿美元以上。企业的广告采取多种形式。其中约有一半的广告支出用于报纸和杂志，有三分之一左右的广告支出用于电视和广播，剩余的支出用于其他让顾客了解产品的方式，例如，直接邮寄、广告牌和气球广告等。

用于广告的资金投入是不是一种社会浪费？或者说广告有没有价值？判断广告的社会价值是困难的，而且往往引起经济学家的激烈争论。

广告的批评者认为，企业做广告是为了操纵人们的偏好。许多广告不是信息性而是心理性的，带有很浓厚的心理暗示，例如某些品牌软饮料的电视广告。该类商业广告并不是要告诉观看者产品的价格或质量，而是通过展现在阳光明媚的海滩上一群快乐的年轻人每人手中都拿一罐那种软饮料来向你传递一个信息："你只有喝我们的产品，才能有这么多朋友和幸福。"广告的批评者认为，这种商业广告创造了一种本来不存在的预期。

批评者还认为，广告抑制了竞争。广告往往努力使消费者相信，产品差别大于实际情况。通过增加对产品差别的感觉和促进品牌忠诚，广告使消费者不太关心相似产品之间的价格差别。在需求曲线缺乏弹性时，每个企业都要收取远远高于边际成本的价格加成。

广告的拥护者则认为，企业用广告向顾客提供信息。广告提供所销售商品的价格、新产品的存在，以及零售店的位置。这种信息可以使顾客更好地选择想购买的商品，从而提高了市场进行有效的资源配置的能力。

拥护者还认为，广告加剧了竞争。因为广告能够使顾客更充分地了解市场上的所有企业，从而更容易地利用价格差别。因此，每个企业拥有的市场势力小了。此外，广告使新企业的进入更加容易，因为它为进入者提供了从现有企业中吸引顾客的一种手段。

随着时间推移，决策者逐渐接受了广告可以使市场更有竞争性的观点。我们以对律师、医师和药剂师这些职业的管制为例来说明。过去，政府禁止这些行业做广告，理由是这些行业的广告都是"非职业性"的。但近年来，法院认识到这些对广告的限制抑制了竞争，因此取消了许多禁止广告的法律。

重要名词解释

1. **Monopolistic competition**：a form of imperfect competition where many competing producers sell products that are differentiated from one another （that is, the products are substitutes, but, with differences such as branding, are not exactly alike）.
2. **Product differentiation**：is the process of distinguishing a product or offering from others, to make it more attractive to a particular target market. This involves differentiating it from competitors' products as well as a firm's own product offerings.
3. **Market power**：is the ability of a firm to alter the market price of a good or service.

主要图表

1.

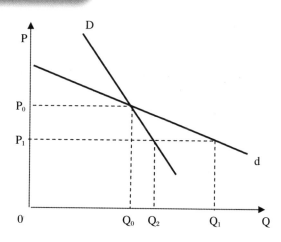

2.

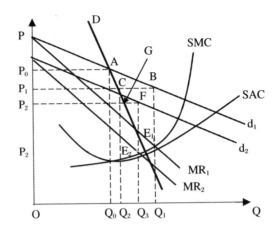

3.

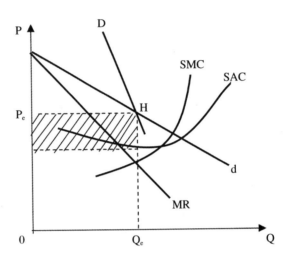

4.

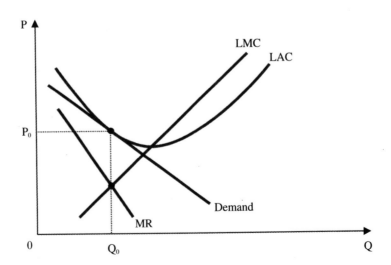

模拟试题

1. Which of the following is a characteristic of monopolistic competition?

    A. Ownership of a key resource by a single firm.

    B. Free entry.

    C. Identical product.

    D. Patents.

    E. Lots of brands.

    Key: B

    Analysis: Attributes of monopolistic competition are many sellers, product differentiation, and free entry and exit.

2. The market for novels is

    A. Perfectly competitive.

    B. A monopoly.

    C. Monopolistically competitive.

    D. An oligopoly.

    E. Depending on the kinds of novels.

    Key: C

    Analysis: The market for novels is a market structure in which many firms sell products that are similar but not identical. Monopolistic competition is the market structure that has some features of competition and some features of monopoly.

3. A monopolistically competitive market has characteristics that are similar to

    A. A monopoly.

    B. A competitive firm.

    C. Both a monopoly and a competitive firm.

    D. Neither a monopoly nor a competitive firm.

    E. Oligopoly.

    Key: C

    Analysis: The monopolistically competitive market has some features of competition and some features of monopoly.

4. Which of the following pairs illustrates the two extreme examples of market structures?

    A. Competition and oligopoly.

    B. Competition and monopoly.

    C. Monopoly and monopolistic competition.

    D. Oligopoly and monopolistic competition.

    E. Monopoly and oligopoly.

Key: B

Analysis: Monopolistic competition, like oligopoly, is a market structure that lies between the extreme cases of competition and monopoly.

5. One way in which monopolistic competition differs from oligopoly is that

   A. There are no barriers to entry in oligopolies.

   B. In oligopoly markets there are only a few sellers.

   C. All firms in an oligopoly eventually earn zero economic profits.

   D. Strategic interactions between firms are rare in oligopolies.

   E. A and C

   Key: B

   Analysis: Attributes of monopolistic competition are many sellers, product differentiation, free entry and exit.

6. Which of the following is an example of a monopolistically competitive industry?

   A. Computer operating systems.

   B. Tennis balls.

   C. Movies.

   D. Cable television.

   E. Running-water.

   Key: C

   Analysis: You should distinguish the difference between four kinds of market structure and understand more profoundly.

7. Monopolistic competition is characterized by which of the following attributes?

   (i) Free entry.

   (ii) Product differentiation.

   (iii) Many sellers.

   A. (i) and (iii).

   B. (i) and (ii).

   C. (ii) and (iii).

   D. (ii) only.

   E. (i), (ii), and (iii).

   Key: E

   Analysis: The three characteristics are many sellers, product differentiation, and free entry and exit.

8. A downward-sloping demand curve

   A. Is a feature of all monopolistically competitive firms.

   B. Means that the firm in question will never experience a zero profit.

   C. Causes marginal revenue to exceed price.

   D. Prohibits firms from earning positive economic profits in the long run.

E. Means that the firm faces the threat of new firms' entry into the market.

Key: A

Analysis: In the monopolistically competitive markets, each firm produces a product that is at least slightly different from those of other firms. Thus, rather than being a price taker, each firm faces a downward-sloping demand curve.

9. For a monopolistically competitive firm, at the profit-maximizing quantity of output,

A. Price exceeds marginal cost.

B. Marginal revenue exceeds marginal cost.

C. Marginal cost exceeds average revenue.

D. Price equals marginal revenue.

E. Marginal revenue exceeds average revenue.

Key: A

Analysis: It examines the understanding of the graph of monopolistic competition in the short run. It has some features of monopoly. As in a monopoly, price exceeds marginal cost.

10. Which of the following conditions is the characteristic of a monopolistically competitive firm in short-run equilibrium?

A. $P = AR$.

B. $MR = MC$.

C. $P > MC$.

D. All of the above.

E. B and C.

Key: D

Analysis: In short-run equilibrium for a monopolistically competitive firm, $P = AR > MC = MR$.

11. An important difference between the situation faced by a profit-maximizing monopolistically competitive firm in the short run and the situation faced by that same firm in the long run is that in the short run,

A. Price may exceed marginal revenue, but in the long run, price equals marginal revenue.

B. Price may exceed marginal cost, but in the long run, price equals marginal cost.

C. Price may exceed average total cost, but in the long run, price equals average total cost.

D. There are many firms in the market, but in the long run, there are only a few firms in the market.

E. A and B

Key: C

Analysis: In the long-run equilibrium, firms will enter and exit until the firms are making exactly zero economic profits. That means in the long run, price equals marginal cost.

The figure is drawn for a monopolistically competitive firm.

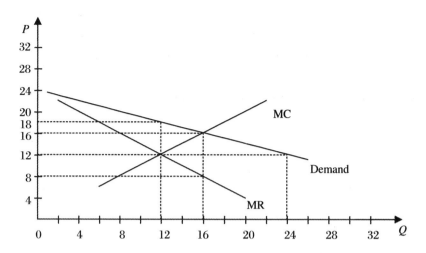

12. Refer to the figure above. The firm's profit-maximizing level of output is

A. 8 units.

B. 12 units.

C. 16 units.

D. 20 units.

E. 24 units.

Key: B

Analysis: According to $MR=MC$, we can choose the point in the intersection of MR curve and MC curve.

13. Refer to the figure above. In order to maximize profit, the firm will charge a price of

A. $8.

B. $12.

C. $16.

D. $18.

E. $24.

Key: D

Analysis: We can find it in the demand curve.

14. Refer to the figure above. Suppose that the average total cost is $18 when Q is 12. What is the profit-maximizing price and resulting profit?

A. $P=\$12$, profit=$0.

B. $P=\$18$, profit=$72.

C. $P=\$18$, profit=$24.

D. $P=\$18$, profit=$0.

E. $P=\$12$, profit=$24.

Key: D

Analysis: Profit=$Q\times(P-ATC)=Q\times(18-18)=0$.

15. Refer to the figure above. If the average total cost is $15 at the profit-maximizing quantity, then the firm's maximum profit is

A. $18.

B. $24.

C. $36.

D. $45.

E. $48.

Key: C

Analysis: Profit=$Q\times(P-ATC)$=$12\times(18-15)$=36.

16. Refer to the figure above. If the average variable cost is $12 at the profit-maximizing quantity and the firm's fixed costs amount to $30, then the firm's maximum profit is

A. $30.

B. $22.

C. $36.

D. $42.

E. $48.

Key: D

Analysis: $12\times(18-12)$-30=42.

17. Refer to the figure above. If the average variable cost is $13 at the profit-maximizing quantity and the firm's profit is $20 at that quantity, then its fixed costs amount to

A. $12.

B. $22.

C. $20.

D. $60.

E. $50.

Key: C

Analysis: FC=40, $12\times(18-13)-FC$=20.

This figure depicts a situation in a monopolistically competitive market.

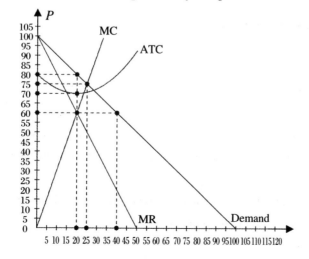

18. Refer to the figure above. How much consumer surplus will be derived from the purchase of this product at the monopolistically competitive price?

   A. $200.

   B. $312.50.

   C. $400.

   D. $800.

   E. $1200.

   Key: A

   Analysis: （100−80)×20/2=200. The top triangle is the consumer surplus.

19. Refer to the figure above. How much profit will the monopolistically competitive firm earn in this situation?

   A. $10.

   B. $200.

   C. $400.

   D. $600.

   E. $0.

   Key: B

   Analysis: （80−70）×20=200.

20. Refer to the figure above. How much output will the monopolistically competitive firm produce in this situation?

   A. 20 units.

   B. 25 units.

   C. 40 units.

   D. 50 units.

   E. 80 units.

   Key: A

   Analysis: According to *MR=MC*, we can get the quantity.

21. When existing firms lose customers and profits due to the entry of a new competitor, a

   A. Predatory-pricing externality occurs.

   B. Consumption externality occurs.

   C. Business-stealing externality occurs.

   D. Product-variety externality occurs.

   E. Production externality occurs.

   Key: C

   Analysis: The business-stealing externality: because other firms lose customers and profits from the entry of a new competitor, the entry of a new firm imposes a negative externality on existing firms.

22. Which of the following is not an argument made by critics of advertising?

   A. Advertising manipulates people's tastes.

B. Advertising impedes competition.

C. Advertising promotes economies of scale.

D. Advertising increases the perception of product differentiation.

E. A and C.

Key: C

Analysis: It examines the understanding of the arguing about advertising.

23. XYZ Co. operates in a monopolistically competitive industry. It produces a leaning product called SmarterKids. XYZ currently produces the profit-maximizing quantity of SmarterKids, but is operating at a loss.

（a）Draw a correctly labeled graph for XYZ Co., and show the following.

（i）The profit-maximizing output and price, labeled as Q_M and P_M

（ii）The area of loss, shaded completely

（b）What must be true in the short run for the company to continue to produce at a loss?

（c）Assume now that the demand for leaning products increases and that XYZ is now earning short-run economic profits. Relative to this short-run situation, how does each of the following change in the long run?

（i）The number of companies

（ii）XYZ's profit

（d）In the long run, if XYZ continues to produce, will it produce the allocatively efficient level of output? Explain.

（e）In the long run, will XYZ be operating in a region where economies of scale exist? Explain.

Key: 11 points $(4 + 1 + 2 + 2 + 2)$

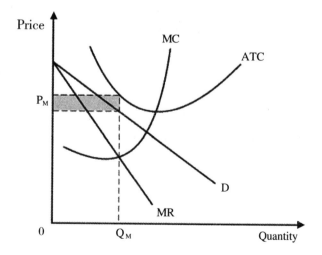

（a）4 points:

One point is earned for a correctly labeled graph with a downward-sloping demand curve, with *MR* below it.

One point is earned for identifying the profit-maximizing output Q_M, at $MC = MR$.

One point is earned for identifying P_M on the demand curve above Q_M.

One point is earned for showing the area of loss shaded completely.

(b) 1 point:

The point is earned for stating that price is greater than average variable cost, or total revenue is greater than total variable cost.

(c) 2 points:

One point is earned for stating that the number of firms will increase.

One point is earned for stating that economic profits will fall to zero or fall to a normal profit.

(d) 2 points:

One point is earned for stating that if XYZ continues to produce in the long run, it will not produce the allocatively efficient level of output.

One point is earned for explaining that XYZ's price is greater than marginal cost.

(e) 2 points:

One point is earned for stating that XYZ will be operating in a region where economics of scale exist.

One point is earned for explaining that the XYZ produces a quantity of output in the declining portion of its long-run ATC.

24. Assume that the mobile phone industry is monopolistically competitive.

(a) Assume that mobile phone manufacturers are earning short-run economic profits. Draw a correctly labeled graph for a typical firm in the industry and show each of the following.

(i) The profit-maximizing output and price

(ii) The area representing economic profit

(b) At the profit-maximizing price you identified in part(a), would the typical firm's demand curve be price inelastic? Explain.

(c) Given the information in part(a), what happens to the demand curve for the typical firm in the long run? Explain.

(d) Using a new correctly labeled graph to show the profit-maximizing output and price for the typical firm in the long run.

(e) Does the typical firm produce an output level that minimizes its average total cost in the long run?

(f) In long-run equilibrium, does the typical firm produce the allocatively efficient level of output? Explain.

Key: 12 points $(4 + 2 + 2 + 1 + 1 + 2)$

（a） 4 points:

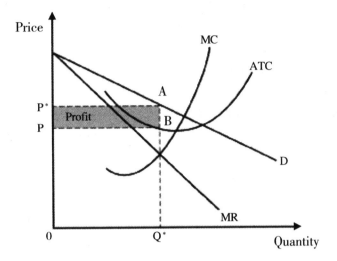

One point is earned for a correctly labeled graph with a downward-sloping demand curve and a marginal revenue curve below the demand curve.

One point is earned for showing the profit-maximizing Q^* at $MC = MR$.

One point is earned for showing P^* on the demand curve above $MC = MR$.

One point is earned for showing the correct area of profit, area P^*PBA.

（b） 2 points:

One point is earned for stating that it is price elastic.

One point is earned for the explanation that MR is positive so that TR rises if P is decreased.

（c） 2 points:

One point is earned for stating that the demand curve for the typical firm would shift to the left.

One point is earned for the explanation that the entry of new firms reduces the market share of existing firms.

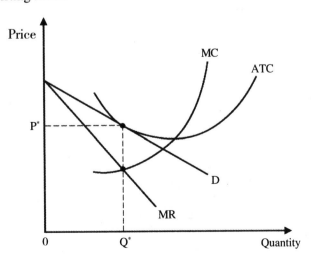

（d）1 point:

The point is earned for showing that long-run equilibrium occurs at the tangency of *ATC* and the demand curve at the profit-maximizing quantity.

（e）1 point:

The point is earned for stating "No".

（f）2 points:

One point is earned for stating "No".

One point is earned for the explanation that at the long-run equilibrium, $P > MC$.

Chapter 16

Public Goods and Common Resources
公共商品和共有资源

　　如果问大家生命中遇到的最幸运的事情是什么，许多人的答案可能都是获得免费的商品，毕竟天上掉馅饼的事情谁不想呢？但是，这种免费商品的出现又对我们原本的经济分析体系提出了新的挑战。在之前的讨论中我们提到，经济体系中的绝大多数商品都是在市场中进行分配，而市场中商品的价格是引导买者与卖者最重要的信号。可是，当商品变为免费的时候，市场的资源配置作用就"英雄无用武之地"了。因为没有价格信号来告诉消费者和生产者交易的合适数量。在这种情况下，政府的角色就显得格外重要。它弥补了由于免费商品的出现而导致的市场失灵，从而提升了人们的经济生活质量。

　　根据上面的情况，我们设想，如果把商品更好地进行分类并加以区别，是不是可以进一步帮助政府管理呢？一般而言，商品的分类依据以下两个特点：一、商品是不是具有排他性（excludability）；二、商品是不是具有竞争性（rivalness）。

　　什么叫排他性呢？排他性是指人们可以阻止其他人享用自己所拥有的商品，它基于的是国家法律对于私人财产的认证和保护；而竞争性则是指一个人的使用会减少其他人对该商品的使用。

　　因此，根据排他性和竞争性，我们可以将商品分为四类：私人商品（private goods），公共商品（public goods），共有资源（common resources）和自然垄断（natural monopolies）。私人商品既具有排他性又具有竞争性；公共商品既无排他性，也无竞争性；共有资源有竞争性但无排他性；自然垄断有排他性，但无竞争性。下面这幅图形象地展示了这四种商品的分类原则：

Rival?

	Yes	No
Yes **Excludable?**	**Private Goods** ·Ice-cream cones ·Clothing ·Congested toll roads	**Natural Monopolies** ·Fire protection ·Cable TV ·Uncongested toll roads
No	**Common Resources** ·Fish in the ocean ·The environment ·Congested nontoll roads	**Public Goods** ·National defense ·Knowledge ·Uncongested nontoll roads

　　我们这里要着重介绍的是公共商品（public goods）。这是每个人都可以免费得到的不具有排他性的商品。由于具有价值的东西没有相应的市场价格，从而导致了外部性，因为人们

从使用稀缺资源中得到了利益却不必向任何人进行支付。

下面我们介绍一种由于公共商品的特性而导致的问题：搭便车问题（the free-rider problem），即得到一种商品的利益但避开为此支付的行为。因为不能排除他人从公共商品中享受利益，所以他们不愿意自己支付成本，而希望他人支付。需要注意的是，这里所讨论的搭便车问题排除了私人市场提供的公共商品。那么政府是如何解决这个问题的呢？如果政府觉得总利益大于总成本，那么它就会提供公共商品，因为政府可以通过税收为其支付，从而使人人受益。国防（national defense）、基础研究（basic research），以及一些扶贫项目（programs to fight poverty）都是重要的公共商品。

在这里，相关的经济学家就提出了一个问题：灯塔（lighthouses）是公共商品吗？我们给出一种分析方法：成本—收益分析（cost-benefit analysis）。成本—收益分析是对提供的某种商品对整个社会带来的总收益（total benefits）和总成本（total costs）进行比较的研究。为了决定是否提供某种公共商品，必须将使用该公共商品的所有人得到的总收益与提供并维护该项公共商品的总成本进行比较。但是，用这种方法来评估一个项目能给整个社会带来多大的收益以及需要付出多少资源成本会面临一个很大的难题，那就是没有用来评估社会收益和资源成本的市场价格。比如生命、时间和艺术的价值要如何评估？因此，这个难题还有待新的方法出现才能得以解决。

最后，我们讨论一下共有资源又有哪些特别之处呢？它与公共商品一样，没有排他性，想使用共有资源的任何一个人都可以免费使用。但是，共有资源具有竞争性，因为一个人使用共有资源就减少了其他人对该资源的享用。共有资源的使用也会出现一系列问题。也即会出现共有的悲剧（tragedy of the commons）。当我们从整个社会的角度来看时，会发现共有资源的使用大于合理的水平，也就是说当个人免费使用共有资源时，共有资源往往被过度使用，从而产生了负外部性。比如清洁的空气和水、拥挤的道路，以及鱼类和其他野生动物等。那么，既然共有资源都被过度使用了，为什么一些珍稀动物还没有绝种呢？是市场在保护他们吗？显然不是，是私人产权（private ownership）和利益驱动（profit motive）的作用。这就体现了产权（property rights）的重要性。当没有很好地建立产权时，比如某些有价值的东西并没有在法律上约定它的所有者，市场就不能有效地配置资源。所以，当由于没有产权而导致市场失灵时，就需要政府来加以解决。

重要名词解释

1. **Excludability:** People can be prevented from enjoying a good.
2. **Rivalness:** One person's use of a good diminishes another person's enjoyment of it.
3. **Private goods:** both excludable and rival
4. **Public goods:** neither excludable nor rival
5. **Common resources:** rival but not excludable
6. **Natural monopolies:** excludable but not rival

模拟试题

1. For private goods allocated in markets,

   A. Prices guide the decisions of buyers and sellers and these decisions lead to an efficient allocation of resources.

   B. Prices guide the decisions of buyers and sellers and these decisions lead to an inefficient allocation of resources.

   C. The government guides the decisions of buyers and sellers and these decisions lead to an efficient allocation of resources.

   D. The government guides the decisions of buyers and sellers and these decisions lead to an inefficient allocation of resources.

   E. Sometimes prices guide the decisions of buyers and sellers, and sometimes the government guides; both decisions lead to an efficient allocation of resources.

   Key: A

   Analysis: Private goods are both excludable and rival. Prices guide the decisions and lead to efficiency.

2. Government policy can potentially raise economic well-being

   A. In all markets for goods and services.

   B. In economic models, but not in reality.

   C. When a good does not have a price attached to it.

   D. In no cases.

   E. In a perfectly competitive market.

   Key: C

   Analysis: When the market failure happens due to the reason of externalities or others, the government can improve the economic well-being.

3. The old lyric "the best things in life are free"

   A. Is not true for any goods.

   B. Is true for some goods that have a price.

   C. Refers to goods provided by nature or the government.

   D. Refers to goods provided by the market.

   E. All of above aren't accurate.

   Key: C

   Analysis: When the goods are provided by nature or the government, they do not have a price attached to it.

4. Governments can improve market outcomes for

   A. Public goods but not common resources.

   B. Common resources but not public goods.

   C. Both public goods and common resources.

   D. Neither public goods nor common resources.

E. Specific public goods and common resources.

Key: C

Analysis: Government policy can potentially remedy the market failure that results in and raises economic well-being.

5. The provision of a public good generates a

   A. Positive externality, as does the use of a common resource.

   B. Positive externality and the use of a common resource generates a negative externality.

   C. Negative externality, as does the use of a common resource.

   D. Negative externality and the use of a common resource generates a positive externality.

   E. Positive externality and the use of a common resource will be more efficient.

   Key: B

   Analysis: It examines the understanding of the public goods. Public Goods are neither excludable nor rival. It can generate a positive externality sometimes, but excessive use will cause the negative externality.

6. When a good is excludable,

   A. One person's use of the good diminishes another person's ability to use it.

   B. People can be prevented from using the good.

   C. No more than one person can use the good at the same time.

   D. Everyone will be excluded from using the good.

   E. One person's use of a good diminishes another person's enjoyment of it.

   Key: B

   Analysis: Excludability means the property of a good whereby a person can be prevented from using it.

7. When a good is rival in consumption,

   A. One person's use of the good diminishes another person's ability to use it.

   B. People can be prevented from using the good.

   C. No more than one person can use the good at the same time.

   D. Everyone will be excluded from obtaining the good.

   E. All of the above are wrong.

   Key: A

   Analysis: Rivalness means the property of a good whereby one person's use diminishes other people's use.

8. An FM radio signal is an example of a good that is

   A. Private.

   B. Non-rival in consumption.

   C. Social.

   D. Non-excludable in production.

   E. Excludable in consumption.

   Key: B

Analysis: One person's use of radio signal cannot diminish other people's use.

9. Goods that are rival in consumption and excludable would be considered as

   A. Natural monopolies.

   B. Common resources.

   C. Public goods.

   D. Private goods.

   E. Normal goods.

   Key: D

   Analysis: Private goods are both excludable and rival.

10. Which of the following would not be considered a private good?

    A. A pair of jeans.

    B. An apple.

    C. A Honda Civic.

    D. Cable TV service.

    E. An apartment.

    Key: D

    Analysis: Cable TV service is not rival, so it is not a private good.

11. Which of the following is not a public good?

    A. National defense.

    B. Patented technological knowledge.

    C. General knowledge.

    D. The elimination of poverty.

    E. Uncongested non-toll roads.

    Key: B

    Analysis: Patented technological knowledge belongs to specific people. It is excludable.

12. Because public goods are

    A. Excludable, people have an incentive to be free riders.

    B. Excludable, people do not have an incentive to be free riders.

    C. Not excludable, people have an incentive to be free riders.

    D. Not excludable, people do not have an incentive to be free riders.

    E. Not excludable, people hate to be free riders.

    Key: C

    Analysis: A free-rider is a person who receives the benefit of a good but avoids paying for it. Public goods meet this condition.

13. Private markets usually fail to provide lighthouses because

    A. Lighthouses cost too much to build relative to their benefits.

    B. Government intervention makes it hard for private lighthouse owners to compete in the market.

    C. Ship captains have incentives to use lighthouses without paying.

    D. Lighthouses are valued very little by ship captains these days.

E. The owner of the lighthouse is able to exclude beneficiaries from enjoying the lighthouse.

Key: C

Analysis: A lighthouse benefits many ship captains, so it is a public good. Ship captains want to use lighthouses for free.

14. National defense is a classic example of a public good because

    A. There is no market for private security services.

    B. It is difficult to exclude people from receiving the benefits from national defense once it is provided.

    C. Everyone agrees that some level of national defense is important, but only the government knows the optimal amount.

    D. There are no private firms willing to supply defense goods such as tanks and weapons.

    E. My enjoyment of the national defense does diminish your enjoyment of the national defense of the United States.

    Key: B

    Analysis: Pubic goods are neither excludable nor rival. National defense has this feature.

15. Reggie, Rachael, and Rudy all enjoy looking at flowers blooming in gardens in their neighborhood. The neighborhood association is considering building a garden around the sign at the entrance to the neighborhood. Reggie values the garden at $20, Rachael at $35, and Rudy at $50. The flowers and labor for the garden cost $85. What should the neighborhood association do?

    A. Build the garden because people like flowers.

    B. Build the garden because the benefits outweigh the costs.

    C. Do not build the garden because the costs outweigh the benefits.

    D. Do not build the garden in order to prevent the "tragedy of the commons" problem of overuse.

    E. Do not build the garden because nobody's benefit exceeds the cost.

    Key: B

    Analysis: 20+35+50=105>85, so the neighborhood can build the garden.

16. Cost-benefit analysts often encounter the problem that those who would benefit from government provision of a public good tend to

    A. Overstate the benefit they would receive from the public good and those who would be harmed by government provision of a public good tend to overstate the costs they would incur from the public good.

    B. Overstate the benefit they would receive from the public good and those who would be harmed by government provision of a public good tend to understate the costs they would incur from the public good.

    C. Understate the benefit they would receive from the public good and those who would be harmed by government provision of a public good tend to overstate the costs they would incur from the public good.

D. Understate the benefit they would receive from the public good and those who would be harmed by government provision of a public good tend to understate the costs they would incur from the public good.

E. All of above are wrong.

Key: A

Analysis: It examines the understanding of cost-benefit analysis. In reality, people often use it unknowingly.

17. The greatest difficulty with cost-benefit analysis of a public project is determining

A. Whether government revenue is sufficient to cover the cost of the project.

B. Which contractor should be awarded the project.

C. The cost of the project.

D. The value or benefit of the project.

E. Who on earth get the benefit.

Key: D

Analysis: Cost benefit analysis estimates the total costs and benefits of a good to society as a whole. For a public project, it is easy to get the cost but difficult to obtain the value or benefit of the project.

18. Which of the following statements is not correct?

A. Environmental degradation is an example of the tragedy of the commons.

B. Cost-benefit analysis is an important tool that economists use to evaluate the benefits of providing a public good.

C. Some goods, such as lighthouses, may be either private or public.

D. The free-rider problem prevents governments from supplying public goods.

E. Regulating the use of the common resource is a typical solution to the tragedy of the commons.

Key: D

Analysis: It examines the understanding of the tragedy of the commons, and we can eliminate the wrong choices one by one. The tragedy of the commons is a story with a general lesson: when one person uses a common resource, he or she diminishes another person's enjoyment of it.

19. Which of the following quotations illustrates the tragedy of the commons?

A. "A bird in the hand is worth two in the bush."

B. "The only difference between the rich and other people is that the rich have more money."

C. "What is common to many is taken least care of, for all men have greater regard for what is their own than for what they possess in common with others."

D. "Anyone who is not a socialist before he is 30 has no heart; anyone who is still a socialist after he is 30 has no head."

E. "There is no free lunch."

Key: C

Analysis: The ancient Greek philosopher Aristotle pointed out the problem with common resources: "What is common to many is taken least care of, for all men have greater regard for what is their own than for what they possess in common with others."

20. One economically efficient way to eliminate the tragedy of the commons is to

   A. Tax the owners of the resource.

   B. Prevent anyone from using the resource.

   C. Reduce the marginal social benefit of the resource.

   D. Establish private ownership of the resource.

   E. None of above is right.

Key: D

Analysis: The market fails to allocate resources efficiently when property rights are not well-established (i.e. some item of value does not have an owner with the legal authority to control it). When the absence of property rights causes a market failure, the government can potentially solve the problem by establishing private ownership of the resource.

主要内容和概念讲解

在之前的章节中，我们讲到了市场如何利用供求的力量配置稀缺资源，并说明了供求均衡在一般情况下还是一种有效率的资源配置方式。用亚当·斯密著名的比喻来讲就是市场中"看不见的手"引导利己的买者和卖者，从而使该市场所产生的社会总收益最大化。其实，我们在之前的讨论中一直有一个隐含的假设：单个消费者或生产者的经济行为对社会其他人的福利没有影响，即不存在所谓的"外部性"（externality），但这种假设是与现实不符的理想状态。

外部性是指某一经济单位的经济活动对其他经济单位所施加的非市场性影响。非市场性是指一种活动所产生的成本或利益未能通过市场价格反映出来，而是无意识地强加于他人的。外部性有正的外部性，称之为外部经济，指的是一个经济主体对其他经济主体产生积极影响，无偿为其他人带来利益。相反，也有负的外部性，称之为外部不经济，指给其他经济单位带来消极影响，对他人施加成本。

外部性与努力解决市场失灵的政策一样，具有多样性。例如，汽车尾气有负外部性，因为它产生了其他人不得不呼吸的烟雾。由于这种外部性，马路或周边环境往往会受到严重污染。许多政府都努力通过规定汽车的尾气排放标准来解决这个问题，同时还对汽油征税，以减少人们开车的次数。修复历史建筑具有正外部性。因为在这些历史建筑物附近散步或骑车的人会享受到这些建筑的美丽，并感受到其所积淀下来的历史内涵。建筑物的所有者得不到修复的全部收益，往往很快遗弃了这些建筑物。许多地方政府对这个问题的处理方法是对拆毁历史建筑物的行为实行管制，并向修复这些建筑物的所有者提供税收减免。狂吠的狗具有负外部性，因为邻居受到了噪音干扰。狗的主人并不承担噪音的全部成本。地方政府通过宣布"干扰平静"为非法行为来解决这个问题。新技术的研究具有正外部性，因为它创造了其他人可以运用的知识；由于发明者并不能占有他们发明的全部收益，所以往往倾向于用很少的资源来从事研究。为此许多政府通过专利制度来解决这个问题，使发明者可以在一定时期内排他地使用自己的发明。在以上各种情况中，决策者没有考虑到自己行为的外部效应。政府的态度则是努力影响这种行为，以便保护旁观者的利益。

如果一个消费者直接关注另一个经济行为人的生产或消费，我们就说这种经济情形包含了消费外部性。例如，邻居在凌晨3点大声吹奏乐器，饭店里邻座在抽廉价的雪茄，当地汽车排放尾气污染环境，都是负的消费外部性的例证。而观赏邻居的花园则是正的消费外部性的一个例子。

同样，如果一个厂商的生产可能性受到另一个厂商或消费者的选择影响，我们就说这种经济情形包含生产外部性。在苹果园和它邻近的养蜂者的那个经典例子中，存在着相互的正生产外部性——每一个厂商的生产对于别的厂商的生产可能性的影响都是正的。相似地，渔场关注倾倒在捕鱼区的污染物的数量是因为这对于它的捕鱼量有负的影响。

外部性最主要的特征是存在着人们关注但又不在市场上出售的商品。没有凌晨3点大声吹奏乐器的市场，没有廉价雪茄烟尘飘绕的市场，也没有把花园料理得漂漂亮亮的邻居的市场。而问题正是由于缺乏外部性的市场才引起的。

外部性对经济效率的影响在于它使得私人行为与社会需要的数量出现差异，这一点可以由私人成本（private cost）和社会成本（social cost）加以说明。

私人成本是指一个经济单位从事某次经济活动所需要支付的费用；一项经济活动的社会成本是指全社会为了这项活动需要支付的费用，包括从事该项经济活动的私人成本加上这一活动给其他经济单位带来的成本。如果一项经济活动产生外部不经济，则社会成本大于私人成本；如果一项经济活动产生外部经济，则社会成本小于私人成本。

同样的分析可以用于私人收益（private revenue）与社会收益（social revenue，即外部经济带来的利益）。

在存在外部不经济的条件下，私人厂商的最优产量大于社会最优产量；在存在外部经济的条件下，私人厂商的最优产量小于社会最优产量。

生产中的负外部性

在前面的分析中，供给与需求曲线包含了有关成本与收益的重要信息。我们以钢铁企业为例。钢铁的需求曲线反映了消费者对钢铁的评价，这种评价用他们愿意支付的价格来衡量。在任何一个既定量时，需求曲线的高表示边际买者的支付意愿。换句话说，它表示购买最后一单位钢铁的价值。同样，供给曲线反映了钢铁生产者的成本。在任何一个既定量时，供给曲线的高表示边际卖者的成本。换句话说，它表示出售最后一单位钢铁的成本。在没有政府干预时，钢铁的价格调整使钢铁的供求平衡，如图17.1所示。

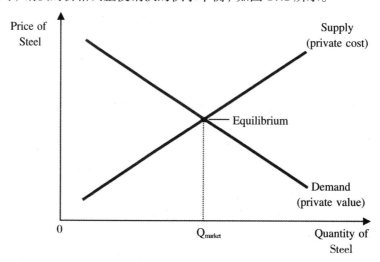

图17.1　没有政府干预的钢铁市场的均衡

现在我们假设钢铁工厂排放污染物：每生产一吨钢铁就有一定量的烟尘进入大气。由于这种污染物对人的健康造成威胁，因此它具有负外部性。这种外部性如何影响市场的效率呢?

由于这种外部性的存在,生产钢铁的社会成本大于钢铁生产者的私人成本。每生产一单位钢铁的社会成本包括钢铁生产者的私人成本和受到污染物不利影响的旁观者的成本。图17.2表示生产钢铁的社会成本。社会成本曲线在供给曲线之上,因为它考虑到了钢铁生产者给社会所带来的外部成本。这两条曲线的差别反映了排放污染物的成本。

应该生产多少钢铁呢?为了回答这个问题,我们需要考虑一个仁慈的社会决策者能做什么。决策者力图使该市场产生的总剩余——钢铁消费者的价值减去生产钢铁的成本——最大化。但决策者知道,生产钢铁的成本包括污染的外部成本。

决策者选择需求曲线与社会成本曲线相交时的钢铁生产水平。从整个社会的角度来看,这个交点决定了钢铁的最优生产量。决策者至少要达到这个生产水平,因为低于这一水平时,钢铁消费者的价值(用需求曲线的高来衡量)大于生产它的社会成本(用社会成本曲线的高来衡量)。决策者也不会使生产大于这一水平,因为生产额外钢铁的社会成本大于消费者的价值。

注意钢铁的均衡数量(即市场量)大于社会的最适当的量(即最适量),这种无效率的原因是市场均衡仅仅反映了生产的私人成本。在市场均衡时,边际消费者对钢铁的评价是私人成本小于生产它的社会成本。这就是说,在市场量时,需求曲线在社会成本曲线之下。因此,使钢铁的生产和消费低于均衡水平增加了社会总福利。

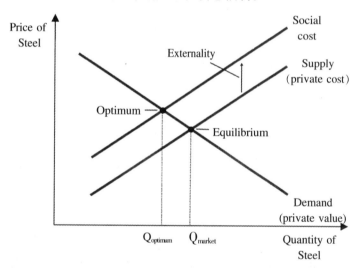

图17.2 钢铁企业的外部性分析

社会决策如何能达到这种最适水平呢?一种方法是对钢铁生产者销售的每一吨钢铁征税。税收使钢铁的供给曲线向上移动,移动量为税收规模。如果税收准确地反映了排入大气的污染物的社会成本,新的供给曲线就与社会成本曲线相一致。在新的市场均衡时,钢铁生产者将生产社会最适量的钢铁。

这种征税的方法被称为外部性的内部化解决方法,因为它给市场买者与卖者以考虑他们行为外部影响的动力。实际上,钢铁生产者在决定供给多少钢铁时会考虑到污染的成本,因为税收会使它们支付这些外部成本。在本章后面我们会看到决策者在解决外部性时能采用的其他方法。

生产的正外部性

当一个生产者采取的经济行为对他人产生了有利的影响,而自己却不能从中得到报酬时,便产生了生产的正外部性。生产的正外部性在原理上与负外部性类似,都是通过对供给曲线的影响来改变最终的均衡结果。例如,一个企业对其所雇佣的工人进行培训,而这些工人却转到其他单位去工作,该企业并不能从其他单位索回培训费用或是得到其他形式的补偿,因此该企业从培训工人中得到的私人利益就小于该活动的社会利益。

消费中的正外部性

对消费外部性的分析类似于对生产外部性的分析。正如图 17.3 所示,需求曲线没有反映一种商品的社会价值,例如教育。在这种情况下,社会价值大于私人价值,而且,社会最适量大于私人市场决定的数量。

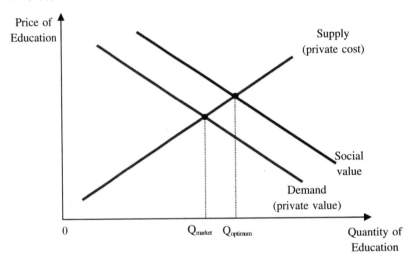

图 17.3 教育的正外部效应

消费的负外部性

当一个消费者采取的行为使他人付出了代价而又未给他人以补偿时,便产生了消费的负外部性。和生产者造成污染的情况类似,消费者也可能造成污染而损害他人。吸烟便是一个明显的例子。吸烟者的行为危害了不吸烟者的身体健康,但并未为此而支付任何成本。此外,在公共场所随意丢弃果皮等垃圾也是常见的例子。

上述几种外部影响可以说是无所不在、无时不在。尽管就单个的生产者或消费者来说,他造成的正的或负的外部性对整个社会也许微不足道;但所有这些消费者和生产者加起来所造成的正的或负的外部性的总的效果将是巨大的。例如,由于扩大生产而引起的污染问题现在已经严重到危及人类自身生存环境的地步了。

政府也可以通过使外部性内部化来纠正市场失灵。消费外部性情况下的适当反应类似于生产外部性的情况。为了使市场均衡接近于社会最适水平,负外部性要有税收,正外部性要有补贴。实际上,这正是政府所遵循的政策:在我们的经济中,含酒精饮料属于纳税最高的商品之一,而对于教育则通过公立学校和政府奖学金进行补贴。

也许你现在会注意到，从这些外部性的例子中可以得出一些一般性的结论：生产或消费的负外部性使市场生产的量大于社会希望的量；生产或消费的正外部性使市场生产的量小于社会希望的量。为了解决这些问题，政府可以通过对有负外部性的商品征税和给有正外部性的商品以补贴来把外部性内部化。

解决外部性的政策

我们讨论了为什么外部性使市场配置资源无效率，但如何纠正由外部性所造成的资源配置不当呢？在现实中，私人行为者和公共政策制定者都以各种方式对外部性做出了反应，所有这些解决方法的目标都是使资源配置接近社会最优的状态。

有时外部性问题可以用道德规范和社会约束来解决。例如，为什么大多数人不乱扔垃圾？尽管有禁止乱扔垃圾的法规，但大多数人不乱扔垃圾只是因为这样做是错误的。道德规范告诉我们，要考虑到我们的行动如何影响其他人。用经济学术语讲就是外部性内部化的必要性。另外，经典的经济学理论所提出的政策建议包括以下几点：

第一，使用税收和补贴。对造成外部不经济的企业，国家应该征税，其数额应该等于该企业给社会其他成员所造成的损失，从而使该企业的私人成本恰好等于社会成本。例如，在生产造成环境污染的情况下，政策向制造污染者收税，其税额等于治理污染所需要的费用。反之，对有正外部性的企业，国家则可以采取补贴的办法，使得企业的私人利益与社会利益相等。无论是哪种情况，只要政府采取措施使得私人成本和私人利益与相应的社会成本和社会利益相等，资源配置就可达到帕累托最优状态。

用于纠正负外部性影响的税收被称为庇古税（Pigou tax），以纪念最早提出这种税收用法的经济学家阿瑟·庇古（Arthur Pigou, 1877–1959）。相对于管制而言，经济学家更倾向于将税收作为解决污染的一种方法，因为税收可以以较低的社会成本减少污染。为了说明其原因，我们来看一个例子。假设有两个工厂——造纸厂和钢铁厂，每家工厂每年向河中倾倒500吨废物。环境保护部门决定在以下两种方法中选择一种来减少污染量。

管制：环境保护部门要求每家工厂把每年的排污量减少为300吨。

庇古税：环境保护部门对每家工厂每排出一吨废物征收5万美元的税收。

管制规定了污染水平，而税收则给工厂所有者一种减少污染的经济激励。你认为哪一种解决方法更好呢？

大多数经济学家倾向于税收。他们首先指出，在减少污染总水平上税收和管制同样有效。环境保护部门可以通过把税收确定在适当的水平上，来达到它想达到的任何污染水平。税收越高，减少的污染也就越多。实际上，如果税收足够高，工厂将关闭，污染减少为零。

经济学家倾向于税收的原因是它对减少污染更有效率。管制要求每个工厂减少等量污染，但等量减少并不一定是清洁水质的最省钱的方法。可能的情况是，造纸厂减少污染的成本比钢铁厂低。如果是这样的话，造纸厂对税收的反应是大幅度地减少污染，以便少交税；而钢铁厂的反应则是减少的污染少，交的税多。

实际上，庇古税规定了污染权的价格。正如市场把商品分配给那些对商品评价最高的买者一样，庇古税把污染权分配给那些减少污染成本最高的工厂。无论环境保护部门选择的污染水平是多少,它都可以通过税收以最低的总成本达到这个目标。

经济学家还认为,庇古税对环境更有利。在命令与控制的管制政策下,一旦工厂达到了300吨污染物的目标就没有动力再减少排污。与此相比,税收激励工厂去开发更清洁的技术,因为更清洁的技术可以减少工厂不得不支付的税收。

庇古税与大多数其他税不同。正如我们在第八章中讨论的,大多数税扭曲了激励,并使资源配置背离社会最优的资源配置。经济福利的减少——即消费者和生产者剩余的减少——大于政府收入的增加量,引起了无谓的损失。与此相比,当存在外部性问题时,社会也关注那些受到影响的旁观者的福利。庇古税是存在外部性时的正确激励,从而使资源配置接近于社会最优。因此,庇古税增加了政府的收入,也提高了经济福利。

第二,使用企业合并的方法。我们假定一个企业的生产影响到了另外一个企业。如果影响是正的,则第一个企业的生产就会低于社会最优水平;反之,如果影响是负的,则第一个企业的生产就会超过社会最优水平。但是如果把这两个企业合并为一个企业,则此时的外部影响就"消失"了,即被"内部化"了。合并后的单个企业为了自己的利益将使自己的生产确定在其边际成本等于边际收益的水平上。而由于此时不存在外部影响,故合并企业的成本与收益就等于社会的成本与收益,于是资源配置达到帕累托最优状态。

第三,使用规定财产权的办法。在许多情况下,外部影响之所以导致资源配置失当,是由于财产权不明确。如果财产权是完全确定的并得到了充分的保障,则有些外部性的影响就可能不会发生。例如,某条河流的上游污染者使下游用水者受到损害。如果给予下游用水者以使用一定质量水源的财产权,则上游污染者将因把下游水质降到特定质量之下而受到惩罚。在这种情况下,上游污染者便会同下游用水者协商,将这种权利从他们那里买过来,然后再让河流受到一定程度的污染。同时,遭到损害的下游用水者也会使用其出售污染权而得到的收入来治理下游的河水。总之,由于污染者为其不好的外部影响付出了代价,故其私人成本与社会成本之间不存在差别。这就是著名的科斯定理。

科斯定理

私人市场在解决这些外部性时的有效性如何呢?最著名的结论提出,在某些情况下,这种方法是极为有效的,这个结论被称为科斯定理(Coase theorem)。这个定理是为纪念提出这个结论的经济学家罗纳德·科斯(Ronald Coase)而命名的。根据科斯定理,如果私人各方可以无成本地就资源配置进行协商,那么,私人市场就将总能解决外部性问题,并最为有效地配置资源。

为了说明科斯定理如何发挥作用,我们来看一个例子。假定迪克有一条狗,狗的狂叫声干扰了迪克的邻居珍妮。迪克从这条狗中得到了收益,但这条狗却给珍妮带来了负外部性。是应该强迫迪克把狗送到动物收留所,还是应该让珍妮继续忍受由于狗狂叫而夜不能眠的痛苦?

先来考虑一下什么结果对社会是有效的。社会计划者通过比较迪克从养狗中得到的收益与珍妮承受狂叫声的成本来确定采取哪种做法。如果收益超过成本,有效的做法就是让迪克养狗而珍妮生活在狂叫声中。但如果成本超过收益,迪克就放弃养狗。

根据科斯定理,私人市场可以自己达到有效的结果。珍妮可以付给迪克一些钱让他放弃养狗。如果珍妮给的钱数大于养狗的收益,迪克就将接受这种做法。通过对价格的协商,迪克和珍妮总可以达到有效率的结果。假设迪克从养狗中得到的收益为 500 美元,而珍妮由于狗的狂叫承受了 800 美元的成本。在这种情况下,珍妮可以给迪克 600 美元,让迪克放弃狗,而迪克也很乐意接受。双方的状况都比以前变好了,也达到了有效率的结果。

当然,珍妮不愿意提供迪克愿意接受的价格也是可能的。假设迪克从养狗中得到的收益是 1000 美元,而珍妮由于狗的狂叫承受了 800 美元的成本。在这种情况下,迪克不会接受任何在 1000 美元以下的出价,而珍妮又不愿意提供任何在 800 美元以上的价格。因此,迪克最终还是养狗。但在这种成本与收益的情况下,这种结果是有效率的。

到现在为止,我们一直假设迪克在法律上有权养一条爱叫的狗。换句话说,我们假设除非珍妮给迪克足够的钱让迪克自愿放弃狗,否则迪克就可以养狗。但是另一方面,如果珍妮在法律上有权要求和平与安宁,结果会有什么不同呢?

根据科斯定理,最初的权利分配对市场达到有效率结果的能力无关紧要。例如,假设珍妮可以通过法律强迫迪克放弃狗。虽然这种权利对珍妮有利,但也许结果并不会改变。在这种情况下,迪克可以向珍妮付钱,让珍妮同意他养狗。如果狗对迪克的收益大于狗狂叫对珍妮的成本,那么迪克和珍妮将就迪克养狗问题进行协商。

虽然最初的权利无论怎样分配,迪克和珍妮都可以达到有效率的结果,但权利分配并不是毫不相关的:它决定了经济福利的分配。是迪克有权养一条爱叫的狗,还是珍妮有权得到和平与安宁,决定了在最后的协商中谁向谁付钱。但是,在这两种情况下,双方都可以互相协商并解决外部性问题。只要收益超过成本,迪克就将以养狗结束。

科斯定理说明,私人经济主体可以解决他们之间的外部性问题。无论最初的权利如何分配,有关各方总可以达成一种协议,在这种协议中每个人的状况都可以变好,而且,结果是有效率的,符合帕累托最优状态。

重要名词解释

1. **Externality**：is a cost or benefit, not transmitted through prices, incurred by a party who did not agree to the action causing the cost or benefit. A benefit in this case is called a positive externality or external benefit, while a cost is called a negative externality or external cost.

2. **Pigou tax**：is a tax levied on a market activity that generates negative externalities. The tax is intended to correct the market outcome. A Pigou tax equals to the negative externality which is thought to correct the market outcome back to efficiency.

3. **Coase theorem**：describes the economic efficiency of an economic allocation or outcome in the presence of externalities. The theorem states that if trade in an externality is possible and there are no transaction costs, bargaining will lead to an efficient outcome regardless of the initial allocation of property rights. In practice, obstacles to bargaining or poorly defined property rights can prevent Coasian bargaining.

主要图表

1.

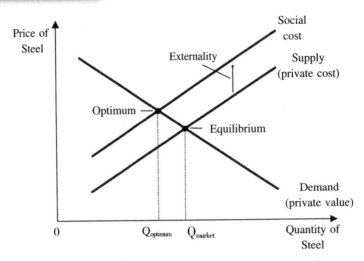

2.

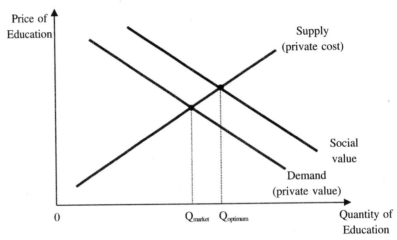

模拟试题

1. In a market economy, government intervention

   A. Will always improve market outcomes.

   B. Reduces efficiency in the presence of externalities.

   C. May improve market outcomes in the presence of externalities.

   D. Is necessary to control individual greed.

   E. Must increase the market efficiency.

   Key: C

   Analysis: It examines the meaning of market failure and externalities.

2. The term "market failure" refers to

   A. A market that fails to allocate resources efficiently.

   B. An unsuccessful advertising campaign which reduces demand.

C. Ruthless competition among firms.

D. A firm that is forced out of business because of losses.

E. The inefficiency caused by externalities.

Key: A

Analysis: A market that fails to allocate resources efficiently is said to have market failure.

3. The impact of one person's actions on the well-being of a bystander is called

A. An economic dilemma.

B. Deadweight loss.

C. A multi-party problem.

D. An externality.

E. Market failure.

Key: D

Analysis: It examines the understanding of externality. When a market outcome affects parties other than the buyers and sellers in the market, side-effects created are called externalities.

4. A cost imposed on someone who is neither the consumer nor the producer is called a

A. Corrective tax.

B. Command and control policy.

C. Positive externality.

D. Negative externality.

E. Neutral externality.

Key: D

Analysis: When the impact on the bystander is adverse, the externality is called a negative externality.

5. Dog owners do not bear the full cost of the noise their barking dogs create and often take too few precautions to prevent their dogs from barking. Local governments address this problem by

A. Making it illegal to "disturb the peace."

B. Having a well-funded animal control department.

C. Subsidizing local animal shelters.

D. Encouraging people to adopt cats.

E. Imposing a fine to dog owners if dogs bark.

Key: A

Analysis: It is an examples of negative externalities. Legal tools are often used to solve the negative externality.

6. Which of the following statements about a well-maintained yard best conveys the general nature of the externality?

A. A well-maintained yard conveys a positive externality because it increases the home's market value.

B. A well-maintained yard conveys a negative externality because it increases the property tax liability of the owner.

C. A well-maintained yard conveys a positive externality because it increases the value of adjacent properties in the neighborhood.

D. A well-maintained yard cannot provide any type of externality.

E. A well-maintained yard conveys a positive externality because it decreases the property tax liability of the owner.

Key: C

Analysis: When the impact on the bystander is beneficial, the externality is called a positive externality. In this example, the neighbor is the bystander.

7. All externalities

A. Cause markets to fail to allocate resources efficiently.

B. Cause equilibrium prices to be too high.

C. Benefit producers at the expense of consumers.

D. Cause equilibrium prices to be too low.

E. Cause some consumers to leave out the market.

Key: A

Analysis: All externalities belong to the market failure. That means it fail to allocate resources efficiently.

8. At any given quantities, the willingness to pay in the market for gasoline is reflected in the

A. Height of the demand curve at that quantity.

B. Height of the supply curve at that quantity.

C. Value to the producer of the last unit of gasoline sold.

D. Total quantity of gasoline exchanged in the market.

E. Total surplus of gasoline.

Key: A

Analysis: The demand curve reflects the buyers' willingness to pay for the goods.

9. The supply curve for a product reflects the

A. Willingness to pay of the marginal buyer.

B. Quantity buyers will ultimately purchase of the product.

C. Cost to sellers of producing the product.

D. Seller's profit from producing the product.

E. Quantity sellers will ultimately produce.

Key: C

Analysis: It examines the understanding of the supply curve.

10. Which of the following statements is correct?

A. Government should tax goods with either positive or negative externalities.

B. Government should tax goods with negative externalities and subsidize goods with positive externalities.

C. Government should subsidize goods with either positive or negative externalities.

D. Government should tax goods with positive externalities and subsidize goods with negative externalities.

E. Government shouldn't intervene the market.

Key：B

Analysis: Taxes are the primary tool used to internalize negative externalities. Government often uses subsidies as the primary method for attempting to internalize positive externalities.

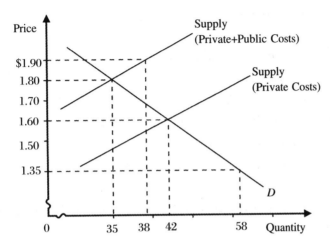

11. Refer to the figure above. This graph represents the tobacco industry. The socially optimal price and quantity are

A. $1.90 and 38 units, respectively.

B. $1.80 and 35 units, respectively.

C. $1.60 and 42 units, respectively.

D. $1.35 and 58 units, respectively.

E. B and C.

Key：B

Analysis: Note the difference between equilibrium and the optimum.

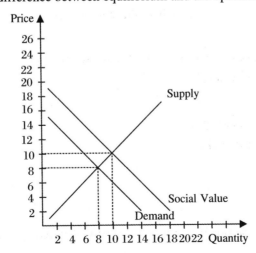

12. Refer to the figure above. If the government wanted to subsidize this market to achieve the socially-optimal level of output, how large would the subsidy need to be?

    A. Less than $2.

    B. $2.

    C. More than $2.

    D. The size of the subsidy cannot be determined from the figure.

    E. $4.

    Key: C

    Analysis: According to the figure above, the demand curve shifts to the social value curve by more than $2.

13. If education produces positive externalities, we would expect

    A. The government to tax education.

    B. The government to subsidize education.

    C. People to realize the benefits, which would increase the demand for education.

    D. Colleges to relax admission requirements.

    E. The government should carry out free education for all people.

    Key: B

    Analysis: Government can use subsidies as the primary method for attempting to internalize positive externalities.

14. Suppose that flu shots create a positive externality equal to $12 per shot. What is the relationship between the equilibrium quantity and the socially optimal quantity of flu shots produced?

    A. They are equal.

    B. The equilibrium quantity is greater than the socially optimal quantity.

    C. The equilibrium quantity is less than the socially optimal quantity.

    D. There is not enough information to answer the question.

    E. A and C are both possible.

    Key: C

    Analysis: Due to the positive externality, the equilibrium quantity must be less than the socially optimal quantity.

15. Which of the following best defines the situation where one firm's research yields knowledge that is used by society as a whole?

    A. Social cost.

    B. Opportunity cost of technology.

    C. Internalization of an externality.

    D. Technology spillover.

    E. Technology policy.

    Key: D

    Analysis: A technology spillover is a type of positive externality that exists when a firm's innovation or design not only benefits the firm, but enters society's pool of technological knowledge and benefits society as a whole.

16. Which of the following is NOT a way of internalizing technology spillovers?

    A. Subsidies.

    B. Patent protection.

    C. Industrial policy.

    D. Taxes.

    E. Technology policy.

Key: D

Analysis: Technology spillovers are the positive externality, so taxes will not be used.

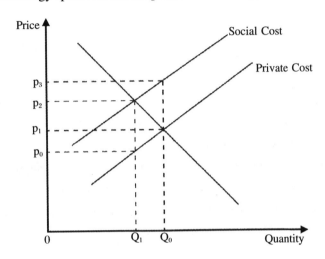

17. Refer to the figure above. Which of the following statements is correct?

    A. To induce firms to internalize the externality in this market, the government should impose a tax measured by P_2-P_0.

    B. To induce firms to internalize the externality in this market, the government should offer a subsidy measured by P_2-P_0.

    C. To induce firms to internalize the externality in this market, the government should impose a tax measured by P_2-P_1.

    D. There is no externality in this market.

    E. To induce firms to internalize the externality in this market, the government should offer a subsidy measured by P_3-P_1.

Key: A

Analysis: $P_2-P_0= P_3-P_1$, it is the social cost; the government should impose a tax by this measurement.

18. Employing a lawyer to draft and enforce a private contract between parties wishing to solve an externality problem is an example of

    A. An opportunity cost.

    B. An implicit cost.

C. A sunk cost.

D. A transaction cost.

E. Production cost.

Key: D

Analysis: Transaction costs are the costs that parties incur in the process of agreeing to and following through a bargain.

19. The proposition that if private parties can bargain without cost over the allocation of resources, they can solve the problem of externalities on their own, is called

A. The Pigouvian theorem.

B. A corrective tax.

C. The externality theorem.

D. The Coase theorem.

E. Market Cleaning

Key: D

Analysis: The Coase Theorem states that if private parties can bargain without cost over the allocation of resources, the private market will always solve the problem of externalities on its own and allocate resources efficiently.

20. John lives in an apartment building and gets a $700 benefit from playing his stereo. Mary lives next door to John and often loses sleep due to the music coming from John's stereo, bearing a $1,000 cost from the noise. At which of the following offers from Mary could both Mary and John benefit from silencing John's stereo?

A. $200.

B. $600.

C. $900.

D. $1,100.

E. $1,300.

Key: D

Analysis: It examines the understanding of the Coase theorem. Just as the transaction cost is more than 700 and less than 1000, both parties can get the benefit.

Chapter 18

The Economics of Labor Markets
劳动力市场

主要内容和概念讲解

完成学业后，你将进入劳动力市场。你以后所赚取的工资水平，很大程度上是由你的工作性质决定的。一般而言，飞行员的工资水平比餐馆服务生的工资水平要高出好几倍。这是为什么呢？我们可以运用第三章所学的需求与供给理论来分析这一问题。

这里所涉及的市场是个特殊的市场，即要素市场。要素市场与一般的产品与劳务市场有共同之处，但也有其特殊性。最重要的要素市场便是劳动市场、土地市场和资本市场。在讨论要素市场的过程中，我们时常面临的一个问题便是不平等与歧视。尤其对于政府而言，它关心的往往不仅仅是经济的有效性，还有社会稳定所必需的公平性。如何客观地衡量不平等？我们将在此章的后半部分回答这个问题。

产品与劳务市场与生产要素市场是密切联系，相互依存的。因此，在研究了产品与劳务市场之后，研究要素市场便是顺理成章的了。研究要素市场主要是研究要素的价格决定，而要素的价格决定问题实际上也就是收入分配问题。

要素市场的特征

要素市场与产品市场非常相似，都是由供求双方的行为共同决定价格，并据此协调资源的配置。和产品市场相比，要素市场具有如下特征：

1. 在产品市场中，需求来自消费者，供给来自生产者；要素市场的情形正好相反，需求来自生产者，供给来自消费者。生产者要进行生产，这样才产生了对生产要素的需求。消费者需要依靠供给要素来得到要素收入，然后才能进行消费。

2. 在产品市场中，产品需求直接来自个人欲望的满足，属于直接需求；在要素市场，要素需求是从产品需求中派生出来的一种间接需求，因而也称之为派生需求。

3. 产品市场的价格是指购买产品本身的价格，产品购买以后即为购买者所有；要素市场的价格一般是指使用要素的价格，购买者仅有一定时期内的使用权。当然，有些要素价格的实现也意味着要素所有权的转让。

4. 在产品市场中，产品的价格决定了厂商的收益；在要素市场中，要素的价格决定了要素所有者的收入。人们一般认为，产品是由劳动、资本、土地和企业家才能这四种要素共同生产出来的，这些要素理应从生产成果中获得报酬。与这四种要素的供求相对应的要素市场可分别称之为劳动市场、资本市场、土地市场及企业家市场。

5. 要素市场与产品市场是相互依存的。要素的价格取决于要素的供求，而要素的供求取决于产品市场。如果产品市场萧条，生产下降，势必降低对要素的需求。而对要素需求的降低又会在其他条件不变时，使得要素市场上要素供给过剩，从而使要素的价格降低。反之，要素价格的变动也会影响产品价格。要素价格上涨会使产品的生产成本提高，从而引起产品价格的上涨。

要素市场利润最大化的原则

在产品市场，厂商为了赢得最大利润，产品的生产必须要满足 MR=MC 的原则。在要素市场，要素的需求也必须满足利润最大化原则。为了进一步分析这一问题，我们先介绍几个概念。

1. 边际产品价值。用 VMP(value of marginal product)表示，它是指投入要素每增加一个单位所增加的产品销售值，即边际产量乘以产品价格。

2. 边际要素成本。用 MFC(marginal cost of factor)表示，它是指追加一单位投入要素而导致的总成本的变化值。

在要素市场上，为了使利润最大化，厂商将按照 VMP=MFC 的原则来使用投入要素。这样做的道理很简单：如果 VMP<MFC，说明厂商使用要素的"边际收益"小于"边际成本"，这时厂商会减少生产要素的使用，直至二者相等；如果 VMP>MFC，说明厂商使用要素的"边际收益"大于"边际成本"，厂商会增加生产要素的使用，直至二者相等。在 VMP=MFC 的条件下，厂商的利润达到最大。

完全竞争条件下的要素供求

这里的完全竞争指的是产品市场和要素市场都处于完全竞争的状态。受边际收益递减规律的支配，边际产品价值曲线向右下方倾斜，如图 18.1 所示。

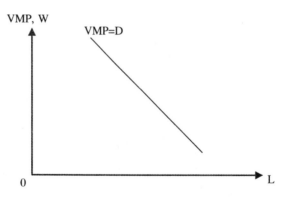

图 18.1 厂商的边际产品价值曲线

由于要素市场为完全竞争，所以厂商使用要素的边际成本就是要素的价格，厂商使用要素的原则可以表示为：VMP=W，在这里 W 表示工资(wage)。在图 18.1 中，对任一要素价格，厂商按 VMP=W 的原则所确定的要素的使用量与对应要素价格的组合均在 VMP 曲线上，所以 VMP 曲线就是完全竞争厂商对生产要素的需求曲线。

在完全竞争条件下，要素的市场供给曲线是一条向右上方倾斜的曲线，而要素的整个市场需求曲线是一条向右下方倾斜的曲线，其交点决定了要素市场的均衡价格，如图 18.2(a)所示。

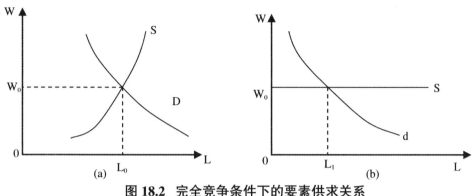

图 18.2　完全竞争条件下的要素供求关系

对于要素所有者来说，他只能在既定的要素价格水平上提供生产要素，即要素的供给曲线为一条水平线。这一曲线对厂商来说就是其 MFC 曲线，其与 VMP 曲线的交点所确定的要素量即为个别厂商在要素价格为 W_0 时所使用生产要素的量，如图 18.2(b)所示。

非完全竞争条件下的要素供求关系

这里的非完全竞争包括产品市场和要素市场都处于非完全竞争状态。

(一)非完全竞争产品市场的要素需求

在产品市场为非完全竞争的条件下，产品价格并非既定不变的。在这里，我们要引入边际收益产品的概念。它是指追加一单位要素投入所带来的产品销售值的增量，用 MRP(marginal revenue product)表示。边际收益产品等于边际产量乘以边际收益，即 MRP=MR×MP。

在前面，我们分析了在完全竞争条件下厂商的边际产品价值 VMP 曲线，知道它是向右下方倾斜的。在非完全竞争条件下厂商的 MRP 曲线也是向右下方倾斜的。但是，MRP 曲线要比 VMP 曲线更陡一些(如图 18.3 所示)，因为在非完全竞争条件下，边际收益产品曲线除了随要素的边际产量曲线下降而下降之外，还随产品的边际收益曲线下降而下降。

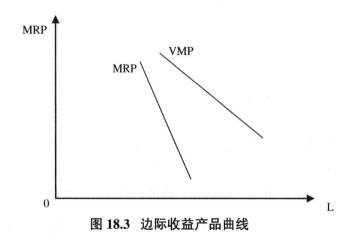

图 18.3　边际收益产品曲线

(二)非完全竞争要素市场的要素供给

假如要素市场存在买方垄断，即要素市场的购买者只有一家厂商时，该厂商所面临的要素供给曲线就相当于全行业的要素供给曲线，这一曲线是向右上方倾斜的。并且，供给曲线与边际成本曲线发生了分离,如图 18.4 所示。

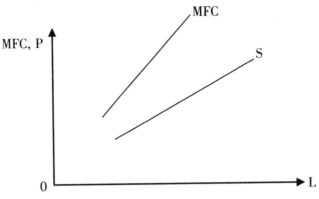

图 18.4 非完全竞争条件下的 MFC 与 S 曲线

值得指出的是,因为产品市场与要素市场既可以为完全竞争,也可能存在垄断势力,所以生产要素市场的均衡就有四种情况:产品市场和要素市场都是完全竞争市场;产品市场为不完全竞争市场,要素市场为完全竞争市场;产品市场为完全竞争市场,要素市场为不完全竞争市场;两个市场均为不完全竞争市场。

工资

(一)劳动供给曲线

劳动者拥有的时间资源是既定的,即每天 24 小时。在这 24 小时中,睡眠占用的时间是不能挪做他用的,我们假定其为 8 小时。在这剩下的 16 小时中,工作以外的时间称为"闲暇"时间。闲暇时间包括除必需的睡眠时间和劳动供给之外的全部活动时间。劳动者选择一部分时间作为闲暇时间来享受,选择其余时间作为劳动供给。闲暇时间可以直接增加劳动者的效用,而工作可以带来收入,收入可以用于消费,从而进一步增加劳动者的效用。

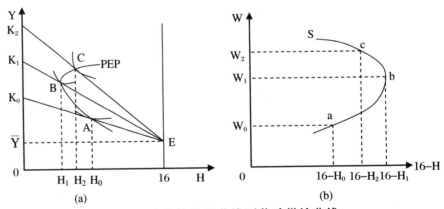

图 18.5 由价格扩展曲线到劳动供给曲线

在图 18.5(a)中,横轴 H 表示闲暇时间,纵轴 Y 表示收入。E 点表示非劳动收入与时间资源总量 16 小时的组合(假设劳动者每天睡觉 8 小时)。K_0 表示当劳动价格为 W_0 时,劳动者把 16 小时全部用于工作所获得的收入和非劳动收入之和,即 $K_0 = 16W_0 + \bar{Y}$。所以劳动者在工资 W_0 条件下的预算线为 EK_0,劳动者获得效用最大化的组合为其无差异曲线和预算线的相切点 A。也就是说当劳动力价格为 W_0 时，劳动者选择的闲暇时间为 H_0，选择的劳动时间为 $16-H_0$，在(b)中相应的点为 a 点；同理可以推出当劳动力价格为 W_1 时，劳动者选择的工作时间为 $16-H_1$，在(b)中相应的点为 b 点；当劳动力价格为 W_2 时，劳动者选择的工作时间为 $16-H_2$，在(b)中相应的点为 c 点；等等。把劳动力价格与劳动者所选择的对应的劳动时间在坐标图中画出，并用平滑的曲线把它们连接起来，就得到了劳动者的劳动供给曲线，如(b)图。在(a)图中，将 A、B、C 等各点连接起来就得到了价格扩展线 PEP。

与一般供给曲线不同的是，劳动供给曲线具有一个鲜明的特点，即它有一段向后弯曲的部分。当工资较低时，随着工资的上升，劳动者会为较高的工资吸引而减少闲暇时间，增加劳动的供给量。在这一阶段，劳动供给曲线向右上方倾斜。但是，工资的上涨对劳动供给的吸引力是有限的。当工资涨到一定程度时，再增加工资，劳动的供给量不但不会增加，反而会减少。于是劳动的供给曲线开始向后弯曲，如图 18.5(b)所示。

(二)替代效应和收入效应

劳动的供给曲线为什么会向后弯曲？下面我们将用替代效应原理和收入效应原理来解释这一问题。

在劳动者时间资源总量给定的条件下，劳动供给的增加就意味着劳动者闲暇时间的减少，劳动和闲暇二者之间存在着反向变化的关系。劳动力价格即工资，实际上就是闲暇的机会成本，增加闲暇就意味着失去收入；相反，减少闲暇就意味着增加收入。于是，工资可以变相地看成是闲暇的价格。对闲暇的需求受到替代效应和收入效应两方面的影响。首先我们来看替代效应。假定闲暇的价格，即工资上涨了，于是相对于其他商品而言，闲暇这个商品变得更加"昂贵"了。于是劳动者会减少对它的"购买"，而转向其他的替代品。因此，由于替代效应，闲暇的需求量与闲暇的价格即工资反方向变化。也就是说，在替代效应的作用下，工资增加，劳动者对闲暇的需求减少；工资减少，劳动者对闲暇需求增加。再来看一下收入效应。相对于普通的商品而言，闲暇是一种特殊的商品。在其他条件不变时，商品价格上升意味着消费者的实际收入下降，但闲暇价格上升却意味着劳动者的实际收入上升。因为此时劳动者享有同样的闲暇，即提供同样的劳动量可以获得更多的收入。随着收入的增加，劳动者将增加对闲暇这种商品的消费。这样，由于收入效应，劳动者对闲暇的需求量与闲暇的价格同方向变化。即在收入效应的作用下，工资增加，劳动者对闲暇的需求量增加；工资降低，劳动者对闲暇的需求量减少。由以上的分析可以看出，随着闲暇价格即工资的上升，劳动者对闲暇的需求量究竟是上升还是下降要取决于这两种效应的大小。如果替代效应大于收入效应，则闲暇的需求量随其价格上升而下降，劳动者会增加劳动的供给；反之，如果收入效应大于替代效应，则闲暇需求量随其价格的上升而上升，劳动者会减少劳动的供给。

通俗地说，当工资的提高使人们富足到一定程度以后，人们会更加珍视闲暇。因此，当工资达到一定程度而又继续提高时，人们的劳动供给量不但不会增加，反而会减少。这就意味着劳动者的劳动供给曲线是向后弯曲的，如图 18.5(b)所示。

(三)劳动的市场供给曲线和均衡工资的决定

整个劳动力市场的劳动供给是由无数个单个劳动者的供给所组成的，将所有单个劳动者的劳动供给曲线水平相加，就得到整个市场的劳动供给曲线。尽管单个劳动者的劳动供给曲线可能会向后弯曲，但整个劳动市场的劳动供给曲线却不一定是向后弯曲的。因为在较高的工资水平上，现有的工人也许会减少劳动的供给，但高工资会吸引来新的工人，所以整个市场的劳动供给一般还是随着劳动工资的上升而增加的，故而市场的劳动供给曲线仍然是向右上方倾斜的。在劳动力市场为完全竞争的情况下，劳动力市场需求曲线总是向右下方倾斜的。将劳动供给曲线和劳动需求曲线结合起来，就可以决定工资水平，如图 18.6 所示。

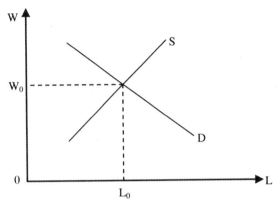

图 18.6 均衡工资的决定

在图 18.6 中，均衡工资水平是由劳动需求曲线 D 和劳动供给曲线 S 共同决定的，且随这两条曲线的变化而变化。其中，劳动供给曲线变化的原因有以下几个方面：第一，非劳动收入财富的增加，较多的财富使消费者可以保留更多的时间自用，这会使其减少劳动供给；第二，劳动者所在地区的社会习俗，例如在某些地方有只许妇女做家务而不许妇女参加工作的习俗，对这一习俗的改变将大大增加当地劳动力的供给；第三，人口、人口的总量及年龄、性别构成都会对劳动供给产生重大影响。

利息

（一）资本

在本章的第一节我们提到了四种生产要素即劳动、土地、资本及企业家才能，这里的资本是与劳动和土地并列的一种生产要素，是指资本物，它是在生产过程中必须使用的各种物品，如机器、厂房、设备、原材料等。据此，可以给资本下一个定义：资本是由经济制度本身产生出来并被用作投入要素以便进一步生产更多的产品和劳务的物品。由资本的定义可以看出资本有三个特点：一是资本的数量是可以改变的，它可以通过人们的经济活动生产出来；二是资本被生产出来的目的是为了以此获得更多的产品和劳务；三是资本是通过用于生产过程来获得更多产品和劳务的。

（二）利息与利率

我们知道，厂商使用土地所有者的土地要付地租，使用劳动力要付工资，而厂商使用资本则要付利息。资本作为生产的要素之一，其本身有一个使用价格，这个价格通常被称为利率，用 r 表示。利率等于资本服务的年收入与资本价值之比，用公式表示为：

$$r = \frac{Z}{P}$$

其中，Z 为资本服务的年收入，P 为资本价值即资本的市场价格。

为了更好地理解上面的公式，我们举一个例子。假设一台设备的价值为 10000 元，这台设备使用一年可得收入 1000 元，则这台设备的（年）利率为 1000÷10000＝10%。

在这里需要说明的是，如果资本价值本身发生变化，比如资本增值或贬值，则利率公式应作相应的修改：

$$r = \frac{Z + \Delta P}{P}$$

其中，ΔP 为资本价值增量，它可以大于、等于或小于 0。

利息的数量在理论分析上一般以利率来表示。利率的高低决定于资本的供求状况。

资本的供给有以下几个基本来源：家庭储蓄、厂商的未分配利润、中央银行新增加的货币发行量、金融体系货币创造机制创造的货币、股票与债券等发行所筹的资本等等。资本的供给曲线自左下方向右上方倾斜（如图 18.7 所示），这表示利率越高，储蓄者愿意提供的储蓄越多，资本的供给越多。

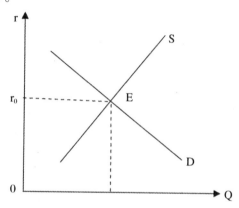

图 18.7　均衡利率的决定

资本需求主要来自以下几方面：厂商投资、技术引进、设备更新；政府的公共支出；个人或家庭进行超过已有收入的购买而申请的贷款等等。资本的需求曲线自左上方向右下方倾斜。

S 与 D 交于 E 点时的 r_0 便为均衡利率，如图 18.7 所示。但实际上，这时的借贷双方被假定为没有任何风险，因而这种利率被称为纯粹利率，纯粹利率不等于实际利率。实际利率的决定还要考虑另外一些因素，例如借贷的风险程度、借贷的期限和长短等等。但纯粹利率是实际利率的基础。

实际上，利率是一种管制价格，政府总是采取措施来影响利率水平。当然，作为管制价格的利率也不能过分偏离均衡利率，否则，便会出现黑市利率同均衡利率拉近甚至相等的情况。

（三）利率的功能

利率的功能主要有：（1）调节储蓄和消费。利率的提高会诱使储蓄增加，从而使资本的供给增加。当然，利率的提高也会提高储蓄者的收入水平，并在某些条件下会使人们的消费适当减少，因为这时消费的机会成本变大了。反过来，利率的降低会减少储蓄，减少储蓄的收入,并适度刺激消费增长。(2)调节投资。利率的高低往往在很大程度上影响资本的需求,影响投资水平。利率的提高,无疑会增加生产成本,其他条件不变时,投资会减少,生产缩减。反过来,利率的降低,会压低生产成本,刺激投资扩大。

利润

与工资、利息相比,利润这种要素报酬形式要复杂一些。对于利润的形成和决定机制,经济学家的看法不尽相同。

(一)利润的性质和来源

在市场经济还不很发达的阶段,资本所有者往往就是企业的管理者,利息与利润是很难区分的。但在现代化大生产中,资本所有者往往并不直接经营、管理企业,而是由专门的高级管理者即企业家来经营、管理。人们通常认为,利润就是企业家才能(管理)的报酬。这种报酬往往很高,有时甚至是普通劳动者工资的几十倍、几百倍。这是因为管理才能被看作一种非常稀缺的要素,并非人人都具备这种才能。这种才能的获得需要昂贵的培训费用。

利润一般分为正常利润和经济利润。前者可看成是企业家的特殊管理才能的价格。后者的来源主要有:

1. 创新。企业家在经营、管理中,不断地进行创新,如引进新的技术和生产方法,开发、生产新产品等等。这些创新活动都会降低成本,增加收益,从而带来经济利润。

2. 风险。生产、经营活动总是有很大的风险性,而这种风险性是由企业家承担的。承担风险需要很高的报酬,以作为可能遭到失败的补偿,否则,将会没有人愿意去从事高风险的事业。

3. 垄断。垄断厂商通过压低生产成本,提高产品销售价格,从中获取超额垄断利润。这种超额垄断利润被认为是一种对劳动者和消费者的剥削。

(二)利润的特点与功能

1. 特点:①企业家才能的质量很难度量,边际生产力也就无法起作用,因此利润无法像其他要素价格那样由边际生产力决定。②利润是收益扣除成本后的余额,不像其他要素的价格都是事先议定的。当事者充其量只能在事先预测和估算利润。③利润不仅可大可小,而且可正可负,不像其他要素价格均为正值。利润为负时便意味着亏损。

2. 功能:①利润不仅是厂商从事生产经营活动的动机,也是评价厂商生产经营活动优劣的标准。②利润不仅影响整个社会的收入分配,也影响整个社会的资源配置。某个行业或某种产品的超额利润,会引导社会资源的流入;反之,负利润即亏损会引导社会资源的流出。③利润也是厂商进一步扩大生产经营活动的基础。

洛伦兹曲线

生产要素价格的决定理论是分配理论的一个重要部分,但并不构成分配理论的全部内容,分配理论还包括收入分配的不平等程度等。收入的分配状况常常是影响一个国家福利水平的重要因素。即便在两个国民收入相同的国家,也可能因为收入分配状况不同而使两国的福利水平产生很大差异。为了研究国民收入在国民之间的分配,美国统计学家 M.O.洛伦兹提出了著名的洛伦兹曲线(Lorenz Curve)。

　　洛伦兹在研究国民收入在国民之间的分配时,首先把一国总人口按收入由低到高排序,然后计算最低的任意百分比人口所得到的收入百分比。再将得到的人口累计百分比和收入累计百分比的对应关系描绘在图形上,即得到洛伦兹曲线,如图18.8所示。

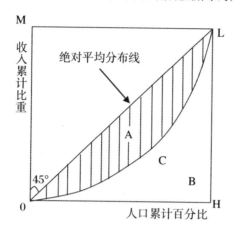

图 18.8　洛伦兹曲线

　　在图18.8中,纵轴表示收入的累计百分比;横轴表示人口累计的百分比;45°线OL为收入绝对平均线,表示人口累计百分比等于收入累计百分比,从而收入分配是完全平等的;OCL即为洛伦兹曲线。显然,洛伦兹曲线OCL位于三角形OHL之内,其弯曲程度反映了分配的不平等程度。如果洛伦兹曲线弯曲程度小,则说明收入分配比较平等,当收入分配绝对平等时,洛伦兹曲线OCL与线OL重合;如果洛伦兹曲线弯曲程度越大则说明收入分配越不平等,当收入都集中在一个人手中时,洛伦兹曲线为折线OHL。

基尼系数(Gini Coefficient)

　　在正常情况下,一个国家的收入分配不会出现两种极端的情况,既不会出现收入分配完全不平等也不会出现收入分配完全平等,而是介于二者之间。相应地,洛伦兹曲线会位于三角形OHL的区域之内。令洛伦兹曲线与45°线OL围成的面积为A,则A可称为"不平等面积",因为A越大说明收入分配越不平等。令B为三角形OHL的面积减去A,则A+B为完全不平等面积,因为洛伦兹曲线OCL与线OL围成的面积为A+B时,收入分配达到完全不平等。所谓基尼系数就是指不平等面积与完全不平等面积之比。基尼系数通常用G表示,则

$$G = \frac{A}{A+B}$$

　　基尼系数是衡量一个国家贫富差距的标准,显然,基尼系数在0和1之间。基尼系数越小,收入越平均;基尼系数越大,收入越不平均。据经济学家钱纳里等人在20世纪70年代初的计算,收入分配高度不均的国家,其基尼系数在0.5~0.7之间;收入分配相对平均的国家,其基尼系数在0.2~0.35之间。

　　据世界银行的测算,在1967年,我国城镇居民个人收入的基尼系数为0.15,这说明当时中国的平均主义非常严重。在1980年,我国城镇居民个人收入的基尼系数为0.33;到

2001 年，基尼系数已达到 0.458，超过了 0.4 的警戒线，说明我国收入不均的现象已比较严重。

重要名词解释

1. **Factors of production:** the input used to produce goods and services

2. **Marginal product of labor:** the increase in the amount of output from an additional unit of labor

3. **Diminishing marginal product:** the property whereby the marginal product of an input declines as the quantity of the input increases

4. **Efficiency wages:** above-equilibrium wages paid by firms to increase worker productivity

5. **Lorenz curve:** It is a graphical representation of the cumulative distribution function of the empirical probability distribution of wealth. It is a graph showing the proportion of the distribution assumed by the bottom y% of the values.

6. **Gini coefficient:** It is a measure of statistical dispersion developed by the Italian statistician and sociologist Corrado Gini. It is a measure of the inequality of a distribution, a value of 0 expressing total equality and a value of 1 maximal inequality.

模拟试题

1. Capital, labor, and land

   A. Have derived demands.

   B. Are factors of production.

   C. Are inputs used in the production of goods and services.

   D. All of the above are correct.

   E. B and C

   Key: D

   Analysis: It examines the understanding of three most important factors of production.

2. The production function is the

   A. Increase in the amount of output from an additional unit of labor.

   B. Marginal product of an input times the price of output.

   C. Relationship between the quantity of input and output.

   D. Shift in labor demand caused by a change in the price of output.

   E. Relationship between quantities of inputs used to make a good and the quantity of derived demand.

   Key: C

   Analysis: It examines the definition of the production function. The production function illustrates the relationship between the quantity of inputs used and the quantity of output of a good.

Number of Workers (L)	Output of Firm A	Output of Firm B	Output of Firm C	Output of Firm D
1	100	100	100	100
2	200	300	190	80
3	300	600	270	60
4	400	1,000	340	40

3. Refer to the table above. Which firm's production function exhibits diminishing marginal product?

A. Firm A

B. Firm B

C. Firm C

D. Firm D

E. None of the above is right.

Key: C

Analysis: The property whereby the marginal product of an input declines as the quantity of the input increases is diminishing marginal product.

4. Which of the following statements is correct?

A. An increase in the supply of other factors, such as capital, will increase the demand for labor.

B. Labor-saving technology will increase the demand for labor.

C. Labor-augmenting technology will decrease the demand for labor.

D. A decrease in the price of output will increase the demand for labor.

E. The value of the marginal product of labor increases when the price of output decreases.

Key: A

Analysis: Three main aspects cause the labor demand curve to shift: output price, technological change and supply of other factors.

5. Suppose that a competitive firm hires labor up to the point at which the value of the marginal product equals the wage. If the firm pays a wage of $700 per week and the marginal product of labor equals 20 units per week, then the marginal cost of producing an additional unit of output is

A. $35.

B. $70.

C. $140.

D. $700.

E. We do not have enough information to answer this question.

Key: A

Analysis: P=W/MPL=700/20=35

6. In the firgure, L represents the quantity of labor and Q represents the quantity of output per week.

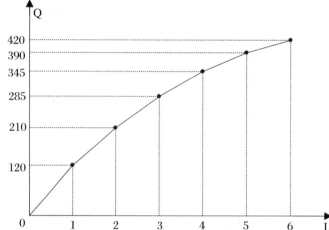

Refer to the figure above. Suppose the firm sells its output for $15 per unit, and it pays each of its workers $750 per week. When output increases from 210 units to 285 units,

A. The marginal cost is $10 per unit of output.

B. The marginal revenue is $5 per unit of output.

C. The value of the marginal product of labor is $4, 275.

D. The firm's profit decreases.

E. The value of the marginal product of labor is $3, 150.

Key: A

Analysis: P=W/MPL=750/(285-210)=10 ∵ P=MC ∴MC=$10

7. The figure shows a particular firm's value-of-marginal-product （VMP） curve. On the horizontal axis, L represents the number of workers. The time frame is daily.

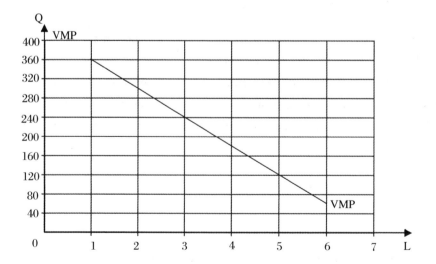

Refer to the figure above. Assume the following:

· Two points on the firm's production function are $(L = 2, Q = 180)$ and $(L = 3, Q = 228)$, Where L = number of workers and Q = quantity of output.

· The firm pays its workers $120 per day.

· The firm's non-labor costs are fixed and they amount to $250 per day.

We can conclude that

A. The firm sells its output for $12 per unit.

B. If the firm is currently employing 2 workers per day, then profit could be increased by $48 per day if a third worker is hired.

C. The marginal cost per unit of output is $2.50 when output is increased from 180 units per day to 228 units per day.

D. The firm's maximum profit occurs when it hires 3 workers per day.

E. All of the above are correct.

Key: C

Analysis: $120/(228 - 180) = 2.5 = MC = P$

8. The factors of production are best defined as the

   A. Output produced from raw materials.

   B. Inputs used to produce goods and services.

   C. Wages paid to the workforce.

   D. Goods and services sold in the market.

   E. Capital and rent.

   Key: B

   Analysis: It examines the definition of the factors of production.

9. Because a firm's demand for a factor of production is derived from its decision to supply a good in the market, it is called a

   A. Differentiated demand.

   B. Secondary demand.

   C. Derived demand.

   D. Hybrid demand-supply.

   E. Excessively demand.

   Key: C

   Analysis: It examines the definition of the derived demand.

10. Factor markets are different from product markets in an important way because

    A. Equilibrium is the exception, and not the rule, in factor markets.

    B. The demand for a factor of production is a derived demand.

    C. The demand for a factor of production is likely to be upward sloping, in violation of the law of demand.

    D. All of the above are correct.

    E. A and B

Key: B

Analysis: It examines the differences between product markets and factor markets.

11. Which of the following best illustrates the concept of "derived demand?"

   A. An increase in the wages of auto workers will lead to an increase in the demand for robots in automobile factories.

   B. An automobile producer's decision to supply more cars will lead to an increase in the demand for automobile production workers.

   C. An automobile producer's decision to supply more minivans results from a decrease in the demand for station wagons.

   D. An increase in the price of gasoline will lead to an increase in the demand for small cars.

   E. None of the above is correct.

Key: B

Analysis: It examines the definition of the derived demand. The demand for a factor of production is a derived demand.

12. For a competitive, profit-maximizing firm, the labor demand curve is the same as the

   A. Marginal cost curve.

   B. Value of marginal product curve.

   C. Production function.

   D. Profit function.

   E. Average cost curve.

Key: B

Analysis: A firm's labor demand curve tells us the quantity of labor that a firm demands at any given wage. We also know that the firm makes that decision by choosing the quantity of labor at which the value of the marginal product equals the wage. As a result, the value-of-marginal-product curve is the labor demand curve for a competitive, profit-maximizing firm.

13. Competitive firms hire workers until the additional benefit they receive from the last worker hired is equal to

   (i) The additional cost of that worker.

   (ii) The wage paid to that worker.

   (iii) the marginal product of that worker.

   A. (i) only

   B. (iii) only

   C. (i) and (ii)

   D. (ii) and (iii)

   E. (i), (ii) and (iii)

Key: C

Analysis: P=W/MPL=MC

14. Labor-saving technology causes which of the following?

   (i) The marginal productivity of labor increases.

(ii) The marginal productivity of labor decreases.

(iii) Labor demand shifts to the right.

(iv) Labor demand shifts to the left.

A. (i) only

B. (ii) only

C. (i) and (iii)

D. (ii) and (iv)

E. (ii), (iii) and (iv)

Key: D

Analysis: Labor-saving technology decreases the demand of labor and the marginal productivity of labor.

15. Labor-augmenting technology causes which of the following?

(i) The marginal productivity of labor increases.

(ii) The marginal productivity of labor decreases.

(iii) Labor demand shifts to the right.

(iv) Labor demand shifts to the left.

A. (i) only

B. (ii) only

C. (i) and (iii)

D. (ii) and (iv)

E. (ii) and (iii)

Key: C

Analysis: Labor-augmenting technology increases the demand of labor and the marginal productivity of labor.

16. Omega Custom Cabinets produces and sells custom bathroom vanities. The firm has determined that if it hires 10 workers, it can produce 20 vanities per week. If it hires 11 workers, it can produce 22 vanities per week. It sells each vanity for $800, and it pays each of its workers $1,000 per week. Which of the following is correct?

A. For the 11th worker, the marginal profit is $600.

B. For the 11th worker, the marginal revenue product is $2,000.

C. The firm is maximizing its profit.

D. If the firm is employing 11 workers, then its profit would increase if it cut back to 10 workers.

E. The firm's profit equals $16,600.

Key: A

Analysis: $800 \times 2 - (1000/2 \times 2) = 600$

17. Your best friend receives a pay raise at her part-time job from $8 to $10 per hour. She used to work 20 hours per week, but now she decides to work 16 hours per week in order to spend more time studying economics. For this price range, her labor supply curve is

A. Vertical.

B. Horizontal.

C. Upward sloping.

D. Backward sloping.

E. Straight line.

Key: D

Analysis: With the wage increasing, the labor supply curve would slope backwards. There is the possibility in terms of conflicting effects on the one's labor-supply decision (called income and substitution effects).

18. For a worker, the opportunity cost of an hour of leisure

A. Rises by \$5 when his or her wage rises by \$5 per hour.

B. Falls by \$5 when his or her wage rises by \$5 per hour.

C. Is the same for a corporate chief executive officer as it is for a garbage-collection worker.

D. Is determined by factors that are unrelated to his or her hourly wage.

E. Is more than his wage.

Key: A

Analysis: It examines the understanding of opportunity cost, wages and the supply of labor.

19. Immigration is an important

A. Explanation for the failure of firms to operate on their labor-demand curves.

B. Explanation for the failure of firms to operate on their output-supply curves.

C. Source of shifts in labor demand.

D. Source of shifts in labor supply.

E. B and D.

Key: D

Analysis: It examines the understanding of labor supply.

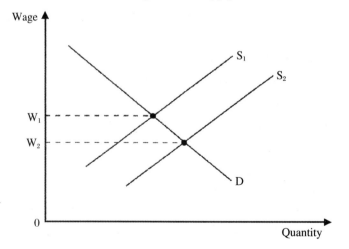

20. Refer to the figure above. If the relevant labor supply curve is S_2 and the current wage is W_1,

A. There is a surplus of labor.

B. The quantity of labor demanded exceeds the quantity of labor supplied.

C. An increase in the minimum wage could be employed to restore equilibrium in the market.

D. Firms will need to raise the wage to restore equilibrium.

E. The quantity of labor supplied will increase.

Key: A

Analysis: It examines the understanding of labor-market equilibrium.

21. In economics, the term capital is used to refer to

A. Money.

B. Stocks and bonds.

C. Equipment and structures used in production.

D. All of the above are correct.

E. B and C.

Key: C

Analysis: Capital refers to the stock of equipment and structures used for production. The economy's capital represents the accumulation of goods produced in the past that are being used in the present to produce new goods and services.

22. Owners of land are compensated according to the

A. Absolute level of production from the land.

B. Number of laborers the land can support.

C. Purchase price of the land stock.

D. Value of the marginal product of land.

E. The location.

Key: D

Analysis: The equilibrium purchase price of a piece of land or capital depends on both the current value of the marginal product and the value of the marginal product expected to prevail in the future.

23. Effective minimum-wage laws will most likely

A. Increase demand for labor.

B. Create a surplus of labor.

C. Increase incomes for all unskilled workers.

D. Decrease incomes for all unskilled workers.

E. Create a shortage of labor.

Key: B

Analysis: Wages are governed by labor supply and labor demand. The minimum-wage laws will cause the deadweight loss. The effective minimum-wage laws must be above equilibrium. So supply will exceed the demand.

24. If we were to observe above-equilibrium wages in a particular labor market, then a possible explanation might be that

A. The theory of efficiency wages holds true for that market.

B. There is a powerful labor union representing workers in that market.

C. Workers are largely unskilled and/or inexperienced and minimum-wage laws are effectively holding wages up in that market.

D. All of the above are correct.

E. B and C

Key: D

Analysis: It examines the understanding of the equilibrium of labor markets. If the wage is above the equilibrium, there must be external interference.

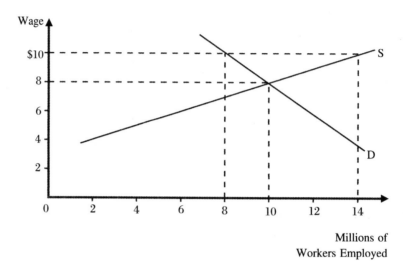

25. Refer to the figure above. Suppose the local labor market was in equilibrium to begin with but then the largest local employer decided to change its compensation scheme to $10 as shown. Which of the following compensation schemes could the graph be illustrating?

A. An efficiency wage.

B. Discrimination.

C. A compensating differential.

D. The superstar phenomenon.

E. Ability, effort, and chance.

Key: A

Analysis: It examines the understanding of some determinants of equilibrium wages. The theory of efficiency wages holds that a firm can find it profitable to pay high wages because doing so increases the productivity of its workers. High wages may reduce worker turnover, increase worker effort, and raise the quality of workers that apply for jobs of the firm.

26. Refer to the figure above. What is the loss associated with wages moving from $8 to $10?

A. 4 million jobs.

B. 6 million jobs.

C. 8 million jobs.

D. 14 million jobs.

E. 2 million jobs.

Key: E

Analysis: 10−8=2

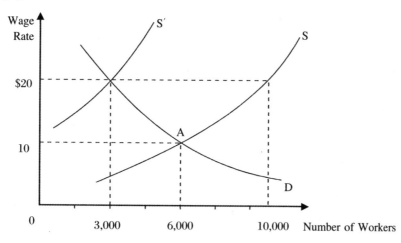

27. Refer to the figure above. This figure depicts labor demand and supply in a nonunionized labor market. The original equilibrium is at point A. If a labor union subsequently establishes a union shop and negotiates an hourly wage of $20, then there will be an excess

    A. Supply of 3, 000 workers.

    B. Demand of 7, 000 workers.

    C. Supply of 4, 000 workers.

    D. Supply of 7, 000 workers.

    E. Demand of 3, 000 workers.

    Key: D

    Analysis: 10000−3000=7000

28. Refer to the figure above. This figure depicts labor demand and supply in a nonunionized labor market. The original equilibrium is at point A. If a labor union subsequently establishes a union shop and negotiates an hourly wage of $20, then the employment level

    A. Increases from 6, 000 to 10, 000.

    B. Increases from 3, 000 to 10, 000.

    C. Decreases from 10, 000 to 3, 000.

    D. Decreases from 6, 000 to 3, 000.

    E. Decrease more than 3, 000.

    Key: D

    Analysis: Excess supply= 6000−3000=3000

29. Suppose that a company hires recent college graduates for two types of jobs, sales people and credit analysts. The hours worked and skill levels are the same for both positions. The sales people must "cold call", which many people find to be unpleasant. When comparing the salaries of the two positions, it is likely that the company pays the

    A. Credit analysts more as a compensating differential.

    B. Sales people more as a compensating differential.

C. Same salary for both positions because they require the same skill level.

D. Same salary for both positions because it would be illegal otherwise.

E. Same salary for both positions because they require the same degree.

Key: B

Analysis: Compensating differentials refer to differences in wage that arise from nonmonetary characteristics of different jobs.

30. Store clerks are known to have low wages. This is likely to reflect the fact that

A. Store clerk jobs are perceived to be relatively easy, thus attracting low-skill workers.

B. Store clerk jobs are perceived to be relatively difficult, thus attracting high-skill workers.

C. Many people perceive the job of store clerk as having significant risk of death on the job.

D. Store clerks are required to have a college degree.

E. Store clerk jobs are more likely to be very dull.

Key: A

Analysis: Human capital is the accumulation of investments in people, such as education and on-the-job training. The most important type of human capital is education.

31. Jo and Flo are identical twins who attended grammar school through high school together. Jo got a job after high school, and Flo got a job after graduating from college. Jo earns $36, 000 a year, and Flo earns $69, 000 a year. Select the best explanation for this wage difference.

A. Jo has less human capital than Flo.

B. Flo has less human capital than Jo.

C. Jo has received a compensating differential

D. Flo has received a compensating differential.

E. Jo has a comparative advantage than Flo.

Key: A

Analysis: The most important type of human capital is education.

32. Which of the following is an economic explanation for the "beauty premium"?

A. Employers pay very attractive women less than average-looking women because they believe them to be less intelligent.

B. Employers pay above-average-looking men more than above-average-looking women.

C. Employers pay above-average-looking women more than average-looking women because customers prefer to deal with better-looking women.

D. Employers pay above-average-looking men more because they signal to the market that they are willing to spend more money on personal grooming, a sign of wealth and stability.

E. Employers pay above-average-looking women more than average-looking women because beautiful people are likely to reflect "good breeding".

Key: C

Analysis: Natural ability is important for workers in all occupations. One interpretation is that good looks are themselves a type of innate ability determining productivity and wages. A second interpretation is that reported beauty is an indirect measure of other types of ability. A third interpretation is that the beauty premium is a type of discrimination.

33. Suppose that a college student receives an offer for a summer internship with a stock brokerage firm. Unfortunately for the student, the internship is unpaid. Is it ever economically beneficial to accept an unpaid job?

    A. Yes, because the experience gained during the internship would increase the student's human capital.

    B. No, because the opportunity cost is too high.

    C. No, because the student is signaling to future employers that he or she is willing to accept low wages.

    D. Yes, because accepting an unpaid job signals to future employers that the student has stable personal finances.

    E. No, because the sunk cost is so high.

    Key: A

    Analysis: It examines the understanding of Human capital and Signaling. Note the difference.

34. A signaling theory of education suggests that educational attainment

    A. Is a signal of high marginal productivity.

    B. Is correlated with natural ability.

    C. Increases the productivity of low-ability workers.

    D. Both A and B are correct.

    E. Both A and C are correct.

    Key: D

    Analysis: It is rational for firms to interpret a college degree as a signal of ability.

35. In the signaling theory of education,

    A. Schooling itself does not lead to more productive workers.

    B. Chance plays more of a role than in the human-capital theory.

    C. Schooling enhances worker productivity.

    D. Compensating differentials do not matter.

    E. Natural ability is important for workers in all occupations.

    Key: A

    Analysis: It examines the understanding of the signaling theory of education.

36. If an employer's behavior is supportive of the theory of efficiency wages, the employer would

    A. Raise wages in an effort to increase worker effort.

    B. Raise wages in an effort to increase worker turnover.

    C. Decrease wages in an effort to increase worker effort.

    D. Decrease wages in an effort to increase worker turnover.

    E. Decrease wages in an effort to raise the quality of workers that apply for jobs at the firm.

    Key: A

Analysis: High wages may reduce worker turnover, increase worker effort, raise the quality of workers that apply for jobs at the firm.

37. Which of the following statements accurately explains the superstar phenomenon in wages?

A. Better carpenters earn more than average carpenters because people are willing to pay higher prices for higher-quality work.

B. Funnier comedians earn more than less funny comedians because they are more talented.

C. Talented athletes earn more than equally talented plumbers because technology allows the delivery of the services provided by the athletes to all interested customers.

D. Athletes get paid for performing services that everyday people perform as hobbies.

E. None of the above is right.

Key: C

Analysis: Superstars arise in markets that exhibit the following characteristics: Every customer in the market wants to enjoy the good supplied by the best producer. The good is produced with a technology that makes it possible for the best producer to supply every customer at a low cost.

38. A union's major source of power is its

A. High-profile leadership.

B. Ability to increase productivity.

C. Ability to threaten a strike.

D. Ability to deny employers the opportunity to bargain over wages.

E. Ability to free withdrawal of labor from a firm.

Key: C

Analysis: Union is a worker association that bargains with employers over wages and working conditions. Strike is the organized withdrawal of labor from a firm by a union.

39. The very high pay earned by the best actors and actresses is partially explained by the fact that

A. They benefit from a compensating differential.

B. Moviegoers all want to see the very best actors, not second-rate actors.

C. They have acting degrees from accredited acting schools.

D. The supply of good actors and actresses is very large.

E. All of the above are wrong.

Key: B

Analysis: It examines the understanding of the superstar phenomenon.

40. Which of the following statements does not accurately describe the market of labor?

A. The characteristics of workers, such as their education and experience, the characteristics of jobs, such as their pleasantness or unpleasantness, and the presence or absence of discrimination by employers all determine equilibrium wages.

B. Labor unions, minimum wage laws, and efficiency wages all may increase wages above their equilibrium level.

C. Firms are willing to pay more for better-educated workers as long as there is an excess supply of this type of worker.

D. Discrimination by employers against a group of workers may artificially lower wages for that group.

E. Discrimination against workers of a certain race or ethnicity is often in conflict with a firm's desire to maximize profits.

Key: C

Analysis: We can eliminate the wrong choices one by one. When the excess supply exists, the price(wage) must decrease.

41. Which of the following explains why soccer players make millions of dollars in Europe but do not in the United States?

A. Discriminatory rules established by the government.

B. Compensating wage differentials for living in Europe.

C. Discriminatory preferences on the part of US sports fans for other sports.

D. Efficiency wages paid to European players to enhance on-field performance.

E. All of the above are right.

Key: C

Analysis: Customer preferences: If customers have discriminatory preferences, a competitive market is consistent with a discriminatory wage differential. This will happen when customers are willing to pay to maintain the discriminatory practice.

42. Economists argue competitive markets provide a "natural remedy" to discriminatory wage practices. Which of the following is widely recognized as a potential limit to the effectiveness of that natural remedy?

A. Some workers are members in unions.

B. Some firms pay efficiency wages; others do not.

C. Some customers are discriminatory in their buying habits.

D. Some employees have accumulated more human capital than other employees.

E. Government always passes laws requiring firms to discriminate.

Key: C

Analysis: Discrimination can persist in competitive markets if customers are willing to pay more to discriminatory firms.

43. A government's policy of redistributing income makes the income distribution

A. more equal, distorts incentives, alters behavior, and makes the allocation of resources more efficient.

B. more equal, distorts incentives, alters behavior, and makes the allocation of resources less efficient.

C. less equal, distorts incentives, alters behavior, and makes the allocation of resources more efficient.

D. less equal, distorts incentives, alters behavior, and makes the allocation of resources less efficient.

E. less equal, distorts incentives, alters behavior, and sometimes makes the allocation of resources more efficient.

Key: B

Analysis: One of the Ten Principles of Economics is that governments can sometimes improve market outcomes. This possibility is particularly important when considering the distribution of income. In doing so, however, the government runs into another of the Ten Principles of Economics: People face tradeoffs.

44. Which of the following is most likely to occur when the government enacts policies to make the distribution of income more equal?

A. A more efficient allocation of resources.

B. A distortion of incentives.

C. Unchanged behavior.

D. Promote incentives.

E. A, B and C are correct.

Key: B

Analysis: When the government enacts policies to make the distribution of income more equitable, it distorts incentives, alters behavior, and makes the allocation of resources less efficient.

45. Which of the Ten Principles of Economics do governments run into when they redistribute income to achieve greater equality?

A. Trade can make everyone better off.

B. The cost of something is what you give up to get it.

C. People face trade-offs.

D. Markets are usually a good way to organize economic activity.

E. People respond to incentives.

Key: C

Analysis: It examines the understanding of the ten principles of economics.

46. Which of the following is not a question that economists try to answer when measuring the distribution of income?

A. How many people live in poverty?

B. How often and how large are people's raises?

C. How often do people move among income classes?

D. What problems arise in measuring the amount of inequality?

E. How much inequality is there in our society?

Key: B

Analysis: A, C, D and E are four questions that economists try to answer.

47. Which of the following is not correct?

A. Poverty is long-term problem for relatively few families.

B. Measurements of income inequality usually do not include in-kind transfers.

C. Measurements of income inequality use lifetime incomes rather than annual incomes.

D. Measurements of income inequality would be more meaningful if they reflected permanent rather than current income.

E. B and C

Key: C

Analysis: Measurements of income inequality use annual incomes rather than lifetime incomes. This is one of the problems in measuring inequality.

48. The normal life cycle pattern of income

A. Contributes to more inequality in the distribution of annual income and to more inequality in living standards.

B. Contributes to more inequality in the distribution of annual income, but it does not necessarily contribute to more inequality in living standards.

C. Contributes to less inequality in the distribution of annual income and in living standards.

D. Has no effect on either the distribution of annual income or on living standards.

E. All of the above are correct.

Key: B

Analysis: This normal life cycle pattern causes inequality in the distribution of annual income, but it does not represent true inequality in living standards.

49. The poverty rate is based on a family's

A. Income, in-kind transfers, and other government aid.

B. Income and in-kind transfers.

C. In-kind transfers only.

D. Income only.

E. In-kind transfers and other government aid.

Key: D

Analysis: The poverty rate is the percentage of the population whose family income falls below an absolute level called the poverty line.

50. Poverty is found to be correlated with

A. Age and race but not family composition.

B. Race only.

C. Race and family composition but not age.

D. Age, race, and family composition.

E. Age only.

Key: D

Analysis: Three facts about poverty: race, age and family composition.

51. Which of the following is not an example of in-kind transfers?

A. Food stamps.

B. Medicare.

C. The Earned Income Tax Credit.

D. Housing vouchers.

E. Old-age pension.

Key: C

Analysis: Transfers to the poor given in the form of goods and services rather than cash are called in-kind transfers. C is the cash form.

52. People have their highest saving rates when they are

A. Retired.

B. Middle-aged.

C. Married with young children.

D. Young and single.

E. At the beginning of the job.

Key: C

Analysis: It examines the understanding of Economic life cycle. The regular pattern of income variation over a person's life is called the life cycle.

53. A family's ability to buy goods and services depends largely on its

A. In-kind transfers.

B. Annual income.

C. Transitory income.

D. Permanent income.

E. Return of investment.

Key: D

Analysis: A family's ability to buy goods and services depends largely on its permanent income, which is its normal, or average, income. Permanent income excludes transitory changes in income.

54. The life cycle effect characterizes a lifetime income profile in which income

A. Tends to follow a seasonal pattern.

B. Rises as a worker gains maturity and experience.

C. Rises and falls in conjunction with the business cycle.

D. Falls during the early years of market activity and peaks at retirement.

E. Falls with the children's growing up.

Key: B

Analysis: It examines the understanding of "the Economic Life Cycle". A young worker has a low income at the beginning of his or her career. Income rises as the worker gains maturity and experience. Income peaks at about age 50. Income falls sharply at retirement, around age 65.

55. Because people can borrow when they are young, the life cycle theory would suggest that one's standard of living depends on

A. Lifetime income rather than annual income.

B. Aggregate income rather than annual personal income.

C. Annual extended family income rather than annual personal income.

D. Income averaged across seasons rather than across years.

E. Lending rather than earnings.

Key: A

Analysis: To the extent that a family saves and borrows to buffer itself from transitory changes in income, these changes do not affect its standard of living. A family's ability to buy goods and services depends largely on its permanent income, which is its normal, or average, income.

56. An example of a transitory change in income is the

A. Annual cost of living adjustment to your salary.

B. Increase in income that results from a job promotion linked to your education.

C. Increase in income of California orange growers that result from an orange-killing frost in Florida.

D. All of the above are correct.

E. A and C

Key: C

Analysis: It examines the differences between the transitory income and permanent income.

57. Economic mobility refers to the

A. Government's attempt to distribute monetary assistance to areas most in need.

B. Ability of families to freely relocate to find good jobs.

C. Movement of people among income classes.

D. Movement of resources from one country to another.

E. Ability of firms to freely allocate resources.

Key: C

Analysis: The movement of people among income classes is called economic mobility.

58. Whether or not policymakers should try to make our society more egalitarian is largely a matter of

A. Economic efficiency.

B. Political philosophy.

C. Egalitarian principles.

D. Enhanced opportunity.

E. Liberalism.

Key: B

Analysis: It examines the understanding of the definition of political philosophy. There are three Political Philosophies: Utilitarianism, Liberalism, and Libertarianism.

59. Which political philosophy believes that the government should equalize the incomes of all members of society?

A. Utilitarianism.

B. Liberalism.

C. Libertarianism.

D. Idealism.

E. None of the above is correct.

Key: E

Analysis: It examines the understanding of three Political Philosophies: Utilitarianism, Liberalism, and Libertarianism.

60. When the government taxes income as part of a redistribution program,

A. The poor pay higher taxes.

B. The rich always benefit more than the poor.

C. The poor are encouraged to work.

D. Incentives to earn income are diminished.

E. Potential gains from greater equality of income can exceed losses.

Key: D

Analysis: People with high incomes pay high taxes, and people with low incomes receive income transfers. Yet, as we have learned, taxes distort incentives and cause deadweight losses. If the government takes away additional income a person might earn through higher income taxes or reduced transfers, the people will have less incentives to work hard.

61. Minimum wage laws

A. Benefit all unskilled workers.

B. Create unemployment, but if demand is relatively elastic, the unemployment effects will be minor.

C. May help the nonpoor, such as teenagers from wealthy families.

D. Reduce poverty by reducing unemployment.

E. Will be in effect if demand for unskilled labor is relatively elastic.

Key: C

Analysis: It examines the overall understanding of Minimum wage laws. Laws setting a minimum wage that employers can pay workers are a perennial source of debate. Advocates view the minimum wage as a way of helping the working poor without any cost to the government. Critics view it as hurting those it is intended to help.

62. Critics of welfare reform argue that

A. Drug addiction has increased among the working poor.

B. The emphasis on work has forced many mothers into low-paying jobs while not providing adequate child care.

C. Homelessness has increased dramatically.

D. The number of people on welfare rolls increased after the reform.

E. Childhood literacy rates have increased.

Key: B

Analysis: A common criticism of welfare programs is that they create incentives for people to become "needy". For example, these programs may encourage families to break up, for many families qualify for financial assistance only if the father is absent. The programs may also encourage illegitimate births, for many poor, single women qualify for assistance only if they have children. Because poor, single mothers are such an important part of the poverty problem and because welfare programs seem to raise the number of poor, single mothers, critics of the welfare system assert that these policies exacerbate the very problems they are supposed to cure.

主要参考文献

1. 高鸿业. 西方经济学(微观部分). 第五版. 北京: 中国人民大学出版社, 2011.
2. 哈尔·R·范里安. 微观经济学: 现代观点. 上海: 上海三联书店、上海人民出版社, 1994.
3. 厉以宁. 西方经济学. 北京: 高等教育出版社, 2000.
4. 梁小民. 微观经济学. 北京: 中国社会科学出版社, 1996.
5. 马克思. 资本论(第三卷). 北京: 人民出版社, 1975.
6. 曼昆. 经济学原理(微观部分). 英文版第三版. 北京: 机械工业出版社, 2003.
7. 平迪克, 鲁宾费尔德. 微观经济学. 第三版. 北京: 中国人民大学出版社, 1997.
8. 萨缪尔森, 诺德豪斯. 经济学. 英文版第16版. 北京: 机械工业出版社, 1998.
9. 萨尔维特. 微观经济理论. 第二版. 纽约: 麦格劳-希尔公司, 1983.
10. 斯蒂格利茨. 经济学(上册、下册). 北京: 中国人民大学出版社, 1997.
11. 宋承先. 现代西方经济学. 上海: 复旦大学出版社, 1994.
12. 尹伯成. 西方经济学简明教程. 上海: 上海人民出版社, 2003.
13. 张培刚. 微观经济学的产生与发展. 长沙: 湖南人民出版社, 1997.
14. 张维迎. 博弈论与信息经济学. 上海: 上海三联书店、上海人民出版社, 1996.